23 NOV 1963

D1580144

HEADQUARTERS
STUDY
SECTION

COUNTY
RESERVE
STOCK

R

1606882 L 828/SW1

Please renew/return this item by the last date shown.

So that your telephone call is charged at local rate,
please call the numbers as set out below:

	From Area codes 01923 or 0208:	From the rest of Herts:
Renewals:	01923 471373	01438 737373 828
Enquiries:	01923 471333	01438 737333 SW1
Minicom:	01923 471599	01438 737599 SW1

L32b

MISCELLANEOUS AND AUTOBIOGRAPHICAL PIECES FRAGMENTS AND MARGINALIA

Bust of Swift by Roubillac in Trinity College, Dublin

JONATHAN SWIFT

MISCELLANEOUS AND AUTOBIOGRAPHICAL PIECES FRAGMENTS AND MARGINALIA

Edited by
Herbert Davis

BASIL BLACKWELL · OXFORD
1962

Basil Blackwell & Mott, Ltd., 1962

Printed in Great Britain for BASIL BLACKWELL & MOTT, LTD.
by A. R. MOWBRAY & CO. LIMITED in the City of Oxford
and bound at the KEMP HALL BINDERY

ACKNOWLEDGMENTS

I AM again under great obligation to a number of libraries, friends and colleagues for help, particularly in giving permission to photograph or transcribe for use in this volume manuscripts and printed books in their possession. I wish therefore here to make due acknowledgment to Trinity College, Dublin; to Marsh's Library; the Royal Irish Academy; and the National Library of Ireland; to the Forster Collection in the Library of the Victoria and Albert Museum; the British Museum; the Bodleian Library; and the Fellows Library, Winchester College; to the university libraries of Harvard, Yale and Johns Hopkins; the Morgan Library, New York, and the Huntington Library, California.

Lord Rothschild and Sir Harold Williams have kindly allowed me to transcribe the marginalia in volumes from Swift's library, now in their possession; and I have constantly consulted the second volume of *The Rothschild Library*, Cambridge, 1954, *Dean Swift's Library*, by Harold Williams, Cambridge, 1932, and the *Catalogue of Dean Swift's Library in 1715*, by T. P. LeFanu. My colleagues, Irvin Ehrenpreis, George Mayhew, and Francis Manley, have generously allowed me to share in the fruits of their special researches. Miss Margaret Pollard has given me great help in searching for volumes in Dublin libraries. As my task now draws to an end I should like also to mention the unfailing and ready support at all times of my publisher, Sir Basil Blackwell, who has provided in this volume the translation of Swift's Latin comment on Herodotus.

It is a particular satisfaction to me that the manuscript of this last Introduction was read, like all the others, by Professor David Nichol Smith, even though it was not improved with his usual rigour. Throughout this undertaking I have had the benefit of his advice and help, and to his memory it is now humbly dedicated.

H. D.

June, 1962.

The CONTENTS

Acknowledgments   v
Introduction   ix

MISCELLANEOUS AND UNFINISHED PIECES
1. Abstract and Fragment of History of England   I
2. Of public Absurdities in England   79
3. Of Mean and Great Figures   83
4. The humble Representation of Clergy of Dublin, 1724   87
5. A Letter to the Writer of the Occasional Paper, 1727   93
6. An Account of the Court and Empire of Japan, 1728   99
7. Preface to Voltaire's *Essay upon the Civil Wars of France*, 1728   109
8. The Answer of William Pulteney to Sir Robert Walpole, 1730   111
9. Preface and Memoirs of Captain Creichton, 1731   120
10. Short Remarks on Bishop Burnet's *History*   183

AUTOBIOGRAPHICAL PIECES
Fragment of Autobiography to 1714   187
Account of his Mother's Death   196
Treaty with Mrs. Anne Long: Death of Mrs. Long   197
Petition against Lord Blayney   199
Holyhead Journal   201

CHARACTERS
Primate Marsh   211
Mrs. Howard   213
Rev. Thomas Sheridan: *Blunders of Quilca: History of Second Solomon*   216
Mrs. Johnson [Stella]—*Bon Mots de* Stella   227

MARGINALIA
Parsons, Robert: *A Conference about the next Succession to the Crown of England*, 1681   241
Herodotus: *Historia Graec.*, 1618   243
Herbert, Thomas: *A Relation of some Yeares Travaile into Africa and greater Asia*, 1634   243

Bodin, Jean: *Les six Livres de la République*, 1579   244
Herbert, Edward, Lord Cherbury: *Life and Raigne of Henry VIII*, 1649   247
Addison, Joseph: *The Freeholder*, 1715   251
Heylin, Peter: *Aerius redevivus, or the History of the Presbyterians*, 1670   255
Browne, John: *Essays on the Trade and Coin of Ireland*, 1729   256
Macky, John: *Characters of the Court of Britain*, etc., 1733   257
Howells, William: *Medulla Historiae Anglicanae*, 1734   262
Burnet, Gilbert: *History of his own Times*, 1724–34   266
Clarendon, Edward Hyde, Earl of: *History of the Rebellion*, 1707   295

APPENDIXES

A. Letter from the Grand Mistress of the Female Free-Masons, 1724   323
B. Memoranda from the book containing the Holyhead Journal, 1727   334
C. A modest Defence of the *Lady's Dressing-Room*, 1732   337
D. Declaration of Inhabitants of St. Patrick's, 1733–4   341
E. Memorandum on Grattan's Walk   344
F. Note on Aristotle   345
G. Advertisements
    (i) From Dublin News Letter, Jan. 4 & 18, 1736–7   346
    (ii) For the Honour of Kingdom of Ireland, 1738   346

Textual notes   349
Index   361

ILLUSTRATIONS

Frontispiece: Photo of Bust of Swift, by Roubillac, in Trinity College, Dublin
Title pages of Voltaire's *Essay*   *facing* p. 108
    Creichton's *Memoirs*   *facing* p. 120
Facsimiles of Manuscript of Autobiography   *facing* p. 192
    Autograph inscription in Swift's copy of Herodotus   *facing* p. 243
    Manuscript of Memoranda from the Holyhead Journal   *facing* p. 334

INTRODUCTION

THE miscellaneous pieces contained in this volume were not included in any of the editions of Swift's works published during his lifetime. They had for the most part remained in manuscript, some of these being first printed by Deane Swift in 1765, twenty years after Swift's death. Some were fragments left unfinished, certainly not intended for publication in this form; others, like the *Autobiography* and the *Holyhead Journal*, and perhaps even the characters of his friends, should be regarded as documents, which though of great interest and importance, are hardly literary works. They are equally varied in date, having been written between 1697—which may be accepted as the likeliest date of the *Abstract of the History of England*—and 1738, when the *Character of Sheridan* was written, some time after his death on October 10.

The *Abstract* covers the period from the Roman invasion of Britain until the reign of William the Conqueror; it is nothing more than notes made from Temple's *Introduction to the History of England* and Samuel Daniel's *Collection of the History of England*.[1] It may possibly have been intended to serve as material for a preliminary chapter to his projected continuation of Temple's history which had broken off at the end of William I's reign. Beginning at this point Swift carried it on only to 1156, having apparently set to work after he had finished his edition of the first two volumes of the *Works of Sir William Temple*, published in 1702. For in his letter to the Count de Gyllenborg of November 2, 1719, he says:

> It is now about sixteen years since I first entertained the design of writing a history of England, from the beginning of William Rufus to the end of Queen Elizabeth; such a history, I mean, as appears to be most wanted by foreigners, and gentlemen of our own country; not a voluminous work, nor properly an

[1] See Irvin Ehrenpreis, *Swift's History of England*, JEGP, 1952, LI, no.2, 177.

abridgment, but an exact relation of the most important affairs and events, without any regard to the rest.[1]

He abandoned the work partly because of the extreme difficulty he found in carrying it out, and partly because he found himself 'engaged in thoughts and business of another kind'. Perhaps he had some intention in 1719 of preparing it for publication, but was again diverted by becoming involved in public affairs in Ireland. Clearly he never became interested in the writing of this sort of history. This fragment is little more than a compilation from the English histories of Holinshed, Daniel and Baker, with further additions from the Latin Chronicles. It has been pointed out that he possessed a copy of Roger Twysden's *Historiae Anglicanae Scriptores decem* and may well have used Charles Ford's copy of Henry Savile's *Rerum Anglicarum scriptores post Bedam*, 1596.[2] These historical pieces provide at least further evidence of Swift's continued preoccupation with the study of history, which had begun when he was a student at Trinity College and is still evident in the latter years of his life, when he was reading and annotating Baronius and Burnet and Clarendon. Whatever view we may take about Swift's qualifications for the office of Historiographer Royal, whatever we may think of the value of his *History of the Last Four Years of Queen Anne*, we must allow that his knowledge of classical and modern historians was not inconsiderable, and he was able to draw upon this effectively in all his political writings. It is this which lends them a force and an authority not often found in controversial pamphlets.

The same preoccupation may be observed in some of the things jotted down for his own amusement or for use when the occasion arose, such as the two next pieces, here printed from his manuscript—*Of public Absurdityes in England* and *Of Mean and Great Figures made by several Persons*. The former is concerned with the ridiculous customs and beliefs to be observed in English political life, which are exposed and condemned. When he gives his reasons for condemnation they are based not only on experience of political life, but are

[1] See below, p. 11.   [2] Ehrenpreis, *op. cit.* pp. 178, 180.

supported by an appeal to history. He is aware that the wisest
states are not exempt from folly, and that this proceeds less
from the nature of their climate than from that of their
government. The latter, however, might seem to indicate an
almost romantic fascination for the dramatic moment in the lives
of the heroes and the villains whose memories have survived. It
is not a composition at all, merely a list of those 'who have
made great Figures in some Particular Action or Circumstances
of their Lives' with a few notes jotted down indiscriminately
just as they occurred to him. Virgil, for instance, is placed
between the Black Prince and Mahomet; Cato between Robert
Harley and Sir Thomas More; and a short statement follows,
recalling the great moment of their lives. The list is incomplete, as it breaks off abruptly with just the name of Sir Jerome
Bows, without any explanation for his inclusion among these
great figures. Swift probably had in mind the rash courage of
Sir Jerome, in upholding the honour of his Queen when he
was ambassador to the Emperor of Muscovia in the year 1583,
as described by Hakluyt;[1] or it may be that he was still the
subject of 'pretty discourse' in good company in London, as
he had been in Pepys day.[2] The second list of contemptible
figures is even more miscellaneous, with such well-known
examples as Antony when he fled after Cleopatra, and Bacon
when convicted of bribery, together with more trivial instances
such as the Earl of Pembroke, who was whipped by a Scotch
lord at Newmarket, and Beau Fielding, who was laughed at
by the ladies when wounded in a quarrel on the stage. Such
instances might well provide material for satire upon human
pride and folly; but these lists show that Swift was equally
aware of and equally concerned with the moments of man's
glory as well as his shame.

The Letter to William King, Archbishop of Dublin, dated
January 1724, was written at the very height of his powers.
He was just finishing the first draft of *Gulliver's Travels* and just
about to begin his *Drapier's Letters*. It was a good moment

---

[1] Hakluyt, Richard, *Principal Navigations, voiages* etc. *of the English Nation*, 1598,
pp. 458f.
[2] Pepys *Diary*, Sep. 5, 1662, ed. Wheatley, II, 308-9.

to compose a 'humble Representation of the Clergy of the City of Dublin', to express in the polite phrases of a formal letter their unwillingness to respond to the Archbishop's appeal for the relief of one Charles McCarthy whose house in College Green was accidentally burnt to the ground, because of the general belief that he had himself set fire to it; and to expose the folly of the Archbishop in allowing himself to be imposed upon, as well as the greed of his officers and those of the great Seal, who receive a large part of such charities in fees and gratuities, and cause trouble to the dignitaries of the church and their church-wardens by the ridiculous demands placed upon them by these letters-patent. It could not have been intended for publication—with its implied criticism of the Archbishop—at a time when they were both concerned in the opposition to Wood's copper coinage. For, although the retionship between them had never been an easy one, during 1724 they were on cordial terms, and in July Swift wrote to King on the death of the Primate to tell him that he should accept the offer of the Primacy if it were made, and giving many reasons why he would wish to see him in that high office.[1]

The next two pieces were first printed by Deane Swift in 1765, and though the manuscripts from which he printed them are not known to have survived, there is no reason to doubt their authenticity. *The Letter addressed to the Writer of the Occasional Paper* was begun during Swift's last visit to London in 1727. A first draft had been shown to Bolingbroke before May 18, when he wrote to Swift and gave him some suggestions:

> In the epistle, a part of which you showed me, mention is made of the author of three Occasional Letters, a person entirely unknown. I would have you insinuate there, that the only reason Walpole can have had to ascribe them to a particular person, is the authority of one of his spies, who wriggles himself into the company of those who neither love, esteem, nor fear the Minister, that he may report, not what he hears, since no man speaks with any freedom before him, but what he guesses.

[1] *Corr.* iii, 199.

Then the next morning he adds:

> I had a hint or two more for you: but they have slipped out of
> my memory. Do not forget the sixty nor the twenty guineas, nor
> the Minister's character transferred into the administration.

Later, on June 6, he writes again:

> I return you the papers, which I have read twice over since you
> was here. They are extremely well; but the Craftsman has not
> only advertised the public, that he intended to turn newswriter,
> he has begun, and for some weeks continued to appear under
> that new character. This consideration inclines me to think, that
> another turn might be given to the introduction;[1]

Elrington Ball suggests 'that Bolingbroke was not altogether
satisfied that the Letter was calculated to assist his designs': and
Swift may therefore have decided not to finish it. But it may
have been abandoned for another reason, since ten days later
Swift is being persuaded that it would be inadvisable for him
to go off to France as he had been planning to do 'when the
opportunity for quitting Ireland for England is fairly before
him'.[2] If there was any thought of his making his peace at
Court, it would not be the moment to attack the scurrilous
methods of the writers employed by Walpole to slander his
opponents, or even to suggest that it would be better to cure
the corruptions complained of, and put an end to the malignity
of parties and encourage persons of merit and virtue. Later,
when he suddenly returned to Ireland, he was too much distressed with anxiety after receiving Sheridan's report of Stella's
illness to concern himself further with such matters.

It is evident that Deane Swift printed it from the unfinished
manuscript, and it is probable that these are the papers which
Bolingbroke had returned. There are adequate reasons why
Swift should have been drawn into the controversy. In
addressing the editor of the *Craftsman*, he refers particularly
to his paper, no. 45, of May 13, in which he had promised to
'subjoin to his usual Dissertation ... a faithful account of all
occurences foreign and domestick; ... to accommodate my
Readers whilst in the Country'. He wished to draw his attention to the scurrility and slander which had been poured out

[1] *Corr.* iii, 392-3 and 393-4.   [2] *Corr.* iii, 397.

in replies to 'The Occasional Writer', the second of whose papers had been advertised in the *Craftsman* of February 20, and the third on March 6, 1727; and he had urged him to 'enquire what real use such a conduct is to the cause they have been so largely paid to defend'. The particular paper he was referring to was entitled *An Answer to the Occasional Writer No. II*; it was addressed 'Worthy Sir, my once Rt Hon. Lord', and proceeded to attack Bolingbroke with great violence and maliciously to draw in Swift as well. He would not have liked this, for example:

> Doubtless by experience you can judge how easy it is for Malice to defame, and how useless a *Venal Pen* is; since even that of Men of the greatest Parts was not able to justify the Proceedings of a more *venal Ministry*, nor blacken the Glories of a successful War. How often has your Friend *Gulliver* lamented that he could say nothing in Harry's commendation, but what must necessarily be taken in an ironical Sense?

Nor would he have been less angered by a further passage in which the Occasional Writer's own words are borrowed to be turned against the *Examiner*:

> Let a Man declaim imperiously, and assert boldly, without regarding Proof, or condescending to Argue; let one of his Tools write a Pamphlet in much the same strain, and the Work is done. . . . This is what happened in the Year 1713 . . . when Numbers were deemed Evidence, and all that the Examiner wrote was received as Gospel.[1]

There can be no doubt that the author of the *Examiner* and of *Gulliver's Travels* began to write this letter with the intention of publishing it.

With it Deane Swift printed for the first time another paper, which he dated 1728, *The Account of the Court and Empire of Japan*, which under the very thin disguise indicated by the title describes the state of the political parties in England and the events which had just occurred when George II succeeded to the crown, and Walpole remained in power in spite of the obvious bribery and corruption which he found necessary to maintain his government. It ends with a speech in which

---

[1] *An Answer to the Occasional Writer No. II.*

Walpole is allowed to justify his past administration and with the utmost cynicism set forth the methods which will be needed to preserve the power of the Whigs. He warns the new monarch that it will be more expensive than hitherto, because the Tories

> from your favourable reception, have begun to reassume a spirit whereof the country had some intelligence; and we know the majority of the people, without proper management, would be still in that fatal interest.

However, for the cost of about a million sterling he promises to return as great a majority of senators of the true stamp as his Majesty can desire. And after his long experience he can assure his Majesty that

> without bribery and corruption, the wheels of government will not turn, or at least will be apt to take fire, like other wheels unless they be greased at proper times.[1]

This paper also must have been intended for publication, and we do not know why Swift never allowed it to appear. For some reason he seems to have decided not to take part openly in the campaign against Walpole. In a letter to the Countess of Suffolk, dated July 27, 1731, he claims that in spite of the usage he had received from Walpole,

> I never offended (him), although he was pleased to quarrel with me very unjustly, for which I showed not the least resentment, whatever I might have in my heart, nor was ever a partaker with those who have been battling with him for some years past.[2]

Elrington Ball maintains that Swift could hardly have made such a statement if he had really been the author of this *Account of the Court of Japan* and particularly if he had been responsible for the *Answer of Pulteney to Walpole*, so recently as October 15, 1730. But as neither of these pieces had been published, and as he had certainly not put his name to anything attacking Walpole, his statement is justifiable. Whatever resentment he had in his heart may have found expression here, but it could not have harmed Walpole any more than the parody of a

[1] See below, pp. 105–6.   [2] *Corr.* iv, 248.

lampoon on Cardinal Fleury, said to be the work of Swift, but
existing only in a few manuscript copies in 1731—

> With favour and fortune fastidiously blest
> he's loud in his laugh and he's coarse in his Jest
> of favour & fortune unmerited vain
> a sharper in trifles a dupe in the main
>
> .   .   .   .   .
>
> Tho I name not the wretch you know whom I mean
> T'is the Cur dog of Brittain & spaniel of Spain.[1]

There has been considerable difference of opinion about the
authenticity of *The Answer of the Right Honourable William
Pulteney Esq. to the Right Honourable Sir Robert Walpole*, which
Deane Swift included later in 1768 in the London edition of
Swift's *Works*. Faulkner had reprinted the other two pieces
from Deane Swift's volume in 1765, and he reprinted this
letter in the last volume of the Dublin edition in 1768.
Elrington Ball notes that it lacks 'the lighter touches which he
introduced into controversy of this kind',[2] and though
there are one or two sentences which sound like Swift,
the letter as a whole seems to me to lack the conciseness
and clarity, which can usually be detected even beneath all his
disguises. It may be said that writing under the name of
Pulteney, Swift might well have imitated something of the
manner of the *Craftsman*, and there is certainly nothing in the
content of the letter which he would not have endorsed. It is
a little dangerous to argue that at that time, in the middle of
October, shortly after returning from his visit to the Achesons,
he was not in a mood for political controversy; but we may
remember that early in November he had said in a letter to
Gay: 'I grow listless, and good for nothing . . . I have left off
writing.'[3]

It must remain a matter of some doubt, but I have followed his
eighteenth-century edition in accepting it. It clearly had nothing
to do with that collection of five letters,[4] with a similar title—
'From the Right Hon. Wm. P——y Esq; To the Right Honourable Sir R——t W——e; With Regard to the Observations on the

---

[1] *Poems*, Oxford, 1937, II, 540.   [2] *Corr.* iv, 248*n*.   [3] *Corr.* iv, 175.
[4] In the library of the Royal Irish Academy, Box 182, Tract 23.

Writings of the *Craftsman*,' advertized in Faulkner's *Dublin Journal*, Dec. 29, 1730. For they were a 'Continuation of Remarks on the History of *England*, from the *Minutes* of Mr. Oldcastle' referred to in the *Answer* as having been published to show

> the bad consequences to the publick, as well as to the prince, from the practices of evil ministers in most reigns, and at several periods, when the throne was filled by wise monarchs as well as by weak.

The main point of the *Answer* is one in which all the critics of Walpole would agree—namely, to draw attention to the great importance of the choice of the person on whom so much depends 'since the Asiatic custom of governing by prime ministers hath prevailed in so many courts of Europe'. They were all concerned to make it clear that attacks on the first minister did not involve any criticism of the Crown; for the wisest and ablest of monarchs may have 'sometimes put too much trust in confident, insinuating, and avaricious ministers'. And then the writer continues:

> Wisdom, attended by virtue and a generous nature, is not unapt to be imposed on. Thus Milton describes *Uriel*, the *sharpest-sighted spirit in heaven*, and *regent of the sun*, deceived by the dissimulation and flattery of the devil, for which the poet gives a philosophical reason, but needless here to quote.[1]

It may seem inconsistent, after having been careful to reject from the canon of Swift's writings everything of which there can be any real doubt of its authenticity, to include here in this volume not only the Preface to Captain Creichton's *Memoirs*, but the text of the *Memoirs* as well. But here we are dealing with something which is admittedly a collaboration; and the only thing we are doubtful about is the extent of the collaboration. According to Faulkner's note, Swift met Captain Creichton at Sir Arthur Acheson's and suggested that he should write his memoirs, at the same time offering to help him 'to place them in Order, prepare them for the Press and endeavour to get for him a Subscription among his Friends'. It seems likely that this is exactly what happened while they were both staying at Market Hill. They had met as early as

B   [1] See below, p. 116.

January 1729, when Swift sent instructions to Mrs. Brent, his housekeeper, to buy a bottle of usquebaugh and leave it at Captain Creichton's house in Capel Street, Dublin, for him to bring down with other things for Lady Acheson.[1] In the summers of 1729 and 1730 Swift spent three months at Market Hill; and the manuscript must have been finished during that time, as it is dated 'in the Year of our Lord, 1730'; it was printed in 1731.

When the volume appeared, it contained an *Advertisement to the Reader* written by Swift, in which he speaks of Captain Creichton as the Author, and commends the great simplicity in his style and manner, resembling

> the Memoirs of Philip de Comines[2] . . . equally natural, and with equal Appearance of Truth, though I confess, upon Affairs in a more obscure Scene, and of less Importance.

Faulkner's statement is rather different—the Dean

> compiled the Memoirs . . . and was particularly attentive to write in the natural, unadorned and even homely Style of a plain old Soldier.

This may be an exaggerated claim of the publisher; but there is evidence enough in the *Memoirs* themselves, that Creichton received considerable assistance from the Dean, who perhaps gives a hint of the amount of trouble he took in these cautious words:

> it was not with little Difficulty, that the Author was persuaded by his Friends, to recollect and put them in Order.

It appears that the Captain was not only accustomed to entertain his friends with accounts of his adventures, but that he had also taken Memoranda of them in writing; it may well be that Swift was able to use some of his manuscripts without much alteration or correction. But in the process of putting them in order and weaving them together it is very unlikely that he did not himself shape and give final form to a large part of the book. The opening paragraphs sound too much like Swift not to have been written by him; and the task of writing

---

[1] *Corr.* iv, 57.
[2] Swift possessed copies of the *Memoirs* of de Comines in both French and English. See Library Sale Catalogue, 1745, nos. 118 and 365.

memoirs would not have been uncongenial to the author of
Gulliver's Travels. He had been a great reader of Memoirs as
well as of Voyages, and I suspect that it was Swift, not the
Captain, who had noticed the infirmity in many writers of
memoirs of 'laying too much weight upon Trifles, which they
are vain enough to conceive the World to be as much concerned in as themselves'. And yet, even as he says this, he
remembers

> that Plutarch, in his Lives of great Men (which I have read in
> the English Translation) says, that the Nature and Disposition
> of a Man's Mind, may be often better discovered by a small
> Circumstance, than by an Action, or Event of the *greatest Im-
> portance*.[1]

I doubt whether Captain Creichton, if he had been referring to
his own reading of Plutarch, would have thought it necessary
to explain that he had read only the English translation; but if
Swift had the pen in hand at this moment, he would have
remembered that Creichton as a boy had only had time for
'some small Progress in Learning at the School of *Dungannon*'
before very inconsiderately marrying his School-master's
daughter at the age of eighteen. A good deal of the account
which the Captain gives of himself and his family is set down
in a way which is surprising for one who had had so little
practice in writing. Even if the story of his adventures may
have been taken from his own narration, or from notes made
in his own justification, it is likely that Swift tampered a good
deal with the materials and was responsible for ordering and
correcting them. We may remember his comment on Marshal
Schomberg's advice to Burnet 'never to meddle in the relation
of military matters'—*very foolish advice, for soldiers cannot write.*[2]
But if Captain Creichton was himself responsible for writing
the character of General Dalziel we might have to admit that
we had discovered a soldier who could write his memoirs, in
a style better than Burnet's, and who was concerned to give a
very different view of the struggle between the parties in
Scotland, without making any pretentions to be a historian:

[1] See below, p. 124.   [2] See below, p. 267.

what I chiefly proposed, was to write my own *Memoirs*, and not a *History of the Times*, further than I was concerned in them.

And in another place, where he can speak from his own experience, he bears witness against the errors of Bishop Burnet, who

> in his History of his own Times, hath in a most false and scandalous Manner, misrepresented the Action at *Bothwell-Bridge*, and the Behaviour of the *Episcopal Clergy* in *Scotland*.[1]

We may remember that when Swift had first read Burnet's remarks on the Episcopal clergy in the Fourth Book of his History he had written in the margin 'Partial Dog';[2] and, moreover, that in his *Advertisement to the Reader* he particularly draws attention to the fact that in this book of Creichton's *Memoirs*

> his plain Narration corrects many mistaken Passages in other Historians, which have too long passed for Truths.

Even if a large part of the narrative owes little more to Swift than editorial supervision, there might be some justification for including it, since he certainly put it in order. But, in addition, there are passages of irony and passages of explanatory comment, which though derived from the situation and experience of Captain Creichton, owe the form in which they are set down wholly to Swift himself. Unless I am very much mistaken Swift sometimes used this old soldier, who was still alive and for whose benefit the book was published, in a way not very different from that in which he had used Lemuel Gulliver, whom he had himself created. Through the voice of the old soldier as through the voice of the sea-captain we can detect the familiar accent of Swift:

> I lye under another Disadvantage, and indeed a very great one, from the wonderful change of Opinions, since I first made any appearance in the World. I was bred under Principles of strictest Loyalty to my Prince, and in an exact Conformity in *Discipline*, as well as *Doctrine*, to the *Church* of *England*; which are neither altered nor shaken to this very Day, and I am now too Old to mend.[3]

[1] See below, p. 146.   [2] See below, p. 285.   [3] See below, p. 124.

And even the paragraph which follows, in which he attempts to give a rational explanation of his dreams, and how he was guided by them in discovering one or two principal covenanters, owes something to Swift's concern to protect Captain Creichton from any taint of that superstition, which was the mark of his adversaries:

> God forbid I should pretend to a spirit of *Divination*, which would make me resemble those very Hipocritical Saints, whom it was both my *Duty* and *Inclination*, to bring to Justice, for their many horrid *Blasphemies* against God, *Rebellions* against their Prince, and *Barbarities* towards their *Countrymen*, and *Fellow-Christians*.

The *Memoirs* were included in the London and Dublin editions of Swift during the eighteenth century, and were accepted by their editors as a compilation of Swift's. Scott also reprinted them on the same grounds:

> To relieve this old gentleman's necessities, Swift compiled his tales of youthful adventure into a distinct narrative, which was published for the Captain's benefit, with considerable success.[1]

Monck Mason, who dislikes Scott's remarks about 'the obvious relish with which (Creichton's brutalities) are handed down to us by Swift' delights to point out that Scott has been deceived by the

> verisimilitude, which gives it the appearance of being expressed in the very words of the narrator himself; so well has Swift personated the character assumed on this occasion . . .[2]

The rest of the pieces in this volume are mainly documents of biographical interest; they are here printed from Swift's autographs, whenever they are available. Though this makes it necessary to dispense with any uniformity in matters of spelling, capitalization and punctuation in this volume, there are two advantages which may justify this procedure. The first is that in following exactly the peculiarities of Swift's manuscript, the character of these informal jottings is preserved, and we are reminded that they were never intended

[1] In his edition of Swift, 1814, I, 390.
[2] *The History and Antiquities of St. Patrick's, Dublin*, 1820, p. 385.

for publication among his literary works. Secondly, if we compare them with the earlier pieces included in this volume, which were edited by Deane Swift, we may observe to what extent the accidentals of spelling, etc., were standardized and the essentials preserved in the printed text.

The manuscript fragment of an autobiography is written on ten quarto leaves, on the right-hand half of the page, with marginal additions in the left-hand column, some of which have been entirely obliterated. It is an unfinished sketch, entitled *Family of Swift*, first printed by Deane Swift as an Appendix to his *Essay upon the Life, Writings and Character of Dr. Jonathan Swift*, in 1755. He says that it had been written 'about six or eight and twenty years ago,' and that it had been given him by Mrs. Whiteway. That would date it between 1727 and 1729, after the death of Stella. The fairer copy which Mrs. Whiteway said she had seen may be the copy preserved among the Orrery Correspondence, now in the Morgan library, with later annotations not by Swift. At the end of this copy there is a note:

> either Indolence, Sickness, Old Age or carelessness hindered the Dean from proceeding further in these Memoirs.

But Swift may never have intended to do more than provide an introductory sketch to the well-known facts of his public career. He seems to have written entirely from memory and has not even taken the trouble to verify all his dates; but this very lack of care shows that there is little justification for the suggestion that has recently been made that it is 'not a reliable foundation for any account of the Dean's background' but rather 'an account of what he wished to have said about himself.'[1] The two mistaken references to his age, which do not agree with the date of his birth, are obviously due to carelessness and not to any intention to deceive. And they were both corrected by Deane Swift, when he printed—very accurately—and carefully annotated the *Family of Swift*. He also corrected other errors in the account of the family of Godwin Swift, and of William and Thomas Swift, who were

[1] Denis Johnson, *In Search of Swift*, Dublin, 1959, pp. 10-14.

both incumbents of the church of St. Andrew in Canterbury. He did not think it necessary to record Swift's erasures and alterations in the manuscript. They will be found indicated below, as well as all the additional material provided in the annotated manuscript copy and in Deane Swift's notes to the printed version.

The notes on the death of his mother and of Mrs. Anne Long were both entered by Swift in his yearly account books for 1710 and 1711–12. They must be regarded as essentially a private expression of his feelings at the moment, intended for no other eyes than his own. He seems concerned to preserve a record of the moment with the utmost precision, the time and the circumstances when the letter was placed in his hands; we may therefore perhaps accept as equally a matter of fact what he then states as his confident belief in his mother's piety and charity, and the strong bond that he felt between them. There is a similar emphasis in the statement he entered in the following year when he heard of the death of Mrs. Anne Long; but here it was not only a private matter, for while he admits to Stella that he was 'never more afflicted at any death' he goes on to say:

> I have ordered a paragraph to be put in the *Post-boy*, giving an account of her death, and making honourable mention of her; but one reason was spite; for, her brother would fain have her death a secret, to save the charge of bringing her up here to bury her, or going into mourning. Pardon all this, for the sake of a poor creature I had so much friendship for.[1]

Some years later, Curll printed in a volume of *Letters, Poems & Tales*, 1718 'A Decree for concluding the Treaty between Dr. Swift and Mrs. Long'. It was probably written during Swift's Christmas visit to Sir Andrew Fountaine at his house in Leicester Fields, 'which began about the middle of the month of December, 1707 . . . and ended early in January, 1708 when Fountaine left town'. This suggestion of Elrington Ball is almost certainly correct, as also his cautious remark that

[1] *Journal to Stella*, Oxford, 1948, II, 446.

The Decree, which was found among Mrs. Long's papers, was not improbably Swift's composition, but purports to be issued by Ginkell Vanhomrigh, on the order of an arbitrator, who perhaps was Fountaine.[1]

The Dean of St. Patrick's Petition to the House of Lords Against the Lord Blayney is here printed from Swift's autograph manuscript—probably a first draft, since there are several alterations and corrections. It is not dated, but as the incident referred to is said to have taken place 'in the last session of Parliament, in the midst of winter', it was probably drawn up early in 1715, at a time when Swift was under suspicion of having had Jacobite sympathies. If Lord Blayney had benefited by Swift's good offices to him earlier in introducing him to Mr. Secretary Addison when Wharton was Lord Lieutenant, he would probably have regarded Swift as an enemy who had abandoned all his earlier Whig friends and had been particularly violent in his attack on Wharton. Ten years later, after the triumph of the Drapier and the acceptance of Swift as the Hibernian patriot, things had entirely changed; and the *Declaration*, dated January 8, 1733, printed here in Appendix D, shows what would have been the fate of anyone who had dared to annoy the Dean of St. Patrick's at that time. In a letter to Pope, dated July 8, 1733, Swift happens to refer specifically to this advantage he enjoys by living in Dublin where everyone gives him the way:

> I am one of the governors of all the hackney coaches, carts, and carriages, round this town, who dare not insult me like your rascally wagoners or coachmen, but give me the way; nor is there one Lord or squire for a hundred of yours, to turn me out of the road, or run over me with their coaches and six.[2]

The *Holyhead Journal*, also printed from the original autograph, dates from September, 1727, when Swift was on his way back to Dublin after his last visit to London. He had set out from the city on September 18, and had reached Chester on the 21st. He then rode on to Holyhead, missed the pacquet boat and was delayed there by the weather for about a week. He happened to have in his pocket a note-book, which he said

[1] *Corr.* iii, 457.　　　　[2] *Corr.* v, 3-4.

he had stolen from the Right Honourable George Dodington, Esq., one of the lords of the Treasury. He had only used it to make some memoranda of things to be done while he was in the City. The rest of the contents[1] were probably entered during these days, and consist of about six pages of verse, the note in which he prides himself on being wiser than Virgil or Horace, and than Pope and Gay, in refusing to attack his worthless enemies by name, and—without any title—what is generally called the *Holyhead Journal*.

It begins with the record of his leaving Chester at eleven in the morning of September 22, 1727, and arriving at Holyhead on Sunday, September 24, where he was delayed until Friday, Michaelmas Day, when they at last were able to put to sea, only to be driven back by fierce winds and again delayed, reaching Dublin finally on October 2. It contains, indeed, a lot of 'strange stuff'—the follies of Wat, his booby servant, the tricks of the guide, the badness of the food and drink and company, even an account of a strange dream he had, in which Pope and Bolingbroke were in the gallery of St. Patrick's Cathedral, and the latter was about to preach the sermon—but he asks a little querulously:

> what would you have me do. I have writt verses, and put down hints till I am weary. I see no creature, I cannot read by candle-light . . . I am now retired to my Chamber to scribble or sit hum-drum.[2]

It recalls certain passages in the *Journal to Stella*; and these scribblings too were doubtless intended to amuse her when Swift got back to Dublin. He knew that she had then not long to live; and four months after his return she was dead. On the night of her funeral, as soon as he was alone, he resolved to set down something of her life and character. Like a good many other pieces in this volume, the character of Stella was written 'for his own satisfaction'.

He wished to record her goodness and her friendship, his delight in educating her from the time she was six years old, his pleasure in her conversation, his approval of her judgment and her conduct. The next day he notes simply—'My head

[1] See Appendix B. [2] See below, p. 204.

aches and I can write no more'. But on January 30, the night of her funeral, which he was too ill to attend, he sat down at nine o'clock to continue his task, and managed to write a few more pages. Then later, as he found time, he added an account of her friends, her charitable deeds, her tastes and her admirable behaviour which had gained for her 'the universal good report of all who ever heard of her'. And finally he gathered up a few examples of her *Bon Mots*.

In 1755, ten years after Swift's death, the *Bon Mots* were printed; and in 1765 Deane Swift also published the Character of Stella. But Swift had allowed Pope to include in the *Last Volume* of their *Miscellanies*, 1727, the birthday verses and one or two other poems which he had written to her. In those lovely lines for her last birthday in 1727 he had tried to offer her some comfort in her illness:

> Yet since from Reason may be brought
> A better and more pleasing Thought,
> Which can in spite of all Delays
> Support a few remaining Days:
> From not the gravest of Divines,
> Accept for once some serious Lines.

And he argues that Virtue

> Looks back with Joy where she has gone,
> And therefore goes with Courage on.

Then he had written to comfort her; now he needs comfort for himself, and seeks it in the same way he had recommended to her:

> Say, *Stella*, feel you no Content,
> Reflecting on a Life well spent?[1]

But these reflections which he had set down in the time of his bereavement remain as a record not unworthy of her.

The other characters that are included here may serve to remind us that Swift was not given to polite eulogy.[2]

The Character of Archbishop Marsh must have been written some time after he was translated to Armagh as Primate of all Ireland in 1703, and before his death in 1713. It may perhaps

----

[1] *Poems*, II, 764.   [2] See also Appendix A.

be dated 1710, at the time when the Archbishop was ill and was not expected to live much longer. It is written with a cold detachment which gives it the quality of a judgment pronounced quite impersonally by one who has never had any real connection with him; and yet it has such a sting that Swift seems not to have been able to forget the two occasions when the Archbishop had shown by his lack of confidence that he had no proper recognition of Swift's qualities. For it was Marsh who, in 1694, when he was Archbishop of Dublin, had insisted on a certificate from Sir William Temple,[1] before allowing Swift to take orders; and it was Marsh again, who after authorizing Swift on October 24, 1710, to 'take the full management' of the business of soliciting the First Fruits for the Church of Ireland, at the very moment when Swift had carried out his mission so speedily by appealing directly to Harley, allowed the bishops to take away his commission so that the matter might be dealt with by the Duke of Ormond, who had just been made Lord Lieutenant.[2]

If, as seems likely, the *Character of Mrs Howard* was written on June 12, 1727,[3] when Swift was staying with Gay in London, it was based on an acquaintance which had begun in the previous year when Dr. Arbuthnot had taken Swift to Leicester House, after repeated invitations from her Royal Highness. But during that summer Swift also met her frequently at Richmond and at her own house, Marble Hill. After his return to Ireland he had sent her a present of Irish plaid, and later 'the crown of Lilliput . . . as a small acknowledgment of your favour to my book and person'.[4] He was obviously much attracted by her as a private person—

> In all offices of life, except those of a courtier, she acts with justice, generosity and truth

but he is already doubtful about 'what part she may act here-after in a larger sphere': even though she may be able to preserve her private virtues to be used later on in her retirement.

---

[1] *Corr.* i, 13 and *n.*   [2] *Corr.* i, 210, 211.
[3] See *Letters to and from Henrietta, Countess of Suffolk*, 1824, p. xxxviii.
[4] *Corr.* iii, 354, 369.

In 1731, in his *Verses on the Death of Dr. Swift*, she appears for a moment, as a courtier, to announce his death:

> Kind Lady Suffolk in the Spleen
> Runs laughing up to tell the Queen:

and he adds a note:

> Mrs Howard, afterwards Countess of Suffolk, then of the Bed-chamber to the Queen, proposed much Friendship for the Dean.[1]

He may well have had in mind what he had written here, that if she had never seen a Court, it is not impossible that she might have been a friend. In August, 1727, during the last weeks that Swift spent in England, they exchanged a number of letters, from which it could only be assumed that she was trying to provide some preferment for Swift in England. Even though he might have refused it, he was evidently annoyed that no offer was ever made. His final opinion of her is very frankly expressed in a letter to Gay of June 29, 1731:

> I always told you Mrs Howard was good for nothing but to be a rank courtier. I care not whether she ever writes to me or no. She has cheated us all.[2]

The *History of the Second Solomon* is a curious performance—a sort of reckoning set down of Sheridan's dealings with his friends, a history in which the judge sums up the case and pronounces judgment, though knowing perfectly well that it will not affect the character or conduct of the accused:

> He is a generous, honest, good-natured man; but his perpetual want of judgment and discretion makes him act as if he were neither generous, honest, nor good-natured.[3]

It was early in their acquaintance that Sheridan had dared to make fun of Swift's poetry. Swift, not wishing to be thought 'a man who could not take a Jest' wrote in verse to Delany, asking him as a young friend of Sheridan's to

> Venture to give him some Advice.
> Few Hints from you will set him right,
> And teach him how to be polite.

          .   .   .   .   .

[1] *Poems*, II, 559.   [2] *Corr.* iv, 233.   [3] See below, p. 225.

> And I no more shall then accuse
> The Flirts of his ill-mannerd Muse.[1]

This was sent to Delany in November, 1718, and meanwhile throughout the year Swift had continued to exchange verses with Sheridan: again in 1719 and 1721 similar exchanges indicate the closeness of their association and the ease of their friendship.

On April 17, 1725, just before leaving Dublin to spend the summer with Stella and Mrs. Dingley at Quilca—'a wild place belonging to Mr. Sheridan'—Swift wrote to Lord Carteret, asking him to bestow a church living on him to the value of one hundred and fifty pounds, in recognition of his excellent work as a schoolmaster. It is probable that it was in this year, as Elrington Ball suggests,[2] that Swift began on April 20, after they had arrived at Quilca, to draw up 'The Blunders, Deficiencies and Misfortunes of Quilca'. This was followed by some verses 'To Quilca a Country House in no very good repair, where the supposed Author and some of his Friends, spent a summer, in the Year 1725'. It was the same summer that Sheridan received preferment from Carteret and advice from Swift on his proper behaviour, backed by the authority of Stella: they were particularly concerned that he should not enlarge his expenses:

> neither let me hear of one rag of better clothes for your wife or brats, but rather plainer than ever. This is positively Stella's advice as well as mine. She says now you need not be ashamed to be thought poor.[3]

When shortly afterwards Sheridan got into trouble for preaching at Cork on the King's birthday from the text, 'Sufficient unto the day is the evil thereof' and was consequently struck off the list of the Lord Lieutenant's chaplains, Swift at once wrote to Tickell, Carteret's Secretary, on behalf of his friend[4] and promised as soon as he returned to Dublin to see the Lord Lieutenant. In the following years nothing seems to have disturbed their friendship, and at Easter, in 1728, they made a tour together through the south-eastern part of Ireland.

---

[1] *Poems*, I, 218-9.   [2] *Corr.* iii, 237*n*.   [3] *Corr.* iii, 246.   [4] *Corr.* iii, 270.

During the following months Swift contributed to Sheridan's new venture, *The Intelligencer*, until it was dropped. But Swift's patience was finally exhausted when Sheridan failed to come to Market Hill in January, 1729, where Swift was waiting to return with him to Dublin; and he seems to have made this misunderstanding the reason for a quarrel. Deane Swift dates the *History of the Second Solomon* at this time. It may also have been prompted by Sheridan's folly in writing a song for the Queen's birthday full of flattery for the Royal Family, 'by which he lost all the esteem of his old friends the Tories, and got not the least interest with the Whigs'. Nevertheless, in spite of their estrangement in these later years, Swift wrote some time after Sheridan's death on October 10, 1738, a *Character of Doctor Sheridan*, with the purpose of appealing to former pupils of his to erect some decent monument in the church where he was buried. Here, though he does not forget his follies and his ignorance of worldly management—

> He was (as it is frequently the case in men of wit and learning) what the French call a *Dupe*, and in a very high degree—

he sets no bounds to his admiration for Sheridan's brilliant gifts as a schoolmaster:

> His chief shining quality was that of a schoolmaster; here he shone in his proper element. . . . He was doubtless the best instructor of youth in these kingdoms, or perhaps in Europe.[1]

MARGINALIA

IN an edition such as this, which is mainly intended to provide the text of Swift's prose writings, it might be thought unnecessary to include some of the informal personal jottings never intended for publication and the notes and marginalia found in some of the books he had read. But since such things have found their way into earlier editions, they may be looked for here; and as in recent years other volumes have come to light containing annotations in Swift's hand it may be convenient that they should be collected here. They are arranged

[1] See below, p. 216.

in the order in which the volumes were read. It should be pointed out also that there are a number of other volumes, which were marked in the Sale Catalogue of 1745 as being annotated, some of which are not now known, and some, now in the library of Lord Rothschild and in the Morgan Library, which bear the signature of Swift on the title-page and sometimes a note giving a price or a date or provenance.[1] His copy of Cicero *de Officiis*, 1517,[2] was inscribed on the verso of the fly-leaf 'The gift of Edw: Pearce, Esqr 1730'. His copy of the English translation of Philip de Comines *Historie*, 1614,[3] has pencil marks throughout, and comments on the passage (p. 54) about the evils caused by an unwise Prince:

> The present state of England
> Where can she find a wise one? except K. George 2ᵈ.

His copy of Robert Parsons' *A Conference about the next Succession to the Crown of England*, 1681,[4] contains a number of unimportant textual corrections and notes which are the first of the Marginalia, being dated Decbr 28. 1705; they are printed here with the permission of Lord Rothschild. His copy of Lucretius (Amsterdam, 1631)[5] contains a label opposite the title-page with a second signature and the date 'Apr. 29 1699' and bears all the marks of having been read with great care, if we may assume that the frequent pencil points in the margins throughout the whole of the five books and the occasional pointing fingers were made by Swift. His copy of Herodotus (Geneva 1618) contains not only the most interesting comment on Herodotus dated July 6, 1720, but beneath it a certificate from George Faulkner, Swift's printer, dated 1762 that 'the above is the Handwriting of the late Dr. Swift'.[6] His copy of *Suetonii Vitæ Cæsarum*, 1574 (Sale Cat. 285) had no

---

[1] See *Catalogue of Dean Swift's Library in* 1715, by T. P. LeFanu (Proceedings of the Royal Irish Academy, July, 1927); *Dean Swift's Library* by Harold Williams, Cambridge 1932; and *The Rothschild Library*, vol. II, Cambridge, 1954.

[2] Sale Cat. 625; Rothschild 2308.   [3] Sale Cat. 365; Rothschild 2309.

[4] Sale Cat. 419; Rothschild 2316.

[5] Morgan Library, New York. This copy probably given to Rev. John Jackson. Another copy of Lucretius, Cantab, 1675. Sale Cat. 30. Caesar, 1635; Sale Cat. 155. (Note in 1715; design'd for D. Jackson.)

[6] Sale Cat. 92; Winchester College Library. See below.

annotations. Some Latin notes on Suetonius have however been recently found in Swift's autograph.[1]

We can determine for the most part when the annotations were made, and some of them are precisely dated. In two letters written in July 1722 to Esther Vanhomrigh and Charles Ford Swift refers to his reading many 'diverting books of history and travels'—'abundance of trash'. But he had evidently begun at least two years before this to prepare for the writing of his own Travels. For in his copy of Thomas Herbert's *A Relation of some Yeares Travaile, begunne Anno 1626. Into Africa and the greater Asia*, 1634,[2] he has written opposite the title his opinion of the book with his signature and the date 1720. He adds further a comment on the reputation which the author had in Ireland where he lived several years after the Restoration. There are also some pencilled markings on several pages of the text, but no marginal annotations.

His copy of Bodin's *Les Six Livres de la Republique*, 1576[3] has his signature on the title-page and the date when he presumably acquired the volume, 1709; but a leaf pasted on the inside of the cover has another signature Jonath: Swift and the date April 2d 1725, with a note below:

Les notes au crayon sur les pages sont aussi de Swift.

These notes are very scanty and often nothing more than outbursts of disapproval—le sot, le coquin!—and if one could be sure that they were all made by Swift's pen, the numerous crosses in the margin, and the underlinings in ink would be more significant.

The notes to *The Life and Raigne of King Henry the Eighth*, 1649, written by Edward, Lord Herbert of Cherbury, were transcribed[4] from Swift's copy, which was very kindly lent

[1] See James Clifford and Irvin Ehrenpreis, *Swiftiana in Rylands Eng Ms.* 659 etc. BJRL, 1955, xxxviii, 368.
[2] Sale Cat. 378; now in Harvard University Library, where there is also a copy of James Puckle, *The Club*, 1713, with the signature of Pope and Swift on the title-page, and on several pages pencilled crosses in the margin and pointing fingers, which look like Swift's markings.
[3] Sale Cat. 591; Yale University Library.
[4] Sale Cat. No. 366; R.2313. An account of the volume and the annotations was published in *Some Unpublished Marginalia of Jonathan Swift*. Privately printed, Cambridge, 1945.

me by Lord Rothschild. On the title-page, in the top right hand corner is the signature, Jon: Swift; and beneath the name of the author he has also written 'with notes by J:S.' Those transcribed below are all quite certainly in the hand of Swift, and express his well-known and unchanging detestation of Henry VIII. A few letters were cut off when the book was rebound. These are supplied within square brackets, and only twice could there be any question of what he has written. The book contains also one or two minor corrections and marginal comments which are not in Swift's hand; they may be due to the former owners, Jo. Heath and Edw. Heath, whose signatures are also on the title-page.

The notes on Addison's *Freeholder* are printed from Scott's transcription of those made in Swift's hand in a copy which belonged to Dr. Bernard, Bishop of Limerick.[1] To one of his notes Swift adds the year in which it was written, 1727; and other notes indicate that Swift's comments were made before King George I's death in the autumn. They are concerned with twenty out of the fifty-five numbers, which ran from December 23, 1715 to June 29, 1716. At that time Swift was still on good terms with Addison, and wrote to him in 1717 to congratulate him on his appointment as Secretary of State—

for no other reason . . . beside that great love and esteem I have always had for you.

Yet when he came to read over these papers later he could not forgive him for some of the opinions he found expressed in them, whether concerned with the clemency of George I and his love for the Church of England, or with the charm of the essays of Sir Richard Blackmore 'so insipid a scoundrel, whom I know he despised'.

The Observations on Heylin's *History of the Presbyterians*, 1670, were first printed in *An Appendix to Dr. Swift's Works*, published in April, 1767. There is no mention of the book either in the Catalogue of Swift's Library in 1715 or in the Sale Catalogue among the annotated volumes; but we may accept the statement that Swift's remarks were written by him

C   [1] See Swift's *Works*, ed. Walter Scott, x, 197.

on one of the blank leaves in the beginning of the book and dated March 6, 1727–8; for, in commenting upon Heylin's 'too high notions of regal power', a mistake into which the clergy fell in the reign of Charles II, he refers to a treatise in which he had explained this. What he has in mind here is evidently what he had written in 1708—*The Sentiments of a Church of England Man*, especially the second section dealing with Government.[1]

Swift's comments on Sir John Browne's *Tracts on Irish Trade* are contained in a presentation copy,[2] bound in Russian leather gilt with an inscription on the cover:

TO THE REVERD.
DEAN SWIFT

The volume contains an *Essay on Trade in General: And, on that of Ireland in Particular*, and *Seasonable Remarks on Trade*. Swift has marked certain passages with a pencilled cross in the margin and has here and there added a comment. The author had been accused in the Third Drapier Letter[3] of great disloyalty to Ireland, and had later appealed to Swift against this harsh judgment in a letter of April 4, 1728,[4] which he sent soon after the presentation of his essays. In that year he had also written the *Memorial of the poor Inhabitants, Tradesmen and Labourers of the Kingdom of Ireland*, to which Swift had replied, though evidently unaware at that time who the author was, for he says:

you appear to write as a stranger, and as of a Country which is left at Liberty to enjoy the Benefits of Nature etc.[5]

There is no record that Swift ever replied to his letter, but at least he remembered it when he came to prepare the text of the *Drapier's Letters* for the Dublin edition of his collected *Works*, and omitted the passages in which Browne had been 'branded as a villain'.

There are a number of copies of the *Memoirs of the Secret*

---

[1] See vol. ii of this ed., p. 13f.
[2] Now in the library of Sir Harold Williams.
[3] Ibid., vol. x, pp. 28, 37, 210.   [4] See *Corr.* iv, 24.
[5] Ibid., vol. xii, p. 23.

Services of John Macky Esq., 1733, in which Swift's Marginalia have been transcribed.[1] I have printed them here from the copy in the Houghton Library, which has the bookplate of John Putland, surgeon, and is the source of several of these later transcriptions, and itself said to be copied from 'the Original in the Dean's own Writing'. They are in some ways the most interesting of all the marginalia, because they are a record of Swift's impression both of the physical appearance and the character of the persons discussed. Sometimes he is concerned mainly to correct some particular point in Macky's description; sometimes he makes only a general comment. Macky is said to have written these characters of the English and Scottish nobility and of the chief naval and military officers about the year 1703 at the request of the Princess Sophia, Electress Dowager of Hanover. His impressions of the persons he describes were probably gained mainly in the years just before the death of William III, when he was employed as a confidential agent and must have had a good opportunity to make his observations on the chief persons at Court. It should be remembered that when Swift made his comments he was drawing upon his memories of the same persons as he had seen them ten or twelve years later from 1710 to 1714; though this would not wholly account for their differences of opinion on such matters as stature and physical appearance.

The comments on Howell's *Medulla Historiae Anglicanae* are found in a copy of the book which Swift had given to Mary Harrison, daughter of Mrs. Whiteway and afterwards Mrs. Deane Swift, on May 29, 1736, 'to encourage her to read usefull and improving Books'. It was a popular Whig history, and Swift took care that she should have plenty of warning against the bias and the nonsense to be found in it. The Marginalia have been fully described in an article by Francis Manley[2] who kindly drew my attention to the volume which is now in the Library of Johns Hopkins University. It was a copy of the ninth edition, published in 1734, and so these annotations must have been made during the years 1734–6, at

---

[1] Not in Sale Cat.; see *Dean Swift's Library*, pp. 63-4.
[2] See P.M.L.A. Sep. 1958, LXXII, 335-8.

a time when Swift was occupied with the final revision of his own history, *The Four Last Years of the Queen*.

Then or later he was reading and marking Burnet's *History of his own Times*, of which the final volume appeared in 1734. Swift's annotated copy came into the possession of Dr. Lyon, and in 1768 was presented by him to Lord Shelburne, afterwards the first Marquis of Landsdowne.[1] It is said to be in the Library at Bowood, but I have not been given the opportunity to examine it. The Marginalia were first printed in part in *The European Magazine*, January 1795–February 1796. They were printed by Scott in his edition of Swift in 1814 and by Routh in his edition of Burnet's *History* in 1823.

In his *Short Remarks on Burnet's History*,[2] which may have been written any time after the publication of the first volume in 1724, Swift condemned Burnet's style and complained of a permanent bias in all his writings:

> He never gives a good character without one essential point, that the person was tender to Dissenters and thought many things in the Church ought to be amended.

But it must be remembered that he also spoke of Burnet as 'a man of generosity and good nature, and very communicative'; and sometimes he admits that 'there is something in this argument' and 'all this is certainly true'. The greater part of the annotations are contained in the first volume of the history and only the last hundred pages of the second volume are commented on here and there. It is not surprising to find that when he is dealing with the events during the last years of the Queen's reign his Whig comments stir Swift to his angriest outbursts—'a false prophet in every particular', 'foolish and factious', or worst of all, 'a vile Scot'.

It was probably when he had returned to London in 1703, and after he had allowed it to be known that he was the author of that remarkable pamphlet, *The Contests and Dissentions of the Nobles and Commons in Athens and Rome etc.*[3] which had been attributed both to Lord Somers and to Burnet himself that

---

[1] The annotations were probably finished in Jan. 1739; see below, p. 294. See also *Dean Swift's Library*, pp. 61-2.

[2] See below, p. 183.   [3] See vol. i of this edit., p. 191.

Swift first met the Bishop, who had 'desired his acquaintance with great marks of esteem and professions of kindness' and it must have been at that time that they discussed together the public affairs in which Burnet had taken part, for Swift says:

> He hath told me many passages not mentioned in this history, and many that are, but with several circumstances suppressed or altered.[1]

It was evidently then that Swift found him 'very communicative'; but their acquaintance cannot have lasted long, for Swift complains that after 1705, in the last years ten of his life, 'he was absolutely party-mad, and fancied he saw Popery under every bush'. His final judgment is a complete condemnation of Burnet as a historian:

> This author is in most particulars the worst qualified for an historian that ever I met with. His style is rough, full of improprieties . . . His observations are mean and trite, and very often false. His secret history is generally made up of coffee house scandals . . . he is the most partial of all writers that ever pretended so much to impartiality.[2]

Like most of his contemporaries, Swift was always much concerned with the study of history, classical and modern. Of the 657 items in the sale catalogue of his library, nearly a hundred were historical works; and if the twenty-nine volumes of Gronovius and Graevius were there mainly for show, a good many of the others were carefully read and annotated; some of the folio volumes of Baronius' *Annales Ecclesiastici* containing marginalia in Swift's hand. And though he was inclined to accept the current view that no great history had yet been written in English, no English Herodotus or Livy had yet appeared, there was nevertheless one book on his shelves, which by the dignity and magnificence of its style, and by its judgments on men and events, must have seemed to him to have almost all the qualities which he required in a historian; and it was a book which he had read and re-read, and marked and annotated more fully than any other, noting finally that he

---

[1] See vol. viii of this edit., p. 119.   [2] See below, p. 183.

had completed his fourth reading of it on April 18, 1741. This book was Clarendon's *History of the Rebellion*.[1]

At first sight many of the comments which Swift has scribbled in the margin seem trivial, mere reiterations of his dislike of the Scots, angry outbursts against them for the part they took in the rebellion, from that sentence that appears already on the very first leaf of Vol. I:

> The cursed, Hellish Vilany, Treachery, Treasons of the Scots, were the chief Grounds and Causes of that execrable Rebellion.

But if we turn over the pages and pay some attention to the passages which are underlined or marked in various ways in the margin, with vertical lines or sometimes a pointing finger, we cannot fail to realize the importance of this book for Swift, and how completely he sometimes surrendered himself to the spell of Clarendon's rhetoric. He is aware of a certain awkwardness and heaviness in some of Clarendon's sentences, a confusion of 'thats' and 'thems', the danger of a sort of official style clogging his Ciceronian periods; he occasionally marks these careless repetitions, or draws attention to an impossibly long parenthesis. But these were minor blemishes, and could easily be corrected like the punctuation, which Swift constantly tinkers with as he reads. Such things did not destroy the dignity of his tone or interfere with the admirable ordering of events and the splendid marshalling of his arguments. Here was one who did possess the requisite qualities of the historian, who could draw upon a wide experience of men and affairs, and was acquainted with the necessary official papers; one who, after the conflict was over and his own active career ended could attempt a calm and careful judgment on the course of the whole sorry business. Swift was able to share in part Clarendon's sense of the tragedy that had befallen his generation, in that the Rebellion had destroyed what should have been a period of the greatest felicity, for he had once written:

> I take the highest period of Politeness in *England* (and it is of the same date in France) to have been the peaceable part of King *Charles* the First's reign.[2]

[1] Sale Cat. 238; now in Marsh's Library, Dublin.
[2] See vol. iv of this edit., p. 94.

But Clarendon is not guarded enough to satisfy Swift's maturer judgment, when he says that it was a period when

> all his Majesty's Dominions . . . enjoy'd the greatest Calm, and the fullest Measure of Felicity, that any People in any Age, for so long time together, have been bless'd with; to the wonder, and envy of all the other parts of Christendom.

And when he ends up with a rhetorical flourish:

> In a word, many wise men thought it a Time, wherein those Two Adjuncts, which Nerva was Deified for uniting, *Imperium & Libertas*, were as well reconciled as is possible.

Swift underlines the word *Libertas* with his pencil, and writes in the margin 'Nego.' Moreover, in his *Presbyterian's Plea of Merit*, 1733, he had explained why he could not agree that there was no thought of making any alteration in religion or government before 1640:

> I have found by often rummaging for old books in Little Britain and Duck-Lane, a great number of pamphlets printed from the year 1630 to 1640, full of as bold and impious railing expressions, against the lawful power of the Crown, and the order of Bishops, as ever were uttered during the Rebellion, or the whole subsequent Tyranny of that fanatic Anarchy.[1]

Sometimes it is Clarendon's caution and understatement that produces the most violent comment, as when he mildly remarks of Sir Anthony Cooper, later Earl of Shaftesbury:

> the flexibility and instability of that Gentleman's nature, not being then understood, or suspected,

Swift writes in the margin 'a great Vilain' and 'an early Rogue'. But generally he is in sympathy with Clarendon's attitude, and it is the events of his tragic story and the unfortunate actors in it which provoke his angry outbursts. When Clarendon comes to that central point of his whole narrative, the death of Lord Falkland at Newbury, which symbolizes the end of that period of great felicity, Swift marks with every sign of approval—pencilled lines and pointing fingers—that noble passage in which Clarendon takes great pains to prepare his readers to

[1] See vol. xii of this edit., p. 264.

pause before the memorial he wished to leave of that great
man—

> if the celebrating the memory of eminent and extraordinary
> Persons, and transmitting their great Virtues, for the imitation of
> Posterity, be one of the principal ends and duties of History it will
> not be thought impertinent in this place, to remember a loss
> which no time will suffer to be forgotten, and no success or
> good fortune could repair.

It is pleasant at this point to observe Swift under the spell of
Clarendon's emotion, himself ready to believe in and admire
such unparalleled goodness and virtue, and to admit that the
death of 'that incomparable young man' 'moves grief to the
highest Excess'.[1]

Swift does not often speak of Clarendon, but when he does
it is in terms that show he fully recognized his great qualities.
He mentions him among the number of great commoners who
from the time of the Restoration had taken the place of the
nobility as chief ministers of State, and in a letter to Bolingbroke he puts him by the side of Bacon and Shaftesbury as
one of those great geniuses, who 'if they had not been so
great, would have been less unfortunate'.[2] And his *History* was
evidently for Swift a book worthy of his quality, which he
could not read without excitement, and which he had in mind
when he wrote his preface to his own *History of the Four Last
Years of Queen Anne.*

[1] See below, p. 304.   [2] *Corr.* iii, 41.

An Abstract of
the History of England
to William the Conqueror

AN

ABSTRACT

OF THE

HISTORY of ENGLAND

From the Invasion of it by Julius Cæsar to William the Conqueror.

T HE most antient account we have of Britain is, that the island was full of inhabitants, divided into several petty kingdoms, as most nations of the world appear to have been at first. The bodies of the Britons were painted Britons. with a sky-coloured blue, either as an ornament or else for terror to their enemies. In their religion they were Heathens, Heathens. as all the world was before Christ, except the Jews.

Their priests were called Druids: These lived in hollow Druids. trees, and committed not their mysteries to writing, but delivered them down by tradition, whereby they were in time wholly lost.

The Britons had wives in common, so many to a particular tribe or society, and the children were in common to that society.

About fifty years before Christ, Julius Cæsar, the first Roman Emperor, having conquered Gaul or France, invaded Britain rather to increase his glory than conquests; for, having overcome the natives in one or two battles, he returned.

The next invasion of Britain by the Romans (then masters of most of the known world) was in the reign of the Emperor Claudius. Claudius; but it was not wholly subdued till that of Nero. Nero. It was governed by lieutenants, or deputies, sent from Rome, as Ireland is now by deputies from England; and continued thus under the Romans for about 460 years; until that empire being invaded by the Goths and Vandals, the Romans were forced not only to recal their own armies, but also to draw from hence the bravest of the Britons, for their assistance against those Barbarians.

The Roman conquests in this island reached no further northward than to that part of Scotland where Stirling and Glasgow are seated: The region beyond was held not worth the conquering: It was inhabited by a barbarous people, Picts. called Caledonians and Picts; who, being a rough fierce nation, daily infested the British borders. Therefore the Emperor Severus built a wall, from Stirling to Glasgow, to prevent the invasions of the Picts: It is commonly called Picts wall. the Picts Wall.

These Picts and Caledonians, or Scots, encouraged by the departure of the Romans, do now cruelly infest and invade A.D. 455. the Britons by sea and land: The Britons chuse Vortigern Saxons. for their king, who was forced to invite the Saxons, (a fierce northern people) to assist him against those Barbarians. The Saxons came over, and beat the Picts in several battles; but, at last, pick quarrels with the Britons themselves; and, after a long war, drive them into the mountains of Wales and Cornwall, and establish themselves in seven kingdoms in Britain, (by them now called England.) These seven kingdoms are usually stiled the Saxon Heptarchy.

A.D. 460. About this time lived King Arthur (if the whole story Arthur. be not a fable) who was so famous for beating the Saxons in several battles.

The Britons received Christianity very early, and, as is reported, from some of the disciples themselves: So that, when the Romans left Britain, the Britons were generally A.D. 600. Christians. But the Saxons were Heathens, till Pope Gregory Austin. the Great sent over hither Austin the Monk, by whom Ethelbert king of the South-Saxons, and his subjects, were converted to Christianity; and the whole island soon followed the example.

After many various revolutions in this island among the Egbert. kingdoms of the Saxons, Egbert, descended from the West-A.D. 819. Saxon kings became sole monarch of England.

The language in Britain was British (now called Welch) or Latin; but, with the Saxons, English came in (although extremely different from what it is now.) The present names of towns, shires, &c. were given by them; and the whole kingdom was called England from the Angles, who were a branch of the Saxons.   Angles.

As soon as the Saxons were settled, the Danes began to trouble and invade them, as they (the Saxons) had before done the Britons.   Danes.

These Danes came out of Germany, Denmark, and Norway, a rough warlike people, little different from the Saxons, to whom they were nigh neighbours.

After many invasions from the Danes, Edgar king of England sets forth the first navy. He was entitled King of all Albion, (an old name of this island) and was the first absolute monarch. He made peace with the Danes, and allowed them to live in his dominions mixt with the English.   Edgar.

In this Prince's time there were five kings in Wales, who all did him homage for their country.

These Danes began first to make their invasions here about the year 800, which they after renewed at several times, and under several leaders, and were as often repulsed. They used to come with vast numbers of ships, burn and ravage before them, as the cities of London, Winchester, &c. Encouraged by success and prey, they often wintered in England, fortifying themselves in the northern parts, from whence they cruelly infested the Saxon kings. In process of time they mixed with the English (as was said before) and lived under the Saxon government: But Ethelred, then king of England, weary of the Danish insolence, a conspiracy is formed, and the Danes are massacred in one day all over England.   A.D. 978. Danes massacred.

Four years after, Sweyn, king of Denmark, to revenge the death of his subjects, invades England; and, after battles fought and much cruelty exercised, he subdues the whole kingdom, forcing Ethelred to fly into Normandy.   Sweyn.

Sweyn dying, his son Canutus succeeds in the Kingdom; but Ethelred returning with an army, Canutus is forced to withdraw to Denmark for succour.   Canutus.

Ethelred dies, and his son Edmond Ironside succeeds; but, Canutus returning with fresh forces from Denmark, after several battles, the kingdom is parted between them both. Edmond dying, his sons are sent beyond sea by Canutus, who now is sole king of England.

Hardicanute, the last Danish king, dying without issue, Edward, son of Ethelred, is chosen king. For his great holiness, he was sirnamed the Confessor, and sainted after his death. He was the first of our princes that attempted to cure the king's evil by touching. He first introduced what is now called the Common Law. In his time began the mode and humour among the English gentry, of using the French tongue and fashions, in compliance with the King, who had been bred up in Normandy.

King's Evil.

The Danish government in England lasted but twenty-six years, under three kings.

Edward the Confessor married the daughter of Earl Godwin, an English nobleman of great power, but of Danish extraction; but, wanting issue, he appointed Edgar Atheling, grandson to his brother, to succeed him, and Harold, son of Earl Godwin, to be governor of the young prince. But, upon Edward's death, Harold neglected Edgar Atheling, and usurped the crown for himself.

Harold.

Edward, while he was in Normandy, met so good reception, that it was said he made a promise to that Duke, that, in case he recovered his kingdom, and died without issue, he would leave it to him. Edward dying, William Duke of Normandy sends to Harold to claim the crown; but Harold, now in possession, resolves to keep it. Upon which Duke William, having prepared a mighty fleet and army, invades England, lands at Hastings, and sets fire to his fleet, to cut off all hope from his men of returning. To Harold he sent his messenger, demanding the kingdom and his subjection: But Harold returned him this answer, That, unless his departed his land, he would make him sensible of his just displeasure. So Harold advanced his forces into Sussex, within seven miles of his enemy. The Norman Duke, to save the effusion of blood, sent these offers to Harold; either wholly to resign the kingdom to him, or to try the quarrel with him in single combat. To this Harold did not agree.

Then the battle joined. The Normans had gotten the worst, if it had not been for a stratagem they invented, which got them the day. In this engagement Harold was killed, and William Duke of Normandy became king of England, under the name of William the Conqueror. A.D. 1066.

A Fragment of the History
from William Rufus

TO THE
COUNT DE GYLLENBORG

Dublin in Ireland, Nov. 2, 1719

SIR,

IT is now about sixteen years since I first entertained the design of writing a history of *England*, from the beginning of *William Rufus* to the end of queen *Elizabeth*; such a history, I mean, as appears to be most wanted by foreigners, and gentlemen of our own country; not a voluminous work, nor properly an abridgment, but an exact relation of the most important affairs and events, without any regard to the rest. My intention was to inscribe it to the king* your late master, for whose great virtues I had ever the highest veneration, as I shall continue to bear to his memory. I confess it is with some disdain that I observe great authors descending to write any dedications at all: and for my own part, when I looked round on all the princes of *Europe*, I could think of none who might deserve that distinction from me, besides the king your master; (for I say nothing of his present *Britannick* majesty, to whose person and character I am an utter stranger, and like to continue so) neither can I be suspected of flattery on this point, since it was some years after that I had the honour of an invitation to his court, before you were employed as his minister in *England*, which I heartily repent that I did not accept; whereby, as you can be my witness, I might have avoided some years uneasiness and vexation, during the last four years of our late excellent queen, as well as a long melancholy prospect since, in a most obscure disagreeable country, and among a most profligate and abandoned people.

I was diverted from pursuing this history, partly by the extreme difficulty, but chiefly by the indignation I conceived at the proceedings of a faction, which then prevailed; and the

---

* Charles XII, King of *Sweden*, who was unfortunately killed by a cannon-ball at the siege of *Frederickshall*, in the year 1718.

papers lay neglected in my cabinet until you saw me in *England*; when you know how far I was engaged in thoughts and business of another kind. Upon her majesty's lamented death, I returned to my station in this kindgom; since which time there is not a northern curate among you who hath lived more obscure than myself, or a greater stranger to the commonest transactions of the world. It is but very lately that I found the following papers, which I had almost forgotten. I publish them now, for two reasons; first, for an encouragement to those who have more youth, and leisure, and good temper than I, towards pursuing the work as far as it was intended by me, or as much further as they please; the second reason is, to have an opportunity of declaring the profound respect I have for the memory of your royal master, and the sincere regard and friendship I bear to yourself; for I must bring to your mind how proud I was to distinguish you among all the foreign ministers, with whom I had the honour to be acquainted. I am a witness of the zeal you shewed not only for the honour and interest of your master, but for the advantage of the Protestant religion in *Germany*, and how knowingly and feelingly you often spoke to me upon that subject. We all loved you, as possessed of every quality that could adorn an *English* gentleman, and esteemed you as a faithful subject to your prince, and an able negociator; neither shall any reverse of fortune have power to lessen you either in my friendship or esteem: and I must take leave to assure you further, that my affection towards persons hath not been at all diminished by the frown of Power upon them. Those whom you and I once thought great and good men, continue still so in my eyes and my heart; only with a * * * * * * * * * * * *

Cætera desiderantur.

[JONATHAN SWIFT]

The REIGN of

WILLIAM the SECOND,

Surnamed RUFUS.

A T the time of the Conqueror's death, his eldest son *Robert*, upon some discontent with his father, being absent in *France*, *William*, the second son, made use of this juncture, and without attending his father's funeral, hastened to *England*, where, pursuant to the will of the deceased prince, the nobility, although more inclined to favour *Robert*, were prevailed with to admit him king, partly by his promises to abate the rigor of the late reign, and restore the laws and liberties which had been then abolished, but chiefly by the credit and solicitations of *Lanfranc*; for that prelate had formerly a share in his education, and always a great affection for his person. At *Winchester* he took possession of his father's treasure, in obedience to whose command, as well as to ingratiate himself with the people, he distributed it among churches and religious houses, and applied it to the redeeming of prisoners, and other acts of popularity.

In the mean time *Robert* returned to *Normandy*, took possession of that duchy, with great applause and content of his people, and spighted at the indignity done him by his father, and the usurpation of his brother in consequence thereof, prepared a great fleet and army to invade *England*; nor did there want an occasion to promote his interest, if the slowness, the softness, and credulity of his nature, could have suffered him to make a right improvement of it.

Odo, bishop of *Baieux*, of whom frequent mention is made in the preceding reign, a prelate of incurable ambition, either on account of his age or character being restored to his liberty and possessions in *England*, grew into envy and discontent, upon seeing *Lanfranc* preferred before him by the new king in his favour and ministry. He therefore formed a conspiracy with several nobles of *Norman* birth to depose the king, and sent an invitation to *Robert* to hasten over. Meantime the conspirators, in order to distract the king's forces, seized on several parts of *England* at once; *Bristol, Norwich, Leicester, Worcester, Shrewsbury, Bath,* and *Durham,* were secured by several noblemen: *Odo* himself seized *Rochester,* reduced the coasts of *Kent,* and sent messages to *Robert* to make all possible speed.

The king, alarmed at these many and sudden defections, thought it his best course to begin his defence by securing the good will of the people. He redressed many grievances, eased them of certain oppressive taxes and tributes, gave liberty to hunt in his forest, with other marks of indulgence, which however forced from him by the necessity of the time, he had the skill or fortune so to order as they neither lost their good grace nor effect; for immediately after he raised great forces both by land and sea, marched into *Kent,* where the chief body of his enemies were in arms, recovered *Tunbridge* and *Pevensey,* in the latter of which *Odo* himself was taken prisoner, and forced to accompany the king to *Rochester.* This city refusing to surrender at the king's summons, *Odo* undertook to prevail with the obstinacy of the inhabitants; but being admitted into the town, was there detained, either by a real or seeming force; however, the king provoked at their stubbornness and fraud, soon compelled them to yield, retook his prisoner, and forcing him for ever to abjure *England,* sent him into *Normandy.*

By these actions, performed with such great celerity and success, the preparations of duke *Robert* were wholly disappointed, himself, by the necessity of his affairs, compelled to a treaty with his brother, upon the terms of a small pension, and a mutual promise of succeeding to each other's dominions on failure of issue, forced to resign his pretensions, and return with a shattered fleet to *Normandy.*

About this time died archbishop *Lanfranc;* by whose death the king, loosed from that awe and constraint he was under, soon began to discover those irregularities of his nature, which till then he had suppressed and disguised, falling into those acts of oppression and extortion that have made his name and memory infamous. He kept the see of *Canterbury* four years vacant, and converted the revenues to his own use, together with those of several other bishopricks and abbies, and disposed all church preferments to the highest bidder. Nor were his exactions less upon the laity, from whom he continually extorted exorbitant fines for pretended transgression of certain penal laws, and entertained informers to observe mens actions and bring him intelligence.

It is here worth observation, that these corrupt proceedings of the prince have, in the opinion of several learned men, given rise to two customs, which are a long time grown to have the force of laws. For, first the successors of this king, continuing the custom of seizing on the accruing rents in the vacancy of sees and abbies, it grew in process of time to be exacted as a right, or acknowledgment to the king as founder; whence the revenues of vacant bishopricks belong at this day to the crown. The second custom had an original not unlike. Several persons, to avoid the persecutions of the king's informers, and other instruments of oppression, withdrew themselves and their effects to foreign countries; upon which the king issued a proclamation, forbidding all men to leave the kingdom without his licence; from whence, in the judgment of the same authors, the writ *ne exeas regno* had its beginning.

By these and the like arbitrary methods having amassed great treasures, and finding all things quiet at home, he raised a powerful army to invade his brother in *Normandy*; but upon what ground or pretext, the writers of that age are not very exact; whether it were from a principle frequent among unjust princes, That old oppressions are best justified by new; or, whether having a talent for sudden enterprises, and justly apprehending the resentments of duke *Robert*, he thought it the wiser course to prevent injuries than to revenge them. In this expedition he took several cities and castles from his brother, and would have proceeded farther, if *Robert* had not desired and obtained the assistance of *Philip* king of *France*, who came with an army to his relief. King *William* not thinking it safe or prudent to proceed further against his enemy supported by so great an ally, yet loth to lose the fruits of his time and valour, fell upon a known and old expedient, which no prince ever practised oftner, or with greater success, and that was, to buy off the *French* king with a sum of money. This had its effect; for that prince not able to oppose such powerful arms, immediately withdrew himself and his forces, leaving the two brothers to concert the measures of a peace.

This was treated and agreed with great advantages on the side of king *William*; for he kept all the towns he had taken, obliged his brother to banish *Edgar Atheling* out of *Normandy*, and, for a further security, brought over with him to *England* the duke himself to attend him in his expedition against *Malcolm* king of *Scotland*, who during his absence had invaded the borders. The king having raised great forces both by sea and land, went in person to repel the inroads of the *Scots*: but the enterprise was without success; for the greatest part of his fleet was destroyed by a tempest, and his army very much diminished by sickness and famine, which forced him to a peace of little honour; by which, upon the condition of homage from that prince, the king of *England* agreed to deliver him up those twelve towns (or manours) in *England* which *Malcolm* had held under *William the Conqueror*; together with a pension of twelve thousand marks.

At this time were sown the seeds of another quarrel between him and duke *Robert*, who soliciting the king to perform some covenants of the last peace, and meeting with a repulse, withdrew in great discontent to *Normandy*.

King *William*, in his return from *Scotland*, fell dangerously sick at *Glocester*, where, moved by the seasonable exhortations of his clergy, or rather by the fears of dying, he began to discover great marks of repentance, with many promises of amendment and retribution, particularly for his injuries to the church. To give credit to which good resolutions, he immediately filled several vacant sees, giving that of *Canterbury* to *Anselm*, a foreigner of great fame for piety and learning. But as it is the disposition of men who derive their vices from their complexions, that their passions usually beat strong and weak

with their pulses, so it fared with this prince, who upon recovery of his health soon forgot the vows he had made in his
sickness, relapsing with greater violence into the same irregularities of injustice and oppression, whereof *Anselm*, the new
archbishop, felt the first effects. This prelate, soon after his
promotion, offered the king a sum of money by way of
present; but took care it should be so small, that none might
interpret it to be a consideration of his late preferment. The
king rejected it with scorn; and as he used but little ceremony
in such matters, insisted in plain terms for more. *Anselm*
would not comply; and the king enraged, sought all occasions
to make him uneasy; until at length the poor archbishop, tired
out with perpetual usurpations (or at least what was then
understood to be such) upon his jurisdiction, privileges, and
possessions, desired the king's licence for a journey to *Rome*;
and upon a refusal, went without it. As soon as he was withdrawn, the king seized on all his revenues, converting them to
his own use, and the archbishop continued an exile until the
succeeding reign.

The particulars of this quarrel between the king and archbishop are not, in my opinion, considerable enough to deserve
a place in this brief collection, being of little use to posterity,
and of less entertainment; neither should I have mentioned it
at all, but for the occasion it gives me of making a general
observation, which may afford some light into the nature and
disposition of those ages. Not only this king's father and
himself, but the princes for several successions, of the fairest
character, have been severely taxed for violating the rights of
the clergy, and perhaps not altogether without reason. It is
true, this character hath made the lighter impression, as proceeding altogether from the party injured, the cotemporary
writers being generally churchmen: and it must be confessed,
that the usurpations of the church and court of *Rome* were in
those ages risen to such heights, as to be altogether inconsistent
either with the legislature or administration of any independant
state; the inferior clergy, both secular and regular, insisting
upon such immunities as wholly exempted them from the civil
power; and the bishops removing all controversies with the

crown by appeal to *Rome*: for they reduced the matter to this short issue, That God was to be obeyed rather than men; and consequently the bishop of *Rome*, who is Christ's representative, rather than an earthly prince. Neither doth it seem improbable that all *Christendom* would have been in utter vassalage, both temporal and spiritual, to the *Roman* see, if the Reformation had not put a stop to those exorbitancies, and in a good measure opened the eyes even of those princes and states who still adhere to the doctrines and discipline of that Church.

While the king continued at *Glocester*, *Malcolm* king of *Scotland* came to his court, with intentions to settle and confirm the late peace between them. It happened that a controversy arose about some circumstances relating to the homage which *Malcolm* was to pay, in the managing whereof king *William* discovered so much haughtiness and disdain, both in words and gestures, that the *Scottish* prince, provoked by such unworthy treatment, returned home with indignation; but soon came back at the head of a powerful army, and, entring *Northumberland* with fire and sword, laid all waste before him. But as all enterprizes have in the progress of them a tincture of those passions by which they were spirited at first, so this invasion begun upon private revenge, which is a blind ungovernable passion, was carried on with equal precipitation, and proved to be ruinous in the event: for *Robert Mowbray*, earl of *Northumberland*, to prevent the destruction of his own country, where he had great possessions, gathering what forces he could suddenly raise, and without waiting any directions from the king, marched against the *Scots*, who were then set down before *Alnwick* castle: there, by an ambush, *Malcolm* and his eldest son *Edward* were slain, and the army, discouraged by the loss of their princes, entirely defeated. This disaster was followed in a few days by the death of queen *Margaret*, who, not able to survive her misfortunes, died for grief. Neither did the miseries of that kingdom end till, after two usurpations, the surviving son of *Malcolm*, who had fled to *England* for refuge, was restored to his crown by the assistance of king *William*.

About this time the hidden sparks of animosity between the two brothers, buried but not extinguished in the last peace, began to flame out into new dissensions: duke *Robert* had often sent his complaints to the king for breach of articles, but without redress, which provoked him to expostulate in a rougher manner, till at length he charged the king in plain terms with injustice and perjury: but no men are found to endure reproaches with less temper than those who most deserve them: the king, at the same time filled with indignation, and stung with guilt, invaded *Normandy* a second time, resolving to reduce his brother to such terms as might stop all further complaints. He had already taken several strong holds, by force either of arms or of money, and intending intirely to subdue the duchy, gave orders to have twenty thousand men immediately raised in *England*, and sent over to him. The duke, to defend himself against these formidable preparations, had recourse again to his old ally the king of *France*, who very readily advanced with an army to his assistance, as an action wherein he could every way find his own accounts; for, beside the appearance of glory and justice by protecting the injured, he fought indeed his own battle, by preserving his neighbouring state in the hands of a peaceful prince, from so powerful and restless an enemy as the king of *England*; and was largely paid for his trouble into the bargain: for king *William*, either loth to engage in a long and dangerous war, or hastened back by intelligence of some troubles from *Wales*, sent offers to his army, just ready to embark for *Normandy*, that upon payment of ten shillings a man they might have leave to return to their own homes. This bargain was generally accepted; the money was paid to the king of *France*, who immediately withdrew his troops; and king *William*, now master of the conditions, forced his brother to a peace upon much harder terms than before.

In this passage there are some circumstances which may appear odd and unaccountable to those who will not give due allowance for the difference of times and manners: that an absent prince, engaged in an unjust war with his own brother, and ill-beloved at home, should have so much power and credit, as by his commission to raise twenty thousand men on a sudden, only as a recruit to the army he had already with him; that he should have a fleet prepared ready, and large enough to transport so great a number; that upon the very point of embarking he should send them so disgraceful an offer; and that so great a number of common soldiers should be able and willing to pay such a sum of money, equal to at least twelve times as much in our times; and that, after being thus deluded and spoiled at once, they should peaceably disband and retire to their several homes. But all this will be less difficult to comprehend, when we reflect on the method of raising and supporting armies, very different from ours, which was then in use, and so continued for many ages after. All men who had lands *in capite* were bound to attend the king in his wars with a proportioned number of soldiers, who were their tenants on easy rents in consideration of military service. This was but the work of a few days, and the troops consisted of such men as were able to maintain their own charges either at home or abroad: neither was there any reason to apprehend that soldiers would ever become instruments for introducing slavery, who held so great a share in the property.

The king, upon his return from *Normandy*, made an unsuccessful expedition against the *Welsh*, who upon the advantages of his absence had, according to their usual custom, made cruel inroads upon the adjoining counties of *Chester*, *Shrewsbury*, and *Hereford*. Upon the king's approach they fled into their fastnesses among the mountains, where he pursued them for some time with great rage and vexation, as well as the loss of great numbers of his men, to no purpose. From hence he was recalled by a more formidable enemy nearer home: for *Robert* earl of *Northumberland*, over-rating his late services against the *Scots*, as much perhaps and as unjustly as they were undervalued by the king, refused to come to his court, which, in those days, was looked on as the first usual mark of discontent in an nobleman; and was often charged by princes as a formal accusation. The earl having disobeyed the king's summons, and concerted matters with other accomplices, broke out into open rebellion, with intentions to depose king *William*, and set up *Stephen* earl of *Albemarle*, son of a sister to *William the*

Conqueror: but all was prevented by the celerity of this active prince; who, knowing that insurrections are best quelled in their beginnings, marched with incredible speed, and surprised the rebels at *Newcastle*, took the castles of *Tinmouth* and *Bamburg*; where the obstinacy of the defendants provoked him, contrary to his nature, to commit cruelties upon their persons, by cutting off their hands and ears, and other the like inhumanities. The earl himself was taken prisoner as he endeavoured to make his escape; but suffered no other punishment than to be confined for the rest of his life.

About this time began the Holy War for recovering of *Palestine*; which having not been the enterprise of any one prince or state, but that wherein most in *Christendom* had a share, it cannot with justice be silently passed over in the history of any nation.

Pope *Urban* the second, in a council at *Clermont*, made a pathetick exhortation, shewing with what danger and indignity to *Christendom* the *Turks* and *Saracens* had, for some ages, not only over-run all *Asia* and *Africa*, where Christianity had long flourished; but had also made encroachments into *Europe*, where they had entirely subdued *Spain*, and some other parts; that *Jerusalem*, the holy city, where our Saviour did so many miracles, and where his sepulchre still remained, to the scandal of the Christian name, lay groaning under the tyranny of Infidels; that the swords which Christian princes had drawn against each other, ought to be turned against the common enemy of their name and religion; that this should be reckoned an ample satisfaction for all their past sins; that those who died in this expedition should immediately go to heaven, and the survivors would be blessed with the sight of our Lord's sepulchre.

Moved by these arguments, and the influence of the person who delivered them, several nobles and prelates immediately took upon them the Cross; and the council dissolving in this high fit of zeal, the clergy, upon their return home, prevailed so far in their several countries, that in most parts of *Europe* some great prince or lord became a votary for *The Holy Land*; as *Hugh the Great*, brother to the king of *France*; *Godfrey* duke of *Lorrain*; *Reimond* count of *Toulouse*; *Robert* duke of *Normandy*, and many others. Neither ought it to be forgotten, that most of these noble and generous princes, wanting money to maintain the forces they had raised, pawned their dominions to those very prelates who had first engaged them in this enterprize: doubtless a notable mark of the force of oratory in the churchmen of those ages, who were able to inspire that devotion into others, whereof they seemed so little sensible themselves.

But a great share in the honour of promoting this religious war, is attributed to the zeal and industry of a certain *French* priest, commonly called *Peter the Hermit*; who being at *Jerusalem* upon pilgrimage some time before, and entering often into private treaty with the patriarch of that city, came back fully instructed in all the measures necessary for such a war: to these was joined the artifice of certain dreams and visions that might pass for divine admonition: all which, added to the piety of his exhortations, gave him such credit with the pope, and several princes of *Christendom*, that he became in his own person the leader of a great army against the Infidels, and was very instrumental for engaging many others in the same design.

What a spirit was thus raised in *Christendom* among all sorts of men, cannot better be conceived than from the vast numbers of these warlike pilgrims; who, at the siege of *Nice*, are said to have consisted of 600,000 foot, and 100,000 horse: and the success at first was answerable to the greatness of their numbers, the valour of their leaders, and the universal opinion of such a cause; for, besides several famous victories in the field, not to mention the towns of less importance, they took *Nice*, *Antioch*, and at last *Jerusalem*, where duke *Godfrey* was chosen king without competition. But zeal, with a mixture of enthusiasm, as I take this to have been, is a composition only fit for sudden enterprises, like a great ferment in the blood, giving double courage and strength for the time, until it sink and settle by nature into its old channel: for, in a few years the piety of these adventurers began to slacken, and give way to faction and envy, the natural corruptions of all confederacies:

however, to this spirit of devotion there succeeded a spirit of honour, which long continued the vein and humour of the times; and the *Holy Land* became either a school, wherein young princes went to learn the art of war, or a scene wherein they affected to shew their valour, and gain reputation, when they were weary of peace at home.

The Christians held possession of *Jerusalem* above eighty years, and continued their expeditions to the *Holy Land* almost as many more, with various events; and after they were entirely driven out of *Asia*, the popes have almost in every age endeavoured in vain to promote new crusadoes; neither does this spirit seem quite extinct among us even to this day; the usual projects of sanguine men for uniting *Christendom* against the *Turk*, being without doubt a traditional way of talk derived to us from the same fountain.

Robert, in order to furnish himself out for this war, pawned his dutchy to the king for 10,000 marks of gold; which sum was levied with so many circumstances of rigour and exaction, towards the church and laity, as very much increased the discontents of both against the prince.

1099. I shall record one act of this king's, which being chiefly personal, may pass rather for a part of his character, than a point of history.

As he was hunting one day in the *New Forest*, a messenger express from *Normandy*, brought him intelligence, that *Helie*, count *de la Fleche*, had laid close siege to *Mans*, and expected to carry the town in a few days; the king leaving his chace, commanded some about him to point whereabout *Mans* lay; and so rode strait on without reflection, until he came to the coast. His attendants advised him to wait until he had made preparations of men and money; to which he only returned; 'They that love me, will follow me.' He entered the ship in a violent storm; which the mariners beholding with astonishment, at length in great humility gave him warning of the danger; but the king commanded them instantly to put off to sea, and not be afraid; for he had never in his life heard of any king that was drowned. In a few days he drove the enemy from before the city, and took the count himself prisoner, who raging at his defeat and captivity, exclaimed, 'That this blow was from Fortune; but Valour would make reprisals, as he should shew, if ever he regained his liberty.' This being told the king, he sent for the count, let him understand that he had heard of his menaces, then gave him a fine horse, bid him begone immediately, and defied him to do his worst.

It would have been an injury to this prince's memory, to let pass an action, by which he acquired more honour than from any other in his life, and by which it appeared that he was not without some seeds of magnanimity, had they been better cultivated, or not overrun by the number or prevalency of his vices.

I have met with nothing else in this king's reign that deserved to be remembered; for, as to an unsuccessful expedition or two against *Wales*, either by himself or his generals; they were very inconsiderable both in action and event, nor attended with any circumstances that might render a relation of them of any use to posterity, either for instruction or example.

His death was violent and unexpected, the effect of casualty; although this perhaps is the only misfortune of life to which the person of a prince is generally less subject than that of other men. Being at his beloved exercise of hunting in the *New Forest* in *Hampshire*, a large stag crossed the way before him, the king hot on his game, cried out in haste to *Walter Tyrrel*, a knight of his attendants, to shoot; *Tyrrel* immediately let fly his arrow, which glancing against a tree, struck the king through the heart, who fell dead to the ground without speaking a word. Upon the surprise of this accident, all his attendants, and *Tyrrel* among the rest, fled different ways; until the fright being a little over, some of them returned, and causing the body to be laid in a collier's cart, for want of other conveniency, conveyed it in a very unbecoming contemptuous manner to *Winchester*, where it was buried the next day without any solemnity, and which is worse, without grief.

I shall conclude the history of this prince's reign, with a description and character of his body and mind, impartially from the collections I have made; which method I shall observe likewise in all the succeeding reigns.

He was in stature somewhat below the usual size, and big bellyed, but he was well and strong knit. His hair was yellow or sandy; his face red, which got him the name of *Rufus*; his forehead flat; his eyes were spotted, and appeared of different colours; he was apt to stutter in speaking, especially when he was angry; he was vigorous and active, and very hardy to endure fatigues, which he owed to a good constitution of health, and the frequent exercise of hunting; in his dress he affected gayety and expence, which having been first introduced by this prince into his court and kingdom, grew, in succeeding reigns, an intolerable grievance. He also first brought in among us the luxury and profusion of great tables. There was in him, as in all other men, a mixture of virtues and vices, and that in a pretty equal degree, only the misfortune was, that the latter, although not more numerous, were yet much more prevalent than the former. For being entirely a man of pleasure, this made him sacrifice all his good qualities, and gave him too many occasions of producing his ill ones. He had one very singular virtue for a prince, which was that of being true to his word and promise: he was of undoubted personal valour, whereof the writers in those ages produce several instances; nor did he want skill and conduct in the process of war. But, his peculiar excellency, was that of great dispatch, which, however usually decried, and allowed to be only a happy temerity, does often answer all the ends of secrecy and counsel in a great commander, by surprising and daunting an enemy when he least expects it; as may appear by the greatest actions and events upon the records of every nation.

He was a man of sound natural sense, as well as of wit and humour, upon occasion. There were several tenets in the *Romish* church he could not digest; particularly that of the saint's intercession; and living in an age over-run with superstition, he went so far into the other extream, as to be censured for an Atheist. The day before his death, a monk relating a terrible dream, which seemed to forebode him some misfortune, the king being told the matter, turned it into a jest; said, The man was a Monk, and dreamt like a Monk, for lucre sake; and therefore commanded *Fitzhamon* to give him an

E

hundred shillings, that he might not complain he had dreamt to no purpose.

His vices appear to have been rather derived from the temper of his body, than any original depravity of his mind; for being of a sanguine complexion, wholly bent upon his pleasures, and prodigal in his nature, he became engaged in great expences. To supply these, the people were perpetually oppressed with illegal taxes and exactions; but that sort of avarice which arises from prodigality and vice, as it is always needy, so it is much more ravenous and violent than the other, which put the king and his evil instruments (among whom *Ralph* bishop of *Durham*, is of special infamy) upon those pernicious methods of gratifying his extravagances by all manner of oppression; whereof some are already mentioned, and others are too foul to relate.

He is generally taxed by writers for discovering a contempt of religion in his common discourse and behaviour; which I take to have risen from the same fountain, being a point of art, and a known expedient, for men who cannot quit their immoralities, at least to banish all reflections that may disturb them in the enjoyment, which must be done either by not thinking of religion at all; or, if it will obtrude, by putting it out of countenance.

Yet there is one instance that might shew him to have some sense of religion as well as justice. When two Monks were outvying each other in canting the price of an abbey, he observed a third at some distance, who said never a word; the king demanded why he would not offer; the Monk said, he was poor, and besides, would give nothing if he were ever so rich; the king replyed, Then you are the fittest person to have it, and immediately gave it him. But this is, perhaps with reason enough, assigned more to caprice than conscience; for he was under the power of every humour and passion that possessed him for the present; which made him obstinate in his resolves, and unsteady in the prosecution.

He had one vice or folly that seemed rooted in his mind, and of all others, most unbefitting a prince: This was, a proud disdainful manner, both in his words and gesture; and having already lost the love of his subjects by his avarice and oppression, this finished the work, by bringing him into contempt and hatred among his servants; so that few among the worst of princes have had the luck to be so ill-beloved, or so little lamented.

He never married, having an invincible abhorrence for the state, although not for the sex.

He died in the thirteenth year of his reign, the forty third of his age, and of *Christ* 1100, *August* 2.

His works of piety were few, but in buildings he was very expensive, exceeding any king of *England* before or since, among which *Westminster-Hall*, *Windsor-Castle*, the *Tower* of *London*, and the whole city of *Carlisle*, remain lasting monuments of his magnificence.

The REIGN of

HENRY the FIRST.

THIS prince was the youngest son of *William the Conqueror*, and bred to more learning than was usual in that age, or to his rank, which got him the surname of *Beauclerc*; the reputation whereof, together with his being born in *England*, and born son of a king, although of little weight in themselves, did very much strengthen his pretensions with the people. Besides, he had the same advantage of his brother *Robert's* absence, which had proved before so successful to *Rufus*, whose treasures he likewise seized on immediately at his death, after the same manner, and for the same end, as *Rufus* did those of his father the *Conqueror*. *Robert* had been now five years absent in the *Holy-War*, where he acquitted himself with great glory; and although he was now in *Apulia*, upon his return homeward, yet the nobles pretending not to know what was become of him, and others giving out that he had been elected king of *Jerusalem*, *Henry* laid hold of the occasion, and calling together an assembly of the clergy, nobles, and people of the realm at *London*, upon his promises to restore king *Edward's* laws, and redress the grievances which had been introduced by his father and brother, they consented to elect him king. Immediately after his coronation, he proceeded upon reforming the abuses of the late reign: he banished dissolute persons from the court, who had long infested it under the protection and example of *Rufus:* he restored the people to the use of lights in the night, which the *Conqueror* had forbidden, after a certain hour, by the ringing of a bell. Then he published his charter, and ordered a copy thereof to be taken for every county in *England*. This charter was in substance; The freedom of Mother Church from former oppressions; leave to the heirs of nobles to succeed in the possession of their lands, without being obliged to redeem them, only paying to the king a moderate relief; abolition of fines for licence of marriage to their heiresses; a promise of not refusing such licence, unless the match proposed be with the king's enemy, *&c.* the next of kin to be guardians of the lands of orphans; punishments for coiners of false money; a confirmation of *St. Edward's* laws; and a general amnesty.

About the same time he performed two acts of justice, which, by gratifying the revenge and the love of the people, gained very much upon their affections to his person: the first was, to imprison *Ralph* bishop of *Durham*, who having been raised by the late king from a mean and sordid birth to be his prime confident and minister, became the chief instrument, as well as contriver, of all his oppressions; the second was, in recalling and restoring archbishop *Anselm*, who having been forced by the continual persecutions of the same prince, to leave *England*, had lived ever since in banishment, and deprived of all his revenues.

The king had not been many months on his throne, when the news came that duke *Robert*, returned from the *Holy Land*, was received by his subjects with great marks of joy and honour, and in universal reputation for his valour and success against the Infidels: soon after which, *Ralph* bishop of *Durham*, either by the negligence or corruption of his keepers, escaped out of prison, and fled over to the duke; whom he stirred up to renew and solicit his pretensions to the crown of *England*, by writing to several nobles who, either through old friendship, or new discontent, or an opinion of his title, gave him promises of their assistance, as soon as he should land in *England:* but the duke having returned exceeding poor from the *Holy Land*, was not yet in a condition for such an undertaking, and therefore thought fit to defer it to a more seasonable opportunity.

As the king had hitherto, with great industry sought all occasions to gratify his people, so he continued to do in the choice of a wife. This was *Matilda*, daughter of *Malcolm* the late king of *Scots*; a lady of great piety and virtue, who, by the power or persuasion of her friends, was prevailed with to leave her cloyster for a crown, after she had, as some writers report, already taken the veil. Her mother was sister to *Edgar Atheling*, the last heir male of the *Saxon* race; of whom frequent mention hath been made in the two preceding reigns: and thus the *Saxon* line, to the great contentment of the *English* nation, was again restored.

Duke *Robert*, having now with much difficulty and oppression of his subjects, raised great forces, and gotten ready a fleet to convey them, resolved once more to assert his title to the crown of *England:* to which end he had for some time held a secret correspondence with several nobles, and lately received fresh invitations. The king, on the other side, who had received timely intelligence of his brother's preparations, gave orders to his admirals to watch the sea-ports, and endeavour to hinder the enemy's landing: but the commanders of several ships, whether *Robert* had won them by his bribes, or his promises, instead of offering resistance, became his guides, and brought his fleet safe into *Portsmouth*, where he landed his men, and from thence marched to *Winchester*, his army hourly encreasing by great numbers of people, who had either an affection for his person, an opinion of his title, or a hatred to the king. In the mean time *Henry* advanced with his forces, to be near the duke, and observe his motions; but, like a wise general, forbore offering battle to an invader, until he might do it with manifest advantage. Besides, he knew very well that his brother was a person whose policy was much inferior to his valour, and therefore to be sooner overcome in a treaty than a fight: to this end, the nobles on both sides began to have frequent interviews; to make overtures; and at last concert the terms of a peace; but wholly to the advantage of the king, *Robert* renouncing his pretensions in consideration of a small pension, and of succeeding to the crown on default of male issue in his brother.

The defection of nobles and other people to the duke was so great, that men generally thought if it had come to a battle, the king would have lost both the victory and his crown. But *Robert*, upon his return to *Normandy* after this dishonourable peace, grew out of all reputation with the world, as well as into perfect hatred and contempt among his own subjects, which in a short time was the cause of his ruin.

The king having thus by his prudence got rid of a dangerous and troublesome rival, and soon after by his valour quelled the insurrections of the earls of *Shrewsbury* and *Mortain*, whom he forced to fly into *Normandy*, found himself in full peace at home and abroad, and therefore thought he might venture a contention with the Church about the right of investing bishops; upon which subject many other princes at that time had controversy with their clergy: but, after long struggling in vain, were all forced to yield at last to the decree of a synod in *Rome*, and to the pertinacy of the bishops in the several countries. The form of investing a bishop, was by delivery of a ring and a pastoral staff; which, at *Rome*, was declared unlawful to be performed by any lay-hand whatsoever; but the princes of *Christendom* pleaded immemorial custom to authorize them; and king *Henry*, having given the investiture to certain bishops, commanded *Anselm* to consecrate them. This the archbishop refused with great firmness, pursuant to what he understood to be his duty, and to several immediate commands of the pope. Both sides adhering to their own sentiments, the matter was carried to *Rome*, where *Anselm* went in person, by the king's desire; who, at the same time, sent ambassadors thither to assert and defend his cause; but the pope still insisting, *Anselm* was forbidden to return to *England*. The king seized on all his revenues, and would not restore him, until upon other concessions of the pope, *Henry* was content to yield up his pretensions to the investiture; but, however, kept the right of electing still in his own hands.

Whatever might have been the method of electing bishops, in the more primitive ages, it seems plain to me that in these times, and somewhat before, although the election was made *per clerum & populum*; yet the king always nominated at first, or approved afterwards, and generally both, as may be seen by the style in which their elections ran, as well as by the persons chosen, who were usually churchmen of the court, or in some employment near the king. But whether this were a gradual encroachment of the regal upon the spiritual power, I had rather leave others to dispute.

1104. About this time duke *Robert* came to *England*, upon a visit to the king, where he was received with much kindness and hospitality; but, at the same time, the queen had private directions to manage his easy temper, and work him to a consent of remitting his pension: this was compassed without much difficulty: but, upon the duke's return to *Normandy*, he was severely reproved for his weakness by *Ralph* bishop of *Durham*, and the two earls of *Mortain* and *Shrewsbury*. These three having fled from *England* for rebellion, and other treasons, lived exiles in *Normandy*; and, bearing an inveterate hatred to the king, resolved to stir up the duke to a resentment of the injury and fraud of his brother. *Robert*, who was various in his nature, and always under the power of the present persuader, easily yielded to their incitements: reproached the king in bitter terms, by letters and messages, that he had cozened and circumvented him; demanding satisfaction, and withal threatening revenge. At the same time, by the advice of the three nobles already mentioned, he began to arm himself as formidably as he could, with design to seize upon the king's possessions in *Normandy:* but as this resolution was rashly taken up, so it was as faintly pursued, and ended in his destruction: neither hath any prince reason to expect better fortune, that engages in a war against a powerful neighbour upon the counsel or instigation of exiles, who having no farther view than to serve their private interest, or gratify their revenge, are sure to succeed in one or t'other, if they can embark princes in their quarrel, whom they fail not to incite by the falsest representations of their own strength, and the weakness of their enemy: for as the king was now settled in his throne too firm to be shaken, so *Robert* had wholly lost all credit and friendship in *England*; was sunk in reputation at home; and, by his unlimited profuseness, reduced so low, that, having pawned most of his dominions, he had offered *Rouen*, his capital city, in sale to the inhabi-

1105 tants. All this was very well known to the king, who, resolving to make his advantage thereof, pretended to be highly provoked at the disgraceful speeches and menaces of his brother; which he made the formal occasion of a quarrel; therefore he first sent over some forces to ravage his country; and, understanding that the duke was coldly supported by his own subjects, many of whom came over to the king's army, he soon followed in person with more; took several towns; and, placing garrisons therein, came back to *England*, designing with the first pretext or opportunity to return with a more potent army, and wholly subdue the duchy to his obedience.

Robert, now grown sensible of his weakness, became wholly dispirited; and following his brother into *England*, in a most dejected manner, begged for peace: but the king, now fully determined upon his ruin, turned away in disdain, muttering at the same time some threatening words. This indignity roused up once more the sinking courage of the duke; who, with bitter words, detesting the pride and insolence of *Henry*, withdrew in a rage, and hasting back to *Normandy*, made what preparations he could for his own defence. The king observing his nobles very ready to engage with him in this expedition; and being assured that those in *Normandy* would, upon his approach, revolt from the duke, soon followed with a mighty army, and the flower of his kingdom. Upon his arrival he was attended, according to his expectation, by several *Norman* lords; and, with this formidable force, sat down before *Tenerchebray*: the duke, accompanied by the two exiled earls, advanced with what strength he had, in hopes to draw the enemy from the siege of so important a place, although at the hazard of a battle. Both armies being drawn out in battalia,

that of the king's trusting to their numbers, began the charge
with great fury, but without any order. The duke, with forces 1106
far inferior, received the enemy with much firmness; and,
finding they had spent their first heat, advanced very regularly
against their main body, before they could recover themselves
from the confusion they were in. He attacked them with so
much courage; that he broke their whole body, and they began
to fly on every side. The king believing all was lost, did what
he could by threats and gentle words to stop the flight of his
men, but found it impossible: then he commanded two bodies
of horse which were placed in either wing, to join, and wheeling about, to attack the enemy in the rear. The duke, who
thought himself so near a victory, was forced to stop his pursuit; and ordering his men to face about, began the fight anew;
mean time the scattered parts of the main body, which had so
lately fled, began to rally, and pour in upon the *Normans*
behind, by which duke *Robert's* army was almost encompassed;
yet they kept their ground awhile, and made several charges,
until at length, perfectly overborne by numbers, they were
utterly defeated. There duke *Robert*, doing all the parts of a
great captain, was taken prisoner, together with the earl of
Mortain, and almost his whole army: for being hemmed in on
all sides, few of them could make their escape. Thus in the 1107
space of forty years, *Normandy* subdued *England*, and *England*
Normandy; which are events perhaps hardly to be paralleled in
any other ages or parts of the world.

The king, having staid awhile to settle the state of *Normandy*,
returned with his brother into *England*, whom he sent prisoner
to *Cardiff* castle, with orders that he should be favourably used,
which, for some time, were duly observed; until being accused
of attempting to make his escape (whether it were real or
feigned) he had his eyes put out with a burning basin, by the
king's express commands; in which miserable condition he
lived for six and twenty years.

It is believed the king would hardly have engaged in this
unnatural and invidious war, with so little pretence or provocation, if the pope had not openly approved and sanctified his
cause, exhorting him to it as a meritorious action; which seems

to have been but an ill return from the vicar of Christ to a prince who had performed so many brave exploits for the service of the Church, to the hazard of his person, and ruin of his fortune. But the very bigotted monks, who have left us their accounts of those times, do generally agree in heavily taxing the *Roman* court for bribery and corruption. And the king had promised to remit his right of investing bishops, which he performed immediately after his reduction of *Normandy*, and was a matter of much more service to the pope, than all the atchievements of duke *Robert* in the Holy Land, whose merits, as well as pretensions, were now antiquated and out of date.

1109   About this time the emperor *Henry* V. sent to desire *Maude* the king's daughter in marriage who was then a child about eight years old: that prince had lately been embroiled in a quarrel with the see of *Rome*, which began upon the same subject of investing bishops, but was carried to great extremities: for invading *Italy* with a mighty army, he took the pope prisoner, forced him to yield to whatever terms he thought fit to impose, and to take an oath of fidelity to him between his hands: however, as soon as *Henry* had withdrawn his forces, the pope assembling a council, revoked all his concessions, as extorted by compulsion, and raised great troubles in *Germany* against the emperor, who, in order to secure himself, sought this alliance with the king.

About this time likewise died archbishop *Anselm*, a prelate of great piety and learning, whose zeal for the see of *Rome*, as well as for his own rights and privileges, should in justice be imputed to the errors of the time, and not of the man. After his death, the king, following the steps of his brother, held the see vacant five years, contenting himself with an excuse, which looked like a jest, That he only waited until he could find another so good a man as *Anselm*.

In the fourteenth year of this king's reign, the *Welsh*, after their usual manner, invaded the Marches with great fury and destruction; but the king, hoping to put a final end to those perpetual troubles and vexations given to his kingdom by that unquiet people, went in person against them with a powerful army; and to prevent their usual stratagem of retreating to their woods and mountains, and other fastnesses, he ordered the woods to be cut down, beset all their places of security, and hunting them like wild beasts, made so terrible a slaughter, that at length observing them to fling down their arms, and beg for quarter, he commanded his soldiers to forbear; then receiving their submissions, and placing garrisons where he thought necessary, he returned, in great triumph and satisfaction, to *London*.

1114. The princess *Maude* being now marriageable, was delivered to the emperor's ambassador; and for a portion to the young lady a tax was imposed of three shillings upon every hide of land in *England*, which grew afterwards into a custom, and was in succeeding times confirmed by acts of parliament, under the name of *Reasonable Aid for marrying the King's Daughter*, although levied after a different manner.

As the institution of parliaments in *England* is agreed by several writers to be owing to this king, so the date of the first hath been assigned by some to the fifteenth year of his reign; which however is not to be affirmed with any certainty: for great councils were convoked not only in the two preceding reigns, but for time immemorial by the *Saxon* princes, who first introduced them into this island, from the same original with the other *Gothick* forms of government in most parts of *Europe*. These councils or assemblies were composed according to the pleasure of the prince who convened them, generally of nobles and bishops, sometimes were added some considerable commoners; but they seldom met, except in the beginning of a reign, or in times of war, until this king came to the crown; who being a wise and popular prince, called these great assemblies upon most important affairs of his reign, and ever followed their advice, which, if it proved successful, the honour and advantage redounded to him, and if otherwise, he was free from the blame: thus when he chose a wife for himself, and a husband for his daughter, when he designed his expedition against *Robert*, and even for the election of an archbishop to the see of *Canterbury*, he proceeded wholly by the advice of such general assemblies, summoned for the purpose.

But the style of these conventions, as delivered by several authors, is very various; sometimes it is *comites, barones, & cleri*; his marriage was agreed on, *consilio majorum natu & magnatum terræ*. One author calls it* *consilium principum, sacerdotum, & reliqui populi*. And for the election of an archbishop, the *Saxon* Chronicle says, That he commanded by letters all bishops, abbots, and thanes to meet him at *Glocester ad procerum conventum*. Lastly, some affirm these assemblies to have been an imitation of the three estates in *Normandy*. I am very sensible how much time and pains have been employed by several learned men to search out the original of parliaments in *England*, wherein I doubt they have little satisfied others or themselves. I know likewise that to engage in the same enquiry, would neither suit my abilities nor my subject. It may be sufficient for my purpose, if I be able to give some little light into this matter, for the curiosity of those who are less informed.

The institution of a state or commonwealth out of a mixture of the three forms of government received in the schools, however it be derided as a solecism and absurdity by some late writers on politicks, hath been very antient in the world, and is celebrated by the gravest authors of antiquity. For although the supreme power cannot properly be said to be divided, yet it may be so placed in three several hands, as each to be a check upon the other; or formed into a balance, which is held by him that has the executive power, with the nobility and people in counterpoise in each scale. Thus the kingdom of *Media* is represented by *Xenophon* before the reign of *Cyrus*; so *Polybius* tells us, the best government is a mixture of the three forms, *regno, optimatium, & populi imperio:* the same was that of *Sparta* in its primitive institution by *Lycurgus*, made up of *reges, seniores, & populus*; the like may be asserted of *Rome, Carthage*, and other states: and the *Germans* of old fell upon the same model, from whence the *Goths* their neighbours, with the rest of those northern people, did perhaps borrow it. But an assembly of the three estates is not properly of *Gothick* institution: for these fierce people, when upon the decline of the *Roman* empire they first invaded *Europe*, and settled so many kingdoms in *Italy*, *Spain*, and other parts, were all heathens; and when a body of them had fixed themselves in a tract of land left desolate by the flight or destruction of the natives, their military government by time and peace became civil; the general was king, his great officers were his nobles and ministers of state, and the common soldiers the body of the people; but these were freemen, and had smaller portions of land assigned them. The remaining natives were all slaves; the nobles were a standing council; and upon affairs of great importance, the freemen were likewise called by their representatives to give their advice. By which it appears, that the *Gothick* frame of government consisted at first but of two states or assemblies, under the administration of a single person. But after the conversion of these princes and their people to the Christian faith, the Church became endowed with great possessions, as well by the bounty of kings, as the arts and industry of the clergy, winning upon the devotion of their new converts: and power, by the common maxim, always accompanying property, the ecclesiasticks began soon to grow considerable, to form themselves into a body, and to call assemblies or synods by their own authority, or sometimes by the command of their princes, who in an ignorant age had a mighty veneration for their learning as well as piety. By such degrees the church arrived at length, by very justifiable steps, to have her share in the commonwealth, and became a third estate in most kingdoms of *Europe*; but these assemblies, as we have already observed, were seldom called in *England* before the reign of this prince, nor even then were always composed after the same manner: neither does it appear from the writers who lived nearest to that age, that the people had any representative at all, beside the barons and other nobles, who did not sit in those assemblies by virtue of their birth or creation, but of the lands or baronies they held. So that the present constitution of the *English* parliament hath, by many degrees and alterations, been modelled to the frame it is now in; which alterations I shall observe in the succeeding reigns as exactly as I can discover them by a diligent search into the histories of the several ages, without engaging in the controverted points of law about this matter, which would rather perplex the reader than inform him.

1116. But to return, *Louis the Gross* king of *France*, a valiant and active prince, in the flower of his age, succeeding to that crown that *Robert* was deprived of, *Normandy*, grew jealous of the neighbourhood and power of king *Henry*, and begun early to entertain designs either of subduing that duchy to himself, or at least of making a considerable party against the king in favour of *William* son of *Robert*, whom for that end he had taken into his protection. Pursuant to these intentions, he soon found an occasion for a quarrel: expostulating with *Henry*, that he had broken his promise by not doing homage for the duchy of *Normandy*, as well as by neglecting to raze the Castle of *Gisors*, which was built on the *French* side of the river *Epte*, the common boundary between both dominions.

But an incident soon offered, which gave king *Henry* a pretext for retaliating almost in the same manner: for it happened that upon some offence taken against his nephew *Theobald* count of *Blois* by the *French* king, *Louis* in great rage sent an army to invade and ravage the earl's territories. *Theobald* defended himself for a while with much valour; but at length in danger to be overpowered, requested aid of his uncle the king of *England*, who supported him so effectually with men and money, that he was able not only to defend his own country, but very much to infest and annoy his enemy. Thus a war was kindled between the two kings; *Louis* now openly asserted the title of *William* the son of *Robert*, and entering into an alliance with the earls of *Flanders* and *Anjou*, began to concert measures for driving king *Henry* out of *Normandy*.

The king having timely intelligence of his enemy's design, began with great vigour and dispatch to prepare himself for war: he raised, with much difficulty and discontent of his people, the greatest tax that had ever been known in *England*; and passing over into *Normandy* with a mighty army, joined his nephew *Theobald*. The king of *France*, who had entertained hopes that he should over-run the duchy before his enemy could arrive, advanced with great security towards the frontiers of *Normandy*; but observing an enemy of equal number and force already prepared to engage him, he suddenly stopt his march. The two armies faced one another for some hours, neither side offering battle; the rest of the day was spent in light skirmishes begun by the *French*, and repeated for some days following with various success; but the remainder of the year passed without any considerable action.

1119. At length the violence of the two princes brought it to a battle: for *Louis*, to give a reputation to his arms, advanced towards the frontiers of *Normandy*, and after a short siege took *Gué Nicaise*; there the king met him, and the fight began, which continued with great obstinacy on both sides for nine hours. The *French* army was divided into two bodies, and the *English* into three; by which means, that part where the king fought in person, being attacked by a superior number began to give way; and *William Crispin*, a *Norman* baron, singling out the king of *England* (whose subject he had been, but banished for treason) struck him twice in the head with so much violence, that the blood gushed out of his mouth. The king inflamed with rage and indignation, dealt such furious blows, that he struck down several of his enemies, and *Crispin* among the rest, who was taken prisoner at his horse's feet. The soldiers encouraged by the valour of their prince, rallied and fell on with fresh vigour, and the victory seemed doubtful, when *William* the son of king *Henry*, to whom his father had intrusted the third body of his army, which had not yet engaged, fell on with this fresh reserve upon the enemy, who was already very much harassed with the toil of the day: this quickly decided the matter; for the *French*, tho' valiantly fighting, were overcome, with the slaughter of several thousand men; their king quitted the field, and withdrew to *Andeli*; but the king of *England* recovering *Gué Nicaise*, returned triumphant to *Rouen*.

This important victory was followed by the defection of the earl of *Anjou* to king *Henry*, and the earl of *Flanders* fell in the battle; by which the king of *France* was at once deprived of two powerful allies. However, by the intercession of the former, a peace was soon after made between both crowns. *William* the king's son did homage to *Louis* for the dukedom of *Normandy*; and the other *William*, following the fortunes of his father, was left to his pretensions and complaints.

It is here observable, that from this time until *Wales* was subdued to the *English* crown, the eldest sons of *England* were called dukes of *Normandy*, as they are now princes of *Wales*.

1120. The king having staid some time in *Normandy*, for the settlement of his duchy after the calamities and confusions of a war, returned to *England*, to the very great satisfaction of his people and himself. He had enlarged his dominions by the conquest of *Normandy*; he had subdued all his competitors, and forced even the king of *France*, their great protector, after a glorious victory, to his own conditions of a peace; he was upon very good terms with the pope, who had a great esteem and friendship for his person, and made him larger concessions than was usual from that see, and in those ages. At home he was respected by the clergy, reverenced by the nobles, and beloved by the people; in his family he was blessed with a son of much hopes, just growing to years of manhood, and his daughter was an empress; so that he seemed to possess as great a share of happiness as human life is capable to admit. But the felicity of man depends upon a conjunction of many circumstances, which are all subject to various accidents, and every single accident is able to dissolve the whole contexture; which truth was never verified more than in this prince, who by one domestick misfortune, not to be prevented or foreseen, found all the pleasure and content he proposed to himself by his prudence, his industry and his valour, wholly disappointed and destroyed: for *William* the young prince having embarked at *Barfleur* some time after his father, the mariners being all drunk, suffered the ship to run upon a rock, where it was dashed to pieces: the prince made a shift to get into the boat, and was making to the shore, until forced back by the cries of his sister, whom he received into the boat, so many others crouded in at the same time, that it was immediately overturned. There perished, beside the prince, a natural son and daughter of the king's, his niece, and many other persons of quality, together with all their attendants and servants, to the number of a hundred and forty, besides fifty mariners, but one person escaping.

Although the king survived this cruel misfortune many years, yet he could never recover his former humour, but grew melancholy and morose; however, in order to provide better for the peace and settlement of the kingdom after his death, about five months after the loss of his son, his former queen having died three years before, he married *Adelais*, a beautiful young lady of the family of *Lorrain*, in hopes of issue by her, but never had any.

The death of the prince gave occasion to some new troubles in *Normandy*; for the earls of *Meulant* and *Evreux*, *Hugh de Montfort*, and other associates, began to raise insurrections there, which were thought to be privately fomented by the *French* king, out of enmity to king *Henry*, and in favour of *William* the son of *Robert*, to whom the earl of *Anjou* had lately given his daughter in marriage. But *William* of *Tankerville*, the 1124 king's lieutenant in *Normandy*, surprizing the enemy's forces by an ambush, intirely routed them, took both the earls prisoners, and sent one of them (*Meulant*) to his master; but the count *d' Evreux* made his escape.

1126. King *Henry* having now lost hopes of issue by his new queen, brought with him, on his return to *England*, his daughter *Maude*, who by the emperor's death had been lately left a widow and childless; and in a parliament or general assembly which he had summoned to *Windsor*, he caused the crown to be settled on her and her children, and made all his nobles take a solemn oath to defend her title. This was performed by none with so much forwardness as *Stephen* earl of *Boulogne*, who was observed to shew a more than ordinary zeal in the matter. This young lord was the king's nephew, being second son of the earl of *Blois* by *Adela* the Conqueror's daughter: he was in high favour with the king his uncle, who had married him to the daughter and heiress of the earl of *Boulogne*, given him great possessions in *England*, and made him indeed too powerful for a subject.

The king having thus fixed the succession of the crown in his daughter by an act of settlement and an oath of fealty,

F

looked about to provide her with a second husband, and at length determined his choice in *Geoffry Plantagenet* earl of *Anjou*, the son of *Fulk* lately deceased.

This prince, whose dominions confined on *France* and *Normandy*, was usually courted for an ally by both kings in their several quarrels; but having little faith or honour, he never scrupled to change sides as often as he saw or conceived it for his advantage. After the great victory over the *French*, he closed in with king *Henry*, and gave his daughter to the young prince *William*; yet at the same time, by the private encouragement of *Louis*, he prevailed on the king of *England* to be easy in the conditions of a peace. Upon the unfortunate loss of the prince, and the troubles in *Normandy* thereupon, he fell again from the king, gave his other daughter to *William* the son of *Robert*, and struck up with *France* to take that prince again into protection. But dying soon after, and leaving his son *Geoffry* to succeed in that earldom, the king was of opinion he could not any where bestow his daughter with more advantage, both for the security and enlargement of his dominions, that by giving her to this earl; by which marriage *Anjou* would become an acquisition to *Normandy*, and thus be a more equal match to so formidable a neighbour as *France*. In a short time the marriage was concluded; and this earl *Geoffry* had the honour to introduce into the royal family of *England* the surname of *Plantagenet*, borne by so many succeeding kings, which began with *Henry* II. who was the eldest son of this marriage.

But the king of *France* was in great discontent at this match: he easily foresaw the dismal consequences to himself and his successors from such an increase of dominion united to the crown of *England:* he knew what impressions might be made in future times to the shaking of his throne by an aspiring and warlike king, if they should happen in a weak reign, or upon any great discontents in that kingdom. Which conjectures being highly reasonable (and since often verified by events) he cast about to find some way of driving the king of *England* intirely out of *France*; but having neither pretext nor stomach in the midst of a peace to begin an open and formal quarrel, there fell out an accident which gave him plausible occasion of pursuing his design.

Charles the Good earl of *Flanders* having been lately murdered by some of his subjects, upon private revenge, the king of *France* went in person to take revenge of the assassins; which he performed with great justice and honour. But the late earl leaving no heir of his body, and several competitors appearing to dispute the succession, *Louis* rejected some others who seemed to have a fairer title, and adjudged it to *William* the son of *Robert*, the better to secure him to his interests upon any design he might engage in against the king of *England*. Not content with this, he assisted the earl in person, subdued his rivals, and left him in peaceable possession of his new dominion.

King *Henry*, on the other side, was very apprehensive of his nephew's greatness, well knowing to what end it was directed; however, he seemed not to regard it, contenting himself to give the earl employment at home, by privately nourishing the discontents of his new subjects, and abetting under-hand another pretender; for *William* had so intirely lost the hearts of his people, by his intolerable avarice and exactions, that the principal towns in *Flanders* revolted from him, and invited *Thierrie* earl of *Alsace* to be their governor. But the king of *France* generously resolved to appear once more in his defence, and took his third expedition into *Flanders* for that purpose. He had marched as far as *Artois*, when he was suddenly recalled to defend his own dominions from the fury of a powerful and provoked invader: for *Henry* king of *England*, moved with indignation to see the *French* king in the midst of a peace so frequently and openly supporting his most dangerous enemy, thought it the best way to divert *Louis* from kindling a fire against him abroad, by forcing him to extinguish one at home: he therefore entered into the bowels of *France*, ravaging and laying waste all before him, and quickly grew so formidable, that the *French* king to purchase a peace was forced to promise never more to assist or favour the earl of *Flanders*; however, as it fell out, this article proved to be wholly needless; for the young earl soon after gave battle to *Thierrie* and put his whole army to the rout; but pursuing his victory, he received a wound in his wrist, which, by the unskilfulness of a surgeon, cost him his life.

This one slight inconsiderable accident did, in all probability, put a stop to very great events; for if that young prince had survived his victory, it is hardly to be doubted but through the justness of his cause, the reputation of his valour, and the assistance of the king of *France*, he would in a little time have recovered *Normandy*, and perhaps his father's liberty, which were the two designs he had in agitation; nor could he well have missed the crown of *England* after the king's death, who was now in his decline, when he had so fair a title, and no competitors in view but a woman and an infant.

1129. Upon the king's return from *Normandy*, a great council of the clergy was held at *London*, for punishing of priests who lived in concubinage, which was the great grievance of the church in those ages, and had been condemned by several canons. This assembly thinking to take a more effectual course against that abomination, as it was called, decreed severe penalties upon those who should be guilty of breaking it, intreating the king to see the law put in execution; which he very readily undertook, but performed otherwise than was expected, eluding the force of the law, by an evasion to his own advantage: for exacting fines of the delinquent priests, he suffered them to keep their concubines without further disturbance. A very unaccountable step in so wise a body for their own concernments, as the clergy of those times is lookt upon to have been; and although perhaps the fact be not worth recording, it may serve as a lesson to all assemblies never to trust the execution of a law in the hands of those who will find it more to their interests to see it broken than observed.

1132. The empress *Maude* was now happily delivered of a son, who was afterwards king of *England* by the name of *Henry* the Second: and the king calling a parliament, had the oath of fealty repeated by the nobles and clergy to her and her issue, which in the compass of three years they all broke or forgot.

1134. I think it may deserve a place in this history to mention the last scene of duke *Robert*'s life, who, either through the poorness or greatness of spirit, having outlived the loss of his honour, his dominions, his liberty, his eye-sight, and his only son, was at last forced to sink under the load of eighty years, and must be allowed for the greatest example either of insensibility or contempt of earthly things, that ever appeared in a sovereign or private person. He was a prince hardly equalled by any in his time for valour, conduct, and courtesy; but his ruin began from the easiness of his nature, which whoever knew how to manage, were sure to be refused nothing they could ask. By such profusion he was reduced to those unhappy expedients of remitting his rights for a pension, of pawning his towns, and multiplying taxes, which brought him into hatred and contempt with his subjects; neither do I think any virtue so little commendable in a sovereign as that of liberality, where it exceeds what his ordinary revenues can supply; where it passes those bounds, his subjects must all be oppressed to shew his bounty to a few flatterers, or he must sell his towns, or basely renounce his rights, by becoming pensioner to some powerful prince in the neighbourhood; all which we have lived to see performed by a late monarch in our own time and country.

1135. Since the reduction of *Normandy* to the king's obedience, he found it necessary for his affairs to spend in that duchy some part of his time almost every year, and a little before the death of *Robert* he made his last voyage there. It was observable in this prince, that having some years past very narrowly escaped shipwreck in his passage from *Normandy* into *England*, the sense of his danger had made very deep impressions on his mind, which he discovered by a great reformation in his life, by redressing several grievances, and doing many acts of piety; and to shew the steadiness of his resolutions, he kept them to the last, making a progress through most parts of *Normandy*, treating his subjects in all places with great familiarity and kindness, granting their petitions, easing their taxes, and, in a word, giving all possible marks of a religious, wise, and gracious prince.

Returning to *St. Denys le Forment* from his progress a little indisposed, he there fell into a fever upon a surfeit of lamprey, which in a few days ended his life. His body was conveyed to *England,* and buried at *Reading* in the abbey-church himself had founded.

It is hard to affirm any thing peculiar of this prince's character; those authors who have attempted it mentioning very little but what was common to him with thousands of other men; neither have they recorded any of those personal circumstances or passages, which only can discover such qualities of the mind as most distinguish one man from another. These defects may perhaps appear in the stories of many succeeding kings; which makes me hope I shall not be altogether blamed for sometimes disappointing the reader in a point wherein I could wish to be the most exact.

As to his person, he is described to be of middle stature; his body strong set and fleshy; his hair black; his eyes large; his countenance amiable, and very pleasant, especially when he was merry. He was temperate in meat and drink, and a hater of effeminacy, a vice or folly much complained of in his time, especially that circumstance of long artificial hair, which he forbid upon severe penalties. His three principal virtues were prudence, valour, and eloquence. These were counterbalanced by three great vices; avarice, cruelty, and lust; of which the first is proved by the frequency of his taxes: the second by his treatment of duke *Robert*; and the last was notorious. But the proof of his virtues doth not depend on single instances, manifesting themselves thro' the whole course of a long reign, which was hardly attended by any misfortune that prudence, justice, or valour could prevent. He came to the crown at a ripe age, when he had passed thirty years, having learned, in his private life, to struggle with hardships, whereof he had his share, from the capriciousness and injustice of both his brothers; and by observing their failures, he had learned to avoid them in himself, being steady and uniform in his whole conduct, which were qualities they both seemed chiefly to want. This likewise made him so very tenacious as he was observed to be in his love and hatred. He was a strict observer of justice, which he seems never to have violated, but in that particular case, which political casuists are pleased to dispense with, where the dispute is about a crown. In that he * * * *

Consider him as a private man, he was perhaps the most accomplished person of his age, having a facetious wit, cultivated by learning, and advanced with a great share of natural eloquence, which was his peculiar talent: and it was no doubt the sense he had of this last perfection in himself, that put him so often upon calling together the great councils of the nation, where natural oratory is of most figure as well as use.

The R E I G N of

S T E P H E N.

THE veneration which people are supposed naturally to pay to a right line, and a lawful title in their kings, must be upheld by a long uninterrupted succession, otherwise it quickly loses opinion, upon which the strength of it, although not the justice, is entirely founded: and where breaches have been already made in the lineal descent, there is little security in a good title (though confirmed by promises and oaths) where the lawful heir is absent, and a popular aspiring pretender near at hand. This, I think, may pass for a maxim, if any consequences drawn from history can pretend to be called so, having been verified successively three times in this kingdom, I mean by the two preceding kings, and by the prince whose reign we are now writing. Neither can this observation be justly controuled by any instances brought of future princes, who being absent at their predecessor's death, have peaceably succeeded, the circumstances being very different in every case, either by the weakness or justice of pretenders, or else by the long establishment of lineal succession.

1135. *Stephen* earl of *Boulogne*, whose descent hath been already shewn in the foregoing reign, as the second of three brothers, whereof the eldest was *Theobald* earl of *Blois*, a sovereign prince, and *Henry* the youngest was bishop of *Winchester*, and the pope's legate in *England*. At the time of king *Henry*'s death, his daughter the empress was with her husband the earl of *Anjou*, a grave and cautious prince, altogether unqualified for sudden enterprizes: but earl *Stephen*, who had attended the king in his last expedition, made so great dispatch for *England*, that the council had not time to meet and make any declaration about a successor. When the lords were assembled, the legate had already, by his credit and influence among them, brought over a great party to his brother's interest; and the earl himself, knowing with what success the like methods were used by his two last predecessors, was very liberal of his promises to amend the laws, support the church, and redress grievances: for all which the bishop undertook to be guarantee. And thus was *Stephen* elected by those very persons who had so lately, and in so solemn a manner, more than once sworn fealty to another.

The motives whereby the nobility was swayed to proceed after this manner, were obvious enough. There had been a perpetual struggle between them and their former kings in the defence of their liberties; for the security whereof, they thought a king elected without other title, would be readier to enter into any obligations, and being held in constant dependance, would be less tempted to break them: therefore, as at his coronation they obtained full security by his taking new and additional oaths in favour of their liberties, their oath of fealty to him was but conditional, to be of force no longer than he should be true to those stipulations.

But other reasons were contrived and given out to satisfy the people: they were told it was an indignity for so noble a nation to be governed by a woman; that the late king had promised to marry his daughter within the realm, and by consent of parliament, neither of which was observed: and lastly, *Hugh Bigod*, steward to king *Henry*, took a voluntary oath, before the archbishop of *Canterbury*, that his master, in his last sickness, had, upon some displeasure, disinherited his daughter.

He received the crown with one great advantage that could best enable him to preserve it; this was the possession of his uncle's treasures, amounting to one hundred thousand pounds, and reckoned as a prodigious sum in those days; by the help of which, without ever raising one tax upon the people, he defended an unjust title against the lawful heir during a perpetual contest of almost twenty years.

In order to defend himself against any sudden invasion, which he had cause enough to expect, he gave all men licence to build castles upon their lands, which proved a very mistaken piece of politicks, although grounded upon some appearance of reason. The king supposed that no invader would venture to advance into the heart of his country without reducing every castle in his way, which must be a work of much time and difficulty, nor would be able to afford men to block them up, and secure his retreat: which way of arguing may be good enough to a prince of an undisputed title, and entirely in the hearts of his subjects: but numerous castles are ill defenders of an usurpation, being the common retreat of malecontents, where they can fly with security, and discover their affections as they please: by which means the enemy, although beaten in the field, may still preserve his footing in the bowels of a country; may wait supplies from abroad, and prolong a war for many years: nor, while he is master of any castles, can he ever be at mercy by any sudden misfortune; but may be always in a condition of demanding terms for himself. These, and many other effects of so pernicious a counsel, the king found through the whole course of his reign; which was entirely spent in sieges, revolts, surprizes, and surrenders, with very few battles, but no decisive action: a period of much misery and confusion, which affords little that is memorable for events, or useful for the instruction of posterity.

1136. The first considerable enemy that appeared against him was *David* king of *Scots*, who having taken the oath of fealty to *Maude* and her issue, being further engaged by the ties of blood, and stirred up through the persuasions of several *English* nobles, began to take up arms in her cause; and invading the northern parts, took *Carlisle* and *Newcastle*; but upon the king's speedy approach with his forces, a peace was presently made, and the towns restored. However, the *Scottish* prince would, by no means, renounce his fidelity to the empress, by paying homage to *Stephen*; so that an expedient was found to have it performed by his eldest son: in consideration of which the king gave, or rather restored, to him the earldom of *Huntington*.

Upon his return to *London* from this expedition, he happened to fall sick of a lethargy, and it was confidently given out that he was dead. This report was with great industry and artifice, dispersed by his enemies, which quickly discovered the ill inclination of several lords, who, although they never believed the thing, yet made use of it for an occasion or pretext to fortify their castles, which they refused to surrender to the king himself; but *Stephen* was resolved, as he said, to convince them that he was alive and well; for coming against them before he was expected, he recovered *Exeter*, *Norwich*, and other fortified places, although not without much difficulty.

It is obvious enough to wonder how a prince of so much valour, and other excellent endowments, elected by the church and state, after a compliance with all conditions they could impose on him, and in an age when so little regard was had to the lineal descent, lastly confirmed by the pope himself, should be soon deserted and opposed by those very persons who had been the most instrumental to promote him. But, beside his defective title, and the undistinguished liberty of building castles, there were three circumstances which very much contributed to those perpetual revolts of the nobles against him: first, that upon his coming to the crown he was very liberal in distributing lands and honours to several young gentlemen of noble birth, who came to make their court, whereby he hoped to get the reputation of a generous prince, and to strengthen his party against the empress: but, by this encouragement, the number of pretenders quickly grew too fast upon him; and when he had granted all he was able, he was forced to dismiss the rest with promises and excuses, who, either out of envy or discontent, or else to mend their fortunes, never failed to become his enemies upon the first occasion that offered. Secondly, when he had reduced several castles and towns which had given the first example of defection from him, he hardly inflicted the least punishment on the authors; which unseasonable mercy, that in another prince and another age would have been called greatness of spirit, passed in him for pusillanimity and fear, and is reckoned, by the writers of those times, to have been the cause of many succeeding revolts. The third circumstance was of a different kind: for, observing how little good effect he had found by his liberality and indulgence, he would needs try the other extream, which was not his talent. He began to infringe the articles of his charter; to recal or disown the promises he had made; and to repulse petitioners with rough treatment, which was the more unacceptable by being new and unexpected.

1137. Mean time the earl of *Anjou*, who was not in a condition to assert his wife's title to *England*, hearing *Stephen* was employed at home, entered *Normandy* with small force, and found it no difficult matter to seize several towns. The *Normans*, in the present distraction of affairs, not well knowing what prince to obey, at last sent an invitation to *Theobald* earl of *Blois*, king *Stephen*'s eldest brother, to accept their dukedom upon the condition of protecting them from the present insults of the earl of *Anjou*. But before this matter could come to an issue, *Stephen*, who, upon reduction of the towns already mentioned, had found a short interval of quiet from his *English* subjects, arrived with unexpected speed into *Normandy*; where *Geoffry* of *Anjou* soon fled before him, and the whole duchy came over to his obedience; for the further settlement whereof he made peace with the king of *France*; constituted his son *Eustace* duke of *Normandy*; and made him swear fealty to that prince, and do him homage. His brother *Theobald*, who began to expostulate upon this disappointment, he pacified with a pension of two thousand marks: and even the earl of *Anjou* himself, who, in right of his wife, made demands of *Stephen* for the kingdom of *England*, finding he was no equal match at present, was persuaded to become his pensioner for five thousand more.

Stephen, upon his return to *England,* met with an account of new troubles from the north; for the king of *Scots,* under pretence of observing his oath of fealty to the empress, infested the borders, and frequently making cruel inroads, plundered and laid waste all before him.

1138. In order to revenge this base and perfidious treatment, the king, in his march northward, sat down before *Bedford,* and took it after a siege of twenty days. This town was part of the earldom of *Huntingdon,* given by *Stephen* in the late peace to the eldest son of the *Scottish* king, for which the young prince did homage to him; and it was upon that account defended by a garrison of *Scots.* Upon intelligence of this surrender, king *David,* overcome with fury, entered *Northumberland,* where, letting loose the rage of his soldiers, he permitted and encouraged them to commit all manner of inhumanities; which they performed in so execrable a manner as would scarce be credible, if it were not attested by almost the universal consent of writers; they ript up women with child, drew out the infants, and tossed them upon the points of their lances: they murdered priests before the altars; then cutting the heads from off the crucifixes, in their stead put on the heads of those they had murdered: with many other instances of monstrous barbarity too foul to relate: but cruelty being usually attended with cowardice, this perfidious prince, upon the approach of king *Stephen,* fled into places of security. The king of *England,* finding no enemy on whom to employ his revenge, marched forward into the country, destroying with fire and sword all the southern parts; and would, in all probability, have made terrible impressions into the heart of *Scotland,* if he had not been suddenly recalled by a more dangerous fire at home, which had been kindled in his absence, and was now broken out into a flame.

Robert earl of *Glocester,* natural son of the late king, came into *England* some time after the advancement of *Stephen* to the crown; and, yielding to the necessity of the time, took the oath of fealty upon the same condition used by the other nobles, to be of force so long as the king should keep his faith with him, and preserve his dignity inviolate: but, being in his heart wholly devoted to the interests of the empress his sister, and moved by the persuasions of several religious men, he had, with great secrecy and application, so far practised upon the levity or discontents of several lords, as to gain them to his party: for the king had, of late, very much alienated the nobles against him; first, by seizing several of their persons, and dispossessing them of their lands; and, secondly, by taking into his favour *William D'Ypres*, a *Flemish* commander of noble birth, but banished by his prince. This man, with many of his followers, the king employed chiefly both in his councils and his armies, and made him earl of *Kent*, to the great envy and displeasure of his *English* subjects. The earl of *Glocester*, therefore, and his accomplices, having prepared all things necessary for an insurrection, it was agreed among them, that while the king was engaged against the *Scots*, each of them should secure what towns and castles they could, and openly declare for the empress. Accordingly earl *Robert* suddenly fortified himself in *Bristol*; the rest followed his example; *Hereford*, *Shrewsbury*, *Ludlow*, *Dover*, and many other places, were seized by several lords, and the defection grew so formidable, that the king, to his great grief, was forced to leave his *Scottish* expedition unfinished, and return with all possible speed to suppress the rebellion begun by his subjects; having first left the care of the north to *Thurstan* archbishop of *York*; with orders carefully to observe the motions of the *Scots*.

Whilst the king was employed in the south, in reducing his discontented lords, and their castles, to his obedience, *David*, presuming upon the distance between them, re-entered *England* with more numerous forces, and greater designs, than before: for, without losing more time than what was necessary to pillage and destroy the country as he marched, he resolved to besiege *York*, which, if he could force to surrender, would serve as a convenient frontier against the *English*. To this end, advancing near the city, and having pitched his tents, he sat down before it with his whole army. In the mean time archbishop *Thurstan*, having already summoned the nobles and gentry of the shire and parts adjacent, had, by powerful persuasions, incited them to defend their country against a treacherous, bloody, and restless enemy: so that before the king of *Scotland* could make any progress in the siege, the whole power of the north was united against him, under the earl of *Albemarle*, and several other nobles. Archbishop *Thurstan* happening to fall sick, could not go in person to the army, but sent the bishop of *Durham* in his stead; by whose encouragements the *English*, although in number far inferior, advanced boldly towards the enemy, and offered them battle, which was as readily accepted by the *Scots*, who, sending out a party of horse to secure the rising ground, were immediately attacked by the *English*, and, after a sharp dispute, entirely defeated. In the heat of the battle the king of *Scots*, and his son *Henry* earl of *Huntington*, gave many proofs of great personal valour. The young prince fell with such fierceness upon a body of the *English*, that he utterly broke and dispersed them; and was pursuing his victory, when a certain man, bearing aloft the head of an enemy he had cut off, cried out, It was the head of the *Scottish* king, which being heard and believed on both sides, the *English*, who had lately fled, rallied again, assaulting their enemies with new vigour; the *Scots*, on the other side, discouraged by the supposed death of their prince, began to turn their backs: the king and his son used all endeavours to stop their flight, and made several brave stands against the enemy; but the greatest part of their army being fled, and themselves almost encompassed, they were forced to give way to fortune, and with much difficulty made their escape.

The loss on the *English* side was inconsiderable; but of *Scots*, by general consent of writers, ten thousand were slain. And thus ended the war of the Standard, as it was usually called by the authors of that age, because the *English*, upon a certain engine, raised the mast of a ship, on the top whereof, in a silver box, they put the consecrated wafer, and fastened the standards of *St. Peter*, and other saints: this gave them courage, by remembering they were to fight in the presence of God; and served likewise for a mark where to re-assemble when they should happen to be dispersed by any accident or misfortune.

1139. Mean time the king was equally successful against his rebellious lords at home, having taken most of their castles and strong holds; and the earl of *Glocester* himself, no longer able to make any resistance, withdrew into *Normandy*, to concert new measures with the empress his sister. Thus the king had leisure and opportunity for another expedition into *Scotland*, to pursue and improve his victory, where he met with no opposition: however, he was at length persuaded with much difficulty to accept his own conditions of a peace; and *David* delivered up to him his eldest son *Henry*, as hostage for performance of articles between them.

The king, in his return homeward, laid siege to *Ludlow* castle, which had not been reduced with the rest: here prince *Henry* of *Scotland*, boiling with youth and valour, and exposing his person upon all occasions, was lifted from his horse by an iron grapple let down from the wall, and would have been hoisted up into the castle, if the king had not immediately flown to his assistance, and brought him off with his own hands by main force from the enemy, whom he soon compelled to surrender the castle.

1140. *Stephen* having thus subdued his inveterate enemies the *Scots*, and reduced his rebellious nobles, began to entertain hopes of enjoying a little ease. But he was destined to the possession of a crown with perpetual disturbance; for he was hardly returned from his northern expedition, when he received intelligence that the empress, accompanied by her brother the earl of *Glocester*, was preparing to come for *England*, in order to dispute her title to the kingdom. The king, who knew by experience what a powerful party she already had to espouse her interests, very reasonably concluded, the defection from him would be much greater, when she appeared in person to countenance and reward it; he therefore began again to repent of the licence he had granted for building castles, which were now like to prove so many places of security for his enemies, and fortifications against himself; for he knew not whom to trust, vehemently suspecting his nobles ever since their last revolt. He therefore cast about for some artifice to get into his hands as many of their castles as he could: in the strength

and magnificence of which kind of structures, the bishops
had far outdone the rest, and were upon that, as well as other
accounts, very much maligned and envied by the temporal
Lords, who were extreme jealous of the church's encreasing
power, and glad upon all occasions to see the prelates humbled.
The king, therefore, having formed his project, resolved to
make trial where it would be least invidious, and where he
could foresee least danger in the consequences. At a parliament or assembly of nobles at *Oxford*, it was contrived to raise
a quarrel between the servants of some bishops and those of
Alan, count of *Dinan* in *Bretagne*, upon a contention of rooms
in their inns. *Stephen* took hold of this advantage, sent for the
bishops, taxed them with breaking his peace, and demanded
the keys of their castles, adding threats of imprisonment if
they dared to disobey. Those whom the king chiefly suspected,
or rather who had built the most and strongest castles, were
Roger bishop of *Salisbury*, with his nephew and natural son the
bishops of *Ely* and *Lincoln*, whom the king, by many circumstances of rigor, compelled to surrender, going himself in
person to seize the *Devizes*, then esteemed the noblest structure
of *Europe*, and built by the forementioned bishop *Roger*, whose
treasure, to the value of forty thousand marks, there likewise
deposited, fell, at the same time, into the king's hand, which in
a few days broke the bishop's heart, already worn with age and
infirmity.

It may, perhaps, not be thought a digression to say something of the fortunes of this prelate, who, from the lowest
beginnings, came to be, without dispute, the greatest church-
man of any subject in his age. It happened that the late king
Henry, in the reign of his brother, being at a village in *Normandy*,
wanted a priest to say mass before him and his train, when this
man, who was a poor curate thereabouts, offered his service,
and performed it with so much dexterity and speed, that the
soldiers who attended the prince recommended him to their
master, upon that account, as a very proper chaplain for
military men; but it seems he had other talents; for having
gotten into the prince's service, he soon discovered great
application and address, much order and œconomy in the

management of his master's fortunes, which were wholly left to his care. After *Henry's* advancement to the crown, this chaplain grew chief in his favour and confidence: was made bishop of *Salisbury*, chancellor of *England*, employed in all his most weighty affairs, and usually left vicegerent of the Realm while the king was absent in *Normandy*. He was among the first that swore fealty to *Maude* and her issue; and among the first that revolted from her to *Stephen*, offering such reasons in council for setting her aside, as, by the credit and opinion of his wisdom, were very prevalent. But the king, in a few years, forgot all obligations, and the bishop fell a sacrifice in his old age to those treasures he had been so long heaping up for its support. A just reward for his ingratitude towards the prince that raised him, to be ruined by the ingratitude of another, whom he had been so very instrumental to raise.

But *Henry* bishop of *Winchester*, the pope's legate, not able to endure this violation of the church, called a council of all the prelates to meet at *Winchester*, where the king being summoned, appeared by his advocate, who pleaded his cause with much learning; and the archbishop of *Rouen* coming to the council, declared his opinion, That although the canons did allow the bishops to possess castles, yet in dangerous times they ought to deliver them up to the king. This opinion *Stephen* followed very steadily, not yielding a tittle, although the legate his brother used all means, both rough and gentle, to work upon him.

The council of bishops broke up without other effect than that of leaving in their minds an implacable hatred to the king, in a very opportune juncture for the interests of *Maude*, who, about this time, landed at *Portsmouth* with her brother *Robert* earl of *Glocester*. The whole force she brought over for this expedition consisted but of one hundred and forty knights; for she trusted altogether in her cause and her friends. With this slender attendance she went to *Arundel*, and was there received into the castle by the widow of the late king; while earl *Robert* accompanied only by twenty men, marched boldly to his own city of *Gloucester*, in order to raise forces for the

G

empress, where the townsmen turned out the king's garrison as soon as they heard of his approach.

King *Stephen* was not surprized at the news of the empress's arrival, being a thing he had always counted upon, and was long preparing himself against. He was glad to hear how ill she was provided, and resolved to use the opportunity of her brother's absence; for, hasting down to *Arundel* with a sufficient strength, he laid siege to the castle, in hopes, by securing her person, to put a speedy end to the war.

But there wanted not some very near about the king, who, favouring the party of *Maude*, had credit enough to prevail with him not to venture time and reputation against an impregnable fortress, but rather by withdrawing his forces, permit her to retire to some less fortified place, where she might more easily fall into his hands. This advice the king took against his own opinion; the empress fled out of *Arundel* by night; and, after frequent shifting her stages through several towns, which had already declared in her favour, fixed herself at last at *Lincoln*; where, having all things provided necessary for her defence, she resolved to continue, and expect either a general revolt of the *English* to her side, or the decision of war between the king and her brother.

1141. But *Stephen*, who had pursued the empress from place to place, hearing she had shut herself up in *Lincoln*, resolved to give her no rest; and to help on his design, it fell out that the citizens in hatred to the earl of *Chester*, who commanded there for the empress, sent a private invitation to the king, with promise to deliver the town and their governor into his hands. The king came accordingly, and possessed himself of the town : but *Maude* and the earl made their escape a few days before. However, many great persons of *Maude's* party remained prisoners to the king, and among the rest the earl of *Chester's* wife, who was daughter to the earl of *Glocester*. These two earls resolving to attempt the relief of their friends, marched with all their forces near *Lincoln*, where they found the enemy drawn up and ready to receive them. The next morning, after battle offered by the lords, and accepted by the king, both sides made ready to engage. The king having disposed his cavalry on each wing, placed himself at the head of his foot, in whom he reposed most confidence. The army of the lords was divided in three bodies; those whom king *Stephen* had banished were placed in the middle, the earl of *Chester* led the van, and the earl of *Glocester* commanded the rear. The battle was fought at first with equal advantage, and great obstinacy on both sides: at length the right wing of the king's horse, pressed by the earl of *Chester*, galloped away, not without suspicion of treachery; the left followed the example. The king beheld their flight, and encouraging those about him, fell with undaunted valour upon the enemy; and being for some time bravely seconded by his foot, did great execution. At length overpowered by numbers, his men began to disperse, and *Stephen* was left almost alone with his sword in his hand, wherewith he opposed his person against a whole victorious army, nor durst any be so hardy to approach him; the sword breaking, a citizen of *Lincoln* put into his hands a *Danish* battle-ax, with which he struck to the ground the earl of *Chester*, who presumed to come within his reach. But this weapon likewise flying in pieces with the force of those furious blows he dealt on all sides, a bold knight of the empress's party, named *William de Keynes*, laid hold on his helmet, and immediately cried out to his fellows, I have got the king. Then the rest ran in, and he was taken prisoner.

The king being thus secured, was presented to the empress, then at *Glocester*, and by her orders conveyed to *Bristol*, where he continued in strict custody nine months, although with honourable treatment for some time, until either upon endeavouring to make his escape, or in malice to the *Londoners*, who had a great affection for their king, he was, by express command from the empress, laid in irons, and used with other circumstances of severity.

This victory was followed by a general defection of almost the whole kingdom; and the earl of *Anjou*, husband to the empress, upon the fame of the king's defeat and imprisonment, reduced without any difficulty the whole duchy of *Normandy* to his obedience.

The legate himself, although brother to king *Stephen*, received her at *Winchester* with great solemnity, accepted her oath for governing with justice, redressing grievances, and supporting the rights of the Church, and took the old conditional one of fealty to her; then in an assembly of bishops and clergy convoked for the purpose, he displayed the miscarriages of his brother, and declared his approbation of the empress to be queen; to which they unanimously agreed. To compleat all, he prevailed by his credit with the *Londoners*, who stood out the last of any, to acknowledge and receive her into the city, where she arrived at length in great pomp, and with general satisfaction.

But it was the misfortune of this princess to possess many weaknesses that are charged to the sex, and very few of its commendable qualities; she was now in peaceable possession of the whole kingdom, except the county of *Kent*, where *William D'Ypres* pretended to keep a small party for the king; when by her pride, wilfulness, indiscretion, and a disobliging behaviour, she soon turned the hearts of all men against her, and in a short time lost the fruits of that victory and success which had been so hardly gained by the prudence and valour of her excellent brother. The first occasion she took to discover the perverseness of her nature, was in the treatment of *Maude*, the wife of king *Stephen*, a lady of great virtue, and courage above her sex, who coming to the empress an humble suitor in behalf of her husband, offered, as a price of his liberty, that he should resign all pretensions to the crown, and pass the rest of his life in exile, or in a convent; but this request was rejected with scorn and reproaches; and the queen finding all intreaties to no purpose, writ to her son *Eustace* to let him understand the ill success of her negociation, that no relief was to be otherwise hoped for than by arms; and therefore advised him to raise immediately what forces he could for the relief of his father.

Her next miscarriage was towards the *Londoners*, who presented her a petition for redressing certain rigorous laws of her father, and restoring those of *Edward the Confessor*. The empress put them off for a time with excuses, but at last discovered some displeasure at their importunity. The citizens, who had with much difficulty been persuaded to receive her against their inclination, which stood wholly for the king, were moved with indignation at her unreasonable refusal of their just demands, and entered into a conspiracy to seize her person. But she had timely notice of their design, and leaving the city by night in disguise, fled to *Oxford*.

A third false step the empress made, was in refusing her new powerful friend the legate a favour he desired in behalf of *Eustace*, the king's son, to grant him the lands and honours held by his father before he came to the crown. She had made large promises to this prelate, that she would be directed in all things by his advice, and to be refused upon his first application a small favour for his own nephew, stung him to the quick; however, he governed his resentments a while, but began at the same time to resume his affection for his brother. These thoughts were cultivated with great address by queen *Maude*, who prevailed at last so far upon the legate, that private measures were agreed between them for restoring *Stephen* to his liberty and crown. The bishop took leave of the empress, upon some plausible pretence, and retired to *Winchester*, where he gave directions for supplying with men and provisions several strong castles he had built in his diocese, while the queen with her son *Eustace* prevailed with the *Londoners* and men of *Kent* to rise in great numbers for the king; and a powerful army was quickly on foot, under the command of *William D'Ypres* earl of *Kent*.

In the mean time the empress began to be sensible of the errors she had committed; and in hope either to retrieve the friendship of the legate, or take him prisoner, marched with her army to *Winchester*, where being received and lodged in the castle, she sent immediately for the legate, spoke much in excuse of what was past, and used all endeavours to regain him to her interests. Bishop *Henry*, on the other side, amused her with dubious answers, and kept her in suspense for some days; but sent privately at the same time to the king's army, desiring them to advance with all possible speed; which was executed with so much diligence, that the empress and her

brother had only time with their troops to march a back way
out of the town. They were pursued by the enemy so close in
the rear, that the empress had hardly time, by counterfeiting
herself dead, to make her escape; in which posture she was
carried as a corpse to *Glocester*; but the earl her brother, while
he made what opposition he could, with design to stop her
pursuers, was himself taken prisoner, with great slaughter of
his men. After the battle, the earl was in his turn presented to
queen *Maude*, and by her command sent to *Rochester* to be
treated in the same manner with the king.

Thus the heads of both parties were each in the power of
his enemy, and fortune seemed to have dealt with great
equality between them. Two factions divided the whole
kingdom, and as it usually happens, private animosities were
inflamed by the quarrel of the publick; which introduced a
miserable face of things throughout the land, whereof the
writers of our *English* story give melancholy descriptions, not
to be repeated in this history; since the usual effects of civil
war are obvious to conceive, and tiresome as well as useless to
relate. However, as the quarrel between the king and the
empress was grounded upon a cause that in its own nature
little concerned the interests of the people, this was thought
a convenient juncture for transacting a peace, to which there
appeared an universal disposition. Several expedients were
proposed; but earl *Robert* would consent upon no other terms
than the deposing of *Stephen*, and immediate delivery of the
crown to his sister. These debates lasted for some months,
until the two prisoners, weary of their long constraint, by
mutual consent were exchanged for each other, and all thoughts
of agreement laid aside.

The king, upon recovery of his freedom, hastened to *London*,
to get supplies of men and money for renewing the war. He
there found that his brother of *Winchester* had, in a council of
bishops and abbots, renounced all obedience to the empress,
and persuaded the assembly to follow his example. The legate
in excuse for his proceeding, loaded her with infamy, produced
several instances wherein she had broken the oath she took
when he received her as queen, and upon which his obedience

was grounded; and said, he had received information that she had a design upon his life.

It must be confessed that oaths of fealty in this prince's reign were feeble ties for binding the subject to any reasonable degree of obedience; and the warmest advocates for liberty cannot but allow, from those examples here produced, that it is very possible for people to run upon great extremes in this matter, that a monarch may be too much limited, and a subject too little; whereof the consequences have been fully as pernicious for the time, as the worst that can be apprehended from arbitrary power in all its heights, although not perhaps so lasting or so hard to be remedied; since all the miseries of this kingdom, during the period we are treating of, were manifestly owing to that continual violation of such oaths of allegiance, as appear to have been contrived on purpose by ambitious men to be broken at pleasure, without the least apprehension of perjury, and in the mean time keep the prince in a continual slavish dependance.

The earl of *Glocester*, soon after his release, went over into *Normandy*, where he found the earl of *Anjou* employed in compleating the conquest of that duchy; there he delivered him the sons of several *English* noblemen, to be kept as hostages for their fathers fidelity to the empress, and used many arguments for persuading him to come over in person with an army to her assistance: but *Geoffry* excused himself by the importance of other affairs, and the danger of exposing the dominions he had newly acquired to rebellions in his absence. However, he lent the earl of *Glocester* a supply of four hundred men, and sent along with him his eldest son *Henry*, to comfort his mother, and be shewn to the people.

During the short absence of the earl of *Glocester*, the empress was closely besieged in *Oxford* by the king; and provisions beginning to fail, she was in cruel apprehensions of falling into his hands. This gave her occasion to put into practice the only talent wherein she seemed to excel, which was that of contriving some little shift or expedient to secure her person upon any sudden emergency. A long season of frost had made the *Thames* passable upon the ice, and much snow lay on the ground; *Maude* with some few attendants clad all in white, to avoid being discovered from the king's camp, crossed the river at midnight on foot, and travelling all night got safe to *Wallingford* castle, where her brother and young son *Henry*, newly returned from *France*, arrived soon after, to her great satisfaction: but *Oxford*, immediately upon the news of her flight, surrendered to the king.

However, this disgrace was fully compensated soon after by another of the same kind, which happened to king *Stephen*; for whilst he and his brother of *Winchester* were fortifying a nunnery at *Wilton*, to bridle his enemies at *Salisbury*, who very much harrassed those parts by their frequent excursions, the earl of *Glocester*, who watched all opportunities, came unaware with a strong body of men, and set fire on the nunnery while the king himself was in it. *Stephen*, upon the sudden surprize of the thing, wholly lost or forgot his usual courage, and fled shamefully away, leaving his soldiers to be cut in pieces by the earl.

During the rest of the war, although it lasted nine years longer, there is little memorable recorded by any writer; whether the parties being pretty equal, and both sufficiently tired with so long a contention, wanted vigor and spirit to make a thorough conquest, and only endeavoured to keep what they had, or whether the multitude of strong castles, whose number daily increased, made it very difficult to end a war between two contending powers almost in ballance; let the cause be what it will, the whole time passed in mutual sieges, surprizes, revolts, surrenders of fortified places, without any decisive action, or other event of importance to be related. By which at length the very genius of the people became wholly bent upon a life of spoil, robbery, and plunder; many of the nobles although pretending to hold their castles for the king or the empress, lived like petty independent princes in a perpetual state of war against their neighbours; the fields lay uncultivated, all the arts of civil life were banished, no veneration left for sacred persons or things; in short, no law, truth, or religion among men, but a scene of universal misery, attended with all the consequences of an embroiled and distracted state.

About the eleventh year of the king's reign, young *Henry*, now growing towards a man, was sent for to *France* by a message from his father, who was desirous to see him; but left a considerable party in *England*, to adhere to his interests; and in a short time after (as some write) the empress herself grown weary of contending any longer in a cause where she had met with nothing but misfortunes of her own procuring, left the kingdom likewise, and retired to her husband. Nor was this the only good fortune that befel *Stephen*; for before the year ended, the main prop and pillar of his enemies was taken away by death; this was *Robert* earl of *Glocester*, than whom there have been few private persons known in the world that deserve a fairer place and character in the registers of time, for his inviolable faith, disinterested friendship, indefatigable zeal, and firm constancy to the cause he espoused, and unparallelled generosity in the conduct thereof: he adhered to his sister in all her fortunes, to the ruin of his own; he placed a crown on her head; and when she had lost it by her folly and perverseness, refused the greatest offers from a victorious enemy, who had him in his power, and chose to continue a prisoner rather than recover his liberty by any hazard to her pretentions: he bore up her sinking title in spight of her own frequent miscarriages, and at last died in her cause by a fever contracted with perpetual toils for her service. An example fit to be shewn the world, although few perhaps are like to follow it; but however, a small tribute of praise, justly due to extraordinary virtue, may prove no ill expedient, to encourage imitation.

But the death of this lord, together with the absence of the empress and her son in *France*, added very little to the quiet or security of the king. For the earl of *Glocester*, suspecting the fidelity of the lords, had with great sagacity, delivered their sons to the earl of *Anjou*, to be kept as pledges for their father's fidelity, as we have before related: by which means a powerful party was still kept up against *Stephen*, too strong to be suddenly broken. Besides, he had, by an unusual strain of his conduct, lately lost much good will, as well as reputation, in committing an act of violence and fraud on the person of the earl of

Chester, a principal adherent of the empress. This nobleman, of great power and possessions, had newly reconciled himself to *Stephen*, and came to his court at *Northamptom*, where, against all laws of hospitality, as well as common faith and justice, he was committed to prison, and forced to buy his liberty with the surrender of *Lincoln*, and all his other places, into the king's hands.

Affairs continued in this turbulent posture about two years, the nobles neither trusting the king nor each other. The number of castles still increased, which every man who had any possessions was forced to build, or else become a prey to his powerful neighbours. This was thought a convenient 1149 juncture, by the empress and her friends, for sending young prince *Henry* to try his fortune in *England*, where he landed at the head of a considerable number of horse and foot, although he was then but sixteen years old. Immediately after his arrival he went to *Carlisle*, where he met his cousin *David* king of *Scots*, by whom he was made knight, after the usual custom of young princes and noblemen in that age. The king of *England*, who had soon intelligence of *Henry's* landing and motion, marched down to secure *York*, against which he expected the first attempt of his enemy was designed. But, whatever the cause might be (wherein the writers of those ages are either 1150 silent or unsatisfactory) both armies remained at that secure distance for three months, after which *Henry* returned back to *Normandy*, leaving the kingdom in the state of confusion he found it at his coming.

The fortunes of this young prince *Henry Fitz-Empress*, now began to advance by great and sudden steps, whereof it will be no digression to inform the reader, as well upon the connexion they have with the affairs at home about this time, as because they concern the immediate successor to the crown.

1151. Prince *Henry's* voyage to *France* was soon followed by the death of his father *Geoffry* earl of *Anjou*, whereby the son became possessed of that earldom, together with the duchy of 1152 *Normandy*; but in a short time after he very much enlarged his dominions by a marriage, in which he consulted his reputation less than his advantage. For *Louis the young*, king of *France*, was lately divorced from his wife *Eleanor*, who, as the *French* writers relate, bore a great contempt and hatred to her husband, and had long desired such a separation. Other authors give her not so fair a character; but whatever might be the real cause, the pretext was consanguinity in the fourth degree. *Henry* was content to accept this lady with all her faults, and in her right became duke of *Aquitain*, and earl of *Poitou*, very considerable provinces, added to his other dominions.

But the two kings of *France* and *England* began to apprehend much danger from the sudden greatness of a young ambitious prince; and their interests were jointly concerned to check his growth. Duke *Henry* was now ready to sail for *England*, in a condition to assert his title upon more equal terms; when the king of *France*, in conjunction with *Eustace*, king *Stephen's* son, and *Geoffry*, the duke's own brother, suddenly entered into his dominions with a mighty army; took the castle of *Neumarchè* by storm and laid siege to that of *Angers*. The duke, by this incident, was forced to lay aside his thoughts of *England*, and marching boldly towards the enemy, resolved to relieve the besieged; but finding they had already taken the castle, he thought it best to make a diversion, by carrying the war into the enemy's country, where he left all to the mercy of his soldiers, surprized and burnt several castles, and made great devastations wherever he came. This proceeding answered the end for which it was designed; the king of *France* thought he had already done enough for his honour, and began to grow weary of a ruinous war, which was likely to be protracted. The conditions of a peace, by the intervention of some religious men, were soon agreed. The duke, after some time spent in settling his affairs, and preparing all things necessary for his intended expedition, set sail for *England*, where he landed the same year in the depth of winter, with a hundred and forty knights, and three thousand foot.

Some time before *Henry* landed, the king had conceived a project to disappoint his designs, by confirming the crown upon himself and his own posterity. He sent for the archbishop of *Canterbury*, with several other prelates, and proposed that his son *Eustace* should be crowned king with all the usual solemnity: but the bishops absolutely refused to perform the office, by express orders from the pope, who was an enemy to *Stephen*, partly upon account of his unjust or declining cause, but chiefly for his strict alliance with the king of *France*, who was then engaged in a quarrel against that see, upon a very tender point relating to the revenues of vacant churches. The king and his son were both enraged at the bishops' refusal, and kept them prisoners in the chamber where they assembled, with many threats to force them to a compliance, and some other circumstances of rigour; but all to no purpose, so that he was at length forced to desist. But the archbishop, to avoid further vexation, fled the realm.

This contrivance of crowning the son during the life and reign of the father, which appears so absurd in speculation, was actually performed in the succeeding reign, and seems to have been taken up by those two princes of *French* birth and extraction, in imitation of the like practice in their native country, where it was usual for kings grown old and infirm, or swayed by paternal indulgence, to receive their eldest son into a share of the administration, with the title of king; a custom borrowed, no doubt, from the later emperors of *Rome*, who adopted their *Cæsars* after the like manner.

1153. The king was employed in his usual exercise of besieging castles when the news was brought of *Henry's* arrival. He left the work he was about, and marched directly against the duke, who was then sat down before *Malmesbury*. But *Stephen* forced him to raise the siege, and immediately offered him battle. The duke, although his army was much encreased by continual revolts, thought it best to gain time, being still in number far inferior to the king, and therefore kept himself strongly entrenched. There is some difference among writers about the particulars of this war: however, it is generally agreed, that in a short time after, the two armies met, and were prepared for battle, when the nobles on both sides, either dreading the consequences, or weary of a tedious war, prevailed with the king and duke to agree to a truce for some days in order to a peace; which was violently opposed by *Eustace*, the king's son, a youth of great spirit and courage, because he knew very well it could not be built but upon the ruin of his interests; and therefore finding he could not prevail, he left the army in a rage, and, attended by some followers, endeavoured to satiate his fury, by destroying the country in his march: But in a few days, as he sat at dinner in a castle of his own, he fell suddenly dead, either through grief, madness, or poison.

The truce was now expired, and the duke began to renew the war with fresh vigour; but the king was wholly dispirited upon this fatal accident, and now first began to entertain real thoughts of a peace. He had lost a son whom he dearly loved, and with him he likewise lost the alliance of the *French* king, to whose sister the young prince was married. He had indeed another son left, but little esteemed by the nobles and people; nor, as it appears, much regarded by his father. He was now in the decline of his age, decayed in his health, forsaken by his friends, who, since the death of *Eustace*, fell daily from him; and having no further care at heart for his posterity, he thought it high time to seek repose for his person. The nobles soon observed this disposition in their king, which was so agreeable to their own; therefore, by general consent, *Theobald* archbishop of *Canterbury* was appointed mediator between both princes. All matters were soon agreed; an assembly of lords was convened at *Winchester*, where the king received the duke with great marks of courtesy and kindness. There the peace was confirmed by the king's charter, wherein are expressed the terms of agreement. But I shall relate only the principal.

The king, by this charter, acknowledged *Henry* for lawful successor to the crown; in which capacity all the nobles paid him homage: and *Henry* himself, with his party, paid homage to *Stephen*. There is likewise a reservation for *William*, the king's son, of all the honours possessed by his father before he came to the crown. The king likewise acknowledges the obedience of his subjects to be no longer due to him than he shall observe the conditions of this charter. And for the performance of these articles, the archbishops and bishops were appointed guarantees. There were some other articles agreed on, which are not mentioned in the charter; as, a general pardon, a restitution, to the right owners, of those lands and possessions, which had been usurped in the time of the troubles; that all castles built during the war should be razed to the ground, which are said to have been above eleven hundred; that the rights of the church should be preserved; with other matters of less moment.

Thus, by the prudence of archbishop *Theobald*, the moderation of the two princes engaged, and the universal inclination of the people, a happy period was put to this tedious and troublesome war: men began to have the prospect of a long peace; nor was it easy to foresee what could possibly arise to disturb it; when discovery was made, by accident, of a most horrible piece of treachery, which if it had met with success, would have once more set the whole nation in a flame. The duke, after the peace, attended the king to *London*, to be shewn to the people as the undoubted successor to the crown; and having made a progress together through some other parts of the kingdom, they came to *Canterbury*; where *Henry* received private notice of a design upon his life. It hath been already observed, that the king employed in his wars a body of *Flemings*, to the great discontent of his own subjects, with whom they were very ungracious. These foreigners were much discontented at the peace, whereby they were likely to become useless and burthensome to the present king, and hateful to the successor. To prevent which, the commanders among them began to practice upon the levity and ambition of *William* the king's son. They urged the indignity he had received in being deprived of his birth-right; offered to support his title by their valour, as they had done that of his father; and, as an earnest of their intentions, to remove the chief impediment by dispatching his rival out of the world. The young prince was easily wrought upon to be at the head of this conspiracy; time and place were fixt; when, upon the day appointed, *William* broke his leg by a fall from his horse; and the conspirators wanting their leader immediately dispersed. This disappointment and delay, as it usually happens among conspirators, were soon followed by a discovery of the whole plot, whereof the duke, with great discretion, made no other use than to consult his own safety; therefore, without any shew of suspicion or displeasure, he took leave of the king, and returned to *Normandy*.

1154. *Stephen* lived not above a year to share the happiness of this peace with his people, in which time he made a progress through most parts of the kingdom, where he gained universal love and veneration, by a most affable and courteous behaviour to all men. A few months after his return he went to *Dover*, to have an interview with the earl of *Flanders*; where, after a short sickness, he died of the *Iliac* passion, together with his old distemper the hœmorrhoids, upon the twenty-fifth day of *October*, in the forty-ninth year of his age, and the nineteenth of his reign.

He was a prince of wonderful endowments, both in body and mind; in his person tall and graceful, of great strength as well as vigour: he had a large portion of most virtues that can be useful in a king towards the happiness of his subjects or himself; courtesy and valour, liberality and clemency, in an eminent degree; especially the last, which he carried to an extreme, though very pardonable, yet hardly consisting with prudence, or his own safety. If we except his usurpation of the crown, he must be allowed a prince of great justice, which most writers affirm to have been always unblemished, except in that single instance: for, as to his treatment of the bishops and the earl of *Chester*, it seems very excuseable by the necessity of the time; and it was the general opinion, if he had not used that proceeding with the latter, it would have cost him his crown. Perhaps his injustice to the empress might likewise admit a little extenuation. Four kings successively had sat on the throne without any regard to lineal descent; a period beyond the memory of most men then alive; whereby the people had lost much of that devotion they were used to bear towards an established succession: besides, the government of a woman was a thing then unknown, and for that reason disliked by all who professed to hate innovations.

But the wisdom of this prince was by no means equal to the rest of his virtues. He came to the crown upon as fair a title as his predecessor, being elected by the general consent of the nobles, through the credit of his brother, and his own personal merit. He had no disturbance for some time, which he might easily have employed in settling the kingdom, and acquiring the love of his people. He had treasure enough to raise and pay armies, without burthening the subject. His competitor was a woman, whose sex was the least of her infirmities, and with whom he had already compounded for his quiet by a considerable pension: yet with all these advantages he seldom was master of above half the kingdom at once, and that by the force of perpetual struggling, and with frequent danger of losing the whole. The principal difficulties he had to encounter, appear to have been manifest consequences of several most imprudent steps in his conduct, whereof many instances have been produced in the history of his reign; such as, the unlimited permission of building castles; his raising the siege of a weak place where the empress was shut up, and must, in a few days, have fallen into his hands; his employing the *Flemings* in his wars, and favouring them above his own subjects; and lastly, that abortive project of crowning his son, which procured him at once the hatred and contempt of the clergy, by discovering an inclination to violence and injustice that he durst not pursue: whereas, it was nothing else but an effect of that hasty and sudden disposition usually ascribed to those of his country, and in a peculiar manner charged to this prince: for authors give it as a part of his character, to be hot and violent in the beginning of an enterprize, but to slacken and grow cold in the prosecution.

He had a just sense of religion, and was frequent in attending the service of the church, yet reported to be no great friend of the clergy; which, however, is a general imputation upon all the kings of this realm in that and some succeeding reigns, and by no means personal to this prince, who deserved it as little as any.

I do not find any alterations during this reign in the meetings of general assemblies, further than that the commons do not seem to have been represented in any of them; for which I can assign no other reason than the will of the king, or the disturbance of the time. I observe the word *Parliament* is used promiscuously among authors, for a general assembly of nobles, and for a council of bishops, or synod of the clergy; which renders this matter too perplexed to ascertain any thing about it.

As for affairs of the church, that deserve particular mention, I have not met with any; unless it should be worth relating, that *Henry*, bishop of *Winchester*, the pope's legate, who held frequent synods during this reign, was the first introducer of appeals to *Rome*, in this kingdom, for which he is blamed by all the monkish historians who give us the account.

The REIGN of

HENRY the SECOND.

A FRAGMENT.

THE spirit of war and contention, which had for a long 1154 time possessed the nation, became so effectually laid during the last year of king *Stephen's* reign, that no alteration or disturbance ensued upon his death, although the new king, after he had received intelligence of it, was detained six weeks by contrary winds: besides, the opinion of this prince's power and virtues, had already begotten so great an awe and reverence for him among the people, that upon his arrival he found the whole kingdom in a profound peace. He landed at *Hostreham*, about the beginning of *December*, was received at *Winchester* by a great number of the nobility, who came there to attend and swear fealty to him, and three weeks after was crowned at *Westminster*, about the twenty-third year of his age.

For the further settling of the kingdom, after the long distractions in the preceding reign, he seized on all the castles

H

which remained undestroyed since the last peace between him and king *Stephen*; whereof some he demolished, and trusted others to the government of persons in whom he could confide.

But that which most contributed to the quiet of the realm, and the general satisfaction of his subjects, was a proclamation published, commanding all foreigners to leave *England*, inforced with a most effectual clause, whereby a day was fixt, after which it should be capital for any of them to appear; among these was *William D'Ypres* earl of *Kent*, whose possessions the king seized in his own hands.

These foreigners, generally called *Flemings* by the writers of the *English* story, were a sort of vagabond soldiers of fortune, who in those ages, under several denominations, infested other parts of *Europe* as well as *England*: they were a mixt people, natives of *Arragon*, *Navarre*, *Biscay*, *Brabant*, and other parts of *Spain* and *Flanders*. They were ready to be hired to whatever prince thought fit to employ them, but always upon condition to have full liberty of plunder and spoil. Nor was it an easy matter to get rid of them, when there was no further need of their service. In *England* they were always hated by the people, and by this prince in particular, whose continual enemies they had been.

After the expulsion of these foreigners, and the forcing a few refractory lords to a surrender of their castles, king *Henry*, like a wise prince, began to consider that a time of settled peace was the fittest juncture to recover the rights of the crown, which had been lost by the war. He therefore resumed, by his royal authority, all crown lands that had been alienated by his predecessor; alledging that they were unalienable in themselves, and besides, that the grants were void, as coming from an usurper. Whether such proceedings are agreeable with justice, I shall not examine; but certainly a prince cannot better consult his own safety than by disabling those whom he renders discontent, which is effectually done no other way but by depriving them of their possessions.

1156. While the king was thus employed at home, intelligence came that his brother *Geoffrey* was endeavouring by force to possess himself of the earldom of *Anjou*, to which he had fair pretentions; for their father considering what vast dominions would fall to his eldest son, bequeathed that earldom to the second in his last sickness, and commanded his nobles then about him, to take an oath that they would not suffer his body to be buried until *Henry* (who was then absent) should swear to observe his will. The duke of *Normandy*, when he came to assist at his father's obsequies, and found that without his compliance he must draw upon himself the scandal of keeping a father unburied, took the oath that was exacted for observance of his will, though very much against his own. But after he was in possession of *England*, whether it were that his ambition enlarged with his dominions, or that from the beginning he had never intended to observe what he had sworn, he prevailed with pope *Adrian* (of *English* birth) to dispense with his oath, and in the second year of his reign went over into *Normandy*, drove his brother intirely out of *Anjou*, and forced him to accept a pension for his maintenance. But the young prince, through the resentment of his unnatural dealing, in a short time died of grief.

Nor was his treatment more favourable to the king of *Scots*, whom, upon a slight pretence, he took occasion to dispossess of *Carlisle*, *Newcastle*, and other places granted by the empress to that prince's father, for his services and assistance in her quarrel against *Stephen*.

Having thus recovered whatever he had any title to demand, he began to look out for new acquisitions. *Ireland* was in that age a country little known in the world. The legates sent sometimes thither from the court of *Rome*, for urging the payment of annats, or directing other Church affairs, represented the inhabitants as a savage people, over-run with barbarism and superstition: for indeed no nation of *Europe*, where the Christian religion received so early and universal admittance, was ever so late or slow in feeling its effects upon their manners and civility. Instead of refining their manners by their faith, they had suffered their faith to be corrupted by their manners; true religion being almost defaced, both in doctrine and discipline, after a long course of time, among a people wholly sunk in ignorance and barbarity. There seem to have been two reasons why the inhabitants of that island continued so long uncultivated; first, their subjection or vassalage to so many petty kings, whereof a great number is mentioned by authors, besides those four or five usually assigned to the several provinces. These princes were engaged in perpetual quarrels, in doing or revenging injuries of violence, or lust, or treachery, or injustice, which kept them all in a continual state of war. And indeed there is hardly any country, how renowned soever in ancient or modern story, which may not be traced from the like original. Neither can a nation come out from this state of confusion, until it is either reduced under one head at home, or by force or conquest becomes subject to a foreign administration.

The other reason why civility made such late entrances into that island, may be imputed to its natural situation, lying more out of the road of commerce or conquest than any other part of the known world. All the intercourse the inhabitants had, was only with the coasts of *Wales* and *Scotland*, from whence, at least in those ages, they were not like to learn very much politeness.

1155. The king, about the second year of his reign, sent ambassadors to pope *Adrian*, with injunctions to desire his licence for reducing the savage people of *Ireland* from their brutish way of living, and subjecting them to the crown of *England*. The king proceeded thus, in order to set up a title to the island, wherein the pope himself pretended to be lord of the see; for in his letter, which is an answer and grant to the king's requests, he insists upon it, that all islands, upon their admitting the Christian faith, become subject to the see of *Rome*; and the *Irish* themselves avowed the same thing to some of the first conquerors. In that fore-mentioned letter, the pope highly praises the king's generous design, and recommends to him the civilizing the natives, the protection of the Church, and the payment of *Peter-pence*. The ill success of all past endeavours to procure from a people so miserable and

irreligious this revenue to the holy fee, was a main inducement
with the pope to be easy and liberal in his grant; for the king
professed a design of securing its regular payment. However,
this expedition was not undertaken until some years after,
when there happened an incident to set it forward, as we shall
relate in its place.   *   *   *   *
*   *   *   *   *   *   *

HENRY the SECOND's Character.

Extracted from the MONKS.

Hard to gather his Character from such bad AUTHORS.

A WISE prince, to whom other princes referred their
differences; and had ambassadors from both empires,
East and West, as well as others, at once in his court.
Strong and brawny body, patient of cold and heat, big head,
broad breast, broken voice, temperate in meat, using much
exercise, just stature, *forma elegantissima, colore subrufo, oculis
glaucis*, sharp wit, very great memory, constancy in adversity
[and] in felicity, except at last he yielded, because almost
forsaken of all; liberal, imposed few tributes, excellent soldier
and fortunate, wise and not unlearned. His vices: mild and
promising in adversity, fierce and hard, and a violator of faith
in prosperity; covetous to his domesticks and children,
although liberal to soldiers and strangers, which turned the
former from him; loved profit more than justice; very lustful,
which likewise turned his sons and others from him. *Rosamond*
and the labyrinth at *Woodstock*. Not very religious; *mortuos
milites lugens plus quam vivos amans; largus in publico, parcus in
privato.* Constant in love and hatred, false to his word, morose,
a lover of ease. Oppressor of nobles, sullen, and a delayer of
justice; *verbo varius & versutus*——Used churchmen well

after *Becket's* death; charitable to the poor, levied few taxes, hated slaughter and cruelty. A great memory, and always knew those he once saw.

Very indefatigable in his travels backwards and forwards to *Normandy*, &c. of most endless desires to increase his dominions.   *   *   *   *   *   *
*   *   *   *   *   *   *

Cætera desiderantur.

OF

PUBLICK ABSURDITYES

IN ENGLAND

IT is a common topick of Satyr, which you will hear
not onely from the mouths of Ministers of State, but of every
whiffler in office, that half a dozen obscure fellows over a
bottle of wine or a dish of coffee shall presume to censure
the actions of Parliaments and Councils, to form Scheams of
government, and new model the commonwealth; and this
usually ridiculed as a pragmatical disposition to politicks in
the very nature and genius of the People. It may possibly
be true: And yet I am grossly deceived if any sober man of
very moderate talents, when he reflects upon the many
ridiculous hurtfull Maximes, customs, and generall rules of
life which prevail in this kingdom, would not with great
reason be tempted, according to the present turn of his
humor, either to laugh, lament, or be angry, or if he were
sanguin enough, perhaps to dream of a remedy. It is the mistake of wise and good men that they expect more Reason
and Virtue from human nature, than taking it in the bulk,
it is in any sort capable of. Whoever hath been present at
Councils or assemblyes of any sort, if he be a man of common
prudence, cannot but have observed such results and opinions
to have frequently passt a majority, as he would be ashamed
to advance in private conversation. I say nothing of Cruelty,
oppression Injustice and the like, because these are fairly
to be accounted for in all assemblyes, as best gratifying the
Passions and interests of Leaders; which is a point of such
high consideration that all others must give place to it. But
I would be understood here to speak onely of opinions
ridiculous foolish and absurd; with conclusions and actions
suitable to them, at the same time when the most reasonable
Propositions are often unanimously rejected.

And, as all assemblyes of men are lyable to this accusation, so likewise there are naturall absurdityes from which the wisest States are not exempt, which proceed less from the nature of their Clymate than that of their government. The Gauls, the Britains, the Spaniards and Italians having retained very little of the Characters given them in antient writings.

By these and the like Reflections I have been often led to consider some publick Absurdityes in our own Country, most of which are in my opinion directly against the rules of right reason, and are attended with great inconveniences to the State. I shall mention such of them as come into memory, without observing any method; and I shall give my reason why I take them to be absurd in their nature, and pernicious in their consequences.

It is absurd that any Person who professeth a different form of worship from that which is national should be trusted with a vote for electing Members in the House of Commons. Because every man is full of zeal for his own Religion, although he regards not morality, and therefore will endeavor to his utmost to bring in a Representative of his own principles, which, if they be popular, may endanger the Religion established, which as it hath formerly happened may alter the whole frame of Government.

A standing army in England whether in time of peace or war is a direct absurdity. For, it is no part of our business to be a warlike nation, otherwise than by our fleets. In forein wars we have no concern, further than in conjunction with Allyes, whom we may either assist by sea, or by forein troops payd with our money. But, mercenary Troops in England can be of no use, except to awe Senates, and thereby promote arbitrary Power in a Monarchy or Oligarchy.

That the Election of Senators should be of any charge to the Candidates, is an absurdity, but that it should be so to a Ministry, is a manifest acknoledgement of the worst designs. If a Ministry intended the Service of their Prince and Country, or well understood wherein their own Security best consisted, they would use the strongest methods to leave the people to their own free choice. [It is impossible that a

Parliament freely elected, according to the original institution, can do any hurt to a tolerable Prince, or a tolerable Ministry.] The members would then consist of Persons who had best estates in the Neighbourhood or the County, or at least never of Strangers. And surely this is full as requisite a Circumstance to a Legislator, as to a Juryman, who ought to be, if possible, *ex vicinia*; since such persons must be supposed the best judges of the wants and desires of their severall burroughs and Countyes. To chuse a representative for Berwick whose estate is at the Lands-end would have been thought in former times a very great solecism, how much more as it is at present, where so many Persons are return[ed] for Burroughs, who do not possess a foot of land in the Kingdom.

By the old constitution, whoever possessed a free-hold in land, by which he was a gainer of forty shillings a year, had the privilege to vote for a Knight of the shire. The good effects of this Law are wholly eluded, partly by the course of time, and partly by corruption. Forty Shillings in those ages were equall to twenty pounds in ours; and therefore it was then a want of Sagacity to fix that priviledge to a determinate Summ, rather than to a certain quantity of land, arable or pasture able to produce a certain quantity of corn or hay. And therefore it is highly absurd and against the intent of the Law that this defect is not regulated.

But the matter is still worse: For any gentleman can upon occasion make as many freeholders as his estate or settlement will allow, by making leases for life of land at a rack rent of forty shillings, where a Tenant, who is not worth one farthing a year when his rent is payd shall be held a legal voter for a Person to represent his County. Neither do I enter into half the frauds that are practised upon this occasion.

It is likewise absurd, that Bouroughs decayd are not absolutely extinguished, because the returned members do in reality represent no body at all, and that severall large Towns are not represented, tho[ugh] full of industrious Townsmen, who much advance the Trade of the Kingdom.

The Claim of Senators to have themselves and Servants exempted from Law-suits and arrests is manifestly absurd. The proceedings at law are already so scandalous a grievance upon account of the delays, that they little need any addition. Whoever is either not able or not willing to pay his just debts, or to keep other men out of their Lands would evade the decision of the Law, is surely but ill qualifyed to be a Legislator. A Criminal with as good reason might sit on the Bench with a power of condemning men to be hanged for their honesty: By the annual sitting of Parliaments, and the days of Priviledge preceding and subsequent, a Senator is one half of the year beyond the reach of common justice.

That the sacred Person of a Senator's footman should be free from arrest although he undoes the poor ale-wife by running on score is a circumstance of equall wisdom and justice, to avoyd the great evil of his master's Lady wanting her complement of liveryes behind the coach.

MEAN AND GREAT FIGURES

MADE BY SEVERAL PERSONS

Of those who have made great FIGURES *in some particular Action or Circumstance of their Lives*

ALEXANDER the great, after his Victory, [at the Streights of Mount Taurus] when he entered the Tent where the Queen and the Princesses of Persia fell at his feet.

Socrates, the whole last Day of his Life, and particularly from the Time he took the Poison to the Moment he expired.

Cicero when he was recalled from his Banishment. The People, through every place he passed meeting him with Shouts of Joy and Congratulation, and all Rome coming out to receive him.

Regulus when he went out of Rome attended by his Friends to the Gates, and returned to Carthage according to his Word of Honor, although he knew he must be put to a cruell Death, for advising the Romans to pursue their War with that Commonwealth.

Scipio the Elder when he dismissed a beautifull Captive Lady, presented to him after a great Victory, turning his Head aside, to preserve his own Virtue.

The same Scipio, when he and Hannibal met before the Battle; if the Fact be true.

Cincinnatus when the Messengers, sent by the Senate to make him Dictator, found him at the Plow.

Epaminondas when the Persian Ambassador came to his House and found him in the midst of Poverty.

The Earl of Strafford the Day that he made his own Defence at his Tryall.

King Charles the Martyr during his whole Tryall, and at his Death.

The Black Prince when he waited at Supper on the King of France, whom he had conquered and taken Prisoner the same Day.

Virgil, when at Rome the whole Audience rose up, out of Veneration, as he entred the Theatre.

Mahomet the great when he cut off his beloved Mistress's head on a Stage erected for that purpose: to convince his Soldiers who taxed him for preferring his Love to his Glory.

Cromwell, when he quelled a mutiny in Hyde-Park.

Harry the Great of France, when he entered Paris, and sate at Cards the same Night with some great Ladyes, who were his mortal Enemyes.

Robert Harley Earl of Oxford, at His Tryall.

Cato of Utica, when he provided for the Safety of his Friends and had determined to dy.

Sir Tho More during his Imprisonment, and at his Execution.

The Earl of Oxford when he was stabbed by Guiscard.

Marius when the Soldier sent to kill him in the Dungeon was struck with so much aw and Veneration that his sword fell from his Hand.

Douglas when the ship he commanded was on Fire, and he lay down to dy in it, because it should not be said that one of his Family ever quitted their Post.

Sr Jerom Bows.

Of those who have made a mean contemptible Figure in some Action or Circumstance of their Life

Antony at Actium when he fled after Cleopatra.

Pompey when he was killed on the seashore in Ægypt.

Nero and Vitellius when they were put to Death.

Lepidus when he was compelled to lay down his Share in the Triumvirate.

Cromwell the Day he refused the Kingship out of Fear.

Perseus K. of Macedon when he was led in Triumph.

Richard the 2d of Engd after he was deposed.

The present K. of Poland, when the K. of Sweden forced him to give up his Kingdom, and when he took it again upon the King of Sweden's Defeat by the Muscovites.

King James 2d of England, when the Pr of Orange sent to him at Midnight to leave London.

King Wm 3rd of England, when he sent to beg the House of Commons to continue his Dutch Guards, and was refused.

The late Queen Ann of Engld, when she sent Whitworth to Muscovy on an Ambassy of Humiliation, for an Insult committed here on that Prince's Ambassador.

The Lord Chancellor Bacon, when he was convicted of Bribery.

The late Duke of Marlborough when he was forced after his own Disgrace, to carry his Dutchesses Gold Key to the Queen.

The old Earl of Pembroke when a Scotch Lord gave him a Lash with a Whip at Newmarket in presence of all the Nobility, and he bore it with Patience.

King Charles 2d of Engd when he entered into the Second Dutch War, and in many other Actions during his whole Reign.

Philip the 2d of Spayn after the Defeat of the Armada.

The Emperor Charles the fifth, when he resigned his Crown, and nobody would believe his Reasons.

K. Charles Ist. of England, when in Gallantry to his Queen, he thought to surprize her with a Present of a Diamond Buckle, which he pushed down her Back, and tore her Flesh with the Tongue; upon which she drew it out, and flung it on the ground.

Fairfax, the Parliament Generall, at the Time of King Charles' Tryall.

Julius Cæsar when Antony offered to put a Diadem on his Head, and the People shouted for Joy to see him Decline it; which he never offered to do till he saw their Dislike in their Countenances.

Coriolanus when he withdrew His Army from Rome at the Intreaty of his Mother.

Hannibal at Antiochus's Court.

Beau Fielding, at fifty years old, when in a Quarrel upon the Stage he was run into his Breast, which he opened and shewed to the Ladyes, that he might move their Love and Pity; but they all fell a laughing.

The Count de Bussy Rabutin when he was recalled to Court after 20 Years banishment into the Country, and affected to make the same Figure he did in his Youth.

The Earl of Sunderland when he turned Papist in the Time of K. James 2d, and underwent all the Forms of a Heretick converted.

Pope [Clement VII] when he was taken Prisoner at Rome by the Emperor Charles the fifth's Forces.

Queen Mary of Scotland when she suffered Bothwell to ravish her, and pleaded that as her Excuse for marrying Him.

K. John of England, when he gave up his Kingdom to the Pope, to be held as a Fief from the See of Rome.

WILLIAM

LORD ARCHBISHOP OF DUBLIN, *&c.*

The humble Representation of the CLERGY of the City of DUBLIN.

Jan. 1724.

MY LORD,

YOUR Grace having been pleased to communicate to us a certain brief, by letters patents, for the relief of one Charles M'Carthy, whose house in College-green, Dublin, was burnt by an accidental fire; and having desired us to consider of the said brief, and give our opinions thereof to your Grace;

We the clergy of the city of Dublin, in compliance with your Grace's desire, and with great acknowledgments for your paternal tenderness towards us, having maturely considered the said brief by letters patents, compared the several parts of it with what is enjoined us by the rubric, (which is confirmed by act of parliament) and consulted persons skilled in the laws of the church; do, in the names of ourselves and of the rest of our brethren, the clergy of the diocess of Dublin, most humbly represent to your Grace:

First, That, by this brief, your Grace is required and commanded, to recommend and command all the parsons, vicars, *&c.* to advance so great an act of charity.

We shall not presume to determine how far your Grace may be commanded by the said brief; but we humbly conceive, that the clergy of your diocess cannot, by any law now in being, be commanded by your Grace to advance the said act of charity, any other ways than by reading the said brief in our several churches, as prescribed by the rubric.

Secondly, Whereas it is said in the said brief, that the parsons, vicars, *&c.* upon the first Lord's-day, or opportunity after the receipt of the copy of the said brief, shall, deliberately and affectionately, publish and declare the tenor thereof to his Majesty's subjects, and earnestly persuade, exhort, and stir them up to contribute freely and chearfully towards the relief of the said sufferer;

We do not comprehend what is meant by the word *opportunity*. We never do preach upon any day except the Lord's-day, or some solemn days legally appointed; neither is it possible for the strongest constitution among us to obey this command (which includes no less than a whole sermon) upon any other opportunity than when our people are met together in the church; and to perform this work in every house where the parishes are very populous, consisting sometimes here in town of 900 or 1000 houses, would take up the space of a year, although we should preach in two families every day; and almost as much time in the country, where the parishes are of large extent, the roads bad, and the people too poor to receive us, and give charity at once.

But, if it be meant that these exhortations are commanded to be made in the church, upon the Lord's-day, we are humbly of opinion, that it is left to the discretion of the clergy, to chuse what subjects they think most proper to preach on, and at what times; and, if they preach either false doctrine or seditious principles, they are liable to be punished.

It may possibly happen, that the sufferer recommended may be a person not deserving the favour intended by the brief; in which case no minister, who knows the sufferer to be an undeserving person, can with a safe conscience, deliberately and affectionately publish the brief, much less earnestly persuade, exhort, and stir up the people to contribute freely and chearfully towards the relief of such a sufferer*.

Thirdly, Whereas in the said brief the ministers and curates are required, on the week-days next after the Lord's-day when the brief was read, to go from house to house, with their

---

* This M'Carthy's house was burnt in the month of August, 1723, and the universal opinion of mankind was, that M'Carthy himself was the person who had set fire to the house.

church-wardens, to ask and receive from all persons the said charity: We cannot but observe here, that the said ministers are directly made collectors of the said charity in conjunction with the church-wardens; which, however, we presume, was not intended, as being against all law and precedent: And therefore, we apprehend, there may be some inconsistency, which leaves us at a loss how to proceed. For, in the next paragraph, the ministers and curates are only required, where they conveniently can, to accompany the church-wardens, or procure some other of the chief inhabitants, to do the same. And, in a following paragraph, the whole work seems left entirely to the church-wardens, who are required to use their utmost diligence to gather and collect the said charity, and to pay the same, in ten days after, to the parson, vicar, &c.

In answer to this, we do represent to your Grace our humble opinion, that neither we nor our church-wardens can be legally commanded or required to go from house to house to receive the said charity; because your Grace hath informed us in your order, at your visitation *An. Dom.* 1712, that neither we nor our church-wardens are bound to make any collections for the poor, save in the church; which also appears plainly by the rubric, that appoints both time and place, as your Grace hath observed in your said order.

We do likewise assure your Grace, that it is not in our power to procure some of the chief inhabitants of our parishes to accompany the church-wardens from house to house in these collections: And we have reason to believe, that such a proposal, made to our chief inhabitants, (particularly in this city, where our chief inhabitants are often peers of the land) would be received in a manner very little to our own satisfaction, or to the advantage of the said collections.

Fourthly, The brief doth will, require, and command the bishops, and all other dignitaries of the church, that they make their contributions distinctly, to be returned in the several provinces to the several archbishops of the same.

Upon which we take leave to observe, that the terms of expression here are of the strongest kind, and in a point

I

that may subject the said dignitaries (for we shall say nothing of the bishops) to great inconveniencies.

The said dignitaries are here willed, required, and commanded to make their contributions distinctly; by which it should seem that they are absolutely commanded to make contributions (for the word *distinctly* is but a circumstance), and may be understood not very agreeable to a voluntary, chearful contribution. And therefore, if any bishop or dignitary should refuse to make his contribution, (perhaps for very good reasons) he may be thought to incur the crime of disobedience to his Majesty, which all good subjects abhor, when such a command is according to law.

Most dignities of this kingdom consist only of parochial tythes, and the dignitaries are ministers of parishes. A doubt may therefore arise, whether the said dignitaries are willed, required, and commanded, to make their contributions in both capacities, distinctly as dignitaries, and jointly as parsons or vicars.

Many dignities in this kingdom are the poorest kind of benefices; and it should seem hard to put poor dignitaries under the necessity either of making greater contributions than they can afford, or of exposing themselves to the censure of wanting charity, by making their contributions public.

Our Saviour commands us, in works of charity, to *let not our left hand know what our right hand doeth*; which cannot well consist with our being willed, required, and commanded by any earthly power, where no law is prescribed, to publish our charity to the world, if we have a mind to conceal it.

Fifthly, Whereas it is said in the said brief, that the parson, vicar, *&c.* of every parish, shall, in six days after the receipt of the said charity, return it to his respective chancellor, *&c.* This may be a great grievance, hazard, and expence to the said parson, in remote and desolate parts of the country, where often an honest messenger (if such a one can be got) must be hired to travel forty or fifty miles going and coming; which will probably cost more than the value of the contribution he carries with him. And this charge, if briefs should happen to be frequent, would be enough to undo many a poor clergyman in the kingdom.

Sixthly, We observe in the said brief, that the provost and fellows of the university, judges, officers of the courts, and professors of laws common and civil, are neither willed, required, nor commanded to make their contributions; but that so good a work is only recommended to them. Whereas we conceive, that all his Majesty's subjects are equally obliged, with or without his Majesty's commands, to promote works of charity according to their power; and that the clergy, in their ecclesiastical capacity, are only liable to such commands as the rubric, or any other law shall enjoin, being born to the same privileges of freedom with the rest of his Majesty's subjects.

We cannot but observe to your Grace, that, in the English act of the fourth year of Queen Anne, for the better collecting charity-money on briefs by letters patent, *&c.* the ministers are obliged only to read the briefs in their churches, without any particular exhortations; neither are they commanded to go from house to house with the church-wardens, nor to send the money collected to their respective chancellors, but pay it to the undertaker or agent of the sufferer. So that, we humbly hope, the clergy of this kingdom shall not, without any law in being, be put to greater hardships in this case than their brethren in England, where the legislature, intending to prevent the abuses in collecting charity-money on briefs, did not think fit to put the clergy under any of those difficulties we now complain of, in the present brief by letters patent, for the relief of Charles M'Carthy aforesaid.

The collections upon the Lord's-day are the principal support of our own numerous poor in our several parishes; and therefore every single brief, with the benefit of a full collection over the whole kingdom, must deprive several thousands of poor of their weekly maintenance, for the sake only of one person, who often becomes a sufferer by his own folly or negligence, and is sure to overvalue his losses double or treble: So that, if this precedent be followed, as it certainly will if the present brief should succeed, we may probably have a new brief every week; and thus, for the advantage of fifty-two persons, whereof not one in ten is deserving, and for the interest of a dozen dextrous clerks and secretaries, the whole poor in the kingdom will be likely to starve.

We are credibly informed, that neither the officers of the Lord Primate, in preparing the report of his Grace's opinion, nor those of the great-seal, in passing the patent for briefs, will remit any of their fees, both which do amount to a considerable sum: And thus the good intentions of well-disposed people are in a great measure disappointed, a large part of their charity being anticipated, and alienated by fees and gratuities.

Lastly, We cannot but represent to your Grace our great concern and grief, to see the pains and labour of our church-wardens so much encreased, by the injunctions and commands put upon them in this brief, to the great disadvantage of the clergy and the people, as well as to their own trouble, damage, and loss of time, to which great additions have been already made, by laws appointing them to collect the taxes for the watch and the poor-house, which they bear with great unwillingness; and, if they shall find themselves further laden with such briefs as this of M'Carthy, it will prove so great a discouragement, that we shall never be able to provide honest and sufficient persons for that weighty office of church-warden, so necessary to the laity as well as the clergy, in all things that relate to the order and regulation of parishes.

Upon all these considerations, we humbly hope that your Grace, of whose fatherly care, vigilance, and tenderness, we have had so many and great instances, will represent our case to his Most Excellent Majesty, or to the Chief Governor in this kingdom, in such a manner, that we may be neither under the necessity of declining his Majesty's commands in his letters patent, or of taking new and grievous burthens upon ourselves and our church-wardens, to which neither the rubric nor any other law in force oblige us to submit.

LETTER

WRITER of the OCCASIONAL PAPER

[Vide the CRAFTSMAN, 1727.]

SIR,

ALTHOUGH, in one of your Papers, you declare an intention of turning them, during the dead season of the year, into accounts of domestic and foreign intelligence; yet I think we, your correspondents, should not understand your meaning so literally, as if you intended to reject inserting any other paper, which might probably be useful for the public. Neither, indeed, am I fully convinced that this new course you resolve to take will render you more secure than your former laudable practice, of inserting such speculations as were sent you by several well-wishers to the good of the kingdom; however grating such notices might be to some, who wanted neither power nor inclination to resent them at your cost. For, since there is a direct law against spreading false news, if you should venture to tell us in one of the Craftsmen, that the Dey of Algiers had got the tooth-ach, or the King of Bantam had taken a purge, and the facts should be contradicted in succeeding pacquets; I do not see what plea you could offer to avoid the utmost penalty of the law, because you are not supposed to be very gracious among those who are most able to hurt you.

Besides, as I take your intentions to be sincerely meant for the public service, so your original method of entertaining and instructing us will be more general and more useful in this season of the year, when people are retired to amusements more cool, more innocent, and much more reasonable than those they have left; when their passions are subsided or suspended; when they have no occasions of inflaming themselves, or each other; where they will have opportunities of hearing common sense, every day in the week, from their tenants or neighbouring farmers, and thereby be qualified, in hours of rain or leisure, to read and consider the advice or information you shall send them.

Another weighty reason why you should not alter your manner of writing, by dwindling to a news-monger, is because there is no suspension of arms agreed on between you and your adversaries, who fight with a sort of weapons which have two wonderful qualities, that they are never to be worn out, and are best wielded by the weakest hands, and which the poverty of our language forceth me to call by the trite appellations of Scurrility, Slander, and Billingsgate. I am far from thinking that these gentlemen, or rather their employers, (for the operators themselves are too obscure to be guessed at) should be answered after their own way, although it were possible to drag them out of their obscurity; but I wish you would enquire what real use such a conduct is to the cause they have been so largely paid to defend. The author of the three first Occasional Letters, a person altogether unknown, hath been thought to glance (for what reasons he best knows) at some public proceedings, as if they were not agreeable to his private opinions. In answer to this, the pamphleteers retained on the other side are instructed by their superiors, to single out an adversary whose abilities they most have reason to apprehend, and to load himself, his family, and friends, with all the infamy that a perpetual conversation in Bridewell, Newgate, and the stews could furnish them; but, at the same time, so very unluckily, that the most distinguishing parts of their characters strike directly in the face of their benefactor, whose idea presenting itself along with his guineas perpetually to their imagination, occasioned this desperate blunder.

But, allowing this heap of slander to be truth, and applied to the proper person; what is to be the consequence? Are our public debts to be the sooner paid; the corruptions that author complains of to be the sooner cured; an honourable peace, or a glorious war the more likely to ensue; trade to flourish; the Ostend company to be demolished; Gibraltar and Port-Mahon left entire in our possession; the balance of Europe to be preserved; the malignity of parties to be for ever at an end; none but persons of merit, virtue, genius and learning to be encouraged? I ask whether any of these effects will follow upon the publication of this author's libel, even sup-posing he could prove every syllable of it to be true?

At the same time, I am well assured, that the only reason of ascribing those papers to a particular person, is built upon the information of a certain pragmatical spy of quality, well known to act in that capacity by those into whose company he insinuates himself; a sort of persons who, although without much love, esteem, or dread of people in present power, yet have too much common prudence to speak their thoughts with freedom before such an intruder; who, therefore, imposes grossly upon his masters, if he makes them pay for anything but his own conjectures.

It is a grievous mistake in a great minister to neglect or despise, much more to irritate men of genius and learning. I have heard one of the wisest persons in my time observe, that an administration was to be known and judged by the talents of those who appeared their advocates in print. This I must never allow to be a general rule; yet I cannot but think it prodigiously unfortunate, that, among the answerers, defenders, repliers, and panegyrists, started up in defence of present persons and proceedings, there hath not yet arisen one whose labours we can read with patience, however we may applaud their loyalty and good-will. And all this with the advantages of constant ready pay, of natural and acquired venom, and a grant of the whole fund of slander, to range over and riot in as they please.

On the other side, a turbulent writer of Occasional Letters, and other vexatious papers, in conjunction perhaps with one or two friends as bad as himself, is able to disconcert, teaze, and sour us whenever he thinks fit, merely by the strength of genius and truth; and after so dextrous a manner, that, when we are vexed to the soul, and well know the reasons why we are so, we are ashamed to own the first, and cannot tell how to express the other. In a word, it seems to me that all the writers are on one side, and all the railers on the other.

However, I do not pretend to assert, that it is impossible for an ill minister to find men of wit who may be drawn, by a very valuable consideration, to undertake his defence; but the misfortune is, that the heads of such writers rebel against their hearts; their genius forsakes them, when they would offer to prostitute it to the service of injustice, corruption, party-rage, and false representations of things and persons.

And this is the best argument I can offer in defence of great men, who have been of late so very unhappy in the choice of their paper-champions; although I cannot much commend their good husbandry, in those exorbitant payments of twenty and sixty guineas at a time for a scurvy pamphlet: since the sort of work they require is what will all come within the talents of any one who hath enjoyed the happiness of a very bad education, hath kept the vilest company, is endowed with a servile spirit, is master of an empty purse, and a heart full of malice.

But, to speak the truth in soberness; it should seem a little hard, since the old Whiggish principle hath been recalled of standing up for the liberty of the press, to a degree that no man, for several years past, durst venture out a thought which did not square to a point with the maxims and practices that then prevailed: I say, it is a little hard that the vilest mercenaries should be countenanced, preferred, rewarded, for discharging their brutalities against men of honour, only upon a bare conjecture.

If it should happen that these profligates have attacked an innocent person, I ask what satisfaction can their hirers give in return? Not all the wealth raked together by the most corrupt rapacious ministers, in the longest course of unlimited power, would be sufficient to atone for the hundredth part of such an injury.

In the common way of thinking, it is a situation sufficient in all conscience to satisfy a reasonable ambition, for a private person, to command the forces, the laws, the revenues of a great kingdom, to reward and advance his followers and flatterers as he pleases, and to keep his enemies (real or imaginary) in the dust. In such an exaltation, why should he be at the trouble to make use of fools to sound his praises, (because I always thought the lion was hard set, when he chose the ass for his trumpeter) or knaves to revenge his quarrels, at the expence of innocent mens reputations?

With all those advantages, I cannot see why persons, in the height of power, should be under the least concern on account of their reputation, for which they have no manner of use; or to ruin that of others, which may perhaps be the only possession their enemies have left them. Supposing times of corruption, which I am very far from doing, if a writer displays them in their proper colours, does he do any thing worse than sending customers to the shop? Here only, at the sign of the Brazen Head, are to be sold places and pensions: beware of counterfeits, and take care of mistaking the door.

For my own part, I think it very unnecessary to give the character of a great minister in the fulness of his power, because it is a thing that naturally doth itself, and is obvious to the eyes of all mankind; for his personal qualities are all derived into the most minute parts of his administration. If this be just, prudent, regular, impartial, intent upon the public good, prepared for present exigencies, and provident of the future; such is the director himself in his private capacity: If it be rapacious, insolent, partial, palliating long and deep diseases of the public with empirical remedies, false, disguised, impudent, malicious, revengeful; you shall infallibly find the private life of the conductor to answer in every point; nay, what is more, every twinge of the gout or gravel will be felt in their consequences by the community: As the thief-catcher, upon viewing a house broke open, could immediately distinguish, from the manner of the workmanship, by what hand it was done.

It is hard to form a maxim against which an exception is not ready to start up: So, in the present case, where the minister grows enormously rich, the public is proportionably poor; as, in a private family, the steward always thrives the fastest when his Lord is running out.

* * * * * * * * * *
* * * * * * * * * *

AN

ACCOUNT

OF THE

COURT and EMPIRE of JAPAN

Written in M DCC XXVIII.

R EGOGE was the thirty-fourth Emperor of Japan, and began his reign in the year 341 of the Christian æra, succeeding to Nena, a Princess who governed with great felicity.

There had been a revolution in that empire about twenty-six years before, which made some breaches in the hereditary line; and Regoge, successor to Nena, although of the royal family, was a distant relation. There were two violent parties in the empire, which began in the time of the revolution above-mentioned; and, at the death of the Empress Nena, were in the highest degree of animosity, each charging the other with a design of introducing new Gods, and changing the civil constitution. The names of these two parties were Husiges and Yortes. The latter were those whom Nena, the late Empress, most favoured towards the end of her reign, and by whose advice she governed.

The Husige faction, enraged at their loss of power, made private applications to Regoge during the life of the Empress; which prevailed so far, that, upon her death, the new Emperor wholly disgraced the Yortes, and employed only the Husiges in all his affairs. The Japanese Author highly blames his Imperial Majesty's proceeding in this affair; because, it was allowed on all hands, that he had then a happy opportunity of reconciling parties for ever by a moderating scheme. But he, on the contrary, began his reign by openly disgracing the principal and most popular Yortes, some of which had been

chiefly instrumental in raising him to the throne. By this
mistaken step he occasioned a rebellion; which, although it
were soon quelled by some very surprising turns of fortune,
yet the fear, whether real or pretended, of new attempts,
engaged him in such immense charges, that, instead of clearing
any part of that prodigious debt left on his kingdom by the
former war, which might have been done by any tolerable
management, in twelve years of the most profound peace;
he left his empire loaden with a vast addition to the old incum-
brance.

This Prince, before he succeeded to the empire of Japan,
was King of Tedsu, a dominion seated on the continent, to the
west-side of Japan. Tedsu was the place of his birth, and more
beloved by him than his new empire; for there he spent some
months almost every year, and thither was supposed to have
conveyed great sums of money, saved out of his imperial
revenues.

There were two maritime towns of great importance
bordering upon Tedsu: Of these he purchased a litigated
title; and, to support it, was forced not only to entrench deeply
on his Japanese revenues, but to engage in alliances very
dangerous to the Japanese empire.

Japan was at that time a limited monarchy, which some
authors are of opinion was introduced there by a detachment
from the numerous army of Brennus, who ravaged a great
part of Asia; and, those of them who fixed in Japan, left behind
them that kind of military institution, which the northern
people, in ensuing ages, carried through most parts of Europe;
the generals becoming kings, the great officers a senate of
nobles, with a representative from every centenary of private
soldiers; and, in the assent of the majority in these two bodies,
confirmed by the general, the legislature consisted.

I need not farther explain a matter so universally known;
but return to my subject.

The Husige faction, by a gross piece of negligence in the
Yortes, had so far insinuated themselves and their opinions
into the favour of Regoge before he came to the empire, that
this Prince firmly believed them to be his only true friends,

and the others his mortal enemies. By this opinion he governed all the actions of his reign.

The Emperor died suddenly, in his journey to Tedsu; where, according to his usual custom, he was going to pass the summer.

This Prince, during his whole reign, continued an absolute stranger to the language, the manners, the laws, and the religion of Japan; and, passing his whole time among old mistresses, or a few privados, left the whole management of the empire in the hands of a minister, upon the condition of being made easy in his personal revenues, and the management of parties in the senate. His last Minister, who governed in the most arbitrary manner for several years, he was thought to hate more than he did any other person in Japan, except his only son, the heir to the empire. The dislike he bore to the former was, because the minister, under pretence that he could not govern the senate without disposing of employments among them, would not suffer his master to oblige one single person, but disposed of all to his own relations and dependents. But, as to that continued and virulent hatred he bore to the Prince his son, from the beginning of his reign to his death, the Historian hath not accounted for it, further than by various conjectures, which do not deserve to be related.

The minister above mentioned was of a family not contemptible, had been early a senator, and from his youth a mortal enemy to the Yortes. He had been formerly disgraced in the senate, for some frauds in the management of a public trust. He was perfectly skilled, by long practice, in the senatorial forms; and dextrous in the purchasing of votes, from those who could find their accounts better in complying with his measures, than they could probably lose by any tax that might be charged on the kingdom. He seemed to fail, in point of policy, by not concealing his gettings, never scrupling openly to lay out vast sums of money in paintings, buildings, and purchasing estates; when it was known, that, upon his first coming into business, upon the death of the Empress Nena, his fortune was but inconsiderable. He had the most boldness, and the least magnanimity, that ever any mortal was endowed with. By enriching his relations, friends, and dependants, in a most exorbitant manner, he was weak enough to imagine that he had provided a support against an evil day. He had the best among all false appearances of courage, which was a most unlimited assurance, whereby he would swagger the boldest men into a dread of his power, but had not the smallest portion of magnanimity, growing jealous, and disgracing every man, who was known to bear the least civility to those he disliked. He had some small smattering in books, but no manner of politeness; nor, in his whole life, was ever known to advance any one person, upon the score of wit, learning, or abilities for business. The whole system of his ministry was corruption; and he never gave bribe or pension, without frankly telling the receivers what he expected from them, and threatning them to put an end to his bounty, if they failed to comply in every circumstance.

A few months before the Emperor's death, there was a design concerted between some eminent persons of both parties, whom the desperate state of the empire had united, to accuse the minister at the first meeting of a new chosen senate, which was then to assemble according to the laws of that empire. And it was believed, that the vast expence he must be at in chusing an assembly proper for his purpose, added to the low state of the treasury, the encreasing number of pensioners, the great discontent of the people, and the personal hatred of the Emperor; would, if well laid open in the senate, be of weight enough to sink the minister, when it should appear to his very pensioners and creatures that he could not supply them much longer.

While this scheme was in agitation, an account came of the Emperor's death, and the Prince his son, with universal joy, mounted the throne of Japan.

The new Emperor had always lived a private life, during the reign of his father; who, in his annual absence, never trusted him more than once with the reins of government, which he held so evenly that he became too popular to be confided in any more. He was thought not unfavourable to the Yortes, at least not altogether to approve the virulence wherewith his father proceeded against them; and therefore, immediately upon his succession, the principal persons of that denomination came, in several bodies, to kiss the hem of his garment, whom he received with great courtesy, and some of them with particular marks of distinction.

The Prince, during the reign of his father, having not been trusted with any public charge, employed his leisure in learning the language, the religion, the customs, and disposition of the Japanese; wherein he received great information, among others, from Nomptoc, master of his finances, and president of the senate, who secretly hated Lelop-Aw, the minister; and likewise from Ramneh, a most eminent senator; who, despairing to do any good with the father, had, with great industry, skill, and decency, used his endeavour to instil good principles into the young Prince.

Upon the news of the former Emperor's death, a grand council was summoned of course, where little passed besides directing the ceremony of proclaiming the Successor. But, in some days after, the new Emperor having consulted with those persons in whom he could chiefly confide, and maturely considered in his own mind the present state of his affairs, as well as the disposition of his people, convoked another assembly of his council; wherein, after some time spent in general business, suitable to the present emergency, he directed Lelop-Aw to give him, in as short terms as he conveniently could an account of the nation's debts, of his management in the senate, and his negotiations with foreign courts: Which that minister having delivered, according to his usual manner, with much assurance and little satisfaction, the Emperor desired to be fully satisfied in the following particulars.

Whether the vast expence of chusing such members into the senate, as would be content to do the public business, were absolutely necessary?

Whether those members, thus chosen in, would cross and impede the necessary course of affairs, unless they were supplied with great sums of money, and continued pensions?

Whether the same corruption and perverseness were to be expected from the Nobles?

Whether the empire of Japan were in so low a condition, that the imperial envoys, at foreign courts, must be forced to purchase alliances, or prevent a war by immense bribes, given to the ministers of all the neighbouring Princes?

Why the debts of the empire were so prodigiously advanced, in a peace of twelve years at home and abroad?

Whether the Yortes were universally enemies to the religion and laws of the Empire, and to the Imperial family now reigning?

Whether those persons, whose revenues consist in lands, do not give surer pledges of fidelity to the public, and are more interested in the welfare of the empire, than others whose fortunes consist only in money?

And because Lelop-Aw, for several years past, had engrossed the whole administration, the Emperor signified, that from him alone he expected an answer.

This minister, who had sagacity enough to cultivate an interest in the young Prince's family, during the late Emperor's life, received early intelligence from one of his emissaries of what was intended at the council, and had sufficient time to frame as plausible an answer as his cause and conduct would allow. However, having desired a few minutes to put his thoughts in order, he delivered them in the following manner.

SIR,
Upon this short unexpected warning, to answer your Imperial Majesty's queries I should be wholly at a loss, in your Majesty's august presence, and that of this most noble assembly, if I were armed with a weaker defence than my own loyalty and integrity, and the prosperous success of my endeavours.

It is well known that the death of the Empress Nena happened in a most miraculous juncture; and that, if she had lived two months longer, your illustrious family would have been deprived of your right, and we should have seen an usurper upon your throne, who would have wholly changed the constitution of this empire, both civil and sacred; and although that Empress died in a most opportune season, yet the peaccable entrance of your Majesty's father was effected by a continual series of miracles. The truth of this appears by that unnatural rebellion which the Yortes raised, without the least provocation, in the first year of the late Emperor's reign, which may be sufficient to convince your Majesty, that every soul of that denomination was, is, and will be for ever, a favourer of the Pretender, a mortal enemy to your illustrious family, and an introducer of new Gods into the empire. Upon this foundation was built the whole conduct of our affairs; and, since a great majority of the kingdom was at that time reckoned to favour the Yortes faction, who, in the regular course of elections, must certainly be chosen members of the senate then to be convoked; it was necessary, by the force of money, to influence elections in such a manner, that your Majesty's father might have a sufficient number to weigh down the scale on his side, and thereby carry on those measures which could only secure him and his family in the possession of the empire. To support this original plan I came into the service: But the members of the senate, knowing themselves every day more necessary, upon the chusing of a new senate, I found the charges to encrease; and that, after they were chosen, they insisted upon an increase of their pensions; because they well knew that the work could not be carried on without them: And I was more general in my donatives, because I thought it was more for the honour of the crown, that every vote should pass without a division; and that, when a debate was proposed, it should immediately be quashed, by putting the question.

SIR, The date of the present senate is expired, and your Imperial Majesty is now to convoke a new one; which, I confess, will be somewhat more expensive than the last, because the Yortes, from your favourable reception, have begun to reassume a spirit whereof the country had some intelligence; and we know the majority of the people, without proper management, would be still in that fatal interest. However, I dare undertake, with the charge only of four hundred thousand sprangs*, to return as great a majority of senators

K   * About a Million Sterling.

of the true stamp, as your Majesty can desire. As to the sums of money paid in foreign courts, I hope, in some years, to ease the nation of them, when we and our neighbours come to a good understanding. However, I will be bold to say, they are cheaper than a war, where your Majesty is to be a principal.

The pensions, indeed, to senators and other persons, must needs increase, from the restiveness of some, and scrupulous nature of others; and the new members, who are unpractised, must have better encouragement. However, I dare undertake to bring the eventual charge within eight hundred thousand sprangs. But, to make this easy, there shall be new funds raised, of which I have several schemes ready, without taxing bread or flesh, which shall be reserved to more pressing occasions.

Your Majesty knows it is the laudable custom of all Eastern princes, to leave the whole management of affairs, both civil and military, to their Visirs. The appointments for your family, and private purse, shall exceed those of your predecessors: You shall be at no trouble, further than to appear sometimes in council, and leave the rest to me: You shall hear no clamour or complaints: Your senate shall, upon occasions, declare you the best of princes, the father of your country, the arbiter of Asia, the defender of the oppressed, and the delight of mankind.

SIR, Hear not those who would most falsely, impiously, and maliciously insinuate, that your government can be carried on without that wholesome, necessary expedient, of sharing the public revenue with your faithful deserving senators. This, I know, my enemies are pleased to call bribery and corruption. Be it so: But I insist, that, without this bribery and corruption, the wheels of government will not turn, or at least will be apt to take fire, like other wheels, unless they be greased at proper times. If an angel from heaven should descend, to govern this empire upon any other scheme than what our enemies call corruption, he must return from whence he came, and leave the work undone.

SIR, It is well known we are a trading nation, and consequently cannot thrive in a bargain where nothing is to be gained. The poor electors, who run from their shops, or the plough, for the service of their country, are they not to be considered for their labour and their loyalty? The candidates, who, with the hazard of their persons, the loss of their characters, and the ruin of their fortunes, are preferred to the senate, in a country where they are strangers, before the very lords of the soil; are they not to be rewarded for their zeal to your Majesty's service, and qualified to live in your metropolis as becomes the lustre of their stations?

SIR, If I have given great numbers of the most profitable employments among my own relations and nearest allies, it was not out of any partiality, but because I know them best, and can best depend upon them. I have been at the pains to mould and cultivate their opinions. Abler heads might probably have been found, but they would not be equally under my direction. A huntsman, who hath the absolute command of his dogs, will hunt more effectually than with a better pack, to whose manner and cry he is a stranger.

SIR, Upon the whole, I will appeal to all those who best knew your royal father, whether that blessed monarch had ever one anxious thought for the public, or disappointment, or uneasiness, or want of money for all his occasions, during the time of my administration? And, how happy the people confessed themselves to be under such a king, I leave to their own numerous addresses; which all politicians will allow to be the most infallible proof how any nation stands affected to their sovereign.

Lelop-Aw, having ended his speech, and struck his forehead thrice against the table, as the custom is in Japan, sate down with great complacency of mind, and much applause of his adherents, as might be observed by their countenances and their whispers. But the Emperor's behaviour was remarkable; for, during the whole harangue, he appeared equally attentive and uneasy. After a short pause, his Majesty commanded that some other counsellor should deliver his thoughts, either to confirm or object against what had been spoken by Lelop-Aw.

AN
ESSAY
UPON THE
CIVIL WARS
OF
FRANCE,

Extracted from curious Manuscripts,

AND ALSO UPON THE

EPICK POETRY

OF THE

EUROPEAN NATIONS

From *HOMER* down to *MILTON*.

With a short Account of the Author.

By Mr. de VOLTAIRE

DUBLIN:
Printed by and for J. HYDE, Bookseller in Dames-
Street, MDCCXXVIII.

PREFACE   TO

VOLTAIRE'S

ESSAY UPON THE
CIVIL WARS OF FRANCE,

MDCCXXVIII

A SHORT ACCOUNT OF THE AUTHOR.

THE Author of the following Discourse, Monsieur *de
Voltaire*, is a young *French* Gentleman, and allowed to
be the most celebrated Poet of that Kingdom.   He
hath been some Years composing an *Heroick Poem* upon *Henry
the Great*: But being falsly accused for writing a Libel, he was
put into the *Bastile*, and confined there in a Dungeon several
Months, till the true Author was discovered.   He there suffered much in his Health, and having been known to some
English Persons of Quality then at *Paris*, he was invited over to
England.   His *Heroic Poem* is finished, and now printing in
London by Subscription, being encouraged by the Crown and
most of the Nobility.   He had not been above eleven Months
in *England*, when he wrote the following Treatise, intended as
an Assistance to those who shall read his *Poem*, and may not
be sufficiently informed in the History of that great Prince.

THE

ANSWER

OF THE

Right Honourable WILLIAM PULTENEY, Esq;

TO THE

Right Honourable Sir ROBERT WALPOLE.

SIR,   Oct. 15, 1730.

A PAMPHLET was lately sent me, entitled, *A Letter from the Right Honourable Sir* R. W. *to the Right Honourable* W. P. *Esq; occasioned by the late Invectives on the King, her Majesty, and all the Royal Family.* By these initial letters of our names, the world is to understand that you and I must be meant. Although the letter seems to require an answer, yet because it appears to be written rather in the style and manner used by some of your pensioners than your own, I shall allow you the liberty to think the same of this answer, and leave the publick to determine which of the two actors can better personate their principals. That frigid and fustian way of haranguing wherewith your representer begins, continues, and ends his declamation, I shall leave to the criticks in eloquence and propriety to descant on; because it adds nothing to the weight of your accusations, nor will my defence be one grain the better by exposing its puerilities.

I shall therefore only remark upon this particular, that the frauds and corruptions in most other arts and sciences, as law, physick (I shall proceed no further) are usually much more plausibly defended than in that of politicks; whether it be, that by a kind of fatality the vindication of a corrupt minister is always left to the management of the meanest and most prostitute writers; or whether it be, that the effects of a wicked or unskilful administration are more publick, visible, pernicious and universal. Whereas the mistakes in other sciences are often matters that affect only speculation; or at worst, the bad consequences fall upon few and private persons. A nation is quickly sensible of the miseries it feels, and little comforted by knowing what account it turns to by the wealth, the power, the honours conferred on those who sit at the helm, or the salaries paid to their pen-men; while the body of the people is sunk into poverty and despair. A *Frenchman* in his wooden shoes may, from the vanity of his nation, and the constitution of that government, conceive some imaginary pleasure in boasting the grandeur of his monarch, in the midst of his own slavery: but a freeborn *Englishman*, with all his loyalty, can find little satisfaction at a minister overgrown in wealth and power from the lowest degree of want and contempt; when that power or wealth are drawn from the bowels and blood of the nation, for which every fellow subject is a sufferer, except the great man himself, his family, and his pensioners. I mean such a minister (if there hath ever been such a one) whose whole management hath been a continued link of ignorance, blunders, and mistakes in every article besides that of enriching and aggrandizing himself.

For these reasons the faults of men, who are most trusted in publick business, are, of all others, the most difficult to be defended. A man may be persuaded into a wrong opinion, wherein he hath small concern: but no oratory can have the power over a sober man against the conviction of his own senses: and therefore, as I take it, the money thrown away on such advocates might be more prudently spared, and kept in such a minister's own pocket, than lavished in hiring a corporation of pamphleteers to defend his conduct, and prove a kingdom to be flourishing in trade and wealth, which every particular subject (except those few already excepted) can lawfully swear, and, by dear experience knows, to be a falshood.

Give me leave, noble Sir, in the way of argument, to suppose this to be your case; could you in good conscience, or moral justice, chide your paper advocates for their ill success in persuading the world against manifest demonstration?

Their miscarriage is owing, alas! to want of matter. Should we allow them to be masters of wit, raillery, or learning, yet the subject would not admit them to exercise their talents; and, consequently, they can have no recourse but to impudence, lying, and scurrility.

I must confess, that the author of your letter to me hath carried this last qualification to a greater height than any of his fellows: but he hath, in my opinion, failed a little in point of politeness from the original which he affects to imitate. If I should say to a prime minister, Sir, you have sufficiently provided that *Dunkirk* should be absolutely demolished and never repaired; you took the best advantages of a long and general peace to discharge the immense debts of the nation; you did wonders with the fleet; you made the *Spaniards* submit to our quiet possession of *Gibraltar* and *Portmahon*; you never enriched yourself and family at the expence of the publick.— Such is the style of your supposed letter, which however, if I am well informed, by no means comes up to the refinements of a fishwife in *Billingsgate*. *You never had a Bastard by* Tom *the waterman*; *you never stole a silver tankard*; *you never were whipped at the cart's tail.*

In the title of your letter, it is said to be *occasioned by the late invectives on the King, her Majesty, and all the Royal Family:* and the whole contents of the paper (stripped from your eloquence) goes on upon a supposition affectedly serious, that their majesties, and the whole royal family, have been lately bitterly and publickly inveighed against in the most enormous and treasonable manner. Now, being a man, *as you well know*, altogether out of business, I do sometimes lose an hour in reading a few of those controversial papers upon politicks, which have succeeded for some years past to the polemical tracts between *Whig* and *Tory*: and in this kind of reading (if it may deserve to be so called) although I have been often but little edified, or entertained, yet hath it given me occasion to make some observations. First, I have observed, that however men may sincerely agree in all the branches of the low-church principle, in a tenderness for dissenters of every kind, in a perfect abhorrence of popery and the pretender, and in the most firm adherence to the protestant succession in the royal house of *Hanover*; yet plenty of matter may arise to kindle their animosities against each other from the various infirmities, follies, and vices inherent in mankind.

Secondly, I observed, that although the vulgar reproach which charges the quarrels between ministers, and their opposers, to be only a contention for power between those who are in, and those who would be in if they could; yet as long as this proceeds no further than a scuffle of ambition among a few persons, it is only a matter of course, whereby the publick is little affected. But when corruptions are plain, open, and undisguised, both in their causes and effects, to the hazard of a nation's ruin, and so declared by all the principal persons and the bulk of the people, those only excepted who are gainers by those corruptions: and when such ministers are forced to fly for shelter to the throne, with a complaint of disaffection to majesty against all who durst dislike their administration: Such a general disposition in the minds of men, cannot, I think, by any rules of reason, be called the *clamour of a few disaffected incendiaries*, grasping after power. It is the true voice of the people; which must and will at last be heard, or produce consequences that I dare not mention.

I have observed thirdly, that among all the offensive printed papers which have come to my hand, whether good or bad, the writers have taken particular pains to celebrate the virtues of our excellent king and queen, even where these were, strictly speaking, no part of the subject: nor can it be properly objected that such a proceeding was only a blind to cover their malice towards you and your assistants; because to affront the king, queen, or the royal family, as it would be directly opposite to the principles that those kind of writers have always professed, so it would destroy the very end they have in pursuit. And it is somewhat remarkable, that those very writers against you, and the regiment you command, are such as most distinguish themselves upon all, or upon no occasions, by their panegyricks on their prince; and, as all of them do this without favour or hire, so some of them continue the same practice under the severest prosecution by you and your janissaries.

You seem to know, or at least very strongly to conjecture, who those persons are that give you so much weekly disquiet. Will you dare to assert that any of these are *Jacobites*, endeavour to alienate the hearts of the people, to defame the prince, and then dethrone him (for these are your expressions) and that I am their patron, their bulwark, their hope, and their refuge? Can you think I will descend to vindicate myself against an aspersion so absurd? God be thanked, we have had many a change of ministry without changing our prince: for if it had been otherwise, perhaps revolutions might have been more frequent. Heaven forbid that the welfare of a great kingdom, and of a brave people, should be trusted with the thread of a single subject's life; for I suppose it is not yet in your view to entail the ministryship in your family. Thus I hope we may live to see different ministers and different measures, without any danger to the succession in the royal protestant line of *Hanover*.

You are pleased to advance a topick, which I could never heartily approve of in any party, although they have each in their turn advanced it while they had the superiority. You tell us, It is hard that while every private man shall have the liberty to chuse what servants he pleaseth, the same privilege should be refused to a king. This assertion, crudely understood, can hardly be supported. If by servants be only meant those who are purely menial, who provide for their master's food and cloathing, or for the convenience and splendour of his family, the point is not worth debating. But the bad or good choice of a chancellor, a secretary, an ambassador, a treasurer, and many other officers, is of very high consequence to the whole kingdom: so is likewise that amphibious race of courtiers between servants and ministers; such as the steward, chamberlain, treasurer of the household, and the like, being all of the privy council, and some of the cabinet, who according to their talents, their principles, and their degree of favour, may be great instruments of good or evil, both to the subject and the prince; so that the parallel is by no means adequate between a prince's court and a private family. And yet if an insolent footman be troublesome in the neighbourhood; if he breaks the people's windows, insults their servants, breaks into other folks houses to pilfer what he can find, although he belong to a duke, and be a favourite in his station, yet those who are injured may, without just offence, complain to his lord, and for want of redress, get a warrant to send him to the stocks, to *Bridewell*, or to *Newgate*, according to the nature and degree of his delinquencies. Thus the servants of the prince, whether menial or otherwise, if they be of his council, are subject to the enquiries and prosecutions of the great council of the nation, even as far as to capital punishment; and so must ever be in our constitution, till a minister can procure a majority even of that council to shelter him; which I am sure you will allow to be a desperate crisis under any party of the most plausible denomination.

The only instance you produce, or rather insinuate, to prove the late invectives against the king, queen, and royal family, is drawn from that deduction of the *English* history, published in several papers by the *Craftsman*; wherein are shewn the bad consequences to the publick, as well as to the prince, from the practices of evil ministers in most reigns, and at several periods, when the throne was filled by wise monarchs as well as by weak. This deduction, therefore, cannot reasonably give the least offence to a *British* king, when he shall observe that the greatest and ablest of his predecessors, by their own candor, by a particular juncture of affairs, or by the general infirmity of human nature, have sometimes put too much trust in confident, insinuating, and avaricious ministers.

Wisdom, attended by virtue and a generous nature, is not unapt to be imposed on. Thus *Milton* describes *Uriel*, *the sharpest-sighted spirit in heaven*, and *regent of the sun*, deceived by the dissimulation and flattery of the devil, for which the poet gives a philosophical reason, but needless here to quote. Is any thing more common, or more useful, than to caution wise men in high stations against putting too much trust in undertaking servants, cringing flatterers, or designing friends?

Since the *Asiatic* custom of governing by prime ministers
hath prevailed in so many courts of *Europe*, how careful should
every prince be in the choice of the person on whom so great
a trust is devolved, whereon depend the safety and welfare
of himself and all his subjects! Queen *Elizabeth*, whose administration is frequently quoted as the best pattern for
English princes to follow, could not resist the artifices of the
earl of *Leicester*, who although universally allowed to be the
most ambitious, insolent, and corrupt person of his age, was
yet her greatest, and almost her only favourite: (his religion
indeed being partly puritan and partly infidel, might have
better tallied with present times) yet this wise queen would
never suffer the openest enemies of that overgrown lord to be
sacrificed to his vengeance; nor durst he charge them with a
design of introducing popery or the *Spanish* pretender.

How many great families do we all know, whose masters
have passed for persons of good abilities, during the whole
course of their lives, and yet the greatest part of whose estates
have sunk in the hands of their stewards and receivers;
their revenues paid them in scanty portions, at large discount,
and treble interest, though they did not know it; while the
tenants were daily racked, and at the same time accused to their
landlords of insolvency. Of this species are such managers,
who, like honest *Peter Waters*, pretend to clear an estate,
keep the owner pennyless, and after seven years, leave him
five times more in debt, while they sink half a plum into their
own pockets.

Those who think themselves concerned, may give you
thanks for that gracious liberty you are pleased to allow them
of *taking vengeance on the ministers, and there shooting their en-
venom'd arrows.* As to myself; I neither owe you vengeance,
nor make use of such weapons: but it is your weakness, or
ill-fortune, or perhaps the fault of your constitution, to convert
wholesome remedies into poison; for you have received better
and more frequent instructions than any minister of your age
and country, if God had given you the grace to apply them.

I dare promise you the thanks of half the kingdom, if you
will please to perform the promise you have made of suffering

the *Craftsman* and company, or whatever other *infamous wretches and execrable villains* you mean, to take their vengeance only on your own sacred ministerial person, without bringing any of your brethren, much less the most remote branch of the royal family, into the debate. This generous offer I suspected from the first; because there were never heard of so many, so unnecessary, and so severe prosecutions as you have promoted during your ministry, in a kingdom where the liberty of the press is so much pretended to be allowed. But in reading a page or two, I found you thought it proper to explain away your grant; for there you tell us, that *these miscreants* (meaning the writers against you) *are to remember that the laws have* ABUNDANTLY LESS *generous, less mild and merciful sentiments* than yourself, and into their secular hands the poor authors must be delivered to fines, prisons, pillories, whippings, and the gallows. Thus your promise of impunity, which began somewhat jesuitically, concludes with the mercy of a *Spanish* inquisitor.

If it should so happen that I am neither *abetter*, *patron*, *protector*, nor *supporter* of these imaginary invectives *against the king, her majesty, or any of the royal family*, I desire to know what satisfaction I am to get from you, or the creature you employed in writing the libel which I am now answering? It will be no excuse to say, that I differ from you in every particular of your political reason and practice; because that will be to load the best, the soundest, and most numerous part of the kingdom with the denominations you are pleased to bestow upon me, that they are, *Jacobites, wicked miscreants, infamous wretches, execrable villains, and defamers of the king, queen, and all the royal family*, and *guilty of high treason*. You cannot know my style; but I can easily know your works, which are performed in the sight of the sun. Your good inclinations are visible; but I begin to doubt the strength of your credit, even at court, that you have not power to make his majesty believe me the person which you represent in your libel: as most infallibly you have often attempted, and in vain, because I must otherwise have found it by the marks of his royal displeasure. However, to be angry with you to whom I am indebted for the greatest obligation I could possibly receive, would be the highest ingratitude. It is to You I owe that reputation I have acquired for some years past of being a lover of my country and its constitution: to You I owe the libels and scurrilities conferred upon me by the worst of men, and consequently some degree of esteem and friendship from the best. From You I learned the skill of distinguishing between a *patriot* and a *plunderer* of his country: and from You I hope in time to acquire the knowledge of being a loyal, faithful, and useful servant to the best of princes, king *George* the second; and therefore I can conclude, by your example, but with greater truth, that I am not only with humble submission and respect, but with infinite gratitude, Sir, your most obedient and most obliged servant.

W. P.

FAULKNER'S NOTE

WHEN Dr. *Swift* was at Sir *Arthur Acheson*'s at *Market-hill* in the County of *Armagh*, an old Gentleman was recommended to him, as being a remarkable Cavalier, in the Reigns of *Charles* II. *James* II. and *William* III. who behaved himself with great Loyalty and Bravery in *Scotland* during the Troubles of those Reigns, but who was neglected by the Government, although he deserved great Rewards from them, and was reduced in his Circumstances, which moved Dr. *Swift* very much, who made him a handsome Present; but said at the same Time, 'Sir, This Trifle cannot support you long, and your friends may grow 'tired of you, and therefore I would have you contrive some 'honest Means of getting a Sum of Money sufficient to put 'you into a Way of Life to support you with Independency 'in your old Age.' To which Captain *Creichton* (for that was the Gentleman's Name) answered, 'I have tired all my Friends, 'and cannot expect any such extraordinary Favours.' Then Dr. *Swift* replied, 'Sir, I have heard much of your Adventures; 'that they are fresh in your Memory; that you can tell them 'with great Humour; and that you have taken Memorandums 'of them in Writing.' To which the Captain said, 'I have, but 'no one can understand them but myself.'——Then Dr. *Swift* rejoined, 'Sir, get your Manuscripts, read them to me, 'and tell me none but genuine Stories, and then I will place 'them in Order for you, prepare them for the Press, and 'endeavour to get you a Subscription among my Friends, 'as you may do with your own.' The Captain, soon after waited on the Dean with his Papers, from whence he compiled the following MEMOIRS, in which he seems particularly attentive to support the Character of the Person in whose Name they were published; and to write in the natural, unadorned, and even in the homely Style of a plain old Soldier. A Subscription was immediately set on Foot, which, by the Dean's Interest and Recommendation, was very considerable, and got the Captain above two hundred Pounds, which made the remaining Part of his Life very happy and easy.

MEMOIRS

O F

Capt. John Creichton,

Written by Himself.

Printed in the Year, 1731.

ADVERTISEMENT
TO THE READER

THE *Author of these* Memoirs, *Capt.* John Creichton, *is still alive, and resides in the Northern Part of this Kingdom. He is a very honest and worthy Man; but of the old Stamp: And it is probable, that some of his Principles will not relish very well, in the present Disposition of the World.* His Memoirs *are therefore to be received like a Posthumous Work, and as containing Facts, which very few alive, except himself, can remember: Upon which Account none of his generous Subscribers are, in the Least, answerable for many Opinions, relating to the Publick, both in Church and State, which he seems to Justify, and in the Vindication of which, to the Hazard of his Life, and the Loss of his Fortune, he spent the most useful Part of his Days. Principles, as the World goes, are little more than Fashion; and the Apostle tells us, that* the Fashion of this World passeth away: *We Read with Pleasure* the Memoirs *of several Authors, whose Party we disapprove; if they be written with Nature and Truth. Curious Men are desirous to see what can be said on both Sides: And even the virulent flat Relation of* Ludlow, *though written in the Spirit of Rage, Prejudice and Vanity, doth not want its Advocates. This inclines me to think, that the* Memoirs *of Capt.* Creichton *may not be unacceptable to the Curious of every Party; because, from my Knowledge of the Man, and the Testimony of several considerable Persons, of different political Denominations, I am confident, that he hath not inserted one Passage or Circumstance, which he did not know, or, from the best Intelligence he could get, believed to be True.*

These Memoirs *are therefore offered to the World in their native Simplicity. And it was not with little Difficulty, that the Author was persuaded by his Friends, to recollect and put them in Order; chiefly for his own Justification, and partly by the Importunity of several eminent Gentlemen, who had a mind that they should turn to some Profit to the Author.*

The *Capt. having made over all his little Estate to a beloved Daughter, upon her Marriage, on the Condition of being entertained in her House, for the small Remainder of his Life, hath put it out of his own Power, either to supply his incidental Wants, to pay some long contracted Debts, or to gratify his generous Nature in being further useful to his Family: on which Accounts, he desires to return his most humble Thanks to his worthy Subscribers; and hopes they will consider him no further than as an honest, well-meaning Man, who by his own personal Courage and Conduct, was able to distinguish himself under many Disadvantages to a Degree, that few private Lives have been attended with so many singular and extraordinary Events.*

Besides the great Simplicity in the Stile and manner of the Author; it is a very valuable Circumstance, that his plain Relation corrects many mistaken Passages in other Historians, which have too long passed for Truths, and whoever impartially compares both, will probably decide in the Captain's Favour. For the Memory of old Men is seldom deceived, in what passed in their Youth and Vigour of Age: And if he hath, at any Time, happened to be mistaken in Circumstances of Time or Place (with neither of which I can charge him) it was certainly against his Will. Some of his own personal Distresses and Actions, which he hath related, might be almost the Subject of a Tragedy.

Upon the whole, comparing great Things to Small; I know not any Memoirs *that more resemble those of* Philip de Comines *(which have received so universal Approbation) than these of Capt.* Creichton, *which are told in a Manner equally Natural, and with equal Appearance of Truth, though I confess, upon Affairs in a more obscure Scene, and of less Importance.*

MEMOIRS

O F

CAPTAIN JOHN CREICHTON

THE former Part of my Life, having been attended with some Passages and Events, not very common to Men of my private and obscure Condition, I have (perhaps induced by the Talkativeness of old Age) very freely and frequently communicated them to several worthy Gentlemen, who were pleas'd to be my Friends, and some of them my Benefactors. These Persons profess'd themselves to be so well entertained with my Story, that they often wished it cou'd be digested into Order, and publish'd to the World, believing that such a Treatise, by the Variety of Incidents, written in a plain unaffected Style, might be, at least, some *Amusement* to indifferent Readers; of some *Example* to those who desire strictly to adhere to their Duty and Principles; and might serve to vindicate *my Reputation* in *Scotland*, where I am well known; that Kingdom having been the chief Scene of my Acting, and where I have been represented by a Fanatick Rebellious Party, as a *Persecutor of the Saints*, and a *Man of Blood*.

Having lost the Benefit of a thorough School-Education by a most indiscreet Marriage, in all *worldly Views*, altho' to a very good Woman; and in Consequence thereof, being forced to seek my Fortune in *Scotland* as a Soldier, where I forgot all the little I had learned, the Reader cannot reasonably expect to be much pleased with my Style, or Method, or Manner of relating: It is enough if I never willfully fail in Point of Truth, nor offend by *Malice* or *Partiality*. My Memory, I thank God, is yet very perfect as to Things long past, although, like an Old Man, I retain but little of what hath happened since I grew into Years.

I am likewise very sensible of an Infirmity in many Authors, who write their own Memoirs, and are apt to lay too much Weight upon *Trifles*, which they are vain enough to conceive the World to be as much concerned in as themselves; yet I remember, that *Plutarch*, in his Lives of great Men (which I have read in the English Translation) says, that the Nature and Disposition of a Man's Mind, may be often better discovered by a *small Circumstance*, than by an Action, or Event of the *greatest Importance*: And besides, it is not improbable that grey Hairs may have brought upon me a *Vanity*, to desire that Posterity may know what Manner of Man I was.

I lye under another Disadvantage, and indeed a very great one, from the wonderful *change of Opinions*, since I first made any Appearance in the World. I was bred under the Principles of the strictest *Loyalty* to my Prince, and in an exact Conformity in *Discipline*, as well as *Doctrine*, to the *Church* of *England*; which are neither altered nor shaken to this very Day, and I am now too Old to mend. However, my different Sentiments, since my last Troubles after the Revolution, have never had the least Influence either upon my Actions, or Discourse. I have submitted my self with entire Resignation, according to St. *Paul*'s Precept, *to the Powers that be*. I converse equally with all Parties, and am equally favoured by all; and, God knows, it is now of little Consequence what my Opinions are, under such a weight of *Age* and Infirmities, with a very scanty Subsistance, which, instead of *Comforting*, will hardly *Support* me.

But there is another Point, which requires a better *Apology* than I am able to give: A judicious Reader will be apt to Censure me, and, I confess, with Reason enough, as Guilty of a very foolish *Superstition* in relating my Dreams, and how I was guided by them with Success, in discovering one or two principal *Covenanters*. I shall not easily allow myself to be either by *Nature*, or *Education*, more *Superstitious* than other Men; but I take the Truth to be this: Being then full of *Zeal* against those *Enthusiastical Rebels*, and better informed of their lurking Holes, than most Officers in the Army, this made so strong an Impression on my Mind, that it affected my

Dreams, when, I was directed to the most probable Places, almost as well as if I had been *Awake*, being guided in the Night by the same *Conjectures* I had made in the Day. There could possibly be no more in the Matter; and God forbid I should pretend to a Spirit of *Divination*, which would make me resemble those very *Hipocritical Saints*, whom it was both my *Duty*, and *Inclination*, to bring to Justice, for their many horrid *Blasphemies* against God, *Rebellions* against their *Prince*, and *Barbarities* towards their *Countrymen*, and *Fellow-Christians*.

My Great-Grand-Father, *Alexander Creichton*, of the House of *Dumfries*, in *Scotland*, in a Feud between the *Maxwells* and the *Johnstons*, (the Chief of the *Johnstons*, being the Lord *Johnston*, Ancestor of the present Marquess of *Anandall*) siding with the latter, and having killed some of the former, was forced to fly into *Ireland*, where he settled near *Kinard*, then a Woody-Country, and now called *Callidon:* But within a Year or two, some Friends and Relations, of those *Maxwells* who had been killed in the Feud, coming over to *Ireland*, to pursue their Revenge, lay in wait for my Grand-Father in the Wood, and shot him dead, as he was going to Church. This Accident happened about the Time that *James* the Sixth of *Scotland* came to the Crown of *England*.

Alexander, my Great-Grand-Father, left two Sons, and as many Daughters; his eldest Son *John*, lived till a Year or two after the breaking out of the Rebellion in 1641. His House was the first in *Ulster* set upon by the *Irish*, who took and imprisoned him at *Dungannon*, but fortunately making his Escape, he went to Sir *Robert Stuart*, who was then in Arms for the King, and dyed in the Service.

This *John*, who was my Grand-Father, left two Sons, *Alexander*, my Father, and a younger Son, likewise named *John*, who being a Child, but two or three Years old at his Father's Death was invited to *Scotland* by the *Lady Dumfries*, there educated by her, and sent to Sea: He made several Voyages to, and from *Barbadoes*, then settled in *Scotland*, where he dyed sometime after the *Restoration*, leaving, beside a Daughter, one Son, who at my Charges, was bred up a *Physitian*, and proved so famous in his Profession, that he was sent, by her late Majesty Q. *Anne*, to cure the King of *Portugal* of the Venereal Disease. He had a Thousand Pounds paid him in Hand, before he began his Journey; but when he arrived at *Lisbon*, the *Portugueze* Council and Physitians dissuaded that King from trusting his Person with a Foreigner. However his Majesty of *Portugal* shewed him several Marks of his Esteem; and, at parting, presented him with a very rich Jewel, which he sold afterwards for five Hundred Guineas. He stayed there not above six Weeks; during which Time, he got very considerable Practice. After living many Years in *London*, where he grew very Rich, he dyed *November* 1726, and, as it is believed, without making a Will, which is very probable, because, although he had no Children, he left me no Legacy, who was his *Cousin-German*, and had been his greatest *Benefactor*, by the Care and Expence of his Education. Upon this Matter, I must add one Circumstance more, how little significant soever it may be to others. Mr. Arch-Deacon *Maurice* being at *London*, in order to his Journey to *France*, on account of his Health, went to visit the Doctor, and put him in mind of me, urging the Obligations I had laid upon him. The Doctor agreed to send me whatever Sum of Money the *ArchDeacon* should think *reasonable*, and deliver it to him on his Return from his Travels; but unfortunately the Doctor died two or three Days before the Arch-Deacon came back.

Alexander, my *Father*, was about eighteen Years old in 1641. The *Irish* Rebellion then breaking out, he went to Captain *Gerrard Irvin*, his Relation, who was then Captain of Horse, and afterwards Knighted by King *Charles* the Second. This Gentleman having a Party for the King, soon after joyned with Sir *Robert Stuart* in the County of *Donegal*; where, in the Course of those Troubles, they continued skirmishing, sometimes with the *Irish Rebells*, and sometimes with those of the *English Parliament*, after the Rebellion in *England* began; till at length *Captain Irvin*, and one Mr. *Stuart*, were taken Prisoners, and put in Jayl in *Derry*; which City was kept for the Parliament against the King, by Sir *Charles Coote*. Here my Father performed a very memorable and gallant Action, in rescuing his Relation *Captain Irvin*, and Mr. *Stuart*. I will relate this Fact in all it's Particulars, not only because it will do some *Honour* to my *Father's Memory*, but likewise because, for its Boldness and Success, it seems to me very well to deserve Recording.

My Father having received Information, that Sir *Charles Coote*, Governor of *Derry*, had publickly declared, that *Captain Irvin* and his *Companion*, should be put to Death, within two or three Days, communicated this Intelligence to seven trusty Friends; who all engaged to assist him, with the Hazard of their *Lives*, in delivering the two Gentlemen from the Danger that threatned them. They all agreed that my Father, and three more, at the Hour of Six in the Morning, when the West-Gate stood open, and the Draw-bridge was let down, for the Governor's Horses to go out to Water, should ride in, one by one, after a Manner as if they belonged to the Town, and there conceal themselves in a Friend's House till Night; at which Time my Father was to acquaint Captain *Irvin*, and his *Fellow Prisoner* with their Design, which was to this Purpose: That, after concerting Measures at the Prison, my Father should repair to a certain Place on the City-Wall, and give Instructions to the Four without, at Twelve at Night: Accordingly, next Morning, as soon as the Gate was open, my Father, with his three Comrades, got into the Town, and the same Night having settled Matters, with the two Gentlemen, that they should be ready at Six next Morning, at which Hour, he and his three Friends should call upon them; He then went to the Wall, and directed the four, who were without, that as soon as they should see the Gate open, and the Bridge drawn, one of them should walk up to the Centry, and secure him from making any Noise, by holding a Pistol to his Breast; after which, the other three should ride up, and secure the Room where the By-guard lay, to prevent them from coming out: Most of the Garrison were in their Beds, which encouraged my Father, and his Friends, and much facilitated the Enterprize: Therefore precisely at six o'Clock, when the By-guard, and Centry at the Western-Gate were secured by the four without, my Father and the other three within, being mounted on Horseback, with one spare

Horse, and in the Habit of Town's-People, with Cudgels in their Hands, called at the Jayl-Door, on Pretence to speak to Captain *Irvin* and Mr. *Stuart*. They were both walking in a large Room in the Jayl, with the Jaylor, and three Soldiers attending them; but these not suspecting the Persons on Horse-back before the Door, whom they took to be Inhabitants of the Town, my Father asked Captain *Irvin*, whether he had any Commands to a certain Place, where he pretended to be going. The Captain made some Answer, but said they should not go before they had drank with him; then, giving a Piece of Money to one of the Soldiers, to buy a Bottle of Sack at a Tavern, a good Way off, and pretending likewise some Errand for another Soldier, sent him also out of the Way; there being now none left to guard the Prisoners but the Jaylor, and the third Soldier; Captain *Irwin* leapt over the Hatch-Door, and as the Jaylor leapt after, my Father knocked him down with his Cudgel. While this was doing, Mr. *Stuart* tript up the Soldier's Heels, and immediately leapt over the Hatch. They both mounted, *Stuart* on the Horse behind my Father, and *Irvin* on the spare one, and in a few Minutes came up with their Companions at the Gate, before the Main-Guard could arrive, although it were kept within twenty Yards of the Jayl-Door.

I should have observed, that as soon as Captain *Irvin*, and his Friend, got over the Hatch, my Father and his Comrades put a Couple of Broad-Swords into their Hands, which they had concealed under their Cloaks, and at the same Time drawing their own, were all six determined to force their Way against any, who offered to obstruct them in their Passage; but the Dispatch was so sudden, that they got clear out of the Gate, before the least *Opposition* could be made. They were no sooner gone, than the Town was alarmed, *Coote the Governor* got out of his Bed, and ran into the Streets in his *Shirt*, to know what the Hubbub meant, and was in a great Rage at the *Accident*. The *Adventurers* met the Governor's Groom, coming back with his Master's Horses from watering; they seized the Horses, and got safe to Sir *Robert Stuart*'s, about four Miles off, without losing one drop of Blood in this *hazardous Enterprize*.

This *Gallant Person* (if I may so presume to call my *Father*) had above *twenty Children* by his Wife *Ann Maxwell*, of the Family of the Earl of *Niddisdale*, of whom I was the eldest; they all died young, except my self, three other Boys, and two Girls; who lived to be Men and Women. My second Brother I took care to have educated at *Glasgow*, but he was drowned at two and twenty Years old, in a Storm, on his return to *Ireland*. The other two dyed Captains abroad, in the Service of King *William*.

I was born on the *Eighth* Day of *May*, 1648, at *Castle-Fin* in the County of *Donegal*. I made some small Progress in Learning at the School of *Dungannon*, but when I was Eighteen Years old, I very inconsiderately marryed Mrs. *Elizabeth Delgarno*, my School-Master's Daughter, by whom I have had *thirteen Children*, who all dyed young, except two Daughters, marryed to two Brothers *James* and *Charles Young* of the County of *Tyrone*.

Having been so very young when I marryed, I could think of no other Course to advance my Fortune, than by getting into the Army. Captain *Irvin*, often mentioned already, had a Brother who was a Physitian at *Edenborough*, to whom he wrote in my Favour, desiring he would recommend me to the Marquess of *Athole* and others, then at the Head of Affairs in *Scotland*; this was in the Year, 1674. There were then, but one Troop of Horse-Guards, (whereof the Marquess was Colonel) and one Regiment of Foot-Guards, commanded by the Earl of *Linlithgow*, in that Kingdom; and they consisted chiefly of Gentlemen.

Dr. *Irvin*, Physitian to the Horse-guards, accordingly presented me to the Marquess of *Athole*, requesting that I might be received into his Troop. His Lordship, pretending there was no Vacancy, was, by the Doctor, threatned, in a free jesting Manner, with a Dose of Poyson, instead of Physick, the first Time he should want his Skill; *weell, weell then*, quoth the Marquess, what is your Friend's Name? *Deel tak' me*, answered the Doctor, *gin I ken*: whereupon I was called in, to write my Name in the Roll. I was then ordered to repair to the Troop at *Sterling*, with Directions to Lieutenant Colonel *Cockburn*, the commanding Officer, to put me into which of the four Squadrons, whereof the Troop consisted, he thought fit. He thereupon placed me in his own, and appointed me my Quarters.

Soon after this, the *Conventicles* growing numerous in the West, several Parties were drawn out to suppress them; among whom I never failed to make One, in hopes thereby to be taken Notice of by my Commanders; for I had nothing to recommend me, except my *Activity, Diligence,* and *Courage,* being a Stranger, and born out of that Kingdom.

My first Action, after having been taken into the Guards, was, with a Dozen Gentlemen more, to go in Quest of Mas *David Williamson,* a noted *Covenanter*; since, made more famous in the Book, called the *Scotch Presbyterian Eloquence.* I had been assured, that this *Williamson* did much frequent the House of my Lady *Cherrytree,* within ten Miles of *Edinborough*; but when I arrived first with my Party about the House, the Lady well knowing our Errand, put *Williamson* to Bed to her Daughter, disguised in a Woman's Night-Dress. When the Troopers went to search in the young Lady's Room, her Mother pretended that she was not well; and *Williamson* so managed the Matter, that when the Daughter raised herself a little in the Bed, to let the Troopers see her, they did not discover him, and so went off disappointed. But the young Lady proved with Child; and *Williamson* to take off the Scandal, married her in some Time after. This *Williamson* married five or six Wives successively, and was alive in the Reign of Queen *Ann*; at which Time, I saw him preaching in one of the Kirks at *Edenborough.* It is said that King *Charles* the Second, hearing of *Williamson*'s Behaviour in Lady *Cherrytree*'s House, wished to see the Man that discovered so much *Vigour,* while his Troopers were in *Search* of him: And, in a merry Way, declared, that when he was in the *Royal-Oak,* he could not have kissed the *bonnyest Lass in Christendom.*

Sometime after this, *Thomas Dalziel,* General of the Forces in *Scotland,* an excellent Soldier, who had been taken Prisoner at the famous Battle of *Worcester,* and sent Prisoner to the *Tower,* escaping from thence into *Muscovy,* was made General to the *Czar*; and returning Home, after the Restoration, was preferred, by the King, to be General of the Forces in *Scotland*, in which Post he continued till his Death, which happened a little before the *Revolution*. This General commanded Fifty of the Foot-Guards, with an Ensign, to accompany me, and to follow my Directions, in the Pursuit of a *notorious Rebel*, one *Adam Stobow*, a Farmer in *Fife*, near *Colross*. This Fellow had gone through the West, endeavouring to stir up Sedition in the People, by his great Skill in *Canting* and *Praying*. There had been several Parties sent out after him, before I and my Men undertook the Business, but they could never discover him. We reached *Colross* at Night, where I directed the Ensign and all the Men to secure three or four *Rebels*, who were in the Place, while I, with two or three of the Soldiers to assist me, went to *Stobow's House*, about a Mile and half from *Colross*, by Break of Day, for fear some of his Friends might give him Notice. Before I got to the House, I observed a *Kiln* in the Way, which I ordered to be searched, because I found there an Heap of Straw in the Passage up to the *Kiln-Pot*. There I found *Stobow* lurking, and carried him to *Colross*, although his Daughter offered me an hundred *Dollars* to let him go. We returned immediately to the General at *Edinborough*, with *Stobow* and the Prisoners taken by the Ensign at *Colross*. They continued a while in Confinement, but *Stobow*, at his Tryal, found Friends enough to save his Life, and was only banished; yet he returned home a Year after, and proved as troublesome and seditious as ever, 'till, at the Fight of *Bothwell-Bridge*, it was thought he was killed, for he was never heard of afterwards.

During the Time I was in the Guards, about two Years after the Affair of Mas *David Williamson*, at the Lady *Cherrytree's*, I was quartered with a Party at *Bath-Gate*, which is a small Village, Twelve Miles from *Edinborough*. One Sunday Morning, by Break of Day, I and my Comrade, a gallant *Highland Gentleman*, of the Name of *Grant*, went out, disguised in *gray Coats* and *Bonnets*, in Search after some *Conventicle*. We travelled on Foot, Eight or Ten Miles into the wild Mountains, where we spyed Three Fellows on the Top of an Hill, whom we conjectured to stand there as Spies, to give Intelligence to a *Conventicle*, when any of the King's Troopers should happen to come that Way. There they stood, with long Poles in their Hands, 'til I and my Friend came pretty near, and then they turned to go down the Hill: When we observed this, we took a little Compass, and came up with them on the other Side; whereupon they stood still, leaning on their Poles: Then I bounced forward upon one of them, and suddenly snatching the Pole out of his Hand, asked him, why he carryed such a Pole on the Lord's-Day, and at the same time knocked him down with it: My Comrade immediately seized on the Second, and laid him flat by a Gripe of his Hair; but the Third took to his Heels, and ran down the Hill. However having left my Friend to guard the Two former, I overtook the Last, and felled him likewise; but the Place being steep, the Violence with which I ran, carried me a good Way down the Hill, before I could recover myself, after the Stroke I had given; and by the Time I could get up again to the Place where he lay, the Rogue had got on his Feet, and was fumbling for a Side-Pistol, that hung at his Belt, under his upper Coat; which as soon as I observed, I fetched him to the Ground a second Time with the Pole, and seized on his Pistol; then leading him up to the other two, I desired my Friend to examine their Pockets, and see whether they carried any Powder or Ball, but we found none.

We then led our Prisoners down the Hill, at the Foot of which there was a Bog, and on the other Side a Man sitting on a Rock; when we advanced near him, leaving our Prisoners in the Keeping of my Friend, I ran up towards the Man, who fled down on the other Side. As soon as I had reached the top of the Rock, there appeared a great Number of People, assembled in a Glin, to hear the preaching of *Mas John King*, as I understood afterwards, whose Voice was so loud, that it reached the Ears of those who were at the greatest Distance, which could not, I think, be less than a Quarter of a Mile; they all standing before him, and the Wind favouring the Strength of his Lungs. When my Friend had brought the Three Prisoners to the Top of the Rock, where I waited for him, they all broke loose and ran down to the *Conventicle*: But my Friend advancing within about Forty Yards of that Rabbel, commanded them in his Majesty's Name, to depart to their own Homes. Whereupon about Forty of their Number, with Poles in their Hands, drew out from the rest, and advanced against us Two, who had the *Courage*, or rather the *Temerity*, to face so great a Company, which could not be fewer than a Thousand. As this Party of theirs was preparing with their long Poles, to attack me and my Friend; it happened very luckily, that a fine *Gelding*, sadled, and bridled, with a Pillion likewise upon him, came up near us, in Search for better Grass; I caught the Horse, and immediately mounted him, which the rest of the *Conventiclers* observing, they broke up, and followed as fast as they could, some on Horseback, and the rest on Foot, to prevent me from going off with the Horse; but I put him to the Gallop, and suffering him to chuse his own Way through the Mountain, which was full of *Boggs* and *Haggs*, got out of Reach. My Friend kept up with me as long as he could, but having run a Mile through such difficult Places, he was quite spent, and the *Conventiclers* hard at his Heels; whereupon he called to me for Assistance, and I alighting put him upon the Horse, bidding him to make the best of his Way to the Laird of *Poddishaw*'s, about Two Miles off. By this Time we saw Twelve *Covenanters* on Horseback, who advanced towards us by a shorter Cut, and blocked up a Gap, through which we were, of necessity, to pass. I undertook to clear the Gap for my Friend, and running towards the Rogues, with my Broad-Sword and Pistol, soon forced them to open to the Right and Left: My Comrade got thorow, and was pursued a good Way; but he so laid about him, with his Broad-Sword, that the Pursuers being unarmed, durst not seize him. In the mean Time, I who was left on Foot, kept the *Covenanters* who followed me, at a proper Distance; but they pelted me with Clods, which I sometimes returned, 'till at last, after chasing me above a Mile, they saw a Party of Troopers in red, passing by, at some Distance; and then they gave over their Pursuit.

The Troopers, observing my Friend galloping and pursued, imagined he was some *Fanatick Preacher*, till they came to an old Woman on a Hill, whom my Friend had desired to deny his being gone that Way; upon which they went off to their Quarters, and he got safe to *Poddishaw*'s, whither I soon after arrived. The Laird of *Poddishaw* had been that Day at Church; from whence returning with the Laird of *Pocammock*, who lived about a Mile off, they both wondered how the Horse got thither, for *Pocammock* was the Owner of the Horse, and his Lady had rode on it that Day to the *Conventicle*, without her Husband's Knowledge, having been seduced thither by some *Fanatick Neighbours*, for she had never been at their Meetings before. My Friend and I acquainted the two Lairds with the whole Adventure of that Day: And, after Dinner, *Pocammock* requested us to let him have the Horse Home, thereby to stifle any *Reflection* his Lady might bring upon *Him*, or *Herself*, by going to a *Conventicle*; He likewise invited us to Dine next Day at his House, where the Horse should again be delivered to me, as justly forfeited by the Folly of his Wife: We went accordingly with the Laird of *Poddishaw*, and dined at *Pocammock*'s, where the Horse was ordered to be led out into the Court, in the same Accoutrements as I found him the Day before: But observing the Lady in Tears, I told her, that if she would give me her Promise, never to go to a *Conventicle* again, I would bestow her the Horse, and conceal what had passed; she readily complyed, and so the Matter was made up: However the Laird, her Husband, assured me, that no Horse in *Scotland* should be better paid for; and, being a leading Man in the Country, and his Lady discovering the Names of those who had been at the *Conventicle*; he sent for them, and persuaded them, as they valued their Quiet, to make up a Purse for me and my Friend, which they accordingly did; and we both lived plentifully a Twelve-Month after, on the Price of that Horse.

This Adventure, making much Noise at *Edenborough*, was the Occasion of my being sent for up thither, by the Marquess of *Athole*, my Colonel, who in a very friendly Manner, expostulated with me upon my *Rashness*; as indeed he had too much

Reason to do; neither was I able to say any Thing in my own Justification. However since what I had done, discovered my *Loyalty* for my Prince, my Zeal for the *Church*, and my *Detestation* of all *Rebellious Principles*; his Lordship ever after gave me many Marks of his Favour and Friendship.

Accordingly, these Services gave me so much Credit with the General, that he promised to apply to the Government, in my favour, for some Preferment in the Army, upon the first Opportunity, which happened about a Year afterwards. For the Seditious Humours in the West still increasing, it was thought proper, that three *Independent Troops of Horse*, and as many *Dragoons*, should be raised to suppress the *Rebels*. Whereupon Mr. *Francis Stuart*, Grandson to the Earl of *Bothwell*, a private Gentleman in the Horse-Guards, like myself, and my intimate Acquaintance, was sent for, in haste, by the General; because the Council of *Scotland* was then writing to the King; that his Majesty would please to grant *Commissions* to those Persons, whose *Names* were to be sent up to *London*, that very Night. Mr. *Stuart* gave me Notice of this: Whereupon, although I was not sent for, I resolved to go up with him to *Edenborough*, and solicit for myself. When I arrived there, and attended the General, his first Question was in an humorous Manner, *wha the Deel sent for you up?* I answered, that I hoped his Excellency would now make good his Promise of preferring me, since so fair an Opportunity offered at present. On this Occasion the General stood my firm Friend, and although the *Sons* and *Brothers* of *Lords* and *Baronets*, and other Persons of *Quality* solicited to be made *Lieutenants* and *Cornets*, in these new raised Troops, yet the General, in Regard to my Services, prevailed with the Council, that I might be appointed *Lieutenant* to Mr. *Stuart*, who was then made *Captain of Dragoons*.

Soon after this, the *Arch-Bishop* of St. *Andrews* was murdered by the Laird of *Hackston* and *Balfour*, assisted by four *poor Weavers*. *Hackston*, before this horrid Action, was reputed an *Honest* and *Gallant Man*, but his Friendship for his Brother-in-Law *Balfour*, drew him in to commit this *inhuman Murder*. *Balfour* who had been the *Arch-Bishop's Chamberlain* (for so in *Scotland* we call a great Man's Steward) whether by *Negligence* or *Dishonesty*, was short in his Payments to his Lord; and the Fear of being called to an Account, was a principal Motive to Assassinate his Master: However, he pretended likewise a great Zeal to the *Kirk*, whereof he looked upon the *Arch-Bishop* as the greatest *Oppressor*. It is certain, that the lower People, mortally hated the *Arch-Bishop*, on Pretence that his Grace had deserted their *Communion*: And the Weavers who were Accomplices of *Balfour*, believed they did *God Service*, in destroying an Enemy of the *Kirk*; and accordingly all the Murderers were esteemed and styled *Saints*, by that *Rebellious Faction*.

After the Murder of the *Arch-Bishop*, several Parties in the West took up Arms, under the leading of *Robert Hamilton*, second Son to Sir *William Hamilton*, of *Preston*; the unworthy son of a most worthy Father: Whereupon the Council met, and sent for *Graham*, then *Laird of Clavers*, afterwards created Viscount *Dundee*, by King *James* the Seventh. This noble Person was, at that Time, Captain of one of those Independent Troops of Horse, which, as I have already mentioned, were raised before the Murder of the *Arch-Bishop*. The Council therefore ordered him to March with a Detachment of one hundred and twenty Dragoons, and a Lieutenant, with his own Troop, in Pursuit of the *Rebels*. *Clavers* was obliged not to open his Commission, till he came in Sight of them. In his March he took Mas *John King*, one of their principal *Preachers*. *Clavers* carried *King* along, until he came in Sight of the Enemy, at *Drumclog*, eight Miles from *Hamilton*. There the *Preacher* was guarded by a Dragoon-Centry, at a little Cabbin, on the top of the Hill, while *Clavers* opening his Commission, found himself commanded to fight the *Rebels*, let their Number be ever so great, with those *hundred and twenty Dragoons*.

But before I proceed to tell the Issue of this Affair, I must digress a little upon the Subject of Mas *John King*, above mentioned. When I was in the Guards, sometime after I had missed *Williamson*, at Lady *Cherritree*'s House: the Government hearing that this *John King* was beginning to hold his *Conventicles* not far from *Sterling*, where the Troop of Horse then lay, ordered the commanding Officer there, to send a Party out to take him, and bring him up to the Council. I was pitched upon, with a small Detachment, to perform this Service. I went to my Lord *Cardrosse*'s House, to whose Lady *King* was Chaplain; there I took him, and delivered him to the Council. This *Preacher* had gotten the Lady's Woman with Child, about four or five Months before, and, it is supposed, had promised her Marriage, provided the Lady would stand his Friend in his present Distress; whereupon she was so far his Friend, as to get him Bailed, on her engaging, he should hold no more *Conventicles*: However he went to the Hills, and there preached the People to Arms; and in several Towns, as *Kirkubry*, *Lanerick*, and *Sanchar* in particular, in Company with *Cameron*, set up *Declarations* on the *Market-Crosses* against the King, whom he *Excommunicated*, with all his *Adherents*. Thus he continued till *Clavers* took him at *Drumclog*, as is above mentioned, where he got off again, 'till I took him a third Time, after the Battle of *Bothwell-Bridge*, which shall be related in its proper Place.

The *Rebels* at *Drumclog* were eight or nine thousand strong: Their Leader, as I have said before, was *Robert Hamilton*, second Brother to the loyal House of *Preston*, but a *Profligate*, who had spent all his *Patrimony*. There were likewise among them the Lairds of *Knockgray* and *Fruah*, with many other Gentlemen of Fortune, whose Names I have forgot. *Clavers*'s Men, with the Addition of some few that came into him, did not exceed One hundred and eighty; yet pursuant to his Orders, he was forced to fight the Enemy; but being so vastly out-numbered, was soon defeated, with the loss of *Cornet Robert Graham*, and about eight or ten private Troopers. The *Rebels* finding the *Cornet*'s Body, and supposing it to be that of *Clavers*, because the Name of *Graham* was wrought in the Shirt-Neck, treated it with the utmost Inhumanity, cutting off the Nose, picking out the Eyes, and stabbing it through in an hundred Places.

Clavers, in his Flight towards *Hamilton* and *Glasgow*, rode an Horse that trailed his Guts for two Miles, from the Place where the Engagement happened, but then overtaking his

M

Groom with some Led-Horses, he mounted one of them, and with the Remains of his small Army, escaped to *Glasgow*. The Rebels, pursuing as far as *Hamilton*, advanced that Evening within a Mile of *Glasgow*, where they encamped all Night. As *Clavers* was marching after his Men up the Hill, where he had left Mas *John King*, under the Guard of a Dragoon, (who ran off with the first that fled) *King*, in a sneering Way, desired him to stay, and take his Prisoner with him.

The Rebels being thus encamped within a Mile of *Glasgow*, *Clavers* commanded his Men in the Town, to stand to their Arms all Night; and having barricadoed the four Streets, to prevent the Rebels Horse from breaking in, ordered Me, at Sun-rise to march with six Dragoons, and discover which Way the Rebels intended to come into the Town. I must here observe, that I, with Captain *Stuart*'s Troop, of Dragoons, and a Battalion of the Foot-Guards, remained in *Glasgow*, while *Clavers* marched to *Drumclog*, where he was defeated. But to return; I followed the Directions which were given me, and having discovered the Enemy from a little Eminence, I was ordered by *Clavers*, who came to me there, to watch at a small House, where the Way divided, and see which of the Roads they would take, or whether they seperated, and each Party took a different Way. I stayed 'till I saw them take two different Roads; some by that from whence I came from the Town, which was over the *Galligate-Bridge*, and the rest by the *High-Church* and *College*, which was more than twice as far as the first Party had to come, and consequently could not both meet at the same time within the Town. This was a great Advantage to *Clavers*, and his little Army. That Party of the Rebels, which took the *Galligate-Bridge* Road, followed me close at the Heels, as I returned to inform *Clavers* what Course they took.

The broad Street was immediately full of them; but advancing towards the Barricade, before their Fellows, who followed the other Road, could arrive to their Assistance, were valiantly received by *Clavers* and his Men, who firing on them at once, and jumping over the Carts and Cars, that composed the Barricade, chased them out of the Town; but were quickly forced to return, and receive the other Party; which, by that time, was marching down by the *High-Church* and *College*; but when they came within Pistol-shot, were likewise fired upon, and driven out of the Town. In this Action many of the Rebels fell, but the King's Party lost not so much as one Man.

The Town's-men being too well affected to the Rebels, concealed many of them in their Houses; the rest who escaped, met and drew up in a Field behind the *High-Church*, where they stayed 'till five in the Afternoon, it being in the Month of *May*, and from thence, marched in a Body to the same Place, where they were in the Morning, about a Mile off the Town. *Clavers* and his Men expecting they would make a second Attack, and discovering, by his *Spyes*, whither they were gone, marched after them; but upon Sight of our Forces, the Rebels retired with a strong Rear-Guard of Horse to *Hamilton*; whereupon *Clavers* returned, and quartered that Night in *Glasgow*.

Next Morning, the Government sent Orders to *Clavers* to leave *Glasgow*, and march to *Sterling*, eighteen Miles further; and three Days after, he was commanded to bring up his Party to *Edenborough*. As soon as he quitted *Glasgow*, the Rebels returned, and having stayed in that Town eight or ten Days, incamped on *Hamilton-Moor*, within a Mile of *Bothwell-Bridge*, where it was said that their Numbers were increased to Fourteen Thousand; although Bishop *Burnet*, in his History of his own Times, most falsly and partially affirms, that they were not more than Four Thousand, or thereabouts.

The Council, finding the *Rebels* daily increasing in their Numbers, gave Information thereof to the King; whereupon, his Majesty sent down the Duke of *Monmouth*, with a Commission, to be *Commander in Chief*, and to take with him four Troops of *English Dragoons*, which were quartered on the Borders: But these, with the Forces in *Scotland*, amounted not to above Three Thousand. Upon the Duke's being made *Commander in Chief*, General *Dalziel* refused to serve under him, and remained at his Lodgings in *Edenborough*, till his Grace was superseded, which happened about a Fortnight after.

The Army was about four Miles forward, on the Road towards *Hamilton*, when the Duke of *Monmouth* came up with his *English Dragoons*, on *Saturday* the 21st of *June:* From thence the whole Forces marched to the *Kirk* of *Shots*, within four Miles of the *Rebels*, where they lay that Night. The next Morning he marched the Army up an Eminence, opposite to the main Body of the Enemy, who were encamped on the *Moor*.

The General Officers, the Earl of *Linlithgow*, Colonel of the Foot-Guards, the Earl of *Mar*, Colonel of a Regiment of Foot, *Clavers*, the Earl of *Hume*, and the Earl of *Ayrly*, all Captains of Horse, the Marquess of *Montrose*, Colonel of the Horse-Guards, (*Athole* having been discarded) *Dalhousie*, with many other Noblemen, and Gentlemen Voluntiers, attending the Duke together, desired his Grace to let them know which Way he designed to take to come at the Enemy; the Duke answered, it must be, by *Bothwell-Bridge*. Now the Bridge lay a short Mile to the Right of the King's Army, was Narrow, and guarded with Three thousand of the *Rebels*, and strongly Barricadoed with great Stones; but, although the Officers were desirous to have passed the River, by *easy Fords*, directly between them and the *Rebels*, and to march to their main Body on the *Moor*, before those Three Thousand, who guarded the Bridge, could come to assist them; yet the Duke was obstinate, and would pass no other Way, than that of the *Bridge*.

Pursuant to this *preposterous* and *absurd Resolution*, he commanded Capt. *Stuart* (whose Lieutenant I was) with his Troop of Dragoons, and eighty Musqueteers, together with four small Field-Pieces, under Cover of the Dragoons, to beat off the Party at the Bridge: The Duke himself, with *David Lesly* and *Melvill*, accompanied us, and ordered the Field-Pieces to be left at the Village of *Bothwell*, within a Musquet Shot of the Bridge: When the Duke and his Men came near the Bridge, the *Rebels* beat a Parley, and sent over a Laird, accompanied with a *Kirk Preacher*. The Duke asking what they came for, was answered, 'That they would have 'the *Kirk established* in the same Manner, as it stood at the King's 'Restoration, and that every Subject should be obliged to 'take the *Solemn League* and *Covenant.*' The Duke told them, their Demand could not be granted, but sent them back to tell their Party, that if they would lay down their Arms, and submit to the King's Mercy, he would intercede for their Pardon.

While this Parly lasted, the Field-Pieces were brought down, and planted over against the *Bridge*, without being perceived by the *Rebels*. The Messengers returned in a short Time, with this Answer; *That they would not lay down their Arms, unless their Conditions were granted them*: Whereupon the *Dragoons* and *Musqueteers* fired all at once, upon those who guarded the *Bridge*, and the Field-Pieces played so warmly, that some Hundreds of the *Rebels* were slain; the rest flying to the main Body on the *Moor*.

The Duke, as soon as he had commanded to Fire, retired into a *Hollow*, from the Enemies Shot; some say by the Persuasion of *Lesly* and *Melvill*, and continued there 'till the Action was over. Then *Captain Stuart* ordered the *Musqueteers* to make Way for the Horse, to pass the *Bridge*, by casting the Stones into the River, which had been placed there to obstruct the Passage over it; but the Army could not pass in less than *five Hours*; and then marched up in order of Battle towards the Enemy, who waited for them on the *Moor*, confiding in the great Superiority of their Number. *Clavers* commanded the Horse on the *Right*, and *Captain Stuart* the Dragoons on the *Left*. The Field-Pieces were carried in the *Center* of the Foot-Guards, while the rest of the Officers commanded at the Head of their Men; and the Duke, after the Enemy was beaten from the *Bridge*, rode at the Head of the Army.

Upon the first Fire, the *Rebels* Horse turned about, and fled upon the *Right* and *Left*; and although the Duke ordered his Men not to stir out of their Ranks to pursue them, yet the Army, not regarding his Commands, followed the flying *Rebels*, killing between Seven and Eight Hundred, and taking Fifteen Hundred Prisoners. Sir *John Bell*, Provost of *Glasgow*, as soon as he saw the *Rebels* fly, rode into the Town; from whence, in a few Hours, he sent all the Bread he could find, together with an Hogshead of Drink to each Troop and

Company in the Army, out of the Cellars of such *Town's-Men* as were found to be Abettors or Protectors of the *Rebels*.

The *Cruelty* and *Presumption* of that *wicked* and *perverse Generation*, will appear evident from a single Instance. These *Rebels* had set up a very large *Gallows*, in the Middle of their Camp, and prepared a *Cart full* of new *Ropes* at the foot of it, in order to hang up the King's Soldiers, whom they already looked upon as vanquished and at Mercy; and it happened, that the Pursuers in the *Royal Army*, returning back with their Prisoners, chose the Place where the *Gallows* stood, to guard them at, without offering to *Hang* one of them, which they justly deserved, and had so much Reason to expect. The Pursuers were no sooner returned, and the whole Action over, than *General Dalziel* arrived at the Camp from *Edenborough*, with a Commission renewed to be *Commander in Chief*, which he received that very Morning by an Express. This Commander having learned how the Duke had conducted the War, told him publickly, and with great Plainness, that he had *betrayed the King*; that he heartily wished his Commission had come a Day sooner, for then said he, *These Rogues should never have troubled his Majesty, or the Kingdom any more.*

Thus the Duke was at the same Time superseded, and publickly Rebuked, before all the Army; yet his Grace forgot his Dignity so far, as to *sneak* among them at the Town of *Bothwell*, (where the Forces encamped) 'till the *Saturday* following; then all the Troops marched back to *Glasgow*, from whence in two or three Days, they were sent to their several Quarters; after which the Duke of *Monmouth* passed by *Sterling* to *Fife* to visit the Duke of *Rothes*.

The same Evening after the Rout on the *Moor*, the Prisoners were sent with a strong Guard towards *Edenborough*. On *Saturday* Morning, when the Army was to march to *Glasgow*, I desired the General's Leave to go with twelve Dragoons, in Search of some of the *Rebels*, who might probably pass the *Clyde*, about *Dunbarton*, to shelter themselves in the *Highlands*, with these Dragoons, clad in gray Coats and Bonnets, I made Haste down the Side of the River; and about Midnight, after travelling twenty four Miles, I came to a Church, and while the Soldiers stayed to refresh their Horses in the Church-Yard, I spyed a Country-Fellow, going by, and asked him in his own Dialect, *Whither gang ye this Time of Night?* He answered, *Wha are ye that Speers?* I replied, *We are your ane Fo'ke*: Upon this the Fellow came up, and told me, there were Eighteen *Friends*, with Horses, at an old Castle, waiting for a Boat to pass over into the Isle of *Arran*. I mounted the Man behind one of my Dragoons, and went towards the Place: But the *Rebels* not finding a Boat, were gone off, and the Guide dismissed. There was a great Dew on the Grass, which directed me and my Party to follow the Track of their Horses, for three or four Miles, 'till the Dew was gone off: I then enquired of a *Cow-herd* on a Hill, whether he saw any of our *poor Fo'ke* travelling that Way; he answered, that they had separated on that Hill, and gone three several Ways, Six in a Party; adding, that in one Party, there was *a bra, muckle Kerl*, with a *white Hat on him, and a great Bob of Ribbons on the Cock o't*. Whereupon I sent four of my *Dragoons* after one Party, four more after another; and myself, with the remaining four, went in Pursuit of him with the *white Hat*. As I went forward, I met another *Cow-Herd*, who told me, that the Fellow with the *Hat*, and one more, (for as the *Rogues* advanced further into the *West*, they still divided into smaller Parties) were just gone down the Hill, to his Master's House. The Good Man of the House returning, from putting the Horses to Grass in the Garden, was going to shut the Door; whereupon myself and two of the *Dragoons* commanded him, with our Pistols at his Breast, to lead us to the Room where the Man lay, who wore a *white Hat*. We entered the Room, and before he awaked, I took away his Arms, and commanded him to Dress immediately: Then finding his Companion asleep in the *Barn*, I forced him likewise to arise, and mounting them both on their own Horses, came at nine o'Clock in the Morning, with my two Prisoners, to the other *Dragoons*, at the Place where we appointed to meet. From thence we rode strait to *Glasgow*, and arrived thither about eight in the Evening, after a Journey of *fifty Miles*, since we left the Army at *Bothwell* the Day before.

This was upon a *Sunday*, and although we met with many hundreds of People on the Road, yet we travelled on to *Glasgow*, without any Opposition. I must here inform the *Reader*, that although I had once before taken this *very Man*, who wore the *white Hat*, yet I did not know him to be Mas *John King* already mentioned, untill I was told so by the Man of the House where I found him. I likewise forgot to mention, that *King* who knew me well enough, as soon as he was taken in the House, entreated me to shew him some Favour, because he had married a Woman of my Name; I answered, *That is true, but first you got her with Bairn, and shall therefore now pay for disgracing one of my Name*.

When we arrived near *Glasgow*, I sent a Dragoon to inform the General, that Mas *John King* was coming to kiss his Hand; whereupon his Excellency, accompanied with all the Noblemen and Officers, advanced as far as the *Bridge* to welcome me and my Prisoners; where it is very observable, that *Graham, Laird of Clavers*, who came among the rest, made not the least Reproach to Mas *John*, in return of his insolent Behaviour, when that Commander fled from *Drumclog*. Mas *John* was sent to *Edenborough* next Morning, under a Guard, and hanged soon after. From hence I went to my Quarters, in *Lanerick*, sixteen Miles from *Glasgow*; and about a Month after, (I hope the Reader will pardon my Weakness) I happened to *Dream* that I found one *Wilson*, a Captain among the *Rebels*, at *Bothwell-Bridge*, in a Bank of Wood, upon the River *Cylde*. This Accident made so strong an Impression upon my Mind, that as soon as I awaked, I took Six and Thirty Dragoons, and got to the Place, by break of Day: Then I caused some of them to alight, and go into the Wood, and set him up, as *Hounds* do a *Hare*, while the rest were ordered to stand Centry to prevent his Escape. It seems I dreamt *Fortunately*, for *Wilson* was actually in the Wood, with five more of his Company, as we afterwards learned; who all seeing me and my Party advancing, hid themselves in a little Island on the River, among the Broom that grew upon it. *Wilson* had not the good Fortune to escape; for as he was trying to get out of one Copse into another, I met him, and guessing by his *good Cloaths*, and by the Description

I had received of him before, that he was the Man I looked for; I seized and brought him to my Quarters; and from thence immediately conveyed him to *Edenborough*, where he was hanged; but might have preserved his Life, if he would have condescended only to say, *God save the King*. This he utterly refused to do, and thereby lost not only his Life, but likewise an Estate, worth Twenty nine thousand Marks *Scots*.

For this Service, the Duke of *Queen'sberry*, then *High Commissioner* of *Scotland*, recommended me to the King, who rewarded me with the Gift of *Wilson's Estate*; but although the Grant passed the Seals, and the *Sheriff* put me in *Possession*, yet I could neither Sell it nor Lett it; no Body daring, for Fear of the Rebels, who had escaped at *Bothwell-Bridge*, either to *Purchase* or *Farm* it; by which Means, I never got a Penny by the Grant; and at the *Revolution* the Land was taken from me, and restored to *Wilson's Heirs*.

The Winter following, General *Dalziel*, with a Battalion of the *Earl of Linlithgow's* Guards, the Earl of *Airly's* Troop of Horse, and Captain *Stuart's* Troop of Dragoons, quartered at *Kilmarnock*, in the West, fifty Miles from *Edenborough*. Here the General, one Day, happened to look on, while I was exercising the Troop of Dragoons, asked me, when I had done, whether I knew any of my Men, who was skilful in praying well in the Style and Tone of the *Covenanters*; I immediately thought upon one *James Gibb*, who had been born in *Ireland*, and whom I made a Dragoon. This Man I brought to the General, assuring his Excellency, that if I had *raked Hell*, I could not find his Match for his Skill in mimicking the *Covenanters*. Whereupon the General gave him Five Pounds, to buy him a gray Coat and a Bonnet, and commanded him to find out the Rebels, but to be sure to take Care of himself among them. The Dragoon went Eight Miles off that very Night, and got Admittance into the House of a notorious *Rebel*, pretending he came from *Ireland* out of *Zeal for the Cause*, to assist at the *Fight of Bothwell-Bridge*, and could not find an Opportunity since, of returning to *Ireland* with Safety; he said he durst not be seen in the Day Time, and therefore, after bewitching the Family with his Gifts of Praying, he was conveyed in the Dusk of the next Evening, with a Guide, to the House of the next adjoyning Rebel; and thus in the same Manner, from one to another, 'till in a Month's time he got through the *principal of them in the West*; telling the General, at his Return, that wherever he came, he made the old Wives, in their devout Fits, *tear off* their *Biggonets* and *Mutches*; he likewise gave the General a List of their Names, and Places of their Abodes; and into the Bargain, brought back a good Purse of Money in his Pocket. The General desired to know how he had *prayed* amongst them; he answered, that it was his Custom, in his Prayers, to send the *King*, the *Ministers of State*, the *Officers of the Army*, with all their Soldiers, and the *Episcopal Clergy*, all *broad-side to Hell*; but particularly the *General himself*: What said the General, did you send me to Hell Sir? *Yea*, replyed the Dragoon, you at the Head of them, as their *Leader*.

And here I do solemnly aver upon my *Veracity and Knowledge*, that *Bishop Burnet*, in his History of his own Times, hath in a most false and scandalous Manner, misrepresented the Action at *Bothwell-Bridge*, and the Behaviour of the *Episcopal Clergy* in *Scotland:* For as to the former, I was *present* in that Engagement, which was performed in the Manner as I have related; and as to the latter, having travelled through most Parts of that Kingdom, particularly the *North* and *West*; I was well acquainted with them, and will take it to my Death, that the Reverse of this Character, which *Burnet* gives of both, is the Truth. And because that Author is so unjust to the *Episcopal Clergy*, and so partial to the *Covenanters*, and their *Teachers*, I do affirm, that I have known several among the latter Sort guilty of those very Vices, wherewith this Bishop brands the *Episcopal Clergy*. Among many others, I will produce one Instance, rather to divert the Reader, than from any Inclination to *Obloquy*. One of those eight *Fanatick Teachers*, who were permitted, at the *Restoration*, to keep their Livings, came to Sir *John Carmichael's House*, within a Mile of *Lanerick*, where I was then upon a Visit to Sir *John*. We drank hard 'till it was late, and all the Company retired, except Sir *John* and myself. The *Teacher* would needs give us

Prayers, but fell a Sleep before he had half done; whereupon Sir *John* and I, setting a Bottle and Glass at his *Nose*, left him upon his *Knees*. The poor Man sneaked off early the next Morning, being, in all Appearance, ashamed of his *Hypocrisy*.

To return from this Digression. The General sent out several Parties, and me with a Party among the rest; where during the *Winter* and the following *Spring*, I secured many of those, whose Names and Abodes, the *Canting Dragoon* had given a List of.

In *July* following, the General, by Order of Council, commanded me to go with a *Detachment of thirty Horse*, and *fifty Dragoons*, in pursuit of about one hundred and fifty *Rebels*, who had escaped at *Bothwell-Bridge*, and ever since kept together in a Body, up and down in *Galloway*. I followed them for five or six Days, from one Place to another; after which, on the 22d of *July*, they stayed for me at *Airs-Moss*, situate in the Shire of *Air*, near the Town of *Cumlock*. The *Moss* is four Miles long from *East* to *West*, and two broad. The *Rebels* drew up at the *East* End, and consisted of thirty Horse and one hundred and twenty Foot. I faced them upon a rising Ground, with my thirty Horse and fifty Dragoons. The Reason why the *Rebels* chose this Place to fight on, rather than a plain Field, was for Fear their *Horse* might desert the *Foot*, as they did on *Hamilton-Moor*, near *Bothwell-Bridge:* And likewise, that in Case they lost the Day, they might save themselves by retreating into the *Moss*.

I placed myself on the *Left* as judging that the best Officer the *Rebels* had, would Command on the *Right*. The Action began about five in the Afternoon, but lasted not long; for I ordered my Men first to receive the Enemy's Fire, then to ride down the Hill upon them, and use their Broad-Swords: They did so, and before the Enemy had Time to draw theirs, cut many of them down in an Instant; whereupon they wheeled about, and Captain *Fowler*, who commanded the *Rebels* on the *Right*, being then in the *Rear*, advancing up to me, I gave him such a Blow over the Head with my Broad Sword, as would have cleaved his Scul, had it not been defended by a *Steel-Cap*. *Fowler* turning about, aimed a Blow at me, but I warded it off, and with a back Stroke, cut the upper Part of his Head clean off, from the Nose upwards.

By this Time, the *Rebels* leaving their Horses, fled to the *Moss*; but the *Royalists* pursuing them, killed about sixty, and took fourteen Prisoners. Here *Cameron*, the *famous Covenanter*, lost his Life; and *Haxton* was taken Prisoner, infamous for embruing his Hands in the Blood of the *Arch Bishop of St. Andrews*, as I have already mentioned; for which *Paricide*, both his Hands were afterwards cut off, and he was hanged at *Edenborough*.

But this Victory cost me very dear; for being then in the Rear, I rode into the *Moss* after the *Rebels*, where I overtook a Dozen of them, hacking and hewing one of my Men, whose Horse was *bogged*; his Name was *Elliot*, a stout Soldier; and one of *Clavers*'s *Troop*. He had received several Wounds, and was at the Point of being killed, when I came to his Relief. I shot one of the *Rogues* dead with my *Carbine*, which obliged the rest to let the poor Man and his Horse creep out of the *Hole*; but at the same Time drew all their Fury upon myself; for *Elliot* made a Shift to crawl out of the *Moss*, leading his Horse in his Hand, but was wholly disabled from assisting his Deliverer, and was not regarded by his Enemies, who probably thought he was mortally wounded, or indeed rather that they had no Time to mind him; for I laid about me so fast, that they judged it best to keep off, and not to venture within my Reach; 'till it unfortunately happened, that my Horse slipped into the same Hole, out of which *Elliot*, and his had just got. When they had me at this Advantage, they began to shew their Courage, and manfully dealt their Blows with their Broad-Swords, from some of which the Carbine that hung down my Back, defended me a little. As I was *paddling in the Hole*, the Horse not able to get out, One of the *Rebels* ran me through the small of the Back with his Broad-Sword, and at the same Instant, two more wounded me under the Ribs with their small ones. Then I threw myself over the Head of my Horse, taking the far Pistol out of the Holster in my left Hand, and holding my Broad-Sword in my *Right*; and as one of the *Villains* was coming hastily up to me, his Foot slipped, and before he could recover himself, I struck my Sword into his Scull; but the Fellow, being big and heavy, snapped it asunder as he fell, within a Span of the Hilt. The *Rebels* had me now at a great Advantage: One of them made a Stroak at me, which I warded off with the Hilt of the Sword, that was left in my Hand; but the Force with which he struck the Blow, and I kept it off, brought us both to the Ground. However I got up before him, clapped my Pistol to his Side, and shot him Dead. As soon as this was done, another came behind me, and with some Weapon or other, struck me such a Blow on the Head, as laid me flat on my Back; in which Posture I remained a good while insensible; the *Rogues* taking it for granted that I was dead, scoured off, fearing that by this Time, some of my Men were returning back from the Pursuit.

After some Time, I a little recovered my Senses, and strove to lift myself up, which one of the *Rogues* happening to see at some Distance, immediately returned, and said in my Hearing, *God, the Dog is no Deed yet*: Then coming up to me, took his Sword, and putting it's Hilt to his Breast, and guiding it with both his Hands, made a Thrust at my Belly; but my Senses were now so far recovered, that I parryed the Thrust with the Piece of the Sword which remained still in my Hand. The Fellow, when he missed his Aim, almost fell on his Face; for the Sword ran up to the Hilt in the Moss; and as he was recovering himself, I gave him a Dab in the Mouth with my broken Sword, which very much hurt him; but he aiming a second Thrust, which I had likewise the good Fortune to put by, and having as before given him another Dab in the Mouth, he immediately went off, for Fear of the Pursuers, whereof many were now returning.

In this Distress, I made a shift with much Difficulty and Pain, to get upon my Feet, but my *Right-Leg* being disabled by the Wound, I received from the Broad-Sword, I was forced to Limp by the Help of the Carbine, which I made Use of as a Staff. I had lost my *Horse*; for one of the *Rogues*, when I had quitted him in the *Hole*, led him away through the *Moss*. I recovered him about a Year after from the Man, to whom the *Rebel* had Sold him; and the said *Rebel*, when he was at the

Gallows, confessed himself to be the same Man, who took away the Horse at *Airs-Moss*.

There was a *Lancashire Gentleman*, one Mr. *Parker*, who came Volunteer to *Airs-Moss*, with Intent, as he expressed himself, to *see the Sport*. This Gentleman, riding on my *Right-Hand*, at the Time when we received the Enemy's Fire, in the Beginning of the Action, was shot with a *Blunderbuss* under the *Left-Shoulder*; the Wound was so large, that a Man might thrust his Fist into it: Yet when I desired him to fall back, and take Care of his Wound, he answered me, that he would first have his *Penny-Worth* out of the *Rogues*; and accordingly followed us on *Horse-back* into the *Moss*, as far as the Horse could go without *Bogging*. But by that Time, his Wound so grievously pained him, with some other Cuts he got in the Pursuit, that he was forced to alight and sit on a dry Spot of Ground, which he found in the *Moss*, from whence he saw all that happened to me, without being able to come to my Assistance, any more than *Elliot*; who having gotten to a rising Ground, saw likewise all that had passed. However Mr. *Parker*, as I came limping towards him, could not forbear *Laughing*, and said, *What a Plague, have you got your Bones well paid too?* Then both of us made a shift to get up to *Elliot* on the rising Ground.

The *Trumpeter* being by this Time returned, with some others from the Pursuit, was ordered to sound a Call, which brought all the rest back, with the fourteen Prisoners, and *Haxton* among the rest, who was that Day *Commander in Chief* among the *Rebels*. Of the King's Party, but two were killed, Mr. *Andrew Kerr*, a Gentleman of *Clavers*'s *own Troop*, and one *Mc. Kabe*, a *Dragoon* in *Captain Stuart's Troop*, where I was *Lieutenant*. The wounded were about Eight or Nine, besides *Parker* and *Elliot*. *Elliot* died the next Day; He, *Kerr*, and *Mc.Kabe*, were honourably buried by Mr. *Brown*, a Gentleman who lived hard by, to whose House their Bodies were carried after the Fight at the *Moss*. An *English Lady*, living about eight Miles off, took Care of Mr. *Parker*, but he died at her House a Year after, of his Wounds, very much lamented on Account of his *Loyalty* and *Valour*.

When the Fight was over, Night coming on, I ordered all my Men, except twelve *Dragoons*, whom I kept to attend myself, to march with the *Prisoners*, and those who were wounded to *Douglass*, fourteen Miles off, and to carry along with them *Cameron*'s *Head*. In the mean time, I and my Party of *Dragoons* went, that Night, sixteen long Miles to *Lanerick*, where the General and all the Foot quartered; as well to acquaint him with what had been done, as to have my own Wounds taken Care of. I sent one of my *Dragoons* before me with my Message: Whereupon the General himself, although it were after Mid-Night, accompanied with the Earls of *Linlithgow*, *Mar*, *Ross*, *Hume*, and the Lord *Dalhousie*, came out to meet me at the Gate: *Dalhousie* forced me to lodge in his *own Chamber*, to which I was accordingly carried by two of my *Dragoons*. After my Wounds had been dressed in the Presence of this *Noble Company*, who stood round about me, being very thirsty through the loss of Blood, I drank the King's Health, and the Company's, in a large *Glass of Wine and Water*; and then was laid in *Dalhousie*'s *own Bed*.

Next Day the General leaving *Lanerick*, with the Forces under his Command, ordered a *Troop of Horse* and another of *Dragoons* to attend me, 'till I should be able to travel up to *Edenborough*, for the better Conveniency of *Physicians* and *Surgeons*. My Wounds did not confine me to my Bed; and in a Month's Time I went to *Edenborough* on *Horse-back* by easy Stages, where I continued 'till *Candlemas* following, lingering of the Wound I had received by the *Broad-Sword*. My *Surgeon* was the Son of the same Dr. *Irvin*, who first got me into the Guards; but having unfortunately neglected to tye a String to the *Tent of Green-Cloath*, which he used for the Wound; the *Tent* slipped into my Body, where it lay under my *Navel* seven Months and five Days, and exceedingly pained me, not suffering me to sleep, otherwise than by taking *Soporiferous Pills*. When the *Tent* was first missing, neither the *Surgeon*, nor any body else ever imagined that it was lodged in my Body; but supposed it to have slipped out of the Wound while I slept, and carried away by some *Rat*, or other *Vermin*: The *Tent* lying thus in my Body, made it impossible that the

Wound could heal: Wherefore, after lingering seven Months, by the Advice of a Gentlewoman in the Neighbourhood, I got Leave to go for *Ireland* with my *Surgeon*, and there try whether my *Native Air* would contribute any thing to my Cure.

However insignificant this Relation may be to the Generality of *Readers*, yet I cannot omit a lucky Accident to which I owe my Cure. While I continued at *Edenborough*, I ordered some *Pipes of Lead* to be made in a *Mold*, through which the thin *Corruption*, which continually issued out of the Wound, caused by the *Tent* remaining in my Body, might be conveyed as through a *Fosset*. These *Pipes* I cut shorter by Degrees, in proportion as I imagined the Wound was healing at the Bottom; 'till at last, by mistaking the true Cause, the *Tent* continuing still where it did, the *Pipes* became too short for the Use intended; Wherefore when I was in *Ireland*, I made a course *Pipe* myself, which was long enough: This *Pipe*, after the Wound was washed with *Brandy*, always remained in my Body 'till the next Dressing; but being made without *Art*, and somewhat jagged at the End, it happened one Morning, when the *Pipe* was drawn out as usual, in order to have the Wound washed, the *Tent* followed, to the great Surprize of my *Father*, who, at that Time, was going to dress the Wound; My *Surgeon* being then at *Castle-Irvin*, where I had left him with his Brother Dr. *Irvin*, at Sir *Gerard Irvin*'s House; the same Gentleman who was delivered out of *Derry-Jayl* by my Father, as I have related in the Beginning of these *Memoirs*.

The Night before the *Tent* was drawn out of my Body, having not slept a Wink, I thought myself in the Morning somewhat *Feverish*, and therefore desired my *Father* to send for Dr. *Lindsey*, to let me *Blood*. In the mean Time, slumbering a little, I dreamed that the *Covenanters* were coming to cut my *Throat*; under this Apprehension I awaked, and found my Neighbour, *Captain Sanderson*, in my *Chamber*, who was come to visit me. I then called for my *Father* to dress my Wound; when the *Tent* followed the *Pipe*, as I have already said, to my great Joy, for then I knew I should soon be well. I therefore ordered my Horse to be got ready, and rode out with *Captain Sanderson* and my *Father*, to *meet* Dr. *Lindsey*, who hearing the joyful News, carried us to a Gentleman's House, where we drank very heartily: Then I returned home and slept almost twenty four Hours. Two Days after, Dr. *Irvin* and his *Brother*, the *Surgeon*, came to my *Father*'s House, where the Dr. being informed in the Circumstances of my Cure, severely chid his *Brother* for his Neglect, swearing he had a mind to shoot him, and that if I had died, my Blood would have been charged on his Head. He then ordered me a Remedy, which would heal up the Wound in twenty Days. This fell out in the Beginning of *May*, at which Time, taking Leave of my *Father* and other *Friends* in *Ireland*, I returned with my *Surgeon Irvin* to *Edenborough*, where before the End of that Month, my Wound was perfectly healed up; but I was never afterwards so able to endure Fatigues, as I had hitherto been.

The *Duke of York* was arrived at *Edenborough* the *Michaelmas* before, where the General, from the Time he left *Lanerick* in *July*, continued with the Guards; the rest of the Forces quartering up and down in other Places. The General, after my Arrival, coming every Day to see me, in his Way, as he went to the *Duke*'s *Court*, did me the Honour to mention me and my Services to his *Royal Highness*, who was desirous to see me; I was admitted to kiss his Hand, and ordered to *sit down*, in Regard to my *honourable Wounds*, which would not Suffer me to *stand*, without *great Pain*. I cannot conceal this mark of Favour and Distinction, shewn me by a great Prince, although I am very sensible it will be imputed to *Vanity*. I must remember likewise, that upon my Return to *Edenborough*, happening to overtake the General in the Street, and gently touching him, his Excellency turning in a great Surprize, cryed out, *O God, Man, are you living*? I answered that I was, and hoped to do the King and his Excellency further Service.

After I had continued a Month with my Friends in *Edenborough*, who all congratulated with me upon my Recovery, I repaired to the Troop at *Lanerick*, where I often ranged with a Party through the *West*, to find out the straggling Remains of the *Covenanting Rebels*, but for some Time without Success, 'till a Week before *Christmas*, after the *Duke of York* succeeded to the Crown, and a Year and half after I was cured. Having

N

drank hard one Night, I *dreamed* that I had found Captain *David Steele*, a notorious *Rebel*, in one of five Farmers Houses on a Mountain in the *Shire* of *Clidesdale*, and Parish of *Lismahego*, within eight Miles of *Hamilton*, a Place that I was well acquainted with. This Man was Head of the Rebels, since the Affair of *Airs-Moss*, having succeeded to *Haxton*, who had been there taken, and afterwards hanged, as the Reader has already heard: For as to *Robert Hamilton*, who was their *Commander in Chief* at *Bothwell-Bridge*, he appeared no more among them, but fled, as it was believed, to *Holland*.

Steele, and his Father before him, held a Farm in the Estate of *Hamilton*, within two or three Miles of that Town. When he betook himself to Arms, the Farm lay waste, and the Duke could find no other Person, who would venture to take it; whereupon his Grace sent several Messengers to *Steele*, to know the Reason why he kept the Farm waste? The Duke received no other Answer, than that he would keep it waste, in *Spight* of him and the *King* too; whereupon his Grace, at whose Table I had always the Honour to be a welcome Guest, desired I would use my Endeavours to destroy that Rogue, and I would oblige him for ever.

I must here take Leave to inform the Reader, that the Duke of *Hamilton*'s Friendship for me, was founded upon the many Services he knew I had done the Publick, as well as upon the Relation I bore to Sir *Gerard Irvin*, the Person, whom of all the World, his Grace most loved and esteemed, ever since the time they had served in Arms together for the *King*, in the *High-lands*, with my *Lord Glankern* and Sir *Arthur Forbes*, (Father to the present *Earl of Granard*) after the King's *Defeat at Worcester*, during the time of the *Usurpation*.

To return therefore to my Story, when I awaked out of my Dream, as I had done before in the Affair of *Wilson*, (and I desire the same Apology, I made in the Introduction to these Memoirs, may serve for both) I presently rose, and ordered Thirty six Dragoons to be at the Place appointed by Break of Day. When we arrived thither, I sent a Party to each of the five Farmers Houses. This *Villain Steele* had murdered above Forty of the King's Subjects *in cold Blood*; and, as I was informed, had often laid Snares to *entrap me*; but it happened, that although he usually kept a Gang to attend him, yet at this Time he had none, when he stood in the greatest Need. One of my Party found him in one of the Farmers Houses, just as I happened to *Dream*. The *Dragoons*, first, searched all the Rooms below without Success, 'till two of them hearing Somebody stirring over their Heads, went up a Pair of *Turnpike-Stairs*. *Steele* had put on his *Cloaths*, while the Search was making below: The Chamber where he lay was called the Chamber of *Deese*, which is the Name given to a Room, where the *Laird* lies when he comes to a *Tenant's House*. *Steele*, suddenly opening the Door, fired a *Blunderbuss* down at the two *Dragoons*, as they were coming up the *Stairs*; but the *Bullets*, grazing against the Side of the *Turnpike*, only wounded, and did not kill them. Then *Steele* violently threw himself down the *Stairs* among them, and made towards the Door to save his Life, but lost it upon the Spot; for the *Dragoons* who guarded the House, dispatched him with their *Broad-Swords*. I was not with the *Party* when he was killed, being at that Time employed in searching at one of the other four Houses, but I soon found what had happened, by hearing the Noise of the Shot made with the *Blunderbuss*: From hence I returned straight to *Lanerick*, and immediately sent one of the Dragoons Express to General *Drummond*, at *Edenborough*.

General *Dalziel* dyed about *Michaelmas* this Year, and was succeeded by *Lieutenant General Drummond*, who was likewise my very good Friend.

But I cannot here let pass the Death of so Brave and Loyal a Commander, as *General Dalziel*, without giving the *Reader* some Account of him, as far as my *Knowledge*, or *Enquiry*, can reach.

Thomas Dalziel, among many other *Officers*, was taken *Prisoner* at the unfortunate Defeat at *Worcester*, and sent to the *Tower*; from whence, I know not by what Means, he made his Escape, and went to *Muscovy*; where the *Czar*, then reigning, made him his *General*: But some Time after the *Restoration* of the *Royal Family*, he gave up his *Commission*, and repairing to King *Charles* the Second, was, in Consideration of his eminent Services, constituted *Commander in Chief, of his Majesty's Forces in Scotland*; in which Post he continued 'till his Death, excepting only one *Fortnight*, when he was superseded by the Duke of *Monmouth*, some Days before the Action at *Bothwell Bridge*, as I have already related. He was bred up very *Hardy* from his Youth, both in *Dyet* and *Cloathing*. He never wore *Boots*, nor above one *Coat*, which was close to his *Body*, with close *Sleeves*, like those we call *Jockey-Coats*. He never wore a *Peruke*; nor did he shave his *Beard* since the Murder of *King Charles the First*. In my Time, his Head was *bald*, which he covered only with a *Beaver-Hat*, the *Brim* of which was not above three *Inches* broad. His *Beard* was white and *Bushy*, and yet reached down almost to his *Girdle*. He usually went to *London* once or twice in a Year, and then only to kiss the *King's Hand*, who had a great Esteem for his *Worth* and *Valour*. His unusual *Dress* and *Figure*, when he was in *London*, never failed to draw after him a great Crowd of Boys, and other young People, who constantly attended at his Lodgings, and followed him with *Huzzas* as he went to *Court*, or returned from it. As he was a *Man of Humour*, he would always thank them for their Civilities, when he left them at the Door, to go into the King; and would let them know exactly, at what Hour he intended to come out again, and return to his Lodgings. When the *King* walked in the *Park*, attended by some of his *Courtiers*, and *Dalziel* in his Company, the same *Crouds* would always be after him, shewing their *Admiration* at his *Beard* and *Dress*, so that the King could hardly pass on for the *Croud*; upon which his Majesty *bid the Devil take Dalziel*, for bringing such a *Rabbel of Boys* together, to have their Guts squeezed out, whilst they gaped at his long *Beard*, and *antick Habit*; requesting him, at the same Time, (as *Dalziel* used to express it) *to Shave and Dress like other Christians*, to keep the *poor Bairns* out of Danger: All this could never prevail on him to part with his *Beard*; but, yet in *Complyance to his Majesty*, he went once to Court in the *very Height of the Fashion*; but as soon as the King and those about him had laughed sufficiently, at the strange Figure he made, he re-assumed his

usual *Habit*, to the great Joy of the Boys, who had not discovered him in his fashionable *Dress*.

When the *Duke of York* succeeded to the Crown, General
Dalziel was resolved still to retain his *Loyalty*, although at
the same Time, he often told his Friends, that all Things were
going wrong at Court; but Death came very reasonably,
to rescue him from the Difficulties he was likely to be under,
between the Notions he had of *Duty to his Prince* on one Side,
and *true Zeal for his Religion* on the other.

I must now resume a little My Discourse upon *Captain Steele*.
Sometime before the Action, in which he was killed, *General
Drummond*, who was then newly made *Commander in Chief*,
sent for me in Haste, to attend him in *Edenborough:* My Way
lay through a very *strong Pass*, hard by *Airs-Moss*, and within
a Mile of *Cumlock:* As I was going through *Cumlock*, a Friend
there told me, that *Steel*, with a *Party*, waited for me at the
Pass. I had with me only *one Dragoon* and a *Drummer*: I ordered
the latter to gallop on straight to the *Pass*, and when he got
thither, to beat a *Dragoon-March*, while I with the *Dragoon*
should ride along the *By-Path*, on the *Edge* of the *Moss*. When
Steel and his Men heard the *Drum*, they scoured cross the *By-
Path* into the *Moss*, apprehending that a *strong Party* was coming
in Search of them: But either I, or the *Dragoon*, (I forget which)
shot one of the *Rebels* dead, as he crossed us to get into the
Moss. To put an End to this Business of *Steel*. When the
Dragoon, whom I sent Express, had delivered his Message to
General Drummond, he was just setting out for his Country-
House at *Dumblane*, but returned to his Lodgings, and wrote
me a Letter, that he would send for me up after the *Holidays*,
and recommend me to the *Government*, to reward me for my
Services. *He* faithfully kept his Word, but I received nothing
more than *Promises*.

Steel was buried in the Church-Yard of *Lithmahegow*, by
some of his Friends; who, after the *Revolution*, erected a fair
Monument, on *Pillars*, over his *Grave*, and caused an *Epitaph*
to be engraved on the *Stone*, in Words to this Effect.

Here lyeth the Body of Captain David Steel, *a Saint, who was
murdered by* John Creichton (*with the Date underneath.*)

Some of my *Friends Burlesqued* this *Epitaph* in the following Manner.

Here lies the Body of Saint Steel,
Murderd by John Creichton, *that Dee'l.*

Duke *Hamilton*, in *Queen Ann*'s Time, informed me of this Honour done to that infamous *Rebel*, and when I had said to his *Grace*, that I wished he had ordered his *Footmen* to *demolish* the *Monument*; the Duke answered, he would not have done so for *Five Hundred Pounds*, because it would be an honour to me as long as it lasted.

The last *Summer*, about the End of *May*, if I remember Right, and I desire to be excused for not always relating Things in the Order when they happened: The *Marquiss* of *Argyle*, after having escaped out of the *Castle* of *Edenborough*, into *Holland*, returned to invade *Scotland*, to support the *Duke of Monmouth*'s *Pretensions* to the *Crown*, as was generally believed. He landed in his own Country, in the *High-lands*, with a Party of *Dutch*, and some *Scottish Gentlemen*, who had fled for *Treason*; among whom Sir *John Cogheran* was of the greatest Note: Whereupon the Government ordered the *Marquess* of *Athole*, and Mr. *Owen Cameron*, Laird of *Logheel*, to raise their *Clans* and march with their Party against *Argyle*. They did so, and, in the *Evening*, pitched their *Camp* close by him. Here, in the Night, *Cameron*, *Patroling with a Party*, met another of his own Men, and taking them for *Enemies*, because they had lost the *Word*, in their *Cups*, killed Eight or Nine; among whom Two or Three happened to be Persons of Note; the Friends of those who were killed, resolving, if possible, to have him hanged, He was obliged to ride *Post* to the King. He went to his Majesty in the Dress he had travelled; and the King, being already informed how the Accident happened; instead of suffering him to tell his Story, commanded him to draw his *Broad-Sword*, intending to *Knight* him therewith: But *Cameron* could not draw it, because the *Scabbard* had got *Wet* on the Way: The King, observing the *Confusion* he was in, said, he knew the Reason that kept the *Sword* in the *Sheath*; adding that he never failed to draw it, in the *Service* of his *Father*, his

Brother, and *Himself*; whereupon he was *knighted* with another *Sword*, with the *Title* of *Sir Owen Cameron*: He returned to *Edenborough*, and from thence went as a *Volunteer*, to serve in the *Standing-Army*, which was then moving towards the *Coast of Galloway*, to prevent *Argyle* from *Landing*. For, upon the *Opposition* he found from the *Marquess* of *Athole* and his Men, with their *Assistants* in the *High-lands*, he shipped his Forces, and sailed round to the *West*, hoping to land there: But the Army moving along the Coast, always in Sight of him, compelled him to return the Way he came, till he landed in his own Country again. From thence, after gathering what Supplies of Men he could, He marched, and encamped, in the *Evening*, within two or three Miles of *Glasgow*. But the King's Army, having sent out *Scouts*, to discover what Way he took, encamped over against him, the same *Evening*, on an *Eminence*; there being a *Bog* between both *Armies*.

The *King*'s *Forces* consisted of the Earl of *Linlithgoe*'s Regiment of *Foot-Guards*, the Earl of *Mar*'s of *Foot*, *Clavers*'s of *Horse*, *Dunmore*'s of *Dragoons*, *Bochan*'s of *Foot*, and *Levingston*'s of *Horse-Guards*, with some Gentlemen of Quality, *Volunteers*; among whom the *Earl of Dunbarton* was of the greatest Note.

Here the Two *Armies* lay in Sight of each other; but, before *Morning*, *Argyle* was gone, his *High-landers* having deserted him; and then the *King*'s *Army* went to refresh themselves at *Glasgow*, waiting 'till it could be known, which Way *Argyle* had fled. It was soon understood that he had crossed the *Clyde* at *Kilpatrick*; and that *Sir John Cogheran* lay with a *Party*, in a *Stone-Dike-Park*, about Ten Miles off. The Lord *Ross* was therefore dispatched, with a *Party* of *Horse*, and Captain *Cleland*, who was now my Captain, (my Friend *Stuart* being Dead) with another of *Dragoons*, to find them out: When they came up to the *Park*, where Sir *John Cogheran* lay with his *Dutch*; they fired at one another, and some of the *King*'s *Soldiers fell*, among whom Captain *Cleland* was one; whereupon the Troop was given to Sir *Adam Blair* (who was likewise wounded in that rash *Engagement*) although, upon Duke *Hamilton*'s Application to the King, *I had been promised* to succeed *Cleland*: But,

Sir *Adam*, and Secretary *Melford*, being *Brothers-in-Law*, that Interest prevailed.

I must desire the *Reader*'s Pardon, for so frequently interspersing my own private Affairs, with those of the Publick; but what I chiefly proposed, was to write my *own Memoirs*, and not a *History of the Times*, further than I was concerned in them.

Night coming on, the *King's Party* withdrew, leaving Sir *John Cogheran* in the *Park*, who, notwithstanding this little Success, desired his Followers to shift for themselves, and left them before Morning. *Argyle* next Evening was found alone, a Mile above *Greenknock*, at the *Water-Side*, endeavouring to get into a little Boat, and grappling with the Owner thereof, (a poor *Weaver*.) It seems he wanted Presence of Mind, to engage the Man with a Piece of Money, to set him on the other Side. In the mean Time, Sir *John Shaw*, riding with some Gentlemen to *Greenknock*, and seeing the *Struggle*, seized the Earl, and carried him to *Glasgow*, from whence he was sent with a strong Guard to *Edenborough*, and sometime after *Beheaded*.

The next Day, the Army marched towards the Borders, against the *Duke of Monmouth*; but, an Express arriving of his Defeat, the Troops were commanded to repair to their several Quarters.

I shall here occasionally relate an unfortunate Accident, which happened this Summer in *Scotland*.

McDonnel, Laird of *Cappagh* in the *High-lands*, within Eight Miles of *Inverloghy*, was unjustly possessed, as most Men believed, for many Years, of an Estate, which in right belonged to the *Laird of Mackintosh*. Both these Gentlemen were *well affected* to the King. The *Laird of Cappagh*, after *Sowing-Time* was over, had gone that *Summer*, as it was his Custom, to make Merry with his *Clans*, on the *Mountains*, 'till the Time of *Harvest* should call him Home: But, in his Absence, *Mackintosh*, and his *Clans*, assisted with a *Party* of the *Army*, by Order from the *Government*, possessed himself of *Cappagh*'s *Estate*; whereupon *McDonnel*, and his Clans, returning from the *Mountains*, sett upon the *Enemy*, killed several Gentlemen among them, and took *Mackintosh* himself *Prisoner*. *McDonnel* had given strict Orders to his Men, not to kill any of the *Army*: But *Captain McKenzy*, who commanded on the other Side, making a Shot at one of *McDonnel*'s *Men*, who was pursuing his *Adversary*, the Man, discharged his *Pistol* at the *Captain*, shot him in the *Knee*, who after having been carried Fifty Miles to *Inverness*, to a *Surgeon*, died of his *Wound*.

Soon after, the *Government* ordered me to detach Sixty *Dragoons*, with a *Lieutenant*, *Cornet*, and *Standard*, and to march with *Captain Streighton*, and Two Hundred of the Foot-Guards, against the *McDonnels*; to destroy *Man*, *Woman*, and *Child*, pertaining to the *Laird of Cappagh*, and to burn his *Houses* and *Corn*. Upon the Approach of our *Party*, *McDonnel*, *Laird of Cappagh*, dismissing his *Prisoners*, retired farther into the *Mountains*: Whereupon we who were sent against him, continued to destroy all the *Houses* and *Corn*, from the Time of *Lammass* to the Tenth of *September*; and then, we advanced towards the *Borders*, to join the *Scotch Army*, which at that Time was marching towards *England*, against the Prince of *Orange*, who then intended an *Invasion*. We arrived thither the First of *October*, after a March of Two Hundred Miles.

General *Drummond* being then dead, *James Douglass*, Brother to the *Duke of Queensberry*, succeeded him as *Commander in Chief*: And *Graham*, *Laird of Clavers* (about this Time created Lord *Dundee*) was *Major-General*. On the First of *October*, the *Army* passed the *Tweede*, and drew up on the *Banks*, on the *English* Side, where the *General* gave a strict Charge to the *Officers*, that they should keep their Men, from offering the least Injury in their March; adding, that if he heard any of the *English* complain, the Officers should answer for the *Faults of their Men*; and so they arrived at *Carlile* that Night.

Next Day, *General Douglass*, by Order from the King, marched the Foot, by *Chester*, towards *London*; and *Dundee* the Horse, by *York*; to which City he arrived in Four or Five Days. The *Army* did not reach *London* 'till about the Five and Twentieth of *October*, being ordered, by the Contrivance of *Douglass*, the *General*, to march slow, on Purpose that the *Prince of Orange* might land, before the *King's Forces* should grow strong enough to oppose him.

The *Scotch Army*, at this Time, consisted of Four Regiments of *Foot*, One of *Horse*, One of *Dragoons*, and One *Troop* of *Horse-Guards*; and it was computed, that the *Earl* of *Feversham*, who was then *General of all the King's Forces*, had under his Command, of *English*, *Scotch* and *Irish*, an *Army* of near Thirty Thousand Men. Soon after the *Prince's Landing*, the King went to *Salisbury*, with a Guard of Two Hundred Horse, commanded by the old *Earl of Airly*, Two Days before the Body of the *Army* came up to him. The *Earl of Airly*, when he was *Lord Ogleby*, had attended the great Marquess of *Montrose* in all his Actions, for *King Charles the First, and Second*. But at this Time being Old, it was reported that he was dead, before the *Scotch Forces* went into *England*, to oppose the *Prince of Orange*; whereupon the King believing the Report, had given his *Troop* in *Dundee*'s *Regiment* to the *Earl of Anandale*: But the *Earl* having overtook the *Army* at *Cambridge*, in their March, went on to *London*, and there presenting himself before the King; his Majesty was so Just and Gracious, that he immediately restored his Lordship to the *Troop*, ordering him at the same Time, to command those Two Hundred Men, who attended him down to *Salisbury*.

When all the *Forces* were arrived at *Salisbury*, the *Earl of Dunmore*, with his *Regiment of Dragoons* (wherein I served) was ordered to a Pass Three Miles below the City, where I commanded the *Guard* that Night.

The same Morning that the *Army* arrived, the Great Men about the King, as the *Lord Churchill*, &c. to the Number of Thirty, advised his Majesty to take the Air on *Horse-Back*, intending, as the *Earl of Dunmore* was informed, to give up their Master to the *Prince*: But the King, probably suspecting the *Design*, returned in Haste to the City. Next Night, at a *Council of War*, called to consult what was fittest to be done in the present Juncture of Affairs, the very same great Men swore to stand by his Majesty with their *Lives* and *Fortunes*; and as soon as he was gone to Rest, mounting on *Horse-Back*, they all went over to the *Prince*, except the *Earl of Feversham*, *Dunbarton*, and a few very more: For the *Earl of Dunbarton* going to his Majesty, for Orders, at Four of the Clock in the Morning, found they were all departed.

Those Few who stayed with the King, advised his Majesty to return immediately to *London*; and the *Lord Dundee* was ordered to bring up the *Scotch-Horse*, and *Dragoons*, with the *Duke of Berwick's Regiment of Horse*, to *Reading*, where he joined *Dunbarton* with his *Forces*, and continued there Nine or Ten Days. They were, in all, about Ten Thousand strong. General *Douglass*, with his *Regiment of Foot Guards*, passing by *Reading*, lay at *Maidenhead*; from whence, one of his *Batallions* revolted to the *Prince*, under the Conduct only of a *Corporal*, whose Name was *Kemp*. However, *Douglass* assured the King, that this Defection happened against his Will; and yet when the Officers were ready to Fire upon the Deserters, his Compassion was such, that he would not permit them.

After this, the *Earl of Dunbarton*, and the *Lord Dundee*, with all the Officers, who adhered to the King, were ordered to meet his Majesty at *Uxbridge*, where he designed to fight the Prince: The *Earl of Feversham* got thither before the King and the Army arrived. When the Forces drew together, every Party sent an Officer to the *Earl of Feversham*, to receive his *Commands*. I attended his Lordship from my *Lord Dundee*, and was ordered with the rest, to wait 'till the King came to *Dinner*, his Majesty being expected within half an Hour; but it fell out otherwise: For the *Earl* to his great Surprize, received a Letter from the King, signifying, that his Majesty was *gone off*, and had no further Service for the *Army*. When I carried this *News* to my *Lord Dundee*, neither his *Lordship*, nor the Lords *Linlithgow* and *Dunmore*, could forbear falling into *Tears*: After which, being at a Loss what Course to take, I said to my *Lord Dundee*, that as he had brought us *out of Scotland*, he should convey us thither back again in a Body; adding, that the Forces might lye that Night at *Watford*, Six Miles off: My *Advice* was followed, and I went before, to get *Billets*, where to Quarter the Men. My *Lord Dundee* ordered all to be ready at Sound of *Trumpet*, and to unbridle their *Horses* no longer, than while they were eating their *Oats*. The Townsmen contrived to give out a *Report*, before Day, that the *Prince of Orange* was approaching, hoping to *affright* us away with a false *Alarm*: Whereupon we marched out, but at the same Time, drew up in a *strong Enclosure*, at the *Town*'s *End*; resolving to fight the *Prince*, if he should advance towards us. My *Lord Dundee* dispatched me immediately, to discover whether the Report of the *Prince*'s Approach were true; but I only met a *Messenger* with a Letter from his *Highness*, to my *Lord Dundee*, which I received and delivered to his Lordship. The Contents of it, as far as I am able to recollect, were as follows.

My *Lord Dundee*,

I understand you are now at Watford, *and that you keep your Men together*; *I desire you may stay there 'till farther Orders, and upon my Honour, none in my Army shall touch you.*

W. H. Prince of Orange.

Upon the Receipt of this *Letter*, our Forces returned into the Town, set up their *Horses*, and refreshed themselves. About Three in the Afternoon, there came *Intelligence*, that the King would be at *Whitehall* that Night, having returned from *Feversham*, whither he had fled in *Disguise*, and was ill treated by the *Rabble*, before they discovered him. Upon this Incident, the *Lords Dundee*, *Dunmore*, *Linlithgow*, and my *Self*, who desired Leave to go with my Colonel, took Horse; and arriving at *Whitehall*, a little after the King, had the *Honour* to kiss *his Majesty*'s *Hand*.

The next Morning, the *Earl of Feversham* was sent by the King, with some *Proposals* to the *Prince of Orange*, who was then at *Windsor*, where his Lordship was put in *Arrest* by the *Prince*'s Command, who sent the *Marquess of Hallifax*, the *Earl of Shrewsbury*, and the *Lord Delamair* (if I rightly Remember) to the King, with his *Highness*'s Order, that his Majesty should *remove* from *Whitehall*, next Day, before *Twelve o'Clock*. This Order was given about One in the Morning: At the same Time, a Barge was brought to *Whitehall-Stairs*, and a *Dutch-Guard* set about the King, without his Knowledge, but with *Directions*, to see him Safe, if he had a Mind to go on Board any *Ship*, in order to his Escape. A *Ship* it seems was likewise prepared, and his Majesty, attended by the *Lords Dunmore*,

Arran, and *Middleton*, went on *Board*; and then the Three *Lords* returned to *London*. The *Prince* arrived at St. *James*'s, about *Two Hours* after his Majesty's Departure; and the *Earl of Arran* went, among the rest, to attend his *Highness*, to whom, being introduced, he told the *Prince*, that the *King*, his *Master*, had commanded him, upon his Departure, to wait upon his *Highness*, and receive his *Commands*. The *Prince* replyed, he was glad to see him, and had an Esteem for *him*, and *all Men of Honour*; then turning aside to some other Persons, who were making their *Court*; Dr. *Burnet*, soon after made *Bishop of Salisbury*, who had been the *Earl of Arran's Governor*, coming up to his Lordship, cryed, *Ay my Lord Arran, you are now come in, and think to make a Merit when the Work is done.* To this Insult, the Earl, in the hearing of many, replyed only, *Come, Dr., we ken one another weel enough*: And the Earl's *own Father* told the *Prince, that if this young* Fellow were not secured, he would perhaps give his *Highness* some *Trouble*. Whereupon this noble young Lord was sent to the *Tower*, where he continued about a Year, and then returned to *Scotland*: And soon after, the young *Lord Forbes*, now *Earl of Granard*, was likewise imprisoned in the same Place. *King William* had made several Advances to his Lordship, as he did to many other Persons of Quality, to engage him in his Service; and sending for him one Day, asked him, why he did not take Care of his Regiment: My *Lord Forbes*, not being provided on a sudden with a better Answer, told the King, that having been born in *Ireland*, he had not Credit enough, he believed, to raise Men to fill up the Places of the *Papists* in his Regiment. *King William* thereupon said, he would take that Charge upon himself. *Lord Forbes*, having now recollected himself, said, he had likewise another Reason, why he found it necessary to decline his Service, but was unwilling to mention it, having not the least Intention to disoblige his *Highness*. The *Prince* desired that he might do it freely, and it should not disoblige him; whereupon my Lord said, that having sworn to retain his *Loyalty* to *King James*, he could not in *Honour* and *Conscience*, without his *Master's Permission*, enter into the *Service* of another *Prince*, during his Majesty's Life: Whereupon

King William, soon after, thought it proper to send him to the *Tower*; but however was so generous, as, in the Time of his *Confinement*, to send one of the *Clerks of the Treasury*, with an Order to pay him *Two Hundred Pounds*, as very reasonably thinking, that under the Loss of his Regiment, as well as of his *Rents* in *Ireland*, he might want Money to support himself. My *Lord Forbes*, having asked the *Clerk*, by whose Direction he brought that Sum; and the other answering, that he was only ordered to pay the Money to his *Lordship*, and to take his Receipt, conjectured this *Present* to have proceeded from *King William*; and therefore desired the *Clerk* to present his most humble *Respects and Thanks* to his *Highness*, and to let him know, that, as he never had done him *any Service*, he could not, *in Honour*, receive any *Marks of his Bounty*.

Upon this Subject I must add one more Particular, that when my *Lord Forbes* arrived with his *Regiment* out of *Ireland*, and attended on *King James*, he advised his *Majesty*, to fight the *Prince* upon the first *Opportunity after his landing*, before his Party should grow *Strong*: But those about the *King*, who had already engaged in the *other Interest*, would not suffer that *Advice* to be *followed*.

I now return to my *Lord Dundee*, and my *Lord Dunmore*. Their *Lordships* acted no longer as *Colonels*, when they understood that the *Prince* intended to place himself on the *Throne*, during his Majesty's Life: But the First, with the Twenty-Four Troopers, who followed him up from *Watford*, left *London*, and repaired, with the utmost Expedition, to his own *Castle*; and the Second, sometime after, to *Edenborough*; lying both quiet, 'till the *Convention* of the States of *Scotland* was called.

After their Lordships were gone to *Scotland*, I went to *Watford*, where my Lord *Kilsythe*, as Lieutenant Colonel, commanded the Lord *Dunmore*'s *Regiment of Dragoons*; the rest of the Army, which had been there, being gone to other Places. Then *Major General McCoy* ordered the Lord *Kilsythe* to march the *Regiment* from *Place* to *Place*, 'till they should come to *Congerton*, a Town in *Cheshire*. Here they quartered, when the *Prince and Princess of Orange* were proclaimed *King and Queen of England*, &c. by the *Sherriff* and *Three* or *Four Bailiffs*. It happened to be a very *stormy Day*; and when the *Sheriff* had done his Office, a *crack-brained Fellow*, at the Head of a great *Rabble*, proclaimed the Duke of *Monmouth* King, to the great Diversion of the *Regiment*, not believing he had been *Beheaded*.

When my *Lord Dunmore* refused to serve *the Prince of Orange*, Sir *Thomas Levingston*, of my *Lord Kilsythe's Family*, got the *Regiment*. This Gentleman was born in *Holland*, and often used to raise *Recruits* in *Scotland*; upon which account, he was well known to the *Regiment*. He came down, Post, to *Congerton*, and at Supper, told the *Officers*, that he was sent to know, which of them would serve *King William*, and which would not? Now the *Oath of Allegiance* to that *Prince*, having not been offered to that *Regiment*, one of the Company answered; that we having sworn *Allegiance* to *King James*, could not, in *Conscience* and *Honour*, draw our *Swords against him*: Whereupon Sir *Thomas*, drinking an *Health to King James, upon his Knees*, answered, that he wished he might be *damned*, whenever he should command them to break *that Oath*: And, in order to ingratiate himself further with the *Regiment*, added, that he would return to *London* next Day, for a Command to march them straight to *Scotland*, where their *Wives* and *Friends* were; and likewise to procure a *Captain's Commission* for *Me*, since Sir *Adam Blair*, who commanded the Troop, in which I was *Lieutenant*, had refused to serve *King William*, both which he accordingly obtained.

When he returned from *London*, he marched, with the *Regiment*, directly through *Berwick*, into *Scotland*: And as they passed by *Edenborough*, (the Castle whereof was kept *for King James*, by the *Duke of Gordon*) Sir *Thomas* and my Lord *Kilsythe* went into the Town, to receive *Duke Hamilton's Commands*, who was then *High Commissioner*; and some other *Officers* went in at the same Time, to see their *Wives* and *Friends*.

The Duke asked Sir *Thomas, where I was*, and, being informed that I was gone to *Sterling*, desired I might be sent for. Upon my attending his *Grace*, he was pleased to say, that he had been *always my Friend*; and that now he had it in his Power to *provide for me*, if I would be *true to my Trust*; (for he supposed I had taken the *Oath to King William*) and, upon my Answer, that *I would be True to what I had Sworn*, the Duke replyed, it was very well.

Upon this Occasion, and before I proceed further, I think it will be proper to make *some Apology for my future Conduct*; because I am conscious, that many People, who are in *another Interest*, may be apt to think and speak hardly of me: But I desire they would please to consider, that the *Revolution* was then an *Event altogether new*, and had put many Men, *much wiser than myself*, at a loss how to proceed. I had taken the *Oath of Allegiance to King James*; and, having been bred up under the strictest Principles of *Loyalty*, could not force my *Conscience* to dispense with that *Oath*, during his *Majesty's Life*. All those Persons of Quality in *Scotland*, to whom I had been most obliged, and on whom I chiefly *depended*, did still adhere to *that Prince*. Those People, whom, from my Youth, I had been taught to *Abhor*; whom, by the Commands of my *Superiors*, I had constantly treated as *Rebels;* and who consequently conceived an *irreconcileable Animosity* against me; were, upon this *great Change*, the highest in *Favour* and *Employments*. And lastly, the *established Religion in Scotland*, which was *Episcopal*, under which I had been educated, and to which I had always born the highest *Veneration*, was now utterly *destroyed* in that Kingdom; (although preserved in the other Two) and the *Presbyterian Kirk*, which had ever been my *greatest Aversion*, exalted in its Stead.

Upon all these Considerations; I hope every candid *Reader* will be so just to believe, that, supposing me in an *Error*, I acted at least *sincerely*, and according to the *Dictates of my Conscience*; and, as it is Manifest, without any *worldly View*: For, I had then considerable Offers made me, and in all Probability should have been greatly advanced, if I could have persuaded myself to accept them.

Having said thus much to excuse my *Conduct*, from that Time forward; I shall now proceed to relate *Facts* and *Passages*, just as they happened; and avoid, as much as possible, giving any *Offence*.

My *Lord Dunmore* being then at *Edenborough*, I thought it my Duty to pay my *Respects* to his *Lordship*, who had been also my *Colonel*. He was pleased to invite me to dine with him, that Day at a *Tavern*; where, he said, *Lieutenant General Douglass,* (who had left *England*, a little before, on some Pretence or other) the *Lord Kilsythe, Captain Levingston, Captain Murray, and Lieutenant Murray, (all his a'ne Lads, as his Lordship expressed himself)* were to meet him. I objected against *Douglass*, that he was not to be *trusted*; (this was the same Man, who afterwards was *Lieutenant General of King William*'s *Army in Ireland*, against *King James*; and whose Name will never be forgot in that *Kingdom*, on Account of his many *Ravages* and *Barbarities* committed there;) but his Lordship answered, that he would *pawn his Life* for his *Honesty*; because my Lord *Dundee* had assured him, that the *Lieutenant General* had given him his *Faith* and *Honour*, to be with him in Five Days, if he marched to the *Hills* to declare for *King James*. Whereupon I submitted my *Scruples* to my *Colonel*'s *Judgment*; and accordingly, we all met together at the *Tavern*.

Dinner was no sooner done, than we heard the News *that King James* was landed in *Ireland:* Then *Douglass* taking a *Beer-Glass*, and looking round him, said, *Gentlemen, we have all eat of his Bread, and here is his Health*; which he drank off, *on his Knees*, and all the Company did the same: Then filling another *Bumper*, He drank *Damnation* to all, who would ever draw a Sword *against* him.

I then returned to *Sterling*, and soon after, the States of *Scotland* met. To this *Convention* my Lord *Dundee* went *incognito*; lest the *Rabble*, who had threatened his *Person*, should *assault* him in the *Streets*. He made a *Speech* to the *House*, to the following Purpose; *That he came thither as a Peer of the Realm, to serve his Majesty; and that if the King had no Service for him, he hoped, that Honourable Assembly would protect him as a peaceable Subject, from the Rage of his Enemies.*

Upon receiving an Answer from the *States*, that they could not possibly do it, he slipt out of the House, and privately withdrew from the Town; followed by the *Twenty Four Troopers*, who had attended him thither: And, as he rode by the *Castle*, seeing the Duke of *Gordon*, who commanded it, walking on the *Walls*; He charged his Grace, to keep the Place

o

for King James, 'till he should hear further from *Him*, who was then going, he said, to appear in the *Field* for his Majesty.

His Lordship had no sooner left the Town, than one Major *Bunting*, with a Party, (by Order from the *Convention*) followed, with Directions to seize him: Whereupon my Lord *Dundee*, commanding his Attendants to march on gently, stopped to speak with the Major; and, understanding his *Errand*, advised him to return, or he would send him back to his Masters, *in a Pair of Blankets*, as he expressed himself. The Major (who perhaps was no *Enemy* to his Lordship) returned accordingly; and my Lord arrived at his *Castle*; where he stayed only that Night: For in the Morning, taking Four Thousand Pounds with him, he went into the *Highlands*, to Sir *Owen Cameron*; where he was soon joyned by the *Laird of Cappagh*, who, sometime before, had been driven out of his Estate by order of *King James*, (as I have already related) and by many other *Gentlemen of Quality*.

Major General McCoy, coming to *Edenborough* at this Juncture, was ordered to march the Forces, which he brought with him, against my Lord *Dundee*. These Forces consisted of Three or Four Regiments of Foot, and one of Horse; besides Sir *Thomas Levingston*'s of Dragoons. They stopped, in their March, a Night or Two at *Dundee*. The first Night, I got privately into the *Castle*, (as it had been agreed between my Lord *Kilsythe and Me*) and there assured my Lady *Dundee*, that the *Regiment of Dragoons*, in which I served, should be at her *Lord's Service*, whenever he pleased to Command, whereof her Ladyship gave Notice next Day to her Husband; who sent Me a Note, by a *ragged Highlander*, which I received as we were on our March, from the Town of *Dundee*, towards the *Highlands*. The Contents of my Lord's Note, were, *That he had written to the* King, *to send him Two Thousand Foot, and One Thousand Horse, out of* Ireland; *and that, as soon as those Forces were arrived, he would expect me with the Regiment of Dragoons.*

When *Major General McCoy* came within Sight of my Lord *Dundee*, Night coming on, obliged him to Halt; which gave Opportunity to his Lordship to retreat in the Morning; but *McCoy* followed him all Day; whereupon, facing about, my

Lord advanced towards him, which caused the *Major General* to retreat in his Turn. Thus we spent about Three Weeks, sometimes pursuing, and sometimes pursued; our Leader, *McCoy*, still writing every Post, for new Supplies; 'till at last, one Regiment of Dragoons, and another of Foot, came to his Assistance, on the Fifth *Day of June*, 1689. When this Reinforcement came, he got Intelligence of my *Lord Kilsythe's Intention, and mine*, of going over with the Regiment to *my Lord Dundee*.

All People agreed, that Lieutenant General *Douglass*, who had made so many *solemn Professions* of his *Loyalty to King James*, and whose *Health* he had *drank on his Knees*, was the very Person, who had given this Intelligence to *McCoy*; because, he alone knew what had passed at the *Tavern*, where we dined; and because, instead of going with *Dundee*, as he had promised him, upon his *Faith* and *Honour*, he had rid Post for *London*.

From this Period, *my Troubles* began; for, I was then sent up to *Edenborough*, and there imprisoned in the *Tolbooth*, together with My Lord *Kilsythe*, Captain *Levingston*, Captain *Murray*, and Lieutenant *Murray*; each of us in a separate Dungeon; with Orders that none should be permitted to speak with us, except through the *Key-Hole*: And in this *miserable Condition*, we lay for *Two Months*.

My Lord *Kilsythe's Friends* were under great Apprehensions, that I would *betray* his Lordship. But my Lord did me the *Justice*, to assure them, that I would suffer the *worst Extremity*, rather than be guilty of so *infamous* an *Action*; which, he said, they should find, upon any *Temptation* that might offer. When we had been close confined in our *Dungeons* for Two Months, we were brought before the Council, One by One, to be examined, concerning our Knowledge of my Lord *Kilsythe's* Intention, to carry off the *Regiment*. *Levingston* and the Two *Murrays*, having not been *privy* to that *Design*, were able to discover nothing to his Lordship's *Prejudice*; and were likewise Gentlemen of too much *Honour*, to purchase their Liberty with a *Lye*; Whereupon they were remanded back to their several *Dungeons*. It was my Turn to be next examined; and I was *strongly suspected*; but notwithstanding my *Liberty* was promised me, if I would discover all I knew of the Matter, the Lord *Advocate*, at the same Time also urging, I must have certainly been *privy* to it; I positively denied any *Knowledge* of that *Affair*; adding, that I believed my Lord *Kilsythe* had never entertained such a *Design*; or if he had, that it was altogether *improbable* his Lordship should impart it to me, a poor *Stranger*, born in *Ireland*; and yet keep it a Secret from Gentlemen *of the Kingdom*, in whom he might much better *confide*. This I still repeated, and stood to, with great Firmness; even after I saw the *Hang-Man*, with the torturing *Boots, standing at my Back:* Whereupon I was likewise returned to my *Dungeon*.

The Council, although they could force no Confession from Me, or my Companions, that might affect my Lord *Kilsythe, on whose Estate their Hearts were much set*, yet resolved to make a Sacrifice of some one among us. But, the other Gentlemen being of their own Kindred and Country, and I a Stranger, as well as much hated for prosecuting the *Covenanters*, (who by the Change of the *Times, Measures* and *Opinions*, were now grown into high Favour with the Government, as I have before mentioned) the Lot fell on me, and they gave out a Report, that I should be hanged within a few Days. But, a Gentleman, then in Town, one Mr. *Buchannan*, who held a *secret Correspondence* with my Lord *Dundee*, sent his Lordship Intelligence of this their Resolution concerning me.

That Lord was then at the Castle of *Blair* of *Athole*; and, having Notice of the Danger I was in, wrote a Letter to Duke *Hamilton*, President of the Council, desiring his Grace to inform the Board, *That if they hanged Captain* Creichton, *or,* (*to use his own homely Expression,*) *if they touched an Hair of his Tail, he would cut the Laird of* Blair, *and the Laird of* Pollock, *Joint by Joint, and would send their Limbs in Hampers to the Council*.

These Two Gentlemen, having been taken Prisoners at St. *Johnstown*, by my Lord *Dundee*, were still kept in Confinement: Whereupon the *Duke*, though it was Night, called the Council, which met immediately, supposing that the Business, which pressed so much, might relate to some *Express from Court*. But when the Clerk read my Lord *Dundee*'s Letter, they appeared in great Confusion: Whereupon the Duke said,

I fear we dare not touch an Hair of Creichton; for, ye all know *Dundee* too well, to doubt whether he will be punctual to his Word; and the Two Gentlemen in his Hands are too nearly allied to some here, that their Lives should be endangered on this Occasion. What his Grace said was very true; for, if I remember right, the Laird of *Blair* had married a Daughter of a *former Duke of Hamilton.* The Issue of the Matter was, that, under this Perplexity, they all cryed out, *Let the Fellow live a while longer.*

Not long after this, happened the Battle of *Gillicranky,* near the *Castle of the Blair of Athole*; where the Forces under the Lord *Dundee,* consisting of no more than Seventeen Hundred Foot, (all *Highlanders,* except Three Hundred, sent him from *Ireland,* under the Command of Colonel *Cannon,* when he expected *Three Thousand,* as I have mentioned,) and *Forty Five Horse,* routed an Army of *Five Thousand* Men, with Major General *McCoy* at their Head; took *Fifteen Hundred* Prisoners, and killed a great Number, among whom *Colonel Balfour* was one. *McCoy* escaped, and fled that Night *Twenty Five* Miles End-Ways, to the Castle of *Drummond.*

But my Lord *Dundee* did not live to see himself *Victorious*: For, as he was wheeling about a Rock, over the Enemy's Heads, and making down the Bray to attack them, (they making a running Fire,) he was killed by a Random Shot, at the Beginning of the Action: Yet his Men discovered not his Fall, 'till they had obtained the Victory. The next Day, though Victorious, they suffered their Prisoners to depart, on *Parole,* that they would never *take up Arms against King James,* Colonel *Fergusson* only accepted, on account of his more than ordinary Zeal for the new Establishment.

King William, having heard of this Defeat, said, *He knew the Lord* Dundee *so well, that he must have been either killed, or mortally wounded; otherwise, before that Time, he would have been Master of* Edenborough.

I now desire Leave to return to my own Affairs. About Four Months after my *Examination,* I was advised, in *plain Words,* by the Dukes of *Hamilton* and *Queensberry,* who were then going up to *London,* that I should bribe *Melvil,* then

Secretary of *Scotland*; with whom their Graces likewise would use their Interest, to get an Order from *King William* for my *Liberty*. But I was so far from having Money to *bribe a Courtier* of the *Secretary*'s *Rank*, that I had hardly enough to support myself: Whereupon my noble Friend, the Lord *Kilsythe*, who thought himself indebted to my *Fidelity* for his *Life* and *Fortune*, was so extremely generous, as to make me a Present of *Five Hundred Pounds*, which I immediately sent to *Melvil*; who thereupon, joyning his Interest with the good Officers of the two Dukes before mentioned, prevailed with *King William*, to send down an Order; upon the Receipt of which, I was to be set at *Liberty* by the Council. But they would not obey it, alledging that the King was misinformed; and, out of the Abundance of their Zeal, wrote to him, that if *Captain Creichton* should obtain his *Liberty*, he would *Murder all Scotland in One Night*.

Thus my Hope of *Liberty* vanished: For, *King William* soon after going to *Flanders*, and not thinking it prudent to discredit the *Representation* which the Council had made of Me, as so very dangerous a Person, left me in the *Tolbooth*; although the Two Dukes, out of their great Friendship, (which I should be most ungrateful ever to forget) had both offered to answer, *Body* for *Body*, for my future peaceable *Demeanour*. But notwithstanding all this, King *William*, for the Reason before mentioned, left me Prisoner in the *Tolbooth*, as I said; where I continued Two Years and an Half longer, without *One Penny of Money*; though not without many Friends, whose *Charity* and *Generosity* supported me under this heavy *Affliction*.

My Wife and two Boys, with as many Daughters, were in Town, all the time of my Confinement. The Boys died young, but the Mother and the two Girls, lived to endure many Hardships; having been twice plundered, by the Rabble, of the little Substance they had left: However, they and my self were still *providentially* relieved by some Friend or other; and particularly once, by the Lady *Carnwath*, (Mother of the *present Earl*) who, when we had not one Penny left to buy Bread, sent us up a Sack of Meal, and a Basket of Fowl, *sixty Miles from Edenborough*.

My fellow Prisoners and I, after the Time of our Examination by the Council, were allowed, for four or five Hours every Day, to converse with each other, and with our Friends; And, when we had been three Years in the *Tolbooth*, my Companions, being related to the best Families in the Kingdom, were at last permitted, on Bail, to lodge in the City, with a Centry at each of their Doors. But I was not allowed the same *Favour*, 'till two Months after; when Duke *Hamilton*, still my Friend, with much Difficulty and strong Application to the Council, obtained it for me: And when the Order was at last granted, I was at a great Loss to find such a Person for my Bail, whom the Council would approve of; 'till the Laird of *Pettencrife*, a Gentleman, whom I had never seen before, sent up his Name (without any *Application from me*) to the Clerk, and was accordingly accepted.

I had not been Two Months discharged out of the *Tolbooth*, and removed to a private Lodging in the Town, with a *Centry* upon me, when the Government, upon some Pretence or other, filled the *Castle* with a great Number of Persons of Quality; among whom were the Lords *Kilsythe*, *Hume*, and several others; and the *Tolbooth* again, with as many of inferior Note, as it could hold.

In a Week, after I had been permitted to live in the City with my Family: I found the *Centry* had Orders to keep me close, without allowing me to stir from my *Lodgings*, upon any *Pretence whatsoever*: But when another Regiment came to relieve that, which was before upon Duty, I bribed *Him*, who had been my *Keeper*, at his going off, that he should tell the first who came in his Place, that his Orders were to *walk with me to any Part of the Town I pleased*. This was accordingly done, and thence forward, I used to take my *Centry* along with me, and visit my old fellow Prisoners, the *Gillicranky-Men*, and sometimes stay with them all Night; at other times, my Friends would do the same at my Lodgings; among whom the Lord *William Douglass* often did me that *Honour*: Nay, sometimes, in Company of some Gentlemen, I would leave the *Centry* drinking with the *Foot-Men* in an *Ale-house*, at the Back of the *Town-Wall*, while we rambled Nine or Ten Miles into the Country, to visit some Acquaintance or other; still taking care to return before *Two in the Afternoon*, which was the Hour of *Parade*, to save the *Centry* from Danger.

Thus I spent about Two Months, 'till the Day the Government had filled the *Castle* and the *Tolbooth* again, as I have mentioned already. As soon as I was told of my Lord *Kilsythe*'s Imprisonment, I knew the Danger I was in, and had just Time to run with the *Centry* to a *Cellar*, where I found Twelve Officers got together, for Shelter, likewise from the Storm, a little before me. We stayed there close 'till Night, and then dispatched my *Centry*, with Captain *Mair*'s *Footman*, to the *Lady Lockhart*'s (who was married to the Captain) Four Miles out of Town, to let her know, that her Husband would be at home that Night, with Twelve other *Cavaliers*, (for so in those Days we affected to Stile ourselves) to avoid being imprisoned in the *Tolbooth*.

When the Message was delivered, the Lady ordered Three or Four of her Servants to take up the *Centry* Four *Pair of Stairs*, and to ply him well with *Drink*. Accordingly they kept him drunk for Twelve Days and Nights together, so that he neither saw me, nor I him, in all that Time. Two Days after we came to Lady *Lockhart*'s, I determined, against her and her Friends *Advice*, to return privately to *Edenborough*, to discourse with the *Laird of Pettencrife*, my *Bail*; resolving, at all Adventures, that so *generous* a Person should not be a Sufferer, *on my Account*. I accordingly repaired, in the Night, to the same *Ale-house*, at the Back of the *Town-Wall*, and thence sent the *Footman*, who attended me, to bring the Laird thither. He presently came, with Two other Gentlemen in his Company; and, after drinking together for Half an Hour *He bid me go whither I pleased, and God's Blessing along with me*; whereupon, thrusting me out of the Door, in a friendly Manner, added, that he would pay the Hundred Pounds he was bound in, to the Council, next Morning, if demanded of him, which they accordingly did, and the Money was paid.

I then returned to the Company, at my Lady *Lockhart*'s, and thence wrote to the Two Dukes before mentioned for their Advice, what Course to take? Their Answer was,

That, in regard to my poor Family, I should make my Escape to my own Country, and there set Potatoes; *'till I saw better Times.* At the End of Twelve Days, Captain *Mairs* and his *Eleven Friends* got over Seas to *St. Germains*; when I likewise took my Leave of them and the Lady, to make the best of my Way for *Ireland*. But I bethought me of the *poor Centry*, (to whom the Twelve Days, we stayed there, seemed no longer than Two or Three, so well was he plyed with Drink) and calling for him, asked, whether he would chuse to share with me and my *Fortunes*, or go back to the Regiment, perhaps to be shot for Neglect of his Duty? He readily answered, that he would go with me whither ever I went; and not long after we came into *Ireland*, I had the good Luck to get him made a *Serjeant of Grenadiers*, in the Regiment, formerly commanded by my Lord *Dunbarton*, by a Captain, who was then gone thither for Recruits; in which Regiment he died a Lieutenant some Years after.

The Lady, at parting, made me a Present of a good Horse, with Ten Dollars, to bear my Charges on the Way; and moreover hired a Tenant's Horse to carry the *Centry* to the *Borders*. I durst not be seen to pass through *Galloway*, and therefore went, by *Carlisle*, to *Whitehaven*. Here I found an Acquaintance, who was Minister of the Town, of the Name of *Marr*; a Gentleman of great *Worth* and *Learning*. Before the *Revolution*, he had been Minister of a Parish in *Scotland*, near the *Borders*: But about the Time of that *Event*, the *Rabble*, as he told me the *Story*, came to his House, in the Night, to Rob and Murder him; having treated others, of his Brethren, the *Episcopal Clergy*, before, in that inhuman Manner. He was a single Man, and had but One Man Servant, whose Business was to dress his *Meat*, and make his *Bed*; and while the *Villains* were breaking into the House, he had just Time to put on his *Breeches*, *Stockings* and *Shoes*, and no more; for by that Time they were got in; when he thought it better to leap out at the *Window*, but half cloathed, as he was, than to expose his Life to the Fury of such, whose very Mercies might be cruel. Thus he saved his Life, and made his Escape to the *English Side*, with only *Four Dollars* in his Pocket; leaving his *Goods*, *House* and *Parish*, as *Plunder*, to those *Saints*; who doubtless looked on such as he was, as no other than an *Usurper* of what, of right, pertained to them; pursuant to the Maxim, *That Dominion is founded in Grace*.

And here I beg Leave to relate the Treatment, which *another Episcopal Clergy-Man* received from that *Tribe*, about the same Time: His Name was *Kirkwood*, whom I likewise knew, before the *Revolution*, Minister of a Parish in *Galloway*, in Scotland, and afterwards Rector in the County of *Fermanagh*, in *Ireland*. Among other good Qualities, this Gentleman was a very *facetious Person*; and by his *Presence of Mind*, in making use of this Talent, he had the good Fortune to save both his *Life* and *Goods*, from the Fury of those *Godly Men*, who then thought all Things their own. When they broke into the House, he was in Bed; and sitting up in his Shirt, desired leave, to speak a few Words before he died; which (I cannot tell how it happened) they granted, and he spoke to this Effect; *That he had always prayed to God, he might die in his Bed, adding, that he had in his House as good* Ale *and* Brandy, *as any in all Scotland; and therefore hoped the* worthy Gentlemen *would do him the* Honour *to drink with him, before they did any thing* rashly.

This *facetious Speech*, which they little expected from him, in the Article of so much Danger as then threatened him, had the Luck to *divert* them from their *bloody Purpose*, and to make them comply with his Request: So that after drinking plentifully, they said he was an *hearty Cheel*; and left him in quiet Possession of his *House* and *Goods*. But he durst not trust his *Talent* to *another Tryal*, lest the next Company might not be influenced, as this First had been; and therefore, as soon as it was Day, made off, with his *Family* and *Effects*, in the best Manner he could; and rested not 'till he was safe in *Ireland*.

I could not forbear relating these *Stories*, from the Gentlemen's own Mouths, as I might do others of the same Kind, upon my own Knowledge; though they are *contradictory* to what the *Preachers of the new established Kirk* have so confidently given out. They would fain have the World believe, that they shewed great *Indulgence* to the *Episcopal Clergy*, at the *Revolution*, and for several Years after. But they must grant me and others Leave not to believe them: Nor ought they to be angry, if I give the *Reader* a further Idea of them, and of the *Spirit* that reigned in the *Synods, Conventions, or General Assemblies of their Kirk.*

During my *Confinement* in the *Tolbooth,* a *General Assembly* was called; to which my Lord *Lothian,* as I was informed afterwards, was sent *Commissioner* from *King William.* His Lordship's Instructions were, to signify to them the King's Desire, that as many of the *Episcopal Clergy,* as would take the *Oath of Allegiance* to him, might keep Possession of their several *Parishes.* To this the Members answered, in a *disdainful Manner, What! shall we suffer any scabbed Sheep among us? Na, na, nat ane*; and thereupon sent Two of their Brethren to *King William,* who was then in *Flanders,* to move him for more *Favours to the Kirk,* and Power, further to *Oppress* the *Episcopal Clergy.* But that Prince told them, in plain Terms, that he had been imposed upon, in granting to the *Kirk,* the *Favours* she had *already got*; and withal commanded them, to let the *General Assembly* know, that it was his *Will* and *Pleasure,* that they should live peaceably with those, who were willing to live so with them; otherwise he would make them know, *that he was their Master.*

With this *unwelcome Answer,* from *King William,* the Two *Spiritual Envoys* returned to those who sent them; and at the same Time, or soon after, that *Prince* dispatched an Order to the *Commissioner* to *Dissolve* the *Assembly,* if he found them persisting in their *Severity,* towards the *Episcopal Clergy.*

As soon as the *Legates* delivered the *Message,* all in the *Assembly* began to speak out, with the greatest Boldness imaginable; saying, *That the King durst not have sent them such an Answer, if he had not an Army at his Back:* Whereupon the *Commissioner* dissolved the *Synod*; and, in the *King's Name,* commanded all the *Members* to depart to their *several Homes.*

But, instead of obeying that Order, they all went, in a Body, with that poor *weak Creature,* the Lord *Crawford,* at their *Head,* to the *Market-Cross*; and there published a *Protestation,* declaring, that the King had no *Authority* in *Church-Affairs,* nor any Right to *Dissolve their General Assembly.*

I relate this *Story*, as it was told me, not only to give the Reader an Idea of the Spirit, that reigned in that *Kirk*, established now in *Scotland*, as I have said, but likewise to do *Justice* to the *Memory* of *King William*, (which may be the more acceptable, as coming from one, who was in a *contrary Interest*.) And indeed I have so good an Opinion *of that Prince*, as to believe he would have acted much better than he did, with Regard to the *Civil and Ecclesiastical Constitution in Scotland*, if he had been permitted to govern by his own Opinions.

But now to come to the Conclusion of my *Story*. The *Hollantide* after I arrived in *Ireland*, my Wife and Two Daughters followed me; and we settled in the *County of Tyrone*, with my Father, (who died Two Years afterwards) on a small *Free-Hold*; where I have made an hard Shift to maintain them with *Industry*, and even *Manual Labour*, for about *Twelve Years*, 'till my Wife died, and my Daughters were married, which happened not very long after I became a *Widower*.

I am at present in the Eighty-Third Year of my Age, still hated by those People, who affirm the old *Covenanters* to have been unjustly dealt with; and therefore believe a great Number of improbable *Stories* concerning me; as that I was a common *Murderer of them*, and their *Preachers*, with many other false and improbable *Stories*. But the *Reader*, I hope, from whom I have not concealed any one *Transaction* or *Adventure*, that happened to me, among *those rebellious People*, or misrepresented the least *Circumstance*, as far as my Memory could serve me; will judge whether, he hath reason to believe me, to have been such a Person as they represented me; and to hate me, as they do, upon that Account. And my Comfort is, that I can appeal from their *unjust Tribunal*, to the *Mercy of God*; before whom, by the Course of Nature, I must soon appear; who knows the Integrity of my Heart, and that my Actions (condemned by them) were, as far as my Understanding could direct me, meant for the *good of the Church*, and the *Service of my King and Country*.

And, although such People hate me, because they give Credit to the false Reports raised concerning me; another

Comfort left me in my old Age is, that I have constantly preserved (and still do so) the Love and Esteem of all honest and good Men, to whom I have had the Happiness, at any Time, to be Known.

JOHN CREICHTON.

The End.

In the Year of our Lord, 1730.

REMARKS

BISHOP BURNET's HISTORY.

THIS author is in most particulars the worst qualified for an historian that ever I met with. His style is rough, full of improprieties, in expressions often Scotch, and often such as are used by the meanest people. He discovers a great scarcity of words and phrases, by repeating the same several hundred times, for want of capacity to vary them. His observations are mean and trite, and very often false. His Secret History is generally made up of coffee-house scandals, or at best from reports at the third, fourth, or fifth hand. The account of the Pretender's birth, would only become an old woman in a chimney-corner. His vanity runs intolerably through the whole book, affecting to have been of consequence at nineteen years old, and while he was a little Scotch parson of 40 pounds a year. He was a gentleman born, and, in the time of his youth and vigour, drew in an old maiden daughter of a Scotch Earl to marry him. His characters are miserably wrought, in many things mistaken, and all of them detracting, except of those who were friends to the Presbyterians. That early love of liberty he boasts of is absolutely false; for the first book that I believe he ever published is an entire treatise in favour of passive obedience and absolute power; so that his reflections on the clergy, for asserting, and then changing those principles, come very improperly from him. He is the most partial of all writers that ever pretended so much to impartiality; and yet I, who knew him well, am convinced that he is as impartial as he could possibly find in his heart; I am sure more than I ever expected from him; particularly in his accounts of the Papist and Fanatic plots. This work may be more properly called,

A History of Scotland during the author's time, with some digressions relating to England, rather than deserve the title he gives it. For I believe two thirds of it relate only to that beggarly nation, and their insignificant brangles and factions. What he succeeds best in, is in giving extracts of arguments and debates in council or parliament. Nothing recommends his book but the recency of the facts he mentions, most of them being still in memory, especially the story of the Revolution; which, however, is not so well told as might be expected from one who affects to have had so considerable a share in it. After all, he was a man of generosity and good-nature, and very communicative; but, in his ten last years, was absolute party-mad, and fancied he saw Popery under every bush. He hath told me many passages not mentioned in this History, and many that are, but with several circumstances suppressed or altered. He never gives a good character without one essential point, that the person was tender to dissenters, and thought many things in the church ought to be amended.

Setting up for a maxim, Laying down for a maxim, Clapt up, Decency, and some other words and phrases, he uses many hundred times.

Cut out for a Court, A pardoning planet, Clapt up, Left in the lurch, The Mob, Outed, A great beauty, Went roundly to work: All these phrases used by the vulgar, shew him to have kept mean or illiterate company in his youth.

Autobiographical Pieces

FAMILY OF SWIFT

THE Family of the Swifts was antient in Yorkshire, from them descended; a noted Person who passed under the name of Cavaliero Swift, a Man of Wit and humor. He was made an Irish peer by King James or K Charles 1. with the Title of Baron Carlingford, but never was in that Kingdom. Many traditionall pleasant Storyes are related of him, which the Family planted in Ireland hath receivd from their parents. [Another of the same *crossed out*] This Lord dyed without Issue male, and his heiress whether of the first or second Descent was married to Robt Fielding Esqr commonly called handsom Fielding, she brought him a considerable Estate [but *crossed out*] in York-shire, which he squandred away, but had no Children: The Earl of Eglington marryed another Coheiress of the same family, as he hath often told me.

Another of the same family was / Sr Edwd. Swift, well p. 2 known in the times of the great Rebellion and usurpation, but I am ignorant whether he left heirs or no.

Of the other branch whereof the greatest part settled in Ireland The Founder was William Swift Prebendary of Canterbury, towards the last years of Qu. Elisab. and during the reign of K. James 1st. He was a Divine of some distinction. There is a Sermon of his extant and the Title is to be seen in the Catalogue of the Bodleyan Library, but I never could get a Copy, and I suppose it would now be of little value.

This William marryed the Heiress of Philpot, I suppose a Yorkshire Gentleman, by whom he got a very considerable estate, which however she kept in her own power, I know not by what artifice. [*Added in the margin*: She was a capricious ill-natured and passionate woman, of which I have been told severall instances] and it hath been a continuall tradition in the family that she absolutely disinherited her onely son Thomas for no greater crime than that of robbing an orchard when he / was a boy. And thus much is certain that Thomas p. 3

187

never enjoyed more than one hundred pounds a year which
was all at Goodrich in Herefordshire, [*added in margin:* except—
above and *crossed out*—a Church or Chaptr Lease, which was not
renewed] whereof not above one half is now in the possession
of a great-great-grandson.

His original picture is now in the hands of Godwin Swift
of Dublin Esqr his great Grandson as well as that of his wife's
[*added in margin:* who seems to have a good deal of the Shrew in
her Countenance] whose [of *erased*] arms as an heiress are
joined with his own, and by the last he seems to have been
a person somewhat fantastick. For there he gives as his
device a Dolphin (in those days called a Swift) twisted about
an Anchor, with this motto, Festine lente.

There is likewise a Seal with the same coat of arms, (but
not joynd with the wifes) which the sd William commonly
made use of, and this is also now in the Possession of Godwin
Swift above mentioned.

p. 4   His eldest son Thomas seems to [be *erased*] have been a
Clergy-man before his Fathers death. He was Vicar of Goodri-[*dge*]ch in Herefordshire, within a mile or two of Ross, he
had likewise another Church-living with about one hundred
pounds a year in Land (part whereof was by Church Leases)
     [N.B. *The phrase in brackets crossed out and three and a half*
     lines in the margin thoroughly obliterated.]
as I have already mentioned. He built a house on his own Land
in the Village of Goodri[*dge*]ch, which by the Architecture,
denotes the builder to have been somewhat whimsical and
singular, and very much towards a Projector. The house is
above an hundred years old and still in good repair, inhabited
by a Tenant of the femal line, but the Landlord a young
Gentleman lives upon his own estate in Ireland. [*Another*
passage entirely obliterated in the margin.]

This Thomas was more [*later:* much] distinguished by his
courage, as well as his loyalty to K. Charles the 1st, and the
Sufferings he underwent for that Prince, more than any person
p. 5 of his condition in England. Some Historians / of those times
relate severall particulars [*in margin:* See a book called Mercurius Rusticus, and another in Folio called the Lives of those

who suffered persecution for K. Ch. 1.] of what he acted, and what hardships he underwent for the Person and cause of that blessed Martyred Prince, He was plundred by the roundheads six and thirty times [*in margin*: Some say above 50]. He engaged his small estate, and gatherd all the money he could get, quilted it in his wastcoat, got off to [*some erasures*] a town held for the King, where [he was askt *erased*] being asked by the Governr who knew him well, what he could do for his Majesty, Mr Swift said he would give the King his Coat, and stripping it off presented it to the Governor, who observing it to be worth little, Mr Swift said, then take my wastcoat, he bid [him *erased and in margin* the Governor] weigh it in his hand, who ordering it to be unripped found it lined with three hundred broad pieces of gold, which as it proved a seasonable relief, must be allowed an extraordinary supply from a private Clergy-man with ten Children of a small Estate, so often plundred and soon after turned out of / his livings in p. 6 the Church.

At another time being inform'd that three hundred horse of the Rebel Party intended in a week to pass over a certain river upon an attempt against the Cavaliers, Mr Swift having a head mechanically turned [with some knowledge in the Mathematicks *crossed out*] he contrived certain pieces of Iron with three Spikes, whereof one must allways be with the point upwards: he placed them over night in the ford where he received notice that the Rebels would pass early the next morning, which they accordingly did, and lost two hundred of their men, who were drownd or trod to death by the falling of their horses, or / torn by the Spikes. p. 7

His Sons, whereof [fore *erased*] four were settled in Ireld (driven thither by their sufferings, and by the death of their father) [had *erased*] related many other passages [from *erased*] which they learned either from their father himself, or from what had been told [related to *erased*] them by the most credible Persons of Herefordshire and some neighboring Countyes, and which some of those Sons often told to their children many of which are still remembred, but many more forgot.

He was deprived of both his Church livings [sooner than most others *erased and in margin*: sooner than most other Loyall Clergymen [for *crossed out*] upon account of his superior zeal for the King's Cause] and his estate sequestred. His Preferments [at least that of Goodridge *added above the line*] were given to a fanatical Saint, who scrupled not / however to conform upon the Restoration, and lived many years, I think till after the Revolution, I have seen many Persons at Goodridge, who knew and told me his name, which I cannot now remembr.

p. 8

[*Added later in the margin:* The Lord Treasurer Oxford told [him *erased*] the Dean that he had among his Father's (Sr Edward Harley's) Papers severall Letters from Mr Thomas Swift writ in those Times, which he promised to give to the Grandson whose life I am writing, but nevr going to his House in Herefordshire while he was Treasurer, and the Queen's death happening in three days after his removal, the Dean went to Ireld, and the Earl being Tryed for his life, and dying while the Dean was in Ireld, he could never get them.]

Mr Thomas Swift dyed in the year 1658, and in the [*number obliterated*] year of his Age, His body lyes under the Altar at Goodri[*dge*]ch with a short inscription. He dyed about two Years before the return of King Charles the Second, who by the reccommendations of some Prelates had promised if ever God should restore him, that he would promote Mr Swift in the Church, and otherways reward his family for [what they had suffered *erased*] his extraordinary Services / and zeal, and persecutions in the royal cause. But Mr Swifts merit dyed with himself.

p. 9

He left ten Sons and three or four Daughters, most of which lived to be Men and Women. His eldest Son, Godwin Swift of the Inner Temple Esqr (so styled by Guillim) [*in margin:* The Herald; in whose book The Family is described at large.] was I think called to the barr before the Restoration. He marryed a relation of the old Marchioness of Ormond, and upon that account as well as his fathers loyalty, the old D of Ormonde made him his attorney generall in the Palatinate of

Tippe[*rar*]y. He had four wives, one of which to the great offence of his family was coheiress to Admiral Deane who was one of the Regicides. [who *erased*] Godwin left severall children who have all estates. He was an / ill pleader, but [perhaps a p. 10 little too *added above the line*] dextrous in the subtil parts of the Law.

The second Son of Mr Thomas Swift was called by the same Name, was bred at Oxford, and took Orders. He marryed the eldest Daughter of Sr Wm D'avenant, but dyed young and left onely one son, who was also called Thomas, and is now Rectr of Puttenham in Surry. His widow lived long, was extremely poor, and in part supported by the famous Dr South who had been her husband's intimate friend.

The rest of his Sons, as far as I [*erasure*] can call to mind were Mr Dryden Swift (called so after the name of his mother, who was a near relation to Mr Dryden the Poet, / William, p. 11 Adam, and Jonathan [*erased and inserted above the line before Adam*] who all lived and dyed in Ireland. But none of them left male issue except Jonathan, who besides a Daughter left one Son born seven Months after his fathers death, of whose life I intend to write a few memorials.

J.S. D.D., and D of St P—— was the onely son of Jonathan Swift, who was the seventh or eighth son of [that eminent Person *erased*] Mr Thomas Swift above mentioned, so eminent for his Loyalty and his sufferings.

His Father dyed young, about two years after his marriage. He had some employments, and agencyes. [had *erased*] his death was much lamented on account of his reputation for integrity with a tolerable good / understanding.   p. 12

He marryed Mrs Abigail Erich of Leicester-shire, descended from the most antient family of [the *added above the line*] Ericks, who derive their Lineage from Erick the Forester, a great Commander, who raised an army to oppose the Invasion of William the Conqueror, by whom he was vanquished, but [was *erased*] afterwards employed to command that Prince's forces, and in his old age retired to his house in Leicester-shire where his family hath continued ever since, but declining every age, and are now in the condition of very private Gentlemen.

This marriage was on both sides very indiscreet, for his wife brought [Mr Swift *erased*] her husband little or no fortune, and p. 13 his death / happening so suddenly before he could make a sufficient establishment for his family: And his son (not then born) hath often been heard to say that he felt the consequences of that marriage not onely through the whole course of his education, but during the greatest part of his life.

He was born in Dublin on St Andrews day, [*a date? completely obliterated in the margin*] and when he was a year old, an event happened to him that seems very unusuall; for his Nurse who was a woman of Whitehaven, [having absolute *crossed out*] being under an absolute necessity of seeing one of her relations, who was then extremely sick, and from whom she expected a Legacy; and being at the same time extremely fond of the infant, she stole him on shipboard unknown to his Mother p. 14 and Uncle, and carryed him with / her to Whitehaven, where he continued for almost [two *erased*] three years. For when the matter was discovered, His Mother sent orders by all means not to hazard a second voyage, till he could be better able to bear it. The nurse was so carefull of him that before he returnd he had learnt to spell, and by the time that he was three years old he could read any chapter in the Bible.

After his return to Ireld, [when *erased*] he was sent at six years old to the School of Kilkenny, from whence at fourteen he was admitted into the University at Dublin, where by the ill Treatment of his nearest Relations, he was so discouraged and sunk in his Spirits, that he too much neglected his [Studyes *erased*] Academical Studyes, for [*in the margin*: some parts of] which he had no great relish by Nature, and turned himself p. 15 to reading History and Poetry. / So that when the time came for taking his degree of Batchlor, although he had lived with great Regularity and due Observance of the Statutes, he was stopped of his Degree, for Dullness and Insufficiency, and at last hardly admitted in a manner little to his Credit, which is called in that Colle[d]ge *Speciali gratia*, [which *erased and in the margin*: And this discreditable mark] as I am told, stands upon record in their Colle[d]ge Registry.

her to Whitehaven, where he
continued for almost ~~two~~ three
years. For when the matter
was discovered, His Mother
sent orders by all means not
to hazard a Second voyage till
he could be better able to bear it.
The Nurse was so carefull of
him that before he return'd he
had learnt to Spell, and by the
time that he was three years old
he could read any chapter in
the Bible.

After his return to Irel~~and~~,
he was sent at Six years old to
the School of Kilkenny, from
whence at fourteen he was
admitted into the University at
Dublin, where by the ill
Treatment of his nearest
Relations, he was so discouraged
and ~~sunk~~ in his Spirits, that
he ~~too much~~ neglected ~~his~~
~~Studyes,~~ Academick Studyes, for
which he had no great relish
by Nature, and turned himself
to reading History and Poetry.

So

The Troubles then breaking out, he went to his Mother, who lived in Leicester, and after continuing there some Months, he was received [into the *erased*] by Sr Wm Temple, whose Father had been a great Friend to the Family, and who was now retired to his House called Moorpark near Farnham in Surrey, where he continued for about two years. For he happened before / twenty years old, by a Surfeit of fruit to p. 16 contract a giddyness and coldness of Stomach, that almost brought him to his Grave, and this disorder [continued *erased*] pursued him with Intermissions of two or thre years to the end of his Life. Upon this Occasion he returned to Ireld by advice of Physicians, who weakly imagined that his native air might be of some use to recover his Health. But growing worse, he soon went back to Sr Wm Temple; with whom growing into some confidence, he was often trusted with matters of great Importance. King William had a high esteem for Sr Wm Temple by a long acquaintance, while that Gentlmn was Ambassador and Mediator of a Generall peace at Nimeguen. The King soon after his Expedition to England, visited his old Friend often at Sheen, and took his advice / in p. 17 affairs of greatest consequence. But Sr W. T. weary of living so near London, and resolving to retire to a more private Scene, bought an Estate near Farnham in Surrey of about 100 ll a year, [*added later in the line*] where Mr Swift [*and in the margin*] accompanied him.

About that time a Bill was brought in to the H. of Commons for Triennial Parlmts, against which the King who was a stranger to our Constitution, was very averse, by the Advice of some [very *erased*] weak People, who persuaded the Earl of Portland that K.Ch. 1st lost his [life and *erased*] Crown and Life by consenting to pass such a bill. The Earl who was a weak man, came down to Moorpark by His Majesty's orders to have Sr Wm Temple's advice, who said much to show him the Mistake. But he continued still to advise the King against passing the Bill. Whereupon Mr Swift was sent to Kensington with the whole Account of that matter, in writing, to convince the King and the Earl how ill they were informed. He told the Earl to whom he was referred by His Majesty, (and gave it in writing) that the

Ruin of K. Charles the 1st was not owing to his passing the Triennial bill, which did not hinder him from dissolving any Parlmt,
continued
in margin
of p. 18 but to the passing another bill, which put it out of his / power
to dissolve the Parliamt then in being, without the consent of
the House. Mr Swift who was well versed in English History
although he were then under [three and *erased*] twenty [one
added above the line] years old, gave the King a short account of
the Matter, but a more large one to the Earl of Portland;
but all in vain: For the King by ill advisers was prevayled
upon [*above the line:* to refuse passing the Bill]. This was the
first time that Mr Swift had ever any converse with [a King
erased] Courts, and he told his friends [that *erased*] it was the
first incident that helped to cure him of vanity. The Consequence of this wrong Step in His Majesty was very unhappy;
For it put that Prince under a necessity of introducing those
People called Whigs into power and Employments, in order
to pacify them. For, although it be held a part of the Kings
Prerogative to refuse passing Bills, Yet the Learned in the
Law, think otherwise, from that Expression used at the
Coronation wherein the Prince obligeth himself to consent to
all Laws *quas vulgus elegerit.*

Mr Swift lived with him some time, but resolving to settle
p. 17
continued himself in some way of [life *erased*] living, was inclined to take
orders. However, although his fortune was very small, he
had a scruple of entring into the Church meerly for support,
and Sr Wm Temple then being Master of the Rolls in Ireland
offered him an Employ of about 120 ll a year in that office,
whereupon Mr Swift told him, that since he had now an
opportunity of living without being driven into the Church
for a maintenance, he was resolved to [go to *above the line*]
Ireld and take holy Orders. He was recommended to the
Lord Capel, then Ld Deputy, who gave him a Prebend in the
p. 18 North, worth about 100 ll a year, of which / growing weary
in a few months, he returned to England; resigned his Living
in favor of a Friend, and continued in Sr W Temple's house
till the Death of that great Man, who besides a Legacy [of a
100 ll *erased*] left him the care and trust and Advantage of
publishing his posthumous Writings.

Upon this Event Mr Swift removed to London, and applyed by Petition to King William, upon the Claym of a Promise his Majesty had mad[e] to Sr W T that he would give Mr Swift a Prebend of Canterbury or Westminster. The Earl of Rumney who professed much friendship for him, promised to second his Petition, but, as he was an old vitious [rake *erased*] illiterate Rake without any sense of Truth or Honor, said not a word to the King: And Mr Swift after long attendance in vain; thought it better to comply with an Invitation given him by the E. of Berkeley to attend him to Ireland as his Chaplain and private Secretary; His Lordship having been appointed one of the Lords Justices of that Kingdom. / He attended p. 19 his Lordship; who landed near Waterford, and Mr. Swift acted as Secretary [till *erased*] the whole Journy to Dublin. But another Person had so far insinuated himself into the Earls favor, by telling him, that the Post of (private *erased*) Secretary was not proper for a Clergyman, nor would be of any advantage to one who aimed onely at Church-preferments, that his Lordship after a poor Apology gave that Office to the other.

In some Months, the Deanry of Derry fell vacant; and it was [my Lord's *erased*, *and in margin* this *erased*, *then added*: the Earl of Berkeley's] turn to dispose of it. Yet things were so ordered that the Secretary having received a Bribe, the Deanry was disposed of to another, and Mr Swift was put off with some other Church-livings not worth above a third part of that rich Deanry, and at this present time, not a sixth. The Excuse [was *erased*] pretended was his being too young, although he / p. 20 were then 30 years old.

SWIFT'S ACCOUNT
OF HIS MOTHER'S DEATH

ON Wednesday, between seven and eight in the evening, May 10, 1710, I received a letter in my chamber at Laracor, (Mr. Percival and John Beaumont being by,) from Mrs. Fenton, dated May 9th, with one enclosed, sent from Mrs. Worrall at Leicester to Mrs. Fenton, giving an account, that my dear mother, Mrs. Abigail Swift, died that morning, Monday, April 24, 1710, about ten o'clock, after a long sickness, being ill all winter, and lame, and extremely ill a month or six weeks before her death. I have now lost my barrier between me and death; God grant I may live to be as well prepared for it, as I confidently believe her to have been! If the way to Heaven be through piety, truth, justice, and charity, she is there.

A DECREE *for Concluding the* TREATY *between Dr.* SWIFT *and Mrs.* LONG.

Text of Decree:

WHEREAS it hath been signifyed to us, that there is now a Treaty of Acquaintance on Foot between Dr. *Swift*, of *Leicester-fields*, on the one Part, and Mrs. *Long* of *Albemarle-street*, on the other Part. And whereas the said Dr. *Swift*, upon the Score of his Merit, and extraordinary Qualities, doth claim the sole and undoubted Right, That all Persons whatsoever, shall make such Advances to him, as he pleases to demand; any Law, Claim, Custom, Privilege of Sex, Beauty, Fortune, or Quality, to the contrary notwithstanding.

And whereas the said Mrs. *Long*, humbly acknowledging and allowing the Right of the said Doctor, doth yet insist upon certain Privileges and Exceptions, as a Lady of the TOAST*, which Privileges, she doth alledge, are excepted out of the Doctor's general Claim, and which she cannot betray, without injuring the whole Body, whereof she is a Member: By which Impediment the said Treaty is not yet brought to a Conclusion; to the great Grievance and Dammage of Mrs. *Van Homrigh*, and her fair Daughter *Hessy*.

And whereas the Decision of this weighty Cause is referred to Us, in our Judicial Capacity; We, out of our tender Regard to Truth and Justice, having heard and duly considered the Allegations of both Parties, do Declare, Adjudge, Decree, and Determine, That the said Mrs. *Long*, notwithstanding any Privileges she may claim as aforesaid, as a Lady of the TOAST, shall, without Essoin or Demurr, in Two Hours after the

---

* *These verses were written by the Lord* Wharton *round one of the* Toasting-Glasses *of the* Kit-Cat-Club, 1703.

> Fill the Glass; let the Hautboys sound,
> Whilst bright *Longy*'s Health goes round:
> With eternal Beauty blest,
> Ever blooming, still the best;
> Drink your Glass, and think the rest.

Publishing of this our DECREE, make all Advances to the said Doctor, that he shall demand; And that the said Advances shall not be made to the said Doctor, as *Un Homme sans Consequence*; but purely upon Account of his great Merit.

And We do hereby strictly forbid the said Mrs. *Van Homrigh*, and her fair Daughter *Hessy*, to aid, abett, comfort or encourage her the said Mrs. *Long*, in her Disobedience for the Future. And in Consideration of the said Mrs. *Long*'s being a TOAST, we think it just and reasonable, That the said Doctor should permit her in all Companies to give her self the Reputation of being one of his Acquaintance; which no other Lady shall presume to do, upon any Pretence whatsoever, without his especial Leave and License first had and obtained.

By Especial Command,

G. V. HOMRIGH.

DEATH OF MRS ANNE LONG

Decbr. 22. 1711

ON Saterday ⟨ at 4 in the morn. dyed Mrs Ann Long at Lynn in Norfolk, where she had retired about 2 years before, and lived under the name of Smyth. the News of it came to Town on Monday night following, wch was Xmas Eve and I heard it on Xmas day at Noon, wch was Tuesday: She was the most beautifull Person of the Age, she lived in, of great Honr and Virtue, infinite Sweetness and Generosity of Temper, and true good Sense.

J. Swift.

DEAN OF ST. PATRICKS PETITION
TO THE H. OF LORDS,
AGAINST THE LORD BLANEY

To the Right Honorable the Lords Spirituall and Temporal
in Parliament assembled

THE humble Petition of Jonathan Swift DD, and Dean
of the Cathedrall of S^t. Patrick's Dublin
Most humbly sheweth

That Your Pet^r is advised by his Physicians on account of
his health, to go often on horse-back, and there being no place in
winter so convenient for riding, as the Strand towards Howth,
Your Pet^r takes all opportunityes that the weather or his
business will permit, to go that road. That, in the last Session
of Parlm^t, in the midst of winter, as Your Pet^r was returning
from Howth, with his two Servants, one before, and the other
behind him, he was pursued by two Gentlemen in a chaise,
drawn by two high mettled horses, in so violent a manner,
that his Servant who rode behind him was forced to give way
with the utmost peril of his life: Whereupon Your Pet^r
made what speed he could, riding to the right and left above
fifty yards to the full extent of the s^d road. But the two Gentlemen driving a light chaise drawn by fleet horses, and intent
upon mischief, turned faster than your Pet^r, endeavoring to
overthrow him. That by great Accident Your Pet^r got to the
side of a ditch, where the chaise could not safely pursue, and
the two Gentlemen, stopping their carriere, Your Pet^r mildly
expostulated with them. Whereupon one of the Gentlemen
said: Damn you is not the road as free for us as for You?
and calling to his servant who rode behind, s^d, Tom (or some
such name) is the Pistol loaden with ball? To which the Servant
answered, Yes, My Lord, and gave him the pistol. Your
Pet^r then s^d to the Gentleman, pray S^r do not shoot, for my
horse is apt to start, by which I shall endanger my life. The

Chaise went forward, and your Pet^r took the opportunity to stay behind.

Your Pet^r is informed that the Person who spoke the words above mentioned, is of Your Lordship's house, under the Stile and Title of Lord Blaney, whom Your Pet^r remembers to have introduced to Mr Secretary Addison in the Earl of Wharton's government and to have done him other good offices at that time, because he was represented as a young man of some hopes and a broken fortune.

That the sd Lord Blaney as Y^r Pet^r is informed is now in Dublin and sometimes attends your Ldships house. And Y^r Pet^{rs} health still requiring that he should often ride, and being confined in winter to go on the same Strand, he is forced to enquire from every one he meets whether the s^d Lord be upon the same Strand; and to order his servants to carry arms to defend himself against the like or a worse insult from the s^d Lord, for the consequences of which, Y^r Pet^r cannot answer.

[*Four lines crossed out here and used in the last sentence.*]

Your Pet^r is informed by his Learned Council, that there is no law now in being which can justify the s^d Lord under colour of his Peerage to assault any of His Majesty's subjects, on the Kings high way, and put them in fear of their lives without provocation, which he humbly conceives, that by onely happening to ride before the sd Lord, he could not possibly give.

Your Pet^r therefore doth humbly implore Your L^{d}shps in Your great Prudence and justice, to provide that he may be permitted to ride with safety on the s^d Strand, or any other of the King's high-ways, for the recovery of his health (so long as he shall demean himself in a peaceable manner)—

And Y^r Pet^r shall ever pray.

HOLYHEAD JOURNAL, 1727

I DO here give notice to posterity, that having been the author of severall writings, both in prose and verse, which have passed with good Success, it hath drawn upon me the censure of innumerable attempters and imitatorers and censurers, many of whose names I know, but shall in this be wiser than Virgil and Horace, by not delivering their names down to future ages; and at the same time disappoint that tribe of writers whose chief end next to that of getting bread, was an ambition of having their names upon record by answring or retorting their Scurrilityes; and would slily have made use of my resentment to let the future world know that there were such Persons now in being. I do therefore charge my Successors in fame, by virtue of being an antient 200 years hence, to follow the same method. Dennis, Blackmore, Bentley, and severall others, will reap great advantage by those who have not observed my rule: And heaven forgive Mr. Pope, who hath so grievously transgressed it, by transmitting so many names of forgotten memory, full at length, to be known by Readers in succeeding times, who perhaps may be seduced to Ducklane and Grubstreet, and there find some of the very Treatises he mentions in his Satyrs. I heartily applaud my own innocency and prudence upon this occasion, who never named above 6 authors of remarkable worthlessness; let the Fame of the rest be upon Mr. Pope and his Children. Mr. Gay, although more sparingly, hath gone upon the same mistake.

THE JOURNAL

Friday, at 11 in the morning I left Chester. It was Sept. 22^d, 1727.

I bated at a blind ale-house 7 miles from Chester. I thence rode to Ridland; in all 22 miles. I lay there, had bad meat, and tolerable wine. I left Ridland a quarter after 4 morn. on Saturday, stopt on Penmenmawr, examined about my sign verses: the Inn is to be on t' other side, therefore the verses to be changed. I baited at Conway, the Guide going to anoth^r Inn, the Maid of the old Inn saw me in the Street, and said that was my House, she knew me; there I dined, and send for Ned Holland, a Squire famous for being mentioned in Mr Lyndsay's verses to Davy Morice. I there again saw Hook's Tomb, who was the 41st Child of his Mother, and had himself 27 Children; he dyed about 1638. There is a nota bene that one of his posterity new furbishd up the Inscription. I had read in A.Bp Williams Life that he was buryed in an obscure Church in North Wales. I enquired, and heard it was at —— Church, within a mile of Bangor, whither I was going; I went to the Church, the Guide grumbling; I saw the Tomb with his Statue kneeling (in marble). It began thus: [Hospes lege et relege quod in hoc obscuro sacello non expectares. Hic jacet omnium Præsulum celeberrimus]. I came to Bangor, and crossed the Ferry a mile from it, where there is an Inn, which if it be well kept will break Bangor. There I lay—it was 22 miles from Holyhead. I was on horseback at 4 in the morning, resolving to be at Church at Holyhead, but to shew Wat Owen Tudor's Tomb at Penmany. We passt the place (being a little out of the way) by the Guides knavery, who had no mind to stay. I was now so weary with riding, that I was forced to stop at Langueveny, 7 miles from the Ferry, and rest 2 hours. Then I went on very weary, but in a few miles more Watt's Horse lost his two fore-shoes, so the Horse was forced to limp after us. The Guide was less concerned than I. In a few miles more, my Horse lost a fore-shoe; and could not go on the rocky ways. I walked above 2 miles to spare him. It was Sunday, and no Smith to be got. At last there was a Smith in the way; we left the Guide to shoe the horses, and walked to a hedge Inn 3 miles from Holyhead; There I stayd an hour, with no ale to be drunk. a Boat offered, and I went by Sea and Sayl in it to Holyhead. The guide came about the same time. I dined with [my *erased*] an old Inkeeper, Mrs. Welch, about 3, on a Loyn of mutton, very good, but the worst ale in the world, and no wine, for the day before I came here, a vast number went to

Ireld after having drank out all the wine. There was Stale beer, and I tryed [Stella's *erased*] a receit of Oyster shells, which I got powderd on purpose; but it was good for nothing. I walked on the rocks in the evening, and then went to bed, and dreamt (he) I had got 20 falls from my Horse.

Monday, Septr. 25. The Captain talks of sailing at 12. The talk goes off; the Wind is fair, but he says it is too fierce; I believe he wants more company. I had a raw chicken for dinner, and Brandy with water for my drink. I walkt morning and afternoon among the rocks. This evening Watt tells me (that) that my Landlady whispered him that the Grafton packet boat, just come in, had brought her 18 bottles of Irish Claret. I secured one, and supped on part of a neat's tongue, which a friend at London had given Watt to put up for me—and drank a pint of the wine, which was bad enough. Not a soul is yet come to Holyhead, except a young fellow who smiles when he meets me, and would fain be my companion; but it is not come to that yet. I writ abundance of verses this day; and severall usefull hints (tho' I say it). I went to bed at 10, and dreamt abundance of nonsense.

Tuesd. 26th. I am forced to wear a shirt 3 days; for fear of being lowsy. I was sparing of them all the way. It was a mercy there were 6 clean when I left London; otherwise Watt (whose blunders would bear an history) would have put them all in the great Box of goods which goes by the Carrier to Chester. He brought but one cravat, and the reason he gave was because the rest were foul, and he thought he should not put foul linnen into the Portmanteau. For, he never dreamt it might be washed on the way. My shirts are all foul now, and by his reasoning, I fear he will leave them at Holyhead when we go. I got anoth^r Loyn of mutton, but so tough I could not chew it, and drank my 2d pint of wine. I walked this morning a great way among the rocks, and to a hole in one of them from whence at certain periods the water spurted up severall foot high. It raind all night, and hath rained since dinner. But now the sun shines, and I will take my afternoons walk. It was fairer and milder weather than yesterday, yet the Captain never dreams of Sailing. To say the

truth Michaelmas is the worst season in the year. Is this
strange stuff? Why, what would you have me do. I have
writt verses, and put down hints till I am weary. I see no
creature, I cannot read by candle-light. Sleeping will make me
sick. I reckon my self fixed here: and have a mind like
Marechall Tallard to take a house and garden. I wish you a
merry Christmas, and expect to see you by Candlemas. I
have walked this evening again about 3 miles on the rocks,
my giddyness God be thanked is almost gone, & my hearing
continues; I am now retired to my Chamber to scribble or
sit hum-drum. The night is fair, and they pretend to have some
hopes of going to-morrow.

Septr. 26th. Thoughts upon being confind at Holyhead.
If this were to be my settlement, during life, I could amuse
my self a while by forming some conveniencyes to be easy;
and should not be frighted either by the solitude, or the
meaness of lodging, eating or drinking. I shall say nothing
upon the suspense I am in about my dearest friend; because
that is a case extraordinary, and therefore by way of amusem^t,
I will speak as if it were not in my thoughts, and only as a
passenger who is in a scurvy unprovided comfortless place
without one companion, and who therefore wants to be at
home, where he hath all conveniences there proper for a
Gentleman of quality. I cannot read at night, and I have no
books to read in the day. I have no subject in my head at
present to write on. I dare not send my Linnen to be washed,
for fear of being called away at half an hour's warning, and
then I must leave them behind me, which is a serious point;
in the mean time I am in danger of being lowsy, which is a
ticklish Point. I live at great expense without one comfortable
bit or sup. I am afraid of joyning with passengers for fear
of getting acquaintance with Irish. The Days are short, and
I have five hours at night to spend by my self before I go to
bed. I should be glad to converse with Farmers or shop-
keepers, but none of them speak English. A Dog is better
company than the Vicar, for I rememb^r him of old. What
can I do but write every thing that comes into my head.
Watt is a Booby of that Species which I dare not suffer to be

familiar with me, for he would ramp on my shoulders in half
an hour. But the worst part is my half hourly longing, and
hopes and vain expectations of a wind; so that I live in
suspense, which is the worst circumstance of human nature.
I am a little dizzy [?] from two scurvy disorders, and if I
should relapse, there is no[t] a welch house curr, that would not
have more care taken of him than I, and whose loss would
not be more lamented. I confine my self to my narrow chambr
in all unwalkable hours. The Master of the pacquet-boat,
one Jones, hath not treated me with the least civility, altho'
Watt gave him my name. In short: I come from being used
like an Emperor to be used worse than a Dog at Holyhead.
Yet my hat is worn to pieces by answering the civilityes of the
poor inhabitants as they pass by. The women might be safe
enough, who all wear hats yet never pull them off, if the dirty
streets did not foul their petticoats by courtisying so low.
Look you; be not impatient, for I onely wait till my watch
marks 10, and then I will give you ease, and my self sleep, if I
can. On my conscience you may know a Welch dog as well
as a Welch man or woman by its peevish passionate way of
barking. This paper shall serve to answer all your questions
about my Journey; and I will have it printed to satisfy the
Kingdom. Forsan et haec olim is a damned lye, for I shall
always fret at the remembrance of this imprisonment. Pray
pity poor Wat, for he is called dunce, puppy, and Lyar 500
times an hour, and yet he means not ill, for he means nothing.
Oh for a dozen bottles of deanry wine and a slice of bread
and butter. The wine you sent us yesterday is a little upon the
sour. I wish you had chosen better. I am going to bed at
ten o'clock, because I am weary of being up.

Wednesday. Last night I dreamt that Ld Bolingbroke and
Mr Pope were at my Cathedrall in the Gallery, and that my
L^d was to preach. I could not find my Surplice, the Church
Servants were all out of the way; the Doors were shut. I sent
to my L^d to come into my Stall for more convcniency to get
into the Pulpit. The Stall was all broken; the[y] s^d the Collegians
had done it. I squeezed among the Rabble, saw my L^d in the
Pulpit. I thought his prayer was good, but I forget it. In his

Sermon, I did not like his quoting Mr. Wycherly by name, and his Plays. This is all, and so I waked. To day we were certainly to sayl; the morning was calm. Wat and I walked up the monstrous mountain properly called Holy head or Sacrum promontorium by Ptolemy, 2 miles from this town. I took breath 59 times. I looked from the top to see the wicklow hills, but the day was too hazy, which I felt to my sorrow; for returning, we were overtaken with a furious shower. I got in to a welch cabin, almost as bad as an Irish one. There was onely an old welch woman sifting flower, who understood no English, and a boy who fell a roaring for fear of me. Wat (otherwise called unfortunate Jack) ran home for my coat, but stayd so long that I came home in worse rain without him, and he was so lucky to miss me, but took care to carry the key of my room where a fire was ready for me. So I coold my heels in the Parlor till he came, but called for a glass of Brandy. I have been cooking my self dry, and am now in my night gown; and this moment comes a Letter to me from one Whelden who tells me he hears I am a lover of the Mathematicks, that he has found out the Longitude, shewn his discourse to D^r. Dobbs of y^r Colledge, and sent Letters to all the Mathematicians in London 3 months ago, but received no answer; and desires I would read his discourse. I sent back his Letter with my answer under it, too long to tell you, onely I said I had too much of the Longitude already, by 2 Projectors, whom I encouraged, one of which was a cheat and the other cut his own throat, and for himself I thought he had a mind to deceive others, or was deceived himself. And so I wait for dinner. I shall dine like a King all alone, as I have done these 6 days. As it happened, if I had gone strait from Chester to Parkgate, 8 miles, I should have been in Dublin on Sunday last. Now Michlmas approaches, the worst time in the year for the Sea, and this rain has made these parts unwalkable, so that I must either write or doze. Bite; when we were in the welch cabin, I order Wat to take a cloath and wipe my wet gown and cassock—it happend to be a meal bag, and as my Gown dryd, it was all dawbed with flower well cemented with the rain. What do I, but see

the Gown and cassock well dryd in my room, and while
Wat was at dinner, I was an hour rubbing the meal out of
them, and did it exactly; He is just come up, and I have gravely
bid him take them down to rub them, and I wait whether he
will find out what I have been doing. The Rogue is come up
in six minutes with my gown, and says there were but few
spots (tho he saw a thousand at first), but neither wonders
at it nor seems to suspect me who labored like a horse to rub
them out. The 3 Pacquet boats are now all on this side;
and the weather grows worse, and so much rain, that there is
an end of my walking. I wish you would send me word how
I shall dispose of my time. If the Vicar could but play at
backgammon I were an Emperor; but I know him not. I am
as insignificant here as parson Brooke is in Dublin; by my
conscience I believe Cæsar would be the same without his
army at his back. Well; the longer I stay here, the more you
will murmur for want of packets. Whoever would wish to
live long, should live here, for a day is longer than a week,
and if the weather be foul, as long as a fortnight. Yet here
I could live with two or three friends in a warm house, and
good wine—much better than being a Slave in Ireld. But
my misery is, that I am in the worst part of wales under the
very worst circumstances; afraid of a relapse; in utmost
solitude; impatient for the condition of our friend; not a soul
to converse with, hinderd from exercise by rain, cooped up
in a room not half so large as one of the Deanry Closets.
My room smoaks into the bargain, and the w'ther is too cold
and moist to be without a fire. There is or should be a
Proverbe here, When M^{rs}. Welch's Chimney smoks, Tis
a sign she'll keep her folks. But, when of smoak the room is
clear, It is a sign we sha'nt stay here. All this is to divert
thinking. Tell me, am not I in a comfortable way? The Yatcht
is to be here for Ld Carteret on the 14th of Octb^r. I fancy he
and I shall come over together. I have opend my door to
let in the wind that it may drive out the smoak. I asked the
wind why [he] is so cross, he assures me 'tis not his fault, but his
cursed master Æolus's. Here is a young Jackanapes in the
same Inn waiting for a wind, who would fain be my companion,

and if I stay here much longer, I am afraid all my pride and grandeur will truckle to comply with him, especially if I finish these leaves that remain; but I will write close, and do as the Devil did at mass, pull the paper with my teeth to make it hold out.

Thursday. 'Tis allowed that we learn patience by suffering. I have now not spirits enough left me to fret: I was so cunning these 3 last days, that whenever I began to rage and storm at the weather, I took special care to turn my face towards Ireland, in hopes by my breath to push the wind forward. But now I give up. However, when upon asking how is the wind, the people answer, Full in y^r teeth, I cannot help wishing a T—— were in theirs. Well, it is now 3 afternoon. I have dined, and invited the Master, the wind and tide serve, and I am just taking boat to go [to] the Ship: so adieu till I see you at the Deanry.

Friday, Mich^{l}mas day. You will now know something of what it is to be at sea. We had not been half an hour in the ship till a fierce wind rose directly against us. We tryed a good while, but the storm still continued: so we turned back, and it was 8 at night, dark and rainy before the ship got back, and at anchor: the other passengers went back in a boat to Holyhead: but to prevent accidents and broken shins I lay all night on board, and came back this morning at 8: am now in my Chamber, where I must stay, and get in a new stock of patience. You all know well enough where I am, for I wrote thrice after your Letter that desired my coming over; the last was from Coventry, 19th instant, but I brought it with me to Chester, and saw it put into the Post, on Thursday 21st, and the next day followed it my self, but the Pacquet boat was gone before I could get here: because I could not ride 70 miles a day.

Characters

A CHARACTER

OF

PRIMATE MARSH

MARSH has the reputation of most profound and universal learning; this is the general opinion, neither can it be easily disproved. An old rusty iron-chest in a banker's shop, strongly lockt, and wonderful heavy, is full of gold; this is the general opinion, neither can it be disproved, provided the key be lost, and what is in it be wedged so close that it will not by any motion discover the metal by the chinking. Doing good is his pleasure; and as no man consults another in his pleasures, neither does he in this; by his aukwardness and unadvisedness disappointing his own good designs. His high station hath placed him in the way of great employments, which, without the least polishing his native rusticity, have given him a tincture of pride and ambition. But these vices would have passed concealed under his natural simplicity, if he had not endeavoured to hide them by art. His disposition to study is the very same with that of an usurer to hoard up money, or of a vicious young fellow to a wench: nothing but avarice and evil concupiscence, to which his constitution has fortunately given a more innocent turn. He is sordid and suspicious in his domesticks, without love or hatred; which is but reasonable, since he has neither friend nor enemy; without joy or grief; in short, without all passions but fear, to which of all others he hath least temptation, having nothing to get or to lose; no posterity, relation, or friend to be solicitous about; and placed by his station above the reach of fortune or envy. He hath found out the secret of preferring men without deserving their thanks; and where he dispenses his favours to persons of merit, they are less obliged to him than to fortune. He is the first of human race, that with great advantages of learning, piety, and station ever escaped being a great man. That which relishes best with him, is mixt liquor and mixt company, and he is seldom unprovided with very bad of both. He is so wise to value his own health more than other mens noses, so that the most honourable place at his table is much the worst, especially in summer. It has been affirmed that originally he was not altogether devoid of wit, till it was extruded from his head to make room for other mens thoughts. He will admit a governor, provided it be one who is very officious and diligent, outwardly pious, and one that knows how to manage and make the most of his fear. No man will be either glad or sorry at his death, except his successor.

CHARACTER

O F

MRS. HOWARD.

Written in the Year 1727.

I SHALL say nothing of her wit or beauty, which are allowed by all persons who can judge of either, when they hear or see her. Besides, beauty being transient, and a trifle, cannot justly make part of a character. And I leave others to celebrate her wit, because it will be of no use in that part of her character which I intend to draw. Neither shall I relate any part of her history; further than, that she went, in the prime of her youth, to the Court of Hanover with her husband, and became of the Bed-chamber to the present Princess of Wales, living in expectation of the Queen's* death: Upon which event she came over with her Mistress, and hath ever since continued in her service; where, from the attendance daily paid her by the ministers, and all expectants, she is reckoned much the greatest favourite of the court at Leicester-house: A situation which she hath long affected to desire that it might not be believed.

There is no politician who more carefully watches the motions and dispositions of things and persons at St. James's, nor can form his language with a more imperceptible dexterity to the present posture of a court, or more early foresee what style may be proper upon any approaching juncture of affairs, whereof she can gather early intelligence without asking it, and often when even those from whom she hath it are not sensible that they are giving it to her, but equally with others admire her sagacity. Sir Robert Walpole and she both think they understand each other, and are both equally mistaken.

* Queen Anne.

With persons where she is to manage, she is very dextrous in that point of skill which the French call *tâter le pavè*; with others she is a great vindicator of all present proceedings, but in such a manner, as if she were under no concern further than her own conviction, and wondering how any body can think otherwise. And the danger is, that she may come in time to believe herself; which, under a change of princes and a great addition of credit, might have bad consequences. She is a most unconscionable dealer; for, in return of a few good words, which she gives to her lords and gentlemen daily waiters before their faces, she gets ten thousand from them behind her back, which are of real service to her character. The credit she hath is managed with the utmost thrift; and, whenever she employs it, which is very rarely, it is only upon such occasions where she is sure to get much more than she spends. For instance, she would readily press Sir Robert Walpole to do some favour for Colonel Churchill, or Doddington; the Prince, for a mark of grace to Mr. Schutz; and the Princess, to be kind to Mrs. Clayton. She sometimes falls into the general mistake of all courtiers, which is that of not suiting her talents to the abilities of others, but thinking those she deals with to have less art than they really possess; so that she may possibly be deceived when she thinks she deceiveth.

In all offices of life, except those of a courtier, she acts with justice, generosity, and truth. She is ready to do good as a private person, and I would almost think in charity that she will not do harm as a courtier, unless to please those in chief power.

In religion she is at least a Latitudinarian, being not an enemy to books written by the Free-thinkers; and herein she is the more blameable, because she hath too much morality to stand in need of them, requiring only a due degree of faith for putting her in the road to salvation. I speak this of her as a private Lady, not as a Court-favourite; for, in the latter capacity, she can shew neither faith nor works.

If she had never seen a Court, it is not impossible that she might have been a friend.

She abounds in good words and expressions of good wishes, and will concert a hundred schemes for the service of those whom she would be thought to favour: Schemes that sometimes arise from them, and sometimes from herself; although, at the same time, she very well knows them to be without the least probability of succeeding. But, to do her justice, she never feeds or deceives any person with promises, where she doth not at the same time intend a degree of sincerity.

She is, upon the whole, an excellent companion for men of the best accomplishments, who have nothing to desire or expect.

What part she may act hereafter in a larger sphere, as Lady of the Bed-chamber to a great Queen, (upon supposing the death of his present Majesty*, and of the Earl of Suffolk, to whose title her husband succeeds) and in high esteem with a King, neither she nor I can foretel. My own opinion is natural and obvious, that her talents as a courtier will spread, enlarge, and multiply to such a degree, that her private virtues, for want of room and time to operate, will be laid up clean (like clothes in a chest), to be used and put on, whenever satiety, or some reverse of fortune, or encrease of ill health, (to which last she is subject) shall dispose her to retire. In the mean-time, it will be her wisdom to take care that they may not be tarnished or moth-eaten, for want of airing and turning at least once a year.

* George the First.

CHARACTER

OF

DOCTOR SHERIDAN

Written in the Year 1738.

DOCTOR THOMAS SHERIDAN died at Rathfarnam the tenth of October 1738, at three of the clock in the afternoon: His diseases were a dropsy and asthma. He was doubtless the best instructor of youth in these kingdoms, or perhaps in Europe; and as great a master of the Greek and Roman languages. He had a very fruitful invention, and a talent for poetry. His English verses were full of wit and humour, but neither his prose nor verse sufficiently correct: However, he would readily submit to any friend who had a true taste in prose or verse. He hath left behind him a very great collection, in several volumes, of stories, humorous, witty, wise, or some way useful, gathered from a vast number of Greek, Roman, Italian, Spanish, French, and English writers. I believe I may have seen about thirty, large enough to make as many moderate books in octavo. But, among those extracts, there were many not worth regard; for five in six, at least, were of little use or entertainment. He was (as it is frequently the case in men of wit and learning) what the French call a *Dupe*, and in a very high degree. The greatest dunce of a tradesman could impose upon him, for he was altogether ignorant in worldly management. His chief shining quality was that of a schoolmaster; here he shone in his proper element. He had so much skill and practice in the physiognomy of boys, that he rarely mistook at the first view. His scholars loved and feared him. He often rather chose to shame the stupid, but punished the idle, and exposed them to all the lads, which was more severe than lashing. Among the gentlemen in this kingdom who have any share of education, the scholars of Dr. Sheridan infinitely excel, in number and knowledge, all their brethren sent from other schools.

To look on the Doctor in some other lights, he was in many things very indiscreet, to say no worse. He acted like too many clergymen, who are in haste to be married when very young; and from hence proceeded all the miseries of his life. The portion he got proved to be just the reverse of 500*l.* for he was poorer by a thousand: So many incumbrances of a mother-in-law, and poor relations, whom he was forced to support for many years. Instead of breeding up his daughters to housewifery and plain cloaths, he got them, at a great expence, to be clad like ladies who had plentiful fortunes; made them only learn to sing and dance, to draw and design, to give them rich silks, and other fopperies; and his two eldest were married without his consent, to young lads who had nothing to settle on them. However, he had one * son, whom the Doctor sent to Westminster-school, although he could ill afford it. The boy was there immediately taken notice of, upon examination; although a mere stranger, he was by pure merit elected a King's scholar. It is true their maintenance falls something short: The Doctor was then so poor, that he could not add fourteen pounds, to enable the boy to finish the year; which, if he had done, he would have been removed to a higher class, and, in another year, would have been sped off (that is the phrase) to a Fellowship in Oxford or Cambridge: But the Doctor was forced to recal him to Dublin, and had friends in our university to send him there, where he hath been chosen of the foundation; and, I think, hath gotten an exhibition, and designs to stand for a fellowship.

The Doctor had a good church-living, in the south parts of Ireland, given him by Lord Carteret; who, being very learned himself, encourageth it in others. A friend of the Doctor's prevailed on his Excellency to grant it. The living was well worth 150*l. per annum.* He changed it very soon for that of

* Thomas Sheridan, M. A. a most celebrated Actor, and Author of several well written Pieces, particularly, BRITISH EDUCATION; or the Source of the Disorders of Great Britain. He hath also written some Tracts on Elocution.

R

Dunboyn; which, by the knavery of the farmers and power of the gentlemen, fell so very low, that he could never get 80*l*. He then changed that living for the free-school of Cavan, where he might have lived well, in so cheap a country, on 80*l*. salary *per annum*, besides his scholars: But the air, he said, was too moist and unwholesome, and he could not bear the company of some persons in that neighbourhood. Upon this he sold the school for about 400*l*. spent the money, grew into diseases, and died.

It would be very honourable, as well as just, in those many persons of quality and fortune, who had the advantage of being educated under Doctor Sheridan, if they would please to erect some decent monument over his body in the church where it is deposited.

THE BLUNDERS, DEFICIENCIES, DISTRESSES, AND MISFORTUNES OF QUILCA.

Proposed to contain one and twenty Volumes in Quarto. Begun April 20, 1724. To be continued Weekly, if due Encouragement be given.

BUT one Lock and a half in the whole House.

THE Key of the Garden Door lost.

THE empty Bottles all uncleanable.

THE Vessels for Drink few and leaky.

THE new House all going to Ruin before it is finished.

ONE Hinge of the Street Door broke off, and the People forced to go out and come in at the Back-door.

THE Door of the Dean's Bed-chamber full of large Chinks.

THE Beauset letting in so much Wind that it almost blows out the Candles.

THE Dean's Bed threatening every Night to fall under him.

THE little Table loose and broken in the Joints.

THE Passages open over Head, by which the Cats pass continually into the Cellar, and eat the Victuals; for which one was tried, condemned, and executed by the Sword.

THE large Table in a very tottering Condition.

BUT one Chair in the House fit for sitting on, and that in a very ill State of Health.

THE Kitchen perpetually crouded with Savages.

NOT a Bit of Mutton to be had in the Country.

WANT of Beds, and a Mutiny thereupon among the Servants, until supplied from *Kells*.

AN egregious Want of all the most common necessary Utensils.

NOT a Bit of Turf this cold Weather, and Mrs. *Johnson* and the Dean in Person, with all their Servants forced to assist at the Bog in gathering up the wet Bottoms of old Clamps.

THE Grate in the Ladies Bed-chamber broke, and forced to be removed, by which they were compelled to be without Fire, the Chimney smoking intolerably; and the Dean's great Coat was employed to stop the Wind from coming down the Chimney, without which Expedient they must have been starved to Death.

A MESSENGER sent a Mile to borrow an old broken Tundish.

BOTTLES stopped with Bits of Wood and Tow, instead of Corks.

NOT one Utensil for a Fire, except an old Pair of Tongs, which travels through the House, and is likewise employed to take the Meat out of the Pot, for Want of a Flesh-Fork.

EVERY Servant an arrant Thief as to Victuals and Drink, and every Comer and Goer as arrant a Thief of every Thing he or she can lay their Hands on.

THE Spit blunted with poking into Bogs for Timber, and tears the Meat to Pieces.

Bellum atque fœminam: Or, a Kitchen war between Nurse and a nasty Crew of both Sexes; she to preserve Order and Cleanliness, they to destroy both; and they generally are Conquerors.

April 28. This Morning the great Fore-door quite open, dancing Backwards and Forwards with all its Weight upon the lower Hinge, which must have been broke if the Dean had not accidentally come and relieved it.

A GREAT Hole in the Floor of the Ladies Chamber, every Hour hazarding a broken Leg.

Two damnable Iron Spikes erect on the Dean's Bedstead, by which he is in Danger of a broken Shin at rising and going to Bed.

THE Ladies and Dean's Servants growing fast into the Manners and Thieveries of the Natives: The Ladies themselves very much corrupted; the Dean perpetually storming, and in Danger of either losing all his Flesh, or sinking into Barbarity for the Sake of Peace.

MRS. *Dingley* full of Cares for herself, and Blunders and Negligence for her Friends. Mrs. *Johnson* sick and helpless:

The Dean deaf and fretting; the Lady's Maid aukward and clumsy; *Robert* lazy and forgetful; *William* a pragmatical, ignorant and conceited Puppy; *Robin* and Nurse the two great and only Supports of the Family.

Bellum lactæum: Or, The milky Battle, fought between the Dean and the Crew of *Quilca*; the latter insisting on their Privilege of not milking until Eleven in the Forenoon; whereas Mrs. *Johnson* wanted Milk at Eight for her Health. In this Battle the Dean got the Victory; but the Crew of *Quilca* begin to rebel again; for it is this Day almost 10 o'Clock, and Mrs. *Johnson* hath not got her Milk.

A PROVERB on the Laziness and Lodgings of the Servants: *The worse their Stye, the longer they lie.*

Two great Holes in the Wall of the Ladies Bed-chamber, just at the Back of the Bed, and one of them directly behind Mrs. *Johnson*'s Pillow, either of which would blow out a Candle in the calmest Day.

THE

HISTORY

OF THE

SECOND SOLOMON*

Written in the Year 1729.

HE became acquainted with a person distinguished for poetical and other writings, and in an eminent station, who treated him with great kindness on all occasions, and he became familiar in this person's house†. In three months time, Solomon, without the least provocation, writ a long poem, describing that person's muse to be dead, and making a funeral solemnity with asses, owls, &c. and gave the copy among all his acquaintance.

Solomon became acquainted with a most deserving lady, an intimate friend of the above person‡, who entertained him also as she would a brother; and, upon giving him a little good advice, in the most decent manner, with relation to his wife, he told her, She was like other women, as bad as she was, and that they were all alike: Although his wife be, in every regard except gallantry, (which no creature would attempt) the most disagreeable beast in Europe.

He lets his wife (whom he pretends to hate as she deserves) govern, insult, and ruin him, as she pleases. Her character is this: Her person is detestably disagreeable; a most filthy slut; lazy, and slothful, and luxurious, ill-natured, envious, suspicious; a scold, expensive on herself, covetous to others: She takes thieves and whores, for cheapness, to be her servants, and turns them off every week: Positive, insolent, an ignorant, prating, overweening fool; a lover of the dirtiest, meanest

* Dr. Sheridan.   † Dean Swift.   ‡ Stella.

company: An abominable tatler, affecting to be jealous of her husband with ladies of the best rank and merit, and merely out of affectation for perfect vanity.

Solomon has no ill-design upon any person but himself, and he is the greatest deceiver of himself on all occasions.

His thoughts are sudden, and the most unreasonable always comes uppermost; and he constantly resolves and acts upon his first thoughts, and then asks advice, but never once before.

The person above-mentioned, whom he lampooned in three months after their acquaintance, procured him a good preferment from the Lord Lieutenant: Upon going down to take possession, Solomon preached, at Cork, a sermon on King George's birth-day, on this text, *Sufficient to the day is the evil thereof.*

Solomon, having been famous for a high Tory, and suspected as a Jacobite, it was a most difficult thing to get any thing for him: But that person, being an old friend of Lord Carteret, prevailed against all Solomon's enemies, and got him made likewise one of his Excellency's chaplains. But, upon this sermon, he was struck out of the list, and forbid the Castle, until that same person brought him again to the Lieutenant, and made them friends.

A fancy sprung in Solomon's head, that a house near Dublin would be commodious for him and his boarders, to lodge in on Saturdays and Sundays: Immediately, without consulting with any creature, he takes a lease of a rotten house at Rathfarnam, the worst air in Ireland, for 999 years, at twelve pounds a year; the land, which was only a strip of ground, not being worth twenty shillings a year. When the same person whom he lampooned heard the thing, he begged Solomon to get a clause of surrender, and at last prevailed to have it done after twenty-one years; because it was a madness to pay eleven pounds a year, for a thousand years, for a house that could not last twenty. But Solomon made an agreement with his landlady that he should be at liberty to surrender his lease in seven years; and, if he did not do it at that time, should be obliged to keep it for 999 years. In the mean time, he expends about one hundred pounds on the house and garden-wall; and in less than three years, contracts such a hatred to the house, that he lets it run to ruin: So that when the seven years are expired, he must either take it for the remainder of the 999 years, or be sued for waste, and lose all the money he laid out: And now he pays twelve pounds a year for a place he never sees.

Solomon has an estate of about thirty-five pounds *per annum*, in the county of Cavan; upon which, instead of ever receiving one penny rent, he hath expended above thirty pound *per annum*, in buildings and plantations, which are all gone to ruin.

Solomon is under-tenant to a Bishop's lease: he is bound by articles to his Lordship to renew and pay a fine, whenever the Bishop renews with his landlord, and to raise his rent as the landlord shall raise it to the Bishop. Seven years expire: Solomon's landlord demands a fine, which he readily pays; then asks for a lease: The landlord says, he may have it at any time. He never gets it. Another seven years elapse: Solomon's landlord demands another fine, and an additional rent: Solomon pays both; asks to have his lease renewed: The steward answers, he will speak to his master. Seventeen years are elapsed: The landlord sends Solomon word that his lease is forfeited, because he hath not renewed and paid his fines according to articles: and now they are at law upon this admirable case.

It is Solomon's great happiness, that, when he acts in the common concerns of life against common sense and reason, he values himself thereupon as if it were the mark of a great genius, above little regards or arts, and that his thoughts are too exalted to descend into the knowledge of vulgar management; and you cannot make him a greater compliment than by telling instances to the company, before his face, how careless he was in any affair that related to his interest and fortune.

He is extremely proud and captious, apt to resent as an affront and an indignity, what was never intended for either.

He is allured as easily by every new acquaintance, especially among women, as a child is by a new play-thing, and is led at will by them to suspect and quarrel with his best friends, of whom he hath lost the greatest part, for want of that indulgency which they ought to allow for his failings.

He is a generous, honest, good-natured man; but his perpetual want of judgment and discretion, makes him act as if he were neither generous, honest, nor good-natured.

The person above-mentioned, whom he lampooned, and to whom he owes his preferment, being in the country and out of order; Solomon had appointed to come for him with a chaise, and bring him to town. Solomon sent him word that he was to set out on Monday, and did accordingly, but to another part of the kingdom, thirty miles wide of the place appointed, in compliment to a lady who was going that way; there staid, with her and her family, a month, then sent the chaise, in the midst of winter, to bring the said person, where Solomon would meet him, declaring he could not venture himself for fear of the frost: And upon the said person's refusing to go in the chaise alone, or to trust to Solomon's appointment, and being in ill health; Solomon fell into a formal quarrel with that person, and foully misrepresented the whole affair to justify himself.

Solomon had published a humorous ballad, called *Balyspellin*, whither he had gone to drink the waters, with a new favourite lady. The ballad was in the manner of Mr. Gay's on *Molly Mogg*, pretending to contain all the rhymes of *Balyspellin*. His friend, the person so often mentioned, being at a gentleman's house in the neighbourhood, and merry over Solomon's ballad, they agreed to make another, in dispraise of Balyspellin-wells, which Solomon had celebrated, and with all new rhymes not made use of in Solomon's. The thing was done, and all in a mere jest and innocent merriment. Yet Solomon was prevailed upon, by the Lady he went with, to resent this as an affront on her and himself; which he did accordingly, against all the rules of reason, taste, good-nature, judgement, gratitude, or common manners.

He will invite six or more people of condition to dine with him on a certain day, some of them living five or six miles from town. On the day appointed he will be absent, and know nothing of the matter, and they all go back disappointed: When he is told of this, he is pleased, because it shews him to be a genius and a man of learning.

Having lain many years under the obloquy of a high Tory and Jacobite, upon the present Queen's birth-day he writ a song, to be performed before the Government and those who attended them, in praise of the Queen and the King, on the common topics of her beauty, wit, family, love of England, and all other virtues, wherein the King and the Royal Children were sharers. It was very hard to avoid the common topics, which were mentioned in abundance. A young collegian, who had done the same job the year before, got some reputation on the account of his wit: Solomon would needs vie with him, by which he lost all the esteem of his old friends the Tories, and got not the least interest with the Whigs; for they are now too strong to want advocates of that kind: And therefore one of the Lords Justices, reading the verses in some company, said, 'Ah, Doctor, this shall not do.' His name was at length in the title-page; and he did this without the knowledge or advice of one living soul, as he himself confesseth.

His full conviction of having acted wrong, in a hundred instances, leaves him as positive in the next instance as if he had never been mistaken in his life: And if you go to him the next day, and find him convinced in the last, he hath another instance ready, wherein he is as positive as he was the day before.

ON THE

DEATH

OF

Mrs. JOHNSON, [STELLA.]

THIS day, being Sunday, January 28th, 1727–8, about eight o'clock at night, a servant brought me a note, with an account of the death of the truest, most virtuous, and valuable friend, that I, or perhaps any other person ever was blessed with. She expired about six in the evening of this day; and, as soon as I am left alone, which is about eleven at night, I resolve, for my own satisfaction, to say something of her life and character.

She was born at Richmond in Surrey on the thirteenth day of March, in the year 1681. Her father was a younger brother of a good family in Nottinghamshire, her mother of a lower degree; and indeed she had little to boast of her birth. I knew her from six years old, and had some share in her education, by directing what books she should read, and perpetually instructing her in the principles of honour and virtue; from which she never swerved in any one action or moment of her life. She was sickly from her childhood until about the age of fifteen: But then grew into perfect health, and was looked upon as one of the most beautiful, graceful, and agreeable young women in London, only a little too fat. Her hair was blacker than a raven, and every feature of her face in perfection. She lived generally in the country, with a family, where she contracted an intimate friendship with another lady* of more advanced years. I was then (to my mortification) settled in Ireland; and, about a year after, going to visit my friends in England, I found she was a little

* Mrs. Dingley.

uneasy upon the death of a person on whom she had some dependance. Her fortune, at that time, was in all not above fifteen hundred pounds, the interest of which was but a scanty maintenance, in so dear a country, for one of her spirit. Upon this consideration, and indeed very much for my own satisfaction, who had few friends or acquaintance in Ireland, I prevailed with her and her dear friend and companion, the other lady, to draw what money they had into Ireland, a great part of their fortune being in annuities upon funds. Money was then at ten *per cent.* in Ireland, besides the advantage of turning it, and all necessaries of life at half the price. They complied with my advice, and soon after came over; but, I happening to continue some time longer in England, they were much discouraged to live in Dublin, where they were wholly strangers. She was at that time about nineteen years old, and her person was soon distinguished. But the adventure looked so like a frolic, the censure held, for some time, as if there were a secret history in such a removal; which, however, soon blew off by her excellent conduct. She came over with her friend on the   in the year 170–; and they both lived together until this day, when death removed her from us. For some years past, she had been visited with continual ill-health; and several times, within these two years, her life was despaired of. But, for this twelve-month past, she never had a day's health; and, properly speaking, she hath been dying six months, but kept alive, almost against nature, by the generous kindness of two physicians, and the care of her friends. Thus far I writ the same night between eleven and twelve.

Never was any of her sex born with better gifts of the mind, or more improved them by reading and conversation. Yet her memory was not of the best, and was impaired in the latter years of her life. But I cannot call to mind that I ever once heard her make a wrong judgment of persons, books, or affairs. Her advice was always the best, and with the greatest freedom, mixt with the greatest decency. She had a gracefulness somewhat more than human in every motion, word, and action. Never was so happy a conjunction of civility, freedom, easiness and sincerity. There seemed to be a combination among all that knew her, to treat her with a dignity much beyond her rank: Yet people of all sorts were never more easy than in her company. Mr. Addison, when he was in Ireland, being introduced to her, immediately found her out; and, if he had not soon after left the kingdom, assured me he would have used all endeavours to cultivate her friendship. A rude or conceited coxcomb passed his time very ill, upon the least breach of respect; for in such a case she had no mercy, but was sure to expose him to the contempt of the standers-by; yet in such a manner as he was ashamed to complain, and durst not resent. All of us, who had the happiness of her friendship, agreed unanimously, that, in an afternoon or evening's conversation, she never failed before we parted of delivering the best thing that was said in the company. Some of us have written down several of her sayings, or what the French call *Bon Mots*, wherein she excelled almost beyond belief. She never mistook the understanding of others; nor ever said a severe word, but where a much severer was deserved.

Her servants loved and almost adored her at the same time. She would, upon occasions, treat them with freedom, yet her demeanour was so awful, that they durst not fail in the least point of respect. She chid them seldom, but it was with severity, which had an effect upon them for a long time after.

January 29th, My Head achs, and I can write no more.

January 30th, Tuesday.

This is the night of the funeral, which my sickness will not suffer me to attend. It is now nine at night, and I am removed into another apartment, that I may not see the light in the church, which is just over against the window of my bed-chamber.

With all the softness of temper that became a lady, she had the personal courage of a hero. She and her friend having removed their lodgings to a new house, which stood solitary, a parcel of rogues, armed, attempted the house, where there was only one boy: She was then about four and twenty: And, having been warned to apprehend some such attempt, she learned the management of a pistol; and the other women and servants being half-dead with fear, she stole softly to her dining-room window, put on a black hood, to prevent being seen, primed the pistol fresh, gently lifted up the sash; and, taking aim with the utmost presence of mind, discharged the pistol loaden with the bullets, into the body of one villain, who stood the fairest mark. The fellow, mortally wounded, was carried off by the rest, and died the next morning, but his companions could not be found. The Duke of Ormond hath often drank her health to me upon that account, and had always an high esteem of her. She was indeed under some apprehensions of going in a boat, after some danger she had narrowly escaped by water, but she was reasoned thoroughly out of it. She was never known to cry out, or discover any fear, in a coach or on horseback, or any uneasiness by those sudden accidents with which most of her sex, either by weakness or affectation, appear so much disordered.

She never had the least absence of mind in conversation, nor given to interruption, or appeared eager to put in her word by waiting impatiently until another had done. She spoke in a most agreeable voice, in the plainest words, never hesitating, except out of modesty before new faces, where she was somewhat reserved; nor, among her nearest friends, ever spoke much at a time. She was but little versed in the common topics of female chat; scandal, censure, and detraction, never came out of her mouth: Yet, among a few friends, in private conversation, she made little ceremony in discovering her contempt of a coxcomb, and describing all his follies to the life; but the follies of her own sex she was rather inclined to extenuate or to pity.

When she was once convinced by open facts of any breach of truth or honour, in a person of high station, especially in the church, she could not conceal her indignation, nor hear them named without shewing her displeasure in her countenance; particularly one or two of the latter sort, whom she had known and esteemed, but detested above all mankind, when it was manifest that they had sacrificed those two precious virtues to their ambition, and would much sooner have forgiven them the common immoralities of the laity.

Her frequent fits of sickness, in most parts of her life, had prevented her from making that progress in reading which she would otherwise have done. She was well versed in the Greek and Roman story, and was not unskilled in that of France and England. She spoke French perfectly, but forgot much of it by neglect and sickness. She had read carefully all the best books of travels, which serve to open and enlarge the mind. She understood the Platonic and Epicurean philosophy, and judged very well of the defects of the latter. She made very judicious abstracts of the best books she had read. She understood the nature of government, and could point out all the errors of Hobbes, both in that and religion. She had a good insight into physic, and knew somewhat of anatomy; in both which she was instructed in her younger days by an eminent physician, who had her long under his care, and bore the highest esteem for her person and understanding. She had a true taste of wit and good sense, both in poetry and prose, and was a perfect good critic of style: Neither was it easy to find a more proper or impartial judge, whose advice an author might better rely on, if he intended to send a thing into the world, provided it was on a subject that came within the compass of her knowledge. Yet, perhaps, she was sometimes too severe, which is a safe and pardonable error. She preserved her wit, judgment, and vivacity to the last, but often used to complain of her memory.

Her fortune, with some accession, could not, as I have heard say, amount to much more than two thousand pounds, whereof a great part fell with her life, having been placed upon annuities in England, and one in Ireland. In a person so extraordinary, perhaps it may be pardonable to mention some particulars, although of little moment, further than to set forth her character. Some presents of gold-pieces being often made to her while she was a girl, by her mother and other friends, on promise to keep them, she grew into such a spirit of thrift, that, in about three years, they amounted to above two hundred pounds. She used to shew them with boasting;

but her mother, apprehending she would be cheated of them, prevailed, in some months, and with great importunities, to have them put out to interest: When the girl lost the pleasure of seeing and counting her gold, which she never failed of doing many times in a day, and despaired of heaping up such another treasure, her humour took quite the contrary turn: She grew careless and squandering of every new acquisition, and so continued until about two and twenty; when, by advice of some friends, and the fright of paying large bills of tradesmen, who enticed her into their debt, she began to reflect upon her own folly, and was never at rest until she had discharged all her shop-bills, and refunded herself a considerable sum she had run out. After which, by the addition of a few years, and a superior understanding, she became, and continued all her life a most prudent œconomist; yet still with a strong bent to the liberal side, wherein she gratified herself by avoiding all expence in cloaths, (which she ever despised) beyond what was merely decent. And, although her frequent returns of sickness were very chargeable, except fees to physicians, of which she met with several so generous, that she could force nothing on them, (and indeed she must otherwise have been undone;) yet she never was without a considerable sum of ready money. Insomuch that, upon her death, when her nearest friends thought her very bare, her executors found in her strong box about a hundred and fifty pounds in gold. She lamented the narrowness of her fortune in nothing so much, as that it did not enable her to entertain her friends so often, and in so hospitable a manner as she desired. Yet they were always welcome; and, while she was in health to direct, were treated with neatness and elegance: So that the revenues of her and her companion, passed for much more considerable than they really were. They lived always in lodgings, their domesticks consisting of two maids and one man. She kept an account of all the family-expences, from her arrival in Ireland to some months before her death; and she would often repine, when looking back upon the annals of her household bills, that every thing necessary for life was double the price, while interest of money was sunk almost to one half; so that the addition made to her fortune was indeed grown absolutely necessary.

[I since writ as I found time.]

But her charity to the poor was a duty not to be diminished, and therefore became a tax upon those tradesmen who furnish the fopperies of other ladies. She bought cloaths as seldom as possible, and those as plain and cheap as consisted with the situation she was in; and wore no lace for many years. Either her judgment or fortune was extraordinary, in the choice of those on whom she bestowed her charity; for it went further in doing good, than double the sum from any other hand. And I have heard her say, she always met with gratitude from the poor: Which must be owing to her skill in distinguishing proper objects, as well as her gracious manner in relieving them.

But she had another quality that much delighted her, although it may be thought a kind of check upon her bounty; however, it was a pleasure she could not resist: I mean that of making agreeable presents, wherein I never knew her equal, although it be an affair of as delicate a nature as most in the course of life. She used to define a present, That it was a gift to a friend of something he wanted or was fond of, and which could not be easily gotten for money. I am confident, during my acquaintance with her, she hath, in these, and some other kinds of liberality, disposed of to the value of several hundred pounds. As to presents made to herself, she received them with great unwillingness, but especially from those to whom she had ever given any; being on all occasions the most disinterested mortal I ever knew or heard of.

From her own disposition, at least as much as from the frequent want of health, she seldom made any visits; but her own lodgings, from before twenty years old, were frequented by many persons of the graver sort, who all respected her highly, upon her good sense, good manners, and conversation. Among these were the late Primate Lindsay, Bishop Lloyd, Bishop Ashe, Bishop Brown, Bishop Stearn, Bishop Pulleyn, with some others of later date; and indeed the greatest number of her acquaintance was among the clergy.

S

Honour, truth, liberality, good-nature, and modesty, were the virtues she chiefly possessed, and most valued in her acquaintance; and where she found them, would be ready to allow for some defects, nor valued them less, although they did not shine in learning or in wit; but would never give the least allowance for any failures in the former, even to those who made the greatest figure in either of the two latter. She had no use of any person's liberality, yet her detestation of covetous people made her uneasy if such a one was in her company; upon which occasion she would say many things very entertaining and humorous.

She never interrupted any person who spoke; she laught at no mistakes they made, but helped them out with modesty; and if a good thing were spoken, but neglected, she would not let it fall, but set it in the best light to those who were present. She listened to all that was said, and had never the least distraction, or absence of thought.

It was not safe nor prudent, in her presence, to offend in the least word against modesty; for she then gave full employment to her wit, her contempt and resentment, under which even stupidity and brutality were forced to sink into confusion; and the guilty person, by her future avoiding him like a bear or a satyr, was never in a way to transgress a second time.

It happened one single coxcomb, of the pert kind, was in her company, among several other ladies; and, in his flippant way, began to deliver some double meanings; the rest flapt their fans, and used the other common expedients practised in such cases, of appearing not to mind or comprehend what was said. Her behaviour was very different, and perhaps may be censured. She said thus to the man: 'Sir, all these ladies and I 'understand your meaning very well, having, in spite of our 'care, too often met with those of your sex who wanted 'manners and good sense. But, believe me, neither virtuous, 'nor even vicious women love such kind of conversation. 'However, I will leave you, and report your behaviour: And, 'whatever visit I make, I shall first enquire at the door whether 'you are in the house, that I may be sure to avoid you.'

I know not whether a majority of ladies would approve of such a proceeding; but I believe the practice of it would soon put an end to that corrupt conversation, the worst effect of dulness, ignorance, impudence, and vulgarity, and the highest affront to the modesty and understanding of the female sex.

By returning very few visits, she had not much company of her own sex, except those whom she most loved for their easiness, or esteemed for their good sense; and those, not insisting on ceremony, came often to her. But she rather chose men for her companions, the usual topics of ladies discourse being such as she had little knowledge of, and less relish. Yet no man was upon the rack to entertain her, for she easily descended to any thing that was innocent and diverting. News, politics, censure, family-management, or town-talk, she always diverted to something else; but these indeed seldom happened, for she chose her company better: And therefore many, who mistook her and themselves, having solicited her acquaintance, and finding themselves disappointed after a few visits, dropt off; and she was never known to enquire into the reason, or ask what was become of them.

She was never positive in arguing, and she usually treated those who were so, in a manner which well enough gratified that unhappy disposition; yet in such a sort as made it very contemptible, and at the same time did some hurt to the owners. Whether this proceeded from her easiness in general, or from her indifference to certain persons, or from her despair of mending them, or from the same practice which she much liked in Mr. Addison, I cannot determine; but when she saw any of the company very warm in a wrong opinion, she was more inclined to confirm them in it, than oppose them. The excuse she commonly gave when her friends asked the reason, was, That it prevented noise, and saved time. Yet I have known her very angry with some whom she much esteemed for sometimes falling into that infirmity.

She loved Ireland much better than the generality of those who owe both their birth and riches to it; and, having brought over all the fortune she had in money, left the reversion of the best part of it, one thousand pounds, to Dr. Stephens's Hospital. She detested the tyranny and injustice of England, in their treatment of this kingdom. She had indeed reason to love a country, where she had the esteem and friendship of all who knew her, and the universal good report of all who ever heard of her, without one exception, if I am told the truth by those who keep general conversation. Which character is the more extraordinary, in falling to a person of so much knowledge, wit, and vivacity, qualities that are used to create envy, and consequently censure; and must be rather imputed to her great modesty, gentle behaviour, and inoffensiveness, than to her superior virtues.

Although her knowledge, from books and company, was much more extensive than usually falls to the share of her sex; yet she was so far from making a parade of it, that her female visitants, on their first acquaintance, who expected to discover it, by what they call hard words and deep discourse, would be sometimes disappointed, and say, they found she was like other women. But wise men, through all her modesty, whatever they discoursed on, could easily observe that she understood them very well, by the judgment shewn in her observations, as well as in her questions.

Bons Mots de STELLA.

A LADY of my intimate Acquaintance both in *England* and *Ireland*, in which last Kingdom she lived from the eighteenth Year of her Age, twenty-six Years, had the most and finest Accomplishments of any Person I ever knew of either Sex. It was observed by all her Acquaintance, that she never failed in Company to say the best Thing that was said, whoever was by; yet her Companions were usually Persons of the best Understanding in the Kingdom. Some of us, who were her nearest Friends, lamented that we never wrote down her Remarks, and what the *French* call *Bons Mots*. I will recollect as many as I can remember.

We were diverting ourselves at a Play called *What is it like?* One Person is to think, and the rest, without knowing the Thing, to say what it is like. The Thing thought on was the Spleen; she had said it was like an Oyster, and gave her Reason immediately, because it is removed by taking Steel inwardly.

Dr. *Sheridan*, who squandered more than he could afford, took out his Purse as he sat by the Fire, and found it was very hot; she said, the Reason was, that his Money burnt in his Pocket.

She called to her Servants to know what ill Smell was in the Kitchen? They answered, they were making Matches: Well, said she, I have heard Matches were made in Heaven, but by the Brimstone, one would think they were made in Hell.

After she had been eating some sweet Thing, a little of it happened to stick on her Lips; a Gentleman told her of it, and offered to lick it off; she said, no Sir, I thank you, I have a Tongue of my own.

In the late King's Time, a Gentleman asked *Jervas* the Painter, Where he lived in *London?* He answered, next Door to the King (for his House was near St. *James*'s.) The other wondering how that could be; she said, you mistake Mr. *Jervas*, for he only means next Door to the *Sign* of a King.

A Gentleman who had been very silly and pert in her Company, at last began to grieve at remembering the Loss of a Child lately dead. A Bishop sitting by comforted him that he should be easy, because the Child was gone to Heaven. No, my Lord, said she, that is it which most grieves him, because he is sure never to see his Child there.

Having seen some Letters writ by a King in a very large Hand, and some Persons wondering at them, she said, it confirmed the old Saying, *That Kings had long Hands.*

Dr. *Sheridan*, famous for punning, and intending to sell a Bargain, said, he had made a very good Pun. Somebody asked, What it was? He answered, my A——. The other taking Offence, she insisted the Doctor was in the right, for every Body knew that punning was his *blind Side*.

When she was extreamly ill, her Physicians said, Madam, you are near the Bottom of the Hill, but we will endeavour to get you up again. She answered, Doctor, I fear, I shall be *out of Breath* before I get up to the Top.

A dull Parson talking of a very smart Thing, said to another Parson as he came out of the Pulpit, he was hammering a long Time, but could not remember the Jest; she being impatient, said, I remember it very well, for I was there, and the Words were these: Sir, you have been blundering at a Story this half Hour, and can neither make Head nor Tail of it.

A very dirty Clergyman of her Acquaintance, who affected Smartness and Repartee, was asked by some of the Company how his Nails came to be so dirty? He was at a Loss; but she solved the Difficulty, by saying, the Doctor's Nails grew dirty by scratching *himself*.

A Quaker Apothecary sent her a Phial corkt; it had a broad Brim, and a Label of Paper about its Neck. What is that, said she, my Apothecary's Son? The ridiculous Resemblance, and the Suddenness of the Question, set us all a Laughing.

Marginalia

MARGINALIA

1. (Parsons, Robert): *A CONFERENCE ABOUT THE NEXT SUCCES-SION TO THE CROWN OF ENGLAND.* Re-printed MDCLXXXI.

On the right hand top corner of the title-page: 'Jon: Swift.' and at the foot of the last page 202, in the margin: Read over Decbr. 28. 1705. J.S.

Page	Parsons	Swift
46	But in the end King *Henry* the Third was admitted, and he proved a very worthy King, after so evil as had gone before him, and had been Deposed, (which is a circumstance that you must always note in this Narration) and he reigned more years than ever King in *England* did before him;	Here he strains the Point, for Henr. 3. was a very bad King.
57–8	many other Kings also (punished) by God himself . . . which had not been Justice on God's part to punish them, if it had been lawful for them to use what manner of proceeding towards their people, as these good Instructers of Princes in our days, most fondly and wickedly do affirm:	A good Opinion weakly defended
70–2	This Otho then . . . named by *Henry* himself to the Inheritance of the said Crown of *Germany,* yet was he not admitted thereunto until he made his Oath and received his new approbation by the people; . . . chosen and admitted again by the Prince and People, and that he Swore to fulfil all those points and conditions, which the signification of the Emperial Ornaments did bind him unto.	It does not appear that he swore.
153	After the Conqueror's death . . . *Robert* being absent in the War of *Hierusalem,* the Holy and Learned man *Lanfranke,* . . . being deceived with vain hope of *William Rufus*'s good nature, persuaded them etc.	that is a mistake
171	certain it is, that unto me and my Conscience he which in any point believeth otherwise than I do, and standeth wilfully in the same, is an *Infidel,* for that he believeth not that which in my Faith and Conscience is the onely and sole Truth, whereby he must be saved.	This is strange Doctrine and hardly sense.
172–3	for any man to give his help, consent or assistance towards the making of a King, whom he judgeth or believeth to be faulty in Religion, and consequently would advance either no Religion, or the wrong, if he were in Authority, is a most grievous and damnable sin	This book was seasonably published about the Time of the Bill for excluding the D. of York.

Page	*Parsons*	*Swift*
175	*(at the end of Part I, cap. 9)*	The latter Part of this Chapter savours much of the Jesuit, and is calculated to raise an inevitable War at the death of Qu. Eliz.

Part II

55 For albeit God had a meaning to punish him, for the sins of his Father *Solomon*, yet suffered he that Rehoboam also should give just occasion himself for the people to leave him, as appeareth by the story; and this is God's high Wisdom, Justice, Providence, and sweet disposition in humane affairs.

from such Examples would not one think he jested

63 the question (whether the Uncle or Nephew should be preferred in Succession of Kingdoms) doubtful among the Wise and Learned of those days.

they were a parcel of Dunces to dispute such a Point.

101 The title to the Crown of the Lady *Arabella*, second branch of the House of *Scotland*—she is a meer stranger; for that her Kindred is only in *Scotland*, and in England she hath only the *Candishes* by her Mothers side; who being but a mean Family, might cause much grudging among the *English* Nobility, . . .

yet now they are Dukes of Devonshire.

116 (A Woman) may be Heir to some particular states of France inheritable by Women, though not to the Crown itself,

this the French deny now.

162 The condition of the Irish under the English—their Taxes and Payments be much less, the Laws of *England* bind them not, except they be allowed and received by their own Parliament in *Ireland*.

Tempora mutantur

172 –3 some external Prince should be admitted upon such Compositions and Agreements, as both the Realm should remain within her ancient Liberties, and perhaps much more than now it enjoyeth (for such Princes commonly and upon such occasions of Preferment would yield to much more in those Cases than a home-born Prince would,)

as Wm. 3 did in our days.

176 they answer to all the Reasons and Arguments . . . against foreign Government, that . . . they are founded for the most part in the errour and prejudice only of the vulgar sort of men, who being once stirred up by the name of Stranger, do consider no further . . ,

Yet K. W.3. was chiefly beloved by the Vulgar.

Judicium De Herodoto post longum
tempus relecto.

Ctesias mendacissimus Herodotum mendaciorum
arguit, exceptis paucissimis, (ut mea fert sententia)
omnimodo excusandum. Caeterum diverticulis
abundans hic pater Historicorum, filum narrationis
ad taedium abrumpit. quam unde oritur (ut par est)
legentibus confusio, et exinde obluvio. Quin et
forsan ipsae narrationes circumstantiis nimium pro
re scatent. Quod ad caetera, hunc Scriptorem inter
apprimè laudandos censeo, neque Graecis neque
Barbaris plus aequo faventem aut iniquum: in
orationibus ferè brevem, simplicem, nec nimis
frequentem. neque absunt dogmata è quibus
creditur lector prudentiam tam moralem quam
civilem haurire poterit.

Julij: 6. 1720. J. Swift.

I do hereby certify that the above is the
Hand Writing of the late Dr. Jonathan Swift,
D.S.P.D. from whom I have had many Letters,
and printed several Pieces from his original MS.
Dublin, August 21, 1762.

George Faulkner

Reproduced from Swift's own copy of Herodotus (Geneva, 1618) by
kind permission of the Warden and Fellows of Winchester College

Facing page 243

Page	Parsons	Swift
201	I said also, that this Lady *Infanta* . . . was likest of all Strangers to bear it away for . . . if her pretence to *England* should be disenabled before this Affair came to be tried, then may her said Father and she, if they list, cast their aforesaid Interests and Titles, (as divers men think they would) upon some other Prince . . .	This is a wild Conjecture.

2. HERODOTUS: *HISTORIA GRAEC.*, GENEVA, 1618

Facing the title-page, the following general comment in Swift's hand:
Judicium de Herodoto post longum tempus relecto

Ctesias mendacissimus Herodotum mendaciorum arguit, exceptis paucissimis, (ut mea fert sententia) omnimodo excusandum. Caeterum diverticulis abundans hic pater Historicorum, filum narrationis ad taedium abrumpit. unde oritur (ut par est) legentibus confusio, et exinde oblivio. Quin et forsan ipsae narrationes circumstantibus nimium pro re scatent. Quod ad caetera, hunc Scriptorem inter apprime laudandos censeo, neque Graecis neque Barbaris plus aequo faventem aut iniquum: in orationibus fere brevem, simplicem, nec nimis frequentem. neque absunt dogmata e quibus eruditus lector prudentiam tam moralem quam civilem haurire poterit.

July 6. 1720   J: Swift

Translation
Judgement on Herodotus, re-read after a long interval.

The archliar Ctesias accuses Herodotus of being a greater liar; but, to my mind, with very few exceptions he should be absolved on all counts. Yet the numerous digressions in this our Father of History do break off the thread of his narrative to the point of tedium; with the natural result that his readers become confused and then forget what has preceded. Moreover the narratives in themselves are perhaps more profuse in detail than their subject-matter demands. For the rest, I rank this writer among those who deserve the very highest praise. To neither Greek nor foreigner is he over-partial or less than fair. His set speeches are mostly short, straight-forward, and not too numerous. He writes, too, not without statements of belief from which a cultivated reader will be able to draw wisdom, both moral and political.

3. HERBERT, THOMAS: *A RELATION OF SOME YEARES TRAVAILE INTO AFRICA AND GREATER ASIA*, 1634

Facing the title-page, in Swift's hand, the following:
> If this Book were stript of its Impertinence, Conceitedness and tedious Digressions, it would be almost worth reading, and would then be two thirds smaller than it is

1720   J: Swift.

> The Author published a new Edition in his older Days with many Additions upon the whole more insufferable than this. He lived severall years after the Restoration and some Friends of mine knew him in Ireld. He seems to have been a Coxcomb both—aevi vitio et sui.

4. BODIN, JEAN: *LES SIX LIVRES DE LA RÉPUBLIQUE*, 1579

On the inner side of the cover is pasted an autograph note, signed Jonath Swift, April 2, 1725.

This Author was a Man of very great Reading, he excells in setting the Arguments on both sides of a Question in the strongest Light: but often (in my Judgment) decides wrong. He handles Government too much like a Lawyer, and grossly mistakes that of England. He shews some Inconveniences in Aristocracyes and Democracyes as necessary, which are easily avoydable. He seems not to have considered the Nature of representing many by few. His Royall Monarchy, which he proposeth as the most Perfect Government is visionary, unless every Country were sure to have always a good King, for he leaves the absolute Power of making and annulling Laws in the Will of the Soverain, although a single Person, contrary to the Judgment of the wisest Writers upon Government. His whimsicall Discourses upon Astrology and the Influence of the Starrs upon human Nature, together with his Digressions upon the Power of Numbers and Harmony are not I think to be otherwise accounted for than by some odd Turn in the Author's Brain, or a Vanity to shew his Acquaintance with Sciences out of his Way.

Page	Bodin	Swift
202	Poland Denmark and Sweden — la resolution de la paix, & de la guerre depend de la noblesse,	la mème chose en Angleterre
205	& en toutes les villes imperiales . . . il n'y a point d'appel a la chābre és causes criminelles	La Chambre des Seigneurs en Angleterre
217	V.S.M. c'est a dire votre majesté sacree.	peut etre serenissime
227	Si doncques il n'y a aucune image de puissance populaire, en l'assemblee des trois estats, qui se sont en ce Royaume, non plus, & encore moins qu'en Espaigne, & Angleterre.	l'ignorant!
235	nous estimons la plus belle chose du monde, de reuerer, seruir, & adorer notre Roy, comme l'image du Dieu viuāt.	le coquin
237	en Angleterre, en Ecosse . . . ou les Ducs, & Comtes estant morts leur enfans, & successeurs, ont bien les terres, mais ils n'ont pas les dignitez prorogatiues, & qualitez de leur predecesseurs.	cela est faux
239	Les vrayes marques d'vn grand Roy.	le sot!
240	H. VIII Roy d'Angleterre, qui laissa le Royaume a son fils Edouart : & a lui substitua Marie etc.	avec le conseil du Parlement
256	si le Prince est absoluement souuerain : comme sont les vrays Monarques de France, d'Espaigne, d'Angleterre	cela est tres faux a l'egard d'Angleterre
261	veu les sainctes loix & ordonnances, & les actions louables de Neron, les CINQ premieres annees qu'il fut Empereur	un erreur vulgaire
263	& la Roygne d'Angleterre sa cousine, qui a tousiours pretendu que les deux Royaumes lui appartiennent	la Reine d'Ecosse etait (?) en vie.

Page	*Bodin*	*Swift*
267	L'estat de Genes est beaucoup plus sujet à changement & à Genefue beaucoup plus asseuré	au contraire
(271)	& n'est pas au pouuoir de l'Empereur d'en leuer vn seul denier, sans la permission des estats. Qui monstre que ceux la sont bien loing de leur opinion qui pensent que l'Empereur soit souuerain.	Par consequence le Roy d'Angleterre n'est pas souuerain qui ne peut lever un denier sans la Permission du Parlement
285	(Marginal heading) S'il est moins dangereux d'auoir vn bon Prince assisté d'vn mauuais cõseil, qu'vn mauuais Prince cõduit par bon cõseil	Le Roy George d'Angleterre
288	Il y en a d'autres qui ne sont poussez, ny d'enuie ny d'inimitié, mais bien d'vne opiniastreté indomitable	le Comte de Notingam d'aujourdhui
291	vn cõseil à part des plus sages senateurs . . . affin d'aduiser aux affaires vrgentes	comme le Cabinet qu('on) appelle en Angleterre
302	. . . il estoit defendu sus peine de leze maiesté, de presenter requeste au peuple, sans auoir pris l'aduis du senat	Le Senat estoit Executeur du Pouvoir du Peuple et l'auteur
348	Mais y a il chose plus dangereuse ny plus pernicieuse, que la desobeissance & mepris du suget enuers le souuerain?	Doctrine detestable
413	toutes ces grandes vertus n'ont peu le maintenir, ny le garantir que son propre fils naturel, avec plusieurs autres coniurez ne le tuassent cruellement	Malice
440	. . . touts arguments, qui monstrent que le monde fut creé au mois de Septembre le Soleil en la Liure l. degré	le sot
460	le pis qu'il y a, c'est que bien souuent en tombant, ils tirent après eux la ruine de la Republique	il se trompe
461	Plusieurs ont empieté la souueraineté par cõtinuatiõ d'offices.	Cesar en Gaul
466	le monarque Royal, qui traitera ses sugets comme le bon père ses enfans.	et qui fiera à un tel Roy?
516	(5th Book) Du Reiglement qu'il faut tenir pour accommoder la forme de République à la Diuersité des hommes, & le moyen de cognoistre le naturel des peuples.	(Two or three crosses in the margin of almost every page, which seem to be Swift's marks.)
541	& Scaliger Veronois escrit, qu'il n'y a point de nation, qui ait l'esprit plus vif à faire tout ce qu'on voudra que le François, soit aux armes, soit aux lettres, soit à la marchandise, soit à bien dire :	cela est faux
629	Car le pensionaire quelquesfois est tel, qu'il ne voudroit pour tous les biẽs du mõde estre descouuert : cõme estoit vn certain milord Anglois, auquel le Roy	

Page	Bodin	Swift
	Loüys XI. dōnoit deux mil escus de pēsion : le porteur demādait aquit . . . le milord lui dist, qu'il recueroit bien la pēsion, mais qu'il n'en bailleroit point d'aquit :	My Ld Hastings
661	Mais il seroit beaucoup plus expedient de n'auoir autre monnoye que d'or, & d'argent, s'il estoit possible de forger monnoye plus petite que le pené	un erreur de tems
664	devant les sols, ou gros d'Angleterre	Groats
678	l'estat populaire est contraire au gens de bien. car la conseruation d'vn Republique populaire, si nous suiuons l'aduis de Xenophon, est d'auancer aux offices, & benefices les plus vicieux et les plus indignes etc.	Mal raisonné par tout
683	les Republiques en forme populaire : qui n'est autre chose en effect que la plus pernicieuse tyrannie qu'on puisse imaginer, si elle n'est gouuernee par gens sages, & vertueux, qui manient le gouuernail comme ceux que j'ay dit.	tous les inconvenients seront oté par une representation du Peuple par election
692	il aduient quelques fois . . . que la loi, ou le prince, ou le magistrat n'est point receu, si tous ceux qui ont voix, ne prestent consentement :	pour la Loy c'est la mème chose en Angleterre ce que cet auteur ne semble d'avoir compris
	mais le Monarque souuerain, se peut ioindre à plus saine & moindre partie :	mais se joindre, s'il est fou ou mal avisé
695	Les loix de honeur sōt plus recommandees à vn Monarque qu'à vn peuple.	le sot !
696	C'est l'exemple duquel usa Suleyman Roy des Turcs ayeul de cestuy-cy, ayant ouy les hautes acclamations, & cris de ioye que fist toute l'armee à Sultan Mustapha son fils retournant de Perse, après l'auoir fait estrāgler en son antichābre, & aussi tost getter mort deuat toute l'armee, il fist crier tout haut, qu'il n'y auoit qu'vn Dieu au ciel, & vn Sultan en la terre	belle exemple
	Aussi voyons nous tous les peuples de la terre de toute ancienneté, et lorsqu'ils estoyent guidez d'vne lumiere naturelle, n'auoir en autre forme de Republique, que la Monarchie, etc.	tant pis pour eux
706	Car le Royaume venant par droit successif comme a tousiours esté le Royaume d'Angleterre, tombe en chois, quand il n'y a proche parēt ny du costé paternel, ny du costé maternel.	et de France et de tout le monde
713	celui qui est né d'vn père, au parauant qu'il fust Roy, ny habile d'y venir par droit successif,	sotise

Page	*Bodin*	*Swift*
	Mais la difficulté est encores demeuree indecise, si le fils de l'aisné, doibt succeder au Roy son ayeul : ou bien si la couronne appartient au frère puisné,	point de difficulté
719	& de nostre aage entre Marie d'Angleterre, & Phillippe de Castile, qu'on appelloit le mari de la ROYNE:	cela est faux car il estoit Roy d'Angleterre &c.
	car si le peuple est genereux, & de bon coeur, il portera impatiēment que la femme commande.	cela est faux

5. HERBERT, EDWARD, LORD CHERBURY: *LIFE AND RAIGNE OF HENRY VIII,* 1649

Page	*Herbert*	*Swift*
36	*Edmund de la Pole,* sonne of John, Duke of *Suffolke* . . . should have his Head struck off;	(H)ellish (Do)g of a King
175	*Henry Fitz-Roy,* son of *Elizabeth Blunt,* avow'd by him and at the Age of six years made Knight publiquely etc.	A Dog, a true Kin(g)
176	Such was the generous disposition of our King, that not onely for *Francis* then a Prisoner, but the expulsed King of *Denmark, Christiern,* he interceded with his best Offices.	One Tyrant intercedes for another.
	But the angry Danes obstinately denyed	(a)nd justly
224	whether he can dispense with the King to have Two Wives, and the Children of both legitimate.	The profligate Dog of a King
226	To which our Ambassadours answered, That our King was a Prince of that piety, that etc.	Lying Rogues
230	nothing but desire of giving satisfaction to his Conscience, and care of establishing the Succession to the Crown . . . had first procur'd him to controvert this Marriage	An impudent perjured true King
258	Mistris *Bolen* whether she . . . had rather be that Lords Wife than a Kings Mistris (*crossed out*)	whore
293	one who had made use of the Evangelliques Doctrine so farre, as to take a reasonable liberty to judge of the present times, . . .	the Author means himself & (?) is his own Style
343	Sir *Thomas More*	The only Man of true Virtue tha(t) ever Engld produced
362	one who much favourd the Papall Authority, spake in this manner. (*This and the following speech marked with a hand drawn in Swift's manner*)	The two following (s)peeches were (c)omposed by the Author

Page	Herbert	Swift
391	he would have been glad not to be compell'd to such violent courses;	Nature alone compelled him
	He condemned *John Frith* a Sacramentary to the fire, . . . so he now caused divers Hollanders in *London* . . . to be burnt in Smithfield.	Barbarous dog!
392	Therefore he resolved now to deferre his Justice no longer (against *Fisher*)	Bloody inhuman Hell-hound of a King
394	Thus ended Sir *Thomas More*	(H)ere the detestable (Ty)rant murdred (Vir)tue her self
396–7	Whereupon, one said thus. To which another, who better understood the Kings Mind, answered thus.	These two Speeches were made by the Author
397	since they are houses dedicated to God, be pleas'd by all means, to convert the profit arising thence, TO SOME OTHER PIOUS USE,	that had been right, much better than give it to whores and Favorites, like an Atheist dog as he was
404	The King having received her (Queen Katherine) Letter, became so compassionate, that he wept	(Hy)pocritical (Vi)lain
399	(N.B. Signature 3C begins wrongly with p. 385 and subsequent pages are thus misnumbered.)	
	so that if in these two Divorces he had not reason, the chief of his Kingdome seem'd to erre with him: Unlesse ill Arts with the Nobility, and undue election of the Knights and Burgesses be suppos'd;	No; they were Slaves not Subjec(ts)
405	Whereas now the common Absolution of Priests, extending (for the most part) no further then to require ATTRITION, or SORROW for their offences past	wrongly defined
444	erected . . . out of the Revenues gotten hereby, divers new Bishopricks,	All beggarly Sees
	the Revenues allotted by the King to these new Bishopricks and Cathedrals amounting to about 8000 l. *per annum.*	hardly half so much even at this day
445	Parliament composed of persons wellaffected to the Kings Service (as his manner was always with great industry to procure such)	As all Rogues of Kings do
	That the King by the advice of his Counsell, or the more part of them might set forth Proclamations under such penalties and pains as to him or them shall seem necessary	Tyrannical
447	Justices of Peace in their Sessions and every Steward, under-steward, and Deputy of Steward in their Leet or Lawday, by the oathes of twelve men have authority to enquire of all the Heresies, Felonies, and offences aforesaid.	barbarous Dogs, and Slaves to that hellish Tyrant

Page	Herbert	Swift
468	the King . . . commanding the said Sir *John Nevil* to be put to death at *York*. Shortly after followed the Countess of *Salisbury's* Execution;	Dog, Villain, King, Viper, Devil Monster
503	And therefore, though some of his Courtiers . . . and others of his Subjects were fallen into the danger of the Six Articles, he voluntarily gave them his pardon;	O wonderful mercy to forgive once in the reign of this beast, what was no crime
508	whereupon our men entering Lieth, found more riches there (they said) then they could have easily imagined.	(1?)o marks (a)t least, as (so)me Scotch (A)uthors (b)oldly assert
561	And thus by her opportune submission she escaped: Though yet some beleeve, it was not so much the Kings intention herein to use the rigour of the Law, as to deter her from reading forbidden Books.	Partial
565	This while the King (though his sicknesse encreased) omitted not to give order to seize on the Duke's goods, and together to inform himself of all which might be materiall against him.	the dying Dog of a King
	The Duke of *Norfolk's* letter to the king— I your most humble Subject prostitute at your foot, do most humbly beseech your Highness to be my good and gracious Lord.	Very mean and abject
569	Notwithstanding all which submissions, joyned with the merits of his Services, it was thought that the Duke would hardly escape, had not the King's death, following shortly after, reserved him to more mercifull times.	The Brute of a King desired to dye in blood as he had lived.
570	Howsoever, it may be collected, that he died religiously and penitently,	yes, just as he lived.
	the course of his Life being commonly held various and diverse from it self, he will hardly suffer any (character)	No no, his whole Life was perfectly of a piece
	without either presuming audaciously to condemn a Prince, heretofore Soveraign of our Kingdom, or omitting the just freedom of a Historian	where is the Presumption? Nero was Emperor of Rome, and was a Saint in comparison of this dying dog Henry
571	At home it was his manner to treat much with his Parliaments; where, if gentle means served not, he came to some degrees of the ROUGH:	That is, he was a Tyrant over his Parliamt.
572	Therefore, without being much troubled at the tumultuous beginnings of the rasher sort, he would give them that leave, which all new things must have, to settle	yes, by hanging or cutting off 5 or 6 heads.
	(especially towards his later end) . . . an intense jealousie almost of all persons and affairs	the quality of all other guilty Vilains.

T

Page	Herbert	Swift
	astiled him both at home and abroad by the name of *Cruell*, which also hardly can be avoyded, especially, if that Attribute be due, not onely to those Princes who inflict capitall punishments frequently . . . but to those who pardon not all that are capable of mercy.	Does the Author question this monster's cruelty?
	and for testimonies in this kinde . . . huge multitudes.	Are not these sufficient?
	He gave some proofs yet that he could forgive, though as they were few and late, they seemed not to recover him the name of a Clement Prince.	What a softner is the Historian!
573	His . . . promiscuous overthrow of Religious Houses	He robbed the Church and then defended him self with the Spoyls.
	he erected divers new BISHOPRICKS,	beggarly ones
	increased the number of Colledges, and the Stipend of Readers	He robbed a Pound and restored a Pin
	his Parliaments were deeply ENGAGED	out of fear of the Tyrant
	his COVETOUSNESS . . . and PRODIGALITY	to gratify his damnable Lusts and Cruelty
574	Whereby it appears, that what in *Henry VII* is call'd by some Covetousness, was a ROYALL VIRTUE.	Oppression, the Author (*sic*) the Author must mean, for so it was in H.7.
	LUST and WANTONNESS	In that he acted like other Kings onely mingling it with blood.
	That concupiscence which in some is a vice,—in others a *necessity of nature*.	as men go to Stool so he was damnably laxative.
	he being more noted for practising PRIVATE PLEASURES, then secret mischiefs: so that if any undue motive did co-operate herein, it may be thought an inordinate desire to have Posterity (especially masculine) which might be the undoubted Heirs of Him and the Kingdom.	Were his private Pleasures followed in order to have Posterity to inherit the Crown
	the chief Potentates of Christendom did court him,	Because in a lower degree they were Rogues like himself
	his Accusers will neither admit Reason of State to cover any where, or Necessity to excuse his Actions	This palliating Author hath increased my Detestation of his Hellish Hero in every Article.
		whose whole Revenue (except a Trifle he gave to his Favorites *word erased*) or squandred on his Lusts.

Page	Herbert	Swift

575 Although one *William Thomas* a Clerk to the Council to Edward the Sixth, did in part defend him in an Italian book, 1552, it hath not availed

So his chief defender was this Wm Thomas.

To conclude; I wish I could LEAVE HIM IN HIS GRAVE.

And I wish he had been Flead, his skin stuffed and hangd on a Gibbet, His bulky guts and Flesh left to be devoured by Birds and Beasts) for a warning to his Successors for ever. Amen.

6. ADDISON, JOSEPH: *THE FREEHOLDER,* 1715-6

Page	Addison	Swift

No. 2. Dec. 26, 1715

16, l. 1 He surmounted those many Difficulties which lay in the Way to His Succession;

What Difficulties were those, or what Methods did he take to surmount them?

b. It is observed by Sir *W. Temple,* that the *English* are particularly fond of a King who is Valiant: Upon which Account His Majesty has a Title to all the Esteem that can be paid to the most Warlike Prince; tho' at the same time . . . He studies to decline all Occasions of Military Glory;

This seems to be a Discovery

18, l. 5 I might here take Notice of His Majesty's more private Virtues, but have rather chosen to remind my Countrymen of the public Parts of his Character,

This is prudent.

19, l. 10 But the most remarkable Interpositions of Providence, in favour of him, have appeared in removing those seemingly invincible Obstacles to his Succession; in taking away . . . the Person who might have proved a dangerous Enemy;

False, groundless, invidious, and ungrateful.

Was the person the Queen?

No. 3. December 30, 1715

21 Memoir of one of our late *Preston* heroes
22 Their grievances.

Could this Author, or his Party, offer as good Reasons for their infamous treatment of our blessed Queen's Person, Government, and Majesty?

l. 13 having been joined by a considerable Reinforcement of *Roman Catholicks,* whom we could rely upon, as knowing them to be the best *Tories* in the Nation,

By this irony, the best Whigs are professed Friends to Fanaticks

27, l. 10 But before we could give the Word, the Trainbands, taking Advantage of our Delay, fled first.

An Argument for a standing Army.

Page	*Addison*	*Swift*

No. 6. Jan. 9, 1715–6

54, l. 12 And tho' I should be unwilling to pronounce the Man who is indolent, or indifferent in the Cause of his Prince, to be absolutely perjured; I may venture to affirm, that he falls very short of that Allegiance to which he is obliged by Oath.

Suppose a King grows a Beast, or a Tyrant, after I have taken an Oath: a'prentice takes an Oath; but if his Master useth him barbarously, the lad may be excused if he wishes for a Better.

No. 7. Jan. 13, 1715–6

61, l. 1 if any Clergyman walks the Streets in his Habit, 'tis ten to one but he is knock'd down by some sturdy Schismatick.

No—but treated like a Dog.

No. 8. Jan. 16, 1715–6

65, l. 17 I will only desire her to think of her Countrey every Time she looks in her Glass

By no means, for if she loves her Country, she will not be pleased with the Sight.

66, l. 6 Every Wife ought to answer for her Man. If the Husband be ingaged in a seditious Club, or drinks mysterious Healths, or be frugal of his Candles on a rejoycing Night,

Will they hang a Man for that?

No. 9. Jan. 20, 1715–6

74, l. 26 and for having removed a General who is now actually in Arms against him,

Driven out by Tyranny, Malice, and Faction.

75, l. 22 The next Grievance is the Parliament of *Great Britain*, against whom you bring a stale Accusation . . . that it was procured by unwarrantable Influences and Corruptions.

The Freeholders will never sign this Paragraph.

77, l. 18 how comes it to pass that the Electorate of *Hanover* is become all of a sudden one of the most inconsiderable Provinces of the Empire?

It is indeed grown considerable by draining of England.

No. 12. Jan. 30, 1715–6

101, l. 14 the present Rebellion is form'd against a King, . . . who has not been charged with one illegal Proceeding;

Are you serious?

No. 13. Feb. 3, 1715–6

106, l. 20 In such a Juncture, a Man . . . is highly culpable, if he does not use all the Means that are suitable to his Station for reducing the Community into its former State of Peace and good Order.

He speaks at his ease, but those who are ill used will be apt to apply what the boy said to his Mother, who told him the Enemy was approaching.

108, l. 6 it was highly probable the Majority would be so Wise as to espouse that Cause which was most agreeable to the publick Weal, and by that Means hinder a Sedition from making a successful Progress.

No—for in England a Faction that governs a weak, or honours a wicked Prince, will carry all against a Majority in the Kingdom, as we have seen by sad experience.

| *Page* | *Addison* | *Swift* |

No. 14. Feb. 6, 1715–6

116, l. 26 Articles of the *Tory* Creed. XIII. That there is an Unwarrantable Faction in this Island, consisting of King, Lords, and Commons.

This Article is too true, with a little alteration.

117, l. 1 XV. That an Act of Parliament to impower the King to Secure Suspected Persons in Times of Rebellion, is . . . a great Infringement of the Liberties of the Subject.

No—but to destroy Liberty.

No. 21. Mar. 2, 1715–6

156, l. 17 When this excellent Princess was yet in her Father's Court, she was so celebrated for the Beauty of her Person,

I have bad Eyes.

159, l. 14 But there is no Part of Her Royal Highness's Character which we observe with greater Pleasure, than that Behaviour by which she has so much endear'd herself to His Majesty:

What would he say now? (i.e. in 1727)

No. 24. Mar. 12, 1715 6

178, l. 10 that submissive Deference of his Royal Highness both from Duty and Inclination to all the Measures of his Royal Father.

Which still continues.

179, l. 20 There is no Question but his Majesty will be as generally valued and beloved in his *British* as he is in his *German* Dominions, when he shall have Time to make his Royal Virtues equally known among us.

How long Time does he require?

No. 26. Mar. 19, 1715–6

191, *b.* the several Inconveniencies which those among the Ladies undergo, who have not yet surrender'd to the Government.

Would he pimp for the Court?

No. 29. Mar. 30, 1716

210, l. 22 Those of our Fellow-Subjects, who are sensible of the Happiness they enjoy in His Majesty's Accession to the Throne, are obliged . . . to adore that Providence which has (led us) through such Difficulties as seemed insuperable;

I wish he had told us any one of those Difficulties.

214, l. 16 it is the Duty of an honest and prudent Man, to sacrifice a doubtful Opinion to the concurring Judgment of those whom he believes to be well intentioned to their Countrey, and who have better Opportunities of looking into all its most complicated Interests.

A motion to make Men go every length with their Party. I am sorry to see such a Principle in this Author.

Page	*Addison*	*Swift*

No. 31. April 6, 1716

228, l. 6 This middle Method (to temper Justice with Mercy) . . . has hitherto been made use of by our Soveraign.   *In trifles.*

l. 17 of several Thousands . . . liable to Death . . . not above Forty have yet suffered?   *A trifle!*

234, l. 22 Has not His Majesty then shewn the least Appearance of Grace . . . in that generous Forgiveness of his Rebellious Subjects etc.   *Prodigious clemency, not to hang all the common Soldiers who followed their Leaders!*

235, l. 20 those who are pardoned would not have known the Value of Grace, if none had felt the Effects of Justice.   *And only hanging the Lords and Gentlemen, and some of the Rabble.*

236, l. 8 their Friends have ever since made use of the most base Methods to infuse those groundless Discontents into the Minds of the Common People   *Hath experience shown those Discontents groundless?*

l. 24 if the Removal of these Person from their Post has produced such popular Commotions, the Continuance of them might . . . have brought about that Revolution   *Very false Reasoning*

243, l. 8 unless his Mind be so blinded with Passion . . . as to assert . . . THAT NO INSTANCES CAN BE PRODUCED OF THE LEAST LENITY . . . FROM THE FIRST HOUR TO THIS DAY,   *Nor to this, 1727*

244, l. 12 God be thanked we have a King who punishes with Reluctancy,   *A great Comfort to the Sufferers!*

l. 25 (Monmouth's Rebellion) had no Tendency either to destroy the National Religion, to introduce an arbitrary Government etc.   *To introduce Fanaticism and destroy Monarchy*

246, l. 22 No Prince has ever given a greater Instance of his Inclinations to rule without a Standing-Army.   *We find this true by experience.*

247, l. 12 What greater Instances could His Majesty have given of his Love to the Church of *England* . . . by his solemn Declarations; by his daily Example; and by his Promotions etc.   *Most undeniable Truth, as any in Rabelais*

No. 44. May 21, 1716

330, b. What still gave him greater Offence was a drunken Bishop, who reeled from one side of the Court to the other, and was very sweet upon an *Indian* Queen.   *Then, that story is true?*

No. 45. May 25, 1716

332, l. 4 I have lately read with much Pleasure, the Essays upon several Subjects published by Sir *Richard Blackmore*;   *I admire to see such praises from this Author to so insipid a Scoundrel, whom I know he despised*

Page	*Addison*	*Swift*

No. 51. June 15, 1716

373, l. 27 History of Free-thinking, Writ by Collins

375, l. 3 the greatest Theorists among the Greeks and Romans . . . have given the Preference to such a Form of Government, as that which obtains in this Kingdom. Yet, this we see is liable to be wholly corrupted.

No. 52. June 18, 1716

380, l. 6 It is plain . . . that such a base ungenerous Race of Men could rely upon nothing for their Safety in this Affront to His Majesty, but the known Gentleness and Lenity of his Government. Then the Devil was in them

No. 54. June 25, 1716

388, *b.* The Whigs tell us . . . that the Tory-Scheme would terminate in Popery and Arbitrary Government. But Tories never writ or spoke so gently and favourably of Popery as Whigs do of Presbytery. Witness a thousand Pamphlets on both sides I will not accept that Condition, nor did I ever see so unfair a one offered

390, l. 17 I shall not impute to any Tory Scheme the Administration of *James* II, on condition that they do not reproach the Whigs with the Usurpation of *Oliver*;

No. 55. June 29, 1716

396, l. 2 The Enemies of His present Majesty find him in a Condition to visit his Dominions in *Germany* without any Danger . . . left under the Protection of a Prince who makes it his Ambition to copy out his Royal Father's Example. Then, why was he never trusted a second time?

398, l. 8 to reduce to Obedience by GENTLE METHODS, which he has declared from the Throne to be MOST AGREEABLE TO HIS INCLINATIONS.

l. 11 May we not hope that all of this kind, who have the least Sentiments of Honour or Gratitude, will be won over to their Duty by so many Instances of Royal Clemency, Not one Instance produced

And is that enough?

7. HEYLIN, PETER: *AERIUS REDEVIVUS, OR THE HISTORY OF THE PRESBYTERIANS*, 1670

This book, by some errors and neglects in the style, seems not to have received the author's last correction. It is written with some vehemence, very pardonable in one who had been an observer and a sufferer, in *England*, under that diabolical fanatic sect which then destroyed church and state. But, comparing in my memory what I have read in other histories, he neither aggravates nor falsifies any facts. His partiality appears chiefly in setting the actions of the Calvinists in the strongest light, without equally dwelling on those of the other side; which, however, to say the truth, was not his proper business. And yet he might have spent some more words on the inhuman massacre of *Paris* and other parts of *France*, which no provocation (and yet the King had the greatest possible) could excuse, or much extenuate. The author, according to the current opinion of the age he lived in, had too high notions of regal power; led by the common mistake of the term *supreme magistrate*, and not rightly distinguishing between the *legislature* and *administration*: into which mistake the clergy fell, or continued, in the reign of Charles II, as shewn and explained in a treatise, *&c.*

March 6, 1727–8   J. Swift.

8. BROWNE, JOHN: *ESSAYS ON THE TRADE AND COIN OF IRELAND*, 1729

Page	Browne	Swift
73	in the 15th section of the Plantation Act, it is ordered, that no Commodities of the Growth or Manufacture of the Plantations, shall be landed in *Ireland* or *Scotland*, unless the same has first been landed in *England*,	Diabolical
74 & 75	(*references to prohibition of woollen manufactures marked*)	
76	by the 1st of *William* and *Mary*, Chap. xxxii, the better to secure the Wooll of *Ireland* to *England*, it was enacted that no Wooll, &c. should be shipp'd off from any Ports of *Ireland* but from *Dublin*, *Waterford etc, etc.* and only to certain ports in *England*.	K. William's kindness to Ireland
77	but soon after, finding that the Restraint laid upon the Exportation of our Wooll, had made us apply with Double Assiduity, to the Manufacture thereof; and that we already exported of such Commodities to foreign Markets, it was thought fit to throw a Damp upon that Branch of our Industry; in order to *incommode* our Manufactures,	Justice to ruin
84	By the 3d of *George, Chap.* viii. so much of the 10th and 11th of *William* III. as vested one half of the Forfeitures for unlawful Exportation of Wooll in the Exchequer of *Ireland*, is repealed . . .	kinder and kinder
85, 87, 88	(*references to further prohibitions marked*)	
89	there remains free for us to work upon, Linnen and Hemp etc. Fish-Oyl, Salt, Corn, *Coals, Marble and Timber*, etc.	I add Oranges, Lemons, Tea, Coffee &c. of Irish growth

Seasonable Remarks on Trade, 1728

1	(under the Head Title, in ink, but may not be Swift's hand) 'an excellent pamphlet'	
9	where the Necessaries of Life are cheap, there also will Labour and Art be cheap,	This is disputed

Page	Browne	Swift
52	Particular Societies are too apt to lay Schemes for agrandizing and enriching themselves at the Expence of the Publick; but alas, it is better even for them in the End, that the general Welfare should be pursued,	whom will you persuade? no Englishman
55	The next great Change was in *Oliver Cromwell*'s Time, where the *Irish* taking Advantage of our Commotions in *England*, under Pretence of assisting the King, took up Arms etc.	this is truly told
58	If we consider the Conduct of that People, since the Revolution, we shall find that we have no Grounds for such a Jealousy of them,	This is bold and handsom
64	it is surely better for us to have the carrying Trade in the Hands of a People who are our Subjects, and whose every Acquisition by Trade flows daily upon us, to encrease our Wealth and Power, than to let it remain in the Hands of those whose every Acquisition by Trade helps to turn the Ballance against us, etc.	The perverse English will ever think otherwise
68	if we bury our Dead in home-spun Linnen, it will at once spare from our Consumption of Wooll enough to supply that Scarcity, and save *England* the Expense of so much as we bury annually in the Ground.	This hint, happily started by Mr. Brown, hath since been successfully put into Execution.

9. MACKY, JOHN: *CHARACTERS OF THE COURT OF BRITAIN* etc.,

1733

N.B.—*The general comments are inserted at the end of each character; particular remarks on the words* IN SMALL CAPS *are written in the margin opposite.*

Page	Macky	Swift
7	John Churchill, Duke of Marlborough, Captain-General	Detestably covetous
10	James, Duke of Ormond, Lord Lieutenant of Ireland	Fairly enough writ
15	Charles, Duke of Shrewsbury: Never was there a greater Mixture of Honour, VIRTUE, and good Sense, in any one Person, than in him;	None
17	Charles, Duke of Somerset, Master of the Horse: Of good JUDGMENT, but by Reason of a great Hesitation in his Speech, wants Expression.	Not a grain, nor hardly common sense
20	John, Duke of Buckinghamshire, Lord Privy Seal	This Charactr is the truest of any

Page	Macky	Swift
26	Daniel, Earl of Nottingham, Secretary of State	He fell in the Whigs was an endless Talker
34	Earl of Romney:	
	was indeed the great *Wheel* on which the *Revolution* rolled.	He had not a wheel to turn a mouse
	He is a Gentleman that hath lived UP to the Employments the King gave him; of great HONOUR and HONESTY, with a MODERATE Capacity	down none at all
35	John, Duke of Newcastle:	
	and hath one only DAUGHTER who will be the richest Heiress in *Europe*.	now Countess of Oxford— cheated by her Father
36	Charles Lenox, Duke of Richmond	A shallow Coxcomb
38	Charles, Duke of Bolton:	
	but does not now make any Figure at Court.	nor anywhere else—a great Booby
39	George Fitzroy, Duke of Northumberland	He was a most worthy Person very good natured and had very good Sense
40	Charles Fitzroy, Duke of Grafton	Almost a Slobber without one good Quality
41	Sir Nathan Wright, Lord Keeper	Very covetous
44	Ralph, Duke of Montagu	As arrant a Knave as any in his time
47	William Cavendish, Marquis of Hartington	A very poor Understanding
48	John, Lord Somers, late Lord Chancellor: Of a CREDITABLE FAMILY	A very mean, his father was a noted Rogue
50	(*at the end*)	I allow him to have possessed all excellent Qualifications except Virtue. He had violent passion(s), and hardly subdued them by his great Prudence
54	Charles, Lord Halifax:	
	He is a great ENCOURAGER OF LEARNING and LEARNED MEN, is the Patron of the *Muses*.	His encouragements were onely good words and dinners —I never heard him say one good thing or seem to tast what was said by another
55	Charles, Earl of Dorset and Middlesex: OF GREAT LEARNING	small or none
	one of the PLEASANTEST COMPANIONS in the World	Not of late years, but a very dull one
59	Charles Howard, Earl of Carlisle: Is a Branch of the noble Family of the *Howards* (Duke of *Norfolk*)	I suppose the present Earl's Father
60	Richard Savage, Earl Rivers	An arrant Knave in common dealing and very prostitute
62	William, Earl of Portland	As great a Dunce as ever I knew
63	James Stanley, Earl of Derby	As arrant a Scoundrel as his Brother

Page	Macky	Swift
66	Charles, Earl of Peterborow	This Character is for the most part true
67	Arnold Joost von Keppel, Earl of Albermarle: King William's constant Companion in all his Diversions and PLEASURES;	very infamous Pleasures
69	Charles Spencer, Earl of Sunderland: Learning VIRTUE, and good Sense	No
70	Algernon Capell, Earl of Essex: whose Throat was cut in the Tower	cut his own Throat
73	Thomas Grey, Earl of Stamford	He lookt and talked like a very weak man but it was said he spake well at Council
80	Thomas Tufton, Earl of Thanet	Of great Piety and Charity
	Edward Montague, Earl of Sandwich	As much a Puppy as ever I saw very ugly and a Fop
82	Richard, Earl of Ranelagh	The vainest Old Fool I ever saw
84	Charles, Lord Lucas	A good plain hum-drum
85	Charles Finch, Earl of Winchelsea	Being very poor he complyed too much with the Party he hated
	He loves Jests and Puns	I never observed it
88	Lord Poulet of Hinton	This Caracter is fair enough
89	Charles, Lord Townshend: is beloved by EVERY Body that KNOWS him	I except one
	William Legg, Lord Dartmouth	This is right enough but he has little Sincerity
92	Thomas, Lord Wharton	The most universal Vilain I ever knew
94	Charles, Lord Mohun	He was little better than a conceited Talker in company
95	Earl of Kent	He seems a good natured man but of very little consequence
	Earl of Lindsey: has both Wit and Learning	I never observed a grain of either
96	Montagu Venables Bertie, Earl of Abingdon	Very covetous
	Philip Stanhope, Earl of Chesterfield	If it be old Chesterfield I have heard he was the greatest Knave in Engld
97	Charles, Earl of Berkeley	Intolerably lazy and Indolent, and somewhat Covetous
100	John, Lord De la Warr	Of very little sense, but formall, and well stockt with the low kind of lowest Politicks
101	Robert, Lord Lexington	A very moderat degree of Understanding

Page	Macky	Swift
103	Ralph, Lord Grey of Werk	had Very little in him
	James, Lord Chandos:	
	his son, Mr Bridges (the present Duke of Chandos) . . . a very worthy Gentleman.	but a great complyer with every Court
104	Francis, Lord Guilford	A mighty silly fellow
106	Lord Griffin	His Son was a plain Drunken Companion
107	Lord Cholmondeley	Good for nothing as far as I ever knew
110	Lord Butler of Weston	
	Earl of Arran in Ireland:	
	of very good Sense, though seldom shews it.	This is right, but he is the most negligent of his own Affairs
114	Mr. Mansel	Of good nature but a very moderate capacity
116	Robert Harley Esq., Speaker of the House of Commons	
	very ELOQUENT	A great Lye
	(*at the end*)	He could not properly be called eloquent, but he knew how to prevail on the House with few words and strong reasons
126	Mr. Boyle, Chancellor of the Exchequer	Had some very Scurvy Qualityes particularly avarice
130	Sir Thomas Frankland, Postmaster General	A fair Character
131	Mr. Smith, one of her Majesty's Privy Council:	
	a very agreeable Companion in Coversation, a bold Orator	I thought him a heavy man
133	Charles D'Avenant, L.L.D.	He was used ill by most Ministryes. He ruined his own Estate, which put him undr necessity to comply with the times
135	Matthew Prior, Esq.	
	Commissioner of Trade	This is near the Truth
136	Thomas, Archbishop of Canterbury	The most good for nothing
	Dr. Tenison	Prelate I ever knew
138	Gilbert, Bishop of Salisbury	
	his Father was LORD of Cremont one of the greatest Orators	Laird Scotch
140	(*at the end*)	His true Character would take up too much time for me (who knew him well) to describe it
142	George Stepney, Esq: Envoy Extraordinary to the Emperor:	
	one of the BEST POETS	scarce of a third rate

Page	*Macky*	*Swift*

143 Mr. Methuen, Ambassador to the King of Portugal

A profligate Rogue, without religion or moralls, but cunning enough yet without abilityes of any kind

146 Lord Raby, Envoy Extraordinary to the King of Prussia:
of FINE UNDERSTANDING

very bad and cannot spell

of LOW STATURE

He is tall

147 Mr. Hill, Envoy Extraordinary to the Duke of Savoy:
took *Deacon's* Orders

Priests

148 PLAINNESS AND SIMPLICITY IN HIS DRESS

Au contraire

Favourite to both Parties

to neither

thin, tall Man,

short, if I remember right

149 Sir Lambert Blackwell, Envoy to the Great Duke of Tuscany

He seemed a very good natured man

151 Mr. Stanhope, Envoy Extraordinary to the States General:
the Son a HANDSOM black man

Ugly

153 Dr. Aglionby, Envoy to Swiss

He had been a Papist

154 Mr. D'Avenant, Agent at Frankfort

He is not worth mentioning

156 John, Lord Cutts, Lieutenant General

The vainest old fool alive

157 Lord Teviot, Lieutenant General,
well-looked MAN

fool

160 Lord Galway, Lieutenant General:
is very modest, vigilant, and SINCERE; a Man of HONOUR and HONESTY

In all directly otherwise

(*at the end*)

A deceitfull Hypocritical factious Knave a damnable Hypocrite of no Religion

162 Earl of Orkney, Lieutenant General

An honest good Natured Gentleman and hath much distinguished himself as a Souldier

163 Sir Charles Haro, Lieutenant General

His Father was a Groom, he was a man of Sense, without one grain of honesty

165 Colonel Matthew Aylmer, Vice-Admiral of the Fleet

A virulent Party-man born in Ireland

167 Colonel Churchill, Vice-Admiral:
a good, but a severe Enemy

friend

178 James, Duke of Hamilton

He was made Master of the Ordnance a worthy good Natured Person very generous but of a middle Understanding, he was murdred by that Villain McCartny an Irish Scot

190 Duke of Argyll

Ambitious, covetous, cunning Scot has no Principle but his own Interest and Greatness. A true Scot in his whole Conduct

Page	Macky	Swift
192	Marquis of Montrose: is very beautiful in his Person, and about twenty-five Years old.	now very homely and makes a sorry appearance
201	Earl of Sutherland	A blundring rattled pated drunken Sot
206	Secretary Johnstoun, now Lord Register: He is very HONEST, . . . and would not tell a Lye for the World.	a treacherous knave
	(*at the end*)	One of the greatest Knaves, even in Scotland
211	Mr. Carstairs	A true Character but not strong enough by a 50th part
218	Earl of Marr	He is crooked He seemed to me a Gentleman of good sense & good nature
223	Andrew Fletcher, of Saltoun	A most arrogant conceited Pedant in Politicks, cannot endure the least Contradiction in any of visions or Paradoxes
240	Earl of Middleton	Sr WmTemple told me he was a very valuable man, and a good Scholar I once saw him
250	Earl of Weems	He was a black man, and handsom for a Scot

10. HOWELLS, WILLIAM: *MEDULLA HISTORIAE ANGLICANAE*
9th ed., 1734

Page	Howells	Swift
v	the Desire of perpetuating . . . one's own Memory is such a glimmering Glance of the *primitive* but OFFUSCATED Light of Nature, that some think it a convincing Argument to prove the Immortality of the Soul.	A Cursed Writer Damned Dunce [*deleted*]
	too weak . . . WITHOUT they were confirmed	unless
v	*History*, and especially the truest and most ancient of *All*, the *Holy Scriptures* . . .	not History
	some (Histories) are *fictitious Romances*, which beside the *Satisfaction* they give the Author's *inventing Head*, are of very little, if of any Use, unless it be to teach young Gallants to strut it in the *Phrase* of *Heroes*, and Ladies to repartee like a *Playbook*.	Aye, They do Sad Dog
vi	the various Changes and MUTATIONS of *elder Times*	changes
vii	without troubling ourselves with our *ancient Relations*, who were not one Drop of Blood a-kin to *William the Conqueror*.	O Jesus

Page	Howells	Swift
x	*The Continuation will we hope, be allow'd to be answerable to the rest.*	Far from it.
4	Iceni, *Suffolk, Norfolk, Cambridge.*	& Huntingdon
39	*Edred* . . . suffered his Royal Body to be chastised at the Will and Direction of *Dunstan,* Abbot of *Glastenbury.*	An Ideot
44	at *Ashdon* . . . the ever-traiterous *Edrick* . . . withdrew his Strength to the *Danes,*	vile Dog
59	*Stephen* Earl of *Bloys,* Son to *Adelicia,* Daughter of the Conqueror . . .	Alice
70	The Castle . . . was taken, and ∧ the King's command none left alive.	at ∧
100	To *James* Lord *Audley* . . . the Prince gave 500 Marks Land in Fee Simple, which said Land the Lord *Audley* bestowed on his four Esquires that had continued with him in all the Brunt and Fury of Danger.	very Noble
	Prince *Edward* . . . took his leave of France, though not of the King thereof; for him he brought with himself a Captive to *London.*	K. of Fra. prisoner.
107	His (Henry IV's) Cousin, the late King EDWARD	Richard
154	A prodigal and merry conceited Nobleman . . . came ruffling into the Court in a new Suit, saying, *Am not I a Mighty Man that bear an hundred Houses on my Back?* Which Cardinal *Woolsey* hearing, said, *You might have better employed it in paying your Debts: Truth my Lord,* said the Nobleman, *you say well, for my Father owed my Master, your Father, Three Half-Pence for a Calf's Head, hold, here is Two-pence for it.*	False—Wolsey's Father was no Butcher, but a private Gentleman
222	The Marquis of Montrose came to the Laird of ASTON's Horse . . but this FALSE *Scot* betrayed this distressed Peer.	true
223	(On Charles I)	
	Great, Good, and Just, could I but rate My Griefs, AND thy too rigid Fate; I'd weep the World to such a Strain, That it should deluge once again.	with
	But ∧ thy loud-tongu'd Blood demands Supplies	since ∧
	More from Briareus's Hands, than Argus's Eyes,	
	I'll THEREFORE sing thy Obsequies with Trumpet Sounds,	(*deleted*)
	And write thy Epitaph with Blood and Wounds.	

Page	Howells	Swift
258	. . . the Dutchess of *York* was brought to Bed of a Son, who was christened by the Name of *Charles*, but died in *December* following	That was a pity
261	That in *March* last *Pickering* had a fair Opportunity (to shoot Charles II) but that the Flint of his Pistol being loose, he could not shoot.	Damned Nonsense
267	A Bill was voted to be brought in to EXCLUDE THE DUKE OF YORK from succeeding to the Crown	Wd to God it had passed.
325	Dr. Hough the VICE-President (of Magdalen College, Oxford)	(*Deleted*)
343	[In 1688, William, Prince of Orange, demanded] That a sufficient Maintenance for his Forces be assigned . . . out of the PUBLICK REVENUE till the sitting of the Parliament.	that was damned unreasonable
353	Mary Eldest Daughter of *James* Duke of *York* . . . now SUCCEEDED HER Father in the Throne.	wrong expressed
356	[Almost a month after William III had been proclaimed King in England, the Scotch Convention met and resolved] 'That King *James* being a profest *Papist*, and acting as King without ever taking the Oaths required by Law . . . had forfeited the Crown, and the Throne was become vacant.'	The Scotch went further than the English: i.e. when the matter was all over.
361	Mr. Walker . . . was sent immediately to *London* with an Address from the Town (Londonderry) to the King, by whom he was bountifully rewarded.	Quid?
372	that great Action wherein the Empire of *Britannia* WAS finally lost by King *James*.	of Ireland and Kingdom were
	Mr. *Pendergrass* . . . was inform'd of the Design (to assassinate William III), and invited to take part in it; but he immediately resolved to discover it.	Coachman to one of the Contrie masters he had been. His Father had been tryed at Clonmel in Ireland for Sheep-stealing
410	(Article 7 of the Peace of Ryswick) . . . the King of *Great Britain* shall also restore all that did belong to *France* before the War.	Qy whether Dutch or English?
421	Everybody knew that the King had a great Affection for that Lady, (Lady Orkney) but those that knew him most intimately discharged him of ANY CRIME IN IT.	for a very good, or rather very bad Reason: however it is certain, that he whored with Her before he attached himself to other Amusements

Page	Howells	Swift
423	July 29 (1700) his Highness Prince William expir'd, to the unspeakable Grief of his Parents. ∧	and the unspeakable Regret of the whole Nation as well as Ruin of the English Interest and Politicks.
428	Captain Kidd . . . set out at the Joint Expence of several Private AdventURES.	rers
543	. . . his Majesty's Succession, when attacked by the late Ministry.	that is false it never was attacked by the immortal Tory Ministry.
568	Citizens of the City of *Chester* . . .	Chichester
573	In the Beginning of *November* (1724) Dr. *Humphrey Prideaux*, Dean of *Norwich*, a Person well known to the Learned World, departed this Life.	however he dyed unbishoped
574	Thomas Earl of Macclesfield fined . . . thirty Thousand Pounds and imprisoned in the Tower of London . . . until he shall pay the said Fine.	An excellent satisfaction to those who had suffered by his Villainy
583	. . . that Limitation was not wholly and for ever to deprive his Majesty's foreign Dominions of any Assistance from this Nation; for if so, his Majesty in THAT respect would be in a worse Condition upon his Accession to the Throne of *Great Britain* than he was before.	what a damned (?) that?
	. . . the House would effectually stand by and support his Majesty against all Attacks . . . upon any of his Territories or Dominions, though not immediately belonging to the Crown of *Great Britain:*	Well sayd My Boy
588	William Cadogan, General of the Foot Forces in SOUTH BRITAIN	England
595	the Castle of *Athlen* in the Electorate of Brunswick Lunenburg, the Place of her (Sophia, divorced wife of George I) Retirement for several Years.	Qy What was the Cause of her Retirement?
	In January (1729) died *Thomas Madox*, Esq; his Majesty's Historiographer, Author of the *Formulare Anglicanum*, and some other Works of Learning.	Many of his Writings Extant
596	His Majesty departed this Life, . . . having reigned twelve years, ten Months, and eleven Days. His Body, being afterwards wrapped in Lead, was privately interred among those of his noble Progenitors.	No Account of his grand Funeral at Hanover.

U

11. BURNET, GILBERT: *HISTORY OF HIS OWN TIMES*, 1724–34

Page	Burnet	Swift

Preface, 3 long experience . . . has inclined me to think generally the worst both of men and parties: and . . . has sharpened my spirits perhaps too much against (the clergy): so I warn my reader to take all that I say on these heads with some grains of allowance . . .

Swift: I will take his warning

4 . . . over and over again retouched and polished by me,
that thereby I may awaken the world to just reflections on their own errors and follies, etc.

Swift: Rarely polished; I never read so ill a style.
This I take to be nonsense

Book I

6 When that king (James I) saw that those who were most in his interests were likewise jealous of his authority, and apt to encroach upon it, . . .

Swift: Nonsense

10 competent provision made by James I for the clergy of Scotland, and in his son's time raised to about fifty pounds a year;

Swift: Scotch pounds, I suppose

11 Colonel Titus assured me that he had from King Charles the first's own mouth, that he (Prince Henry) was poisoned by the Earl of Somerset's means.

Swift: Titus was the greatest Rogue in England

18 my father did always believe (Gowry's) was a real conspiracy, not a contrivance to get rid of that earl.

Swift: Melvil makes nothing of it

20 I turn now to the affairs of Scotland, which are but little known.

Swift: Not worth knowing

23 the Archbishop of St. Andrews . . . beginning his journey to London on a Sunday, which was a very odious thing in that country.

Swift: Poor Malice

24 it was believed (the earl of Traquair) died of hunger.

Swift: A strange death: perhaps it was of want of *meat*

26 My father preserved the papers relating to the trial (of Lord Balmerinoch) . . . the whole record was copied for me . . . and is indeed a very noble piece, full of curious matter.

Swift: Puppy

28 The Earl of Argyle was . . . free of all scandalous vices,

Swift: As a man is free of a corporation, he means

29 and were clapt up upon it.

Swift: Dignity of Expression

30 (King Charles I) loved high and rough methods . . . hated all that offered prudent and moderate counsels, etc.

Swift: Not one good quality named

Page	Burnet	Swift
31	The queen loved . . . to be IN INTRIGUES OF ALL SORTS,	Not of love, I hope
	By the concessions that he made, especially of the triennial Parliament, the honest and quiet part of the Nation was satisfied . . . so they broke off from those violenter propositions that occasioned the war.	Dark, or nonsense
	The King did not come into those concessions . . . with a good grace: (there were grounds for the belief) that he intended not to stand to them any longer than he lay under that force that visibly drew them from him contrary to his own inclinations.	Sad trash
33	the first volume of the Earl of Clarendon's History gives a faithful representation of the beginnings of the troubles, though writ in favour of the Court . . .	Writ with the spirit of an historian, not of (a raker) into scandal
34	some of them (the leading Scotch preachers) affected a strain of stating cases of conscience not with relation to moral actions, but to some reflexions on their condition and temper.	Great Nonsense. Rutherford was half fool, half mad
40	Lord Montrose's expedition . . . alienated the Scots much from the King: Now they seemed to have some colour for all those aspersions they had cast on the King etc.	Lord Clarendon differs from all this
41	The Earl of Essex told me he could . . . never see any reason to believe the King had any accession to the (Irish massacre).	And who but *a Beast* ever believed it?
42	Cromwell argues with the Scots concerning the King's death. Drumond said, 'Cromwell had plainly the better of them at their own weapon, and upon their own principles.'	And Burnet thought as Cromwell did
46	. . . impossible to set up a Commonwealth in England: for that cannot be brought about but by a military force: and they will ever keep the Parliament in subjection to them, and so keep up their own authority.	Weak.
	Fairfax was much distracted in his mind, and changed purposes often every day.	Fairfax had hardly common sense
49	I will not enter farther into the military part: for I remember an advice of Marshal Schomberg's, never to meddle in the relation of military matters.	Very foolish advice, for Soldiers cannot write.
50	Archbishop Laud . . . a hot, indiscreet man: His severity and injustice . . . were such visible blemishes, that nothing but	

Page	Burnet	Swift
	the putting him to death in so unjust a manner could have raised his character . . . his defence of himself . . . a very mean performance.	All this is full of malice and ill Judgment
	Eikon Basilike universally believed to be by King Charles I.	I think it a poor treatise, and that the King did not write it.
51	Upon the King's death, the Scots proclaimed his son King, and sent over Sir George Wincam, THAT MARRIED MY GREAT-AUNT, to treat with him while he was in the Isle of Jersey.	Was that the reason he was sent?
53	I was there myself, and not a little weary of so tedious a service.	Burnet was not then eight years old
61	Scotland during the usurpation—we always reckon those eight years of usurpation a time of great peace and prosperity.	No doubt you do.
63	The crowds were far beyond the capacity of their churches, or the reach of their voices,	I believe the Church had as much capacity as the minister
64	The resolutioners sent up one Sharp . . . an active and eager man:	Afterwards Archbishop, and murdered
66	CLAPT them up for a short while:	Pox of his *Claps*
86	Care taken to manage the Army: Of all this Monk had both the praise and the reward; though I have been told a very small share of it belonged to him.	Malice

Book II

92	I will therefore enlarge . . . on the affairs of Scotland; out of the inbred love that all men have for their native country,	Could not he keep his inbred love to himself?
	Sharp's protestations . . . of his sincerity for the presbytery . . . while he was indeed undermining it. . . . nothing could ever bring people to any tolerable thoughts of a man, whose dissimulation and treachery was so well known etc.	Sure there was some secret personal cause of all this malice against Sharp
93	The great art of keeping him long was, the being easy, and the making every thing easy to him. (of Charles II)	Eloquence
99	His (Bennet, afterwards Earl of Arlington) parts were solid, but not quick.	They were very quick
100	He (the Duke of Buckingham) was true to nothing, for he was not true to himself. He could keep no secret, nor execute any design without spoiling it.	No consequence Nonsense
117	they could only fix the nullity (of the Puritan Parliaments) upon the pretence of force and violence. Yet . . . it was visible that neither the late king nor the present were under any force when they passed them.	Both kings were under a force

Page	*Burnet*	*Swift*

118 To annul a Parliament was a terrible precedent, which destroyed the whole security of government:

Wrong arguing

so that distress on his affairs was really equivalent to a force on his person:

It was so

119 we went into it (the Parliament of 1648) as knaves, and therefore no wonder if we miscarried in it as fools.

True

the Act (annulling those Parliaments) must for ever take away all the security that law can give: no government was so well established, as not to be liable to a revolution: this would cut off all hopes of peace and submission, if any disorder should happen thereafter.

Wrong weak reasoning

120 Such care was taken that no public application should be made in favour of presbytery. Any attempt that was made on the other hand met with great encouragement.

Does the man write like a bishop?

126 And after some time spent in his private devotions he (the Marquis of Argyle) was beheaded.

He was the greatest Villain of his age

The doctrine delivered in their sermons did not fall under the cognizance of the temporal courts, till it was first judged by the church.

Popery

127 The proceedings against Waristoun were soon despatched, he being absent.

Waristoun was an abominable Dog

135 Of Bishop Leightoun—His style was rather too fine:

Burnet is not guilty of that.

140 He did not THINK orders given without bishops were null and void. He THOUGHT, the forms of government were not settled by such positive laws as were unalterable; but only by apostolical practices, which, as he THOUGHT, authorized Episcopacy as the best form. Yet he did not THINK it necessary to the being of a church. But he THOUGHT . . .

Think, thought, thought, think, thought

154 This was suitable enough to a maxim that he (Sharp) and all that sort of people set up, that the execution of laws was that by which all governments maintained their strength, as well as their honour.

Dunce, can there be a better maxim?

157 Burnet's character of the Scottish ministers

Strange inconsistent stuff

160 The king had not been many days at Whitehall, when one Venner . . . who thought it was not enough to believe etc., but added to this, that the saints were to take the kingdom themselves.

This wants grammar

Page	Burnet	Swift
163	John Goodwin and Milton did also escape all censure, to the surprise of all people.	He censures even mercy
163	Paradise Lost, though in blank verse without rhyme, yet it was esteemed the beautifullest and perfectest poem that ever was writ, at least in OUR language.	A mistake, for it is *in English*
164	but above all the great opinion that was had of his (Sir Henry Vane) parts and capacity to embroil matters again, made the Court think it necessary to put him out of the way. When he saw his death was designed, he composed himself to it, with a resolution that surprised all who knew how little of that was natural to him. Some instances of this were very extraordinary, though they cannot be mentioned with decency.	A malicious turn. Vane was a dangerous enthusiastic beast His lady *conceived* of him the night before his execution
	It was generally thought the government had lost more than it had gained by his death.	Vane was beheaded for new attempts, not here mentioned
179	So the Papists had this generally spread among them, that they should . . . animate the church party to maintain their ground against all the sectaries . . . But at the same time they spoke of toleration, as necessary both for the peace and quiet of the nation, and for the encouragement of trade.	This is inconsistent
180	Mr. Baxter, a man of great piety; and, if he had not meddled in too many things, would have been esteemed one of the learned men of the age: he writ near 200 books:	Very sad ones
184	The Convocation added some new holy days . . . took in more lessons out of the Apocrypha, in particular the story of Bel and the Dragon: Reports were spread . . . of the plots of the Presbyterians in several counties. Many were taken up on those reports: but none were ever tried for them.	I think they acted wrong A common Practice
	Those who did not conform to the liturgy by St Bartholomew's Day, 1662, were deprived of all ecclesiastical benefices . . . without any provision for the maintenance of those so deprived: a severity neither practised by Queen Elizabeth . . . nor by Cromwell, in both of which a fifth part of the benefice was reserved for their subsistence.	But by King William

Page	*Burnet*	*Swift*
186	The great fines then raised on the church estates ill applied. If the half had been applied to the buying of tithes or glebes for small vicarages, here a foundation had been laid for a great and effectual reformation.	He judges here right, in my opinion
	With this great accession of wealth there broke in upon the church a great deal of luxury and high living, on the pretence of hospitality; while others made purchases, and left great estates, most of which we have seen melt away.	Uncharitable aggravation
189	Patrick was a great preacher . . . but a little too severe against those who differed from him. . . . He became afterwards more moderate.	A base innuendo

Yes, for he turned a rank Whig |
190	(Archbishop Tenison) was a very learned man, held in very high esteem	The dullest, good for nothing man I ever knew
191	The reform in preaching from the old manner—This was both long and heavy, when all was PYE-BALLED, full of many sayings of different languages.	A noble epithet
	The king had little or no literature, but true and good sense; and had got a right notion of style.	How came Burnet not to learn this style?
193	He who laboured most, at the greatest charge and with the most success at experiments (in the Royal Society) was Robert Boyle. . . . He neglected his person, despised the world, and lived abstracted from all pleasures, designs, and interests.	Boyle was a very silly writer
195	there was nothing the whole popish party feared more than an union of those of the Church of England with the presbyterians: they knew, we grew the weaker, the more our breaches were widened; and that, the more we were set against one another, we would mind them the less.	
202	one Mrs Steward, reckoned a very GREAT BEAUTY,	Rogue

A pretty phrase |
203	One of the first things that was done in this session of Parliament was the execution of my unfortunate uncle, Waristoun.	Was he hanged or beheaded? A fit uncle for such a Bishop
211	in Ulster . . . they were well received, and had all manner of liberty as to their way of religion.	The more the pity
214	The blame of all this was cast upon Sharp . . . the King looked on him as one of the worst of men.	Surely there was some secret cause for this perpetual malice against Sharp

Page	*Burnet*	*Swift*
220	De Witt had the notions of a commonwealth from the Greeks and Romans. And from them he came to fancy that an army commanded by officers of their own country was both more in their own power, and would serve them with the more zeal, since they themselves had such an interest in their success.	He ought to have judged the contrary
235	The rebels defeated at Pentland Hill—they were a poor harmless company of men, become mad by oppression.	A fair historian!
237	They might all have saved their lives, if they would have renounced the Covenant: so they were really a sort of martyrs for it.	Decent term
238	Sir John Cunningham . . . one of the PIOUSEST men of the nation.	Is that Scotch?
242	the King . . . communicated THAT to them; and with THAT signified, THAT it was his pleasure THAT the army should be disbanded.	Four *thats* in one line
243	Archbishop Sheldon's letter to Sir R. Murray—which I read, and found more temper and moderation in it, than I could have expected from him.	Sheldon was a very great and excellent man
245	Cromwell was certainly fond of her (the Countess of Dysert), and she took care to entertain him in it; till he, finding what was said upon it, broke it off.	Cromwell had gallantries with her
247	The Scottish clergy saw designs were forming to turn them all out: and, hearing that they might be better provided in Ireland, they were in many places bought out, and prevailed on to desert their cures.	So Ireland was well provided
252	In the afternoon he heard him with more temper, as he himself told me.	Who told him?
253	the King and Sheldon had gone into such expostulations upon it, that from that day forward Sheldon could never recover the King's confidence.	Sheldon had refused the Sacrament to the King for living in adultery
	He (Sir Orlando Bridgman) had been always on the side of the church:	What side should he be of?
256	It seemed against the common course of justice, to make all corresponding with him treason, when he himself was not attainted of treason:	Bishop of Rochester's case
257	Thus the Lord Clarendon fell under the common fate of great ministers etc. etc. Their friends do generally shew, that they are only the friends of their fortunes . . . by turning as violently against them as they formerly fawned abjectly upon them.	Stupid moralist

His judgment (Clarendon's elder son) was not to be MUCH depended on; for he was MUCH carried by vulgar prejudices and false notions. He was MUCH in the Queen's favour . . .   —   much, much, much

258 He (the Earl of Rochester) has a VERY GOOD PEN, but speaks not gracefully.   —   I suppose it was of gold or silver

(The King) told me, he had a chaplain, that was a very honest man, but a very great blockhead, to whom he had given a living in Suffolk, that was full of that sort of people: . . . but his nonsense suited their nonsense, for he had brought them all to church: and, in reward of his diligence, he had given him a bishopric in Ireland.   —   Bishop Woolly of Clonfert

259 but it was unworthy of the Church to go and court or treat with enemies . . . to confess we had been in the wrong . . . to bring scorn and contempt on ourselves.   —   I think so too.

260 The three volumes of the Friendly Debate, though writ by a very good man . . .   —   Writ by Bishop Patrick

(Bishop Parker) was attacked by the liveliest droll of the age . . . the author of   —   What is a droll?

the *Rehearsal Transprosed* had all the men of wit on his side.   —   Andrew Marvel

263 But after all, he never treated her (Nell Gwyn) with the DECENCIES of a mistress.   —   Pray what decencies are those?

Another mistress, the daughter of a clergyman . . . was never easy in an ill course, and died with a great sense of her former ill life. I was OFTEN WITH HER the last three months of her life.   —   Was she handsome then?

264 The King loved his (Rochester) company for the diversion it afforded, better than his person; and there was no love lost between them.   —   A noble phrase

265 Sedley . . . was not so correct as Lord Dorset, nor so sparkling as Lord Rochester.   —   No better a critic in wit than style

266 Lord Roberts, afterwards Earl of Radnor —as wise as a CYNICAL humour could allow him to be.   —   How does that hinder wisdom?

273 The Prince (of Orange) told me, that he never spake of this (that Charles II was a papist) till AFTER HIS DEATH: —   That is, his own death

277 This was the single expression savouring of piety that ever fell from him (Sharp) in all the conversation that passed between him and me.   —   Rank malice

Page	Burnet	Swift
285	And nobody could ever tell me how the words *ecclesiastical matters* were put in the Act. Leightoun thought he was sure it was put in after the draught and form of the act was agreed on.	
287	(Archbishop Burnet) was not cut out for a court or for the ministry:	Nonsense A phrase of dignity
	At this time the University of Glasgow chose me, though unknown to them all, to be professor of divinity there. There was no sort of artifice or management to bring this about: it came of themselves; and they did it without any recommendation of any person whatsoever.	Modest
288	The episcopal party thought I intended to make myself popular at their cost: so they began that strain of fury and calumny that has pursued me ever since from THAT SORT OF PEOPLE,	A civil term for all who are episcopal
298	I did indeed conceal several things that related to the King: I left out some passages that were in his letters . . .	The letters, if they had been published, could not have given a worse character
300	They (those recommended for the Scottish bishoprics) had an ill opinion of the court, and could not be brought to leave their retirement.	For that very reason they should have accepted Bishopricks
301	a story told me by a person of distinction, who had it from some who were well informed of the matter.	Poor authority
303	He came afterwards out into the world. I saw him often. He was a man of a very sweet temper, only a little too formal for a Frenchman. But he was very sincere. He was a Jansenist. He hated the Jesuits.	Pretty jumping periods
304	And therefore he blamed him, . . .	Who blamed whom?
	. . . the Duke of Savoy was encouraged to make a conquest of Genoa;	Geneva
	the king consented; but with this severe reflection, that he believed he would be true to any body but himself.	Does he mean Lockhart would not be true to Lockhart?
305	. . . they corrupted him (the Dutch Ambassador) into a belief that they had no design on them,	Who on whom?
306	The Earl of Shaftesbury was the chief man in this advice] (to stop bank payments for a year).	Clifford had the merit of this
318	. . . as also his (William II, Prince of Orange) death, . . . in the most unhappy time possible for the Princess Royal's big belly.	A pretty contrast

Page	Burnet	Swift
	that which WAS most particular WAS, that he WAS to have a son by a widow, and WAS …	Was, was, was, was
320	They set it also up for a maxim, …	He can vary a phrase; set up for a maxim, and lay down for a maxim
321	since his oath was made to them, and by consequence it was in their power to release the obligation that did arise from it to themselves.	Bad casuist
321	(The Prince saw he could not depend upon DeWitt.) When he told me this, he added that he was certainly one of the greatest men of the age, and he believed he served his country faithfully.	Yet the Prince contrived that he should be murdered
	Now I come to give an account of the fifth crisis brought on the whole reformation, which has been of the longest continuance, since we are yet in the agitations of it.	Under the Queen and Lord Oxford's ministry
322	in the management of that run of success …	A metaphor, but from gamesters
326	The infamy of (De Wit's murder) cast on him and his party, to make them all odious; though the Prince spoke of it always to me with the greatest horror possible:	Yet he was guilty enough
328	Prince Waldeck was their chief general: a man of a great compass and a true judgment:	*i.e.* very fat
330	Van Beuning was a man of great notions; He broke twice with the Prince, after he came into a confidence with him. He employed me to reconcile him to him for the third time:	Perspicuity
	In the end of his days, he set himself wholly to mind the East India trade … the actions sinking on the sudden on the breaking out of a new war, that sunk him into a melancholy, …	Eloquent
335	I will complete the transactions of this memorable year …	
337	Thus I have gone far into the state of affairs of Holland in this memorable year.	Why, you called it so but just now before
	The French released twenty-five thousand Dutch prisoners … for fifty thousand crowns.	What! ten shillings a piece! By much too dear for a Dutchman
	A French mistress made Duchess of Portsmouth. She had come over with the King's sister to Dover where the king expressed such a regard to her, that the Duke of Buckingham, who hated the Duchess of Cleveland, intended to PUT HER ON THE KING.	Surely he means the contrary

Page	Burnet	Swift
341	Duke Lauderdale . . . put me in mind of the project I had laid before him, of putting all the outed ministers by couples into parishes . . . and every one might have the half of a benefice.	A Scottish project: instead of feeding *fifty*, you starve one *hundred*

Book III

346	Lord Clifford stuck firm to the Duke, and was heated with the design of bringing in Popery, even to enthusiasm. It was believed, if the design had succeeded, he had agreed with his wife to take orders, and to aspire to a cardinal's hat.	Was he or she to take orders?
362	I told him, what afterwards happened, that most of these would make their own terms, and leave him in the lurch.	True sublime
370	I was ever of Nazianzen's opinion, who never wished to see any more synods of the clergy.	Dog
372	But the King said, he was afraid I had been too busy;	The King knew him right
	I preached in many of the churches of London; and was so well received, that it was probable I might be accepted of in any that was to be disposed of by A POPULAR ELECTION.	Much to his honour
373	Duke Lauderdale had gone so far in opening some wicked designs to me, that I perceived he could not be satisfied unless I was undone. So I told what was mentioned before of the discourses that passed between him and me.	A Scotch Dog
374	He (Lord Howard) went over in the beginning of the war, and offered to serve De Wit. But he told me, he found him a dry man.	Who told who? I guess Howard told Burnet
378	At least he (Sir William Temple) thought religion was fit only for the mob.	A word of dignity for an historian.
	He was a corrupter of all that came near him. And he delivered himself up wholly to study, ease, and pleasure.	Sir William Temple was a man of virtue, to which Burnet was a stranger
380	Upon this I yielded, and gave (the house) an account of the discourse formerly mentioned (between Lauderdale and himself).	Treacherous villain
	My love to my country, and my private friendships, carried me perhaps too far;	Right
382	(Sir Harbottle Grimstone) had always A TENDERNESS TO THE DISSENTERS,	Burnet's test of all virtues
	His second wife, whom I knew . . . had all the high notions for the church and the	

Page	*Burnet*	*Swift*

crown, in which she had been bred; but was the humblest, the devoutest, and best tempered person I ever KNEW OF THAT SORT.

Rogue

384 for if a Parliament thought any law inconvenient for the good of the whole, they must be supposed still free to alter it:

Wrong arguing

387 It was said, a standing Parliament changed the constitution of England.

The present case under King George

It was said that a Parliament of a long continuance ... was like to be destructive to the constitution.

Tempora mutantur; for nothing now will do but septennial Parliaments

388 (Lord Russell) had from his first education an inclination to favour the nonconformists;

So have all the author's favourites

392 But with these good qualities Compton was a weak man, wilful, and strangely wedded to a party.

He means to the church

Sancroft ... was a dry, cold man, reserved and peevish; so that none loved him, and few esteemed him:

False and detracting

396 Burnet's friendship with Sir William Jones, the Attorney-General—My way of writing history pleased him. And so he pressed me to undertake the history of England.

Very modest

399 The Duke of Lauderdale had mastered the opposition made to him so entirely, that men were now though silent, not quiet.

Nonsense, or printer's mistake. It should be, *silent, though not quiet*

One Carstairs, a loose and vicious gentleman,

Epithets well placed

404 It was an extraordinary thing that a random cannon shot should have killed him (Turenne).

How extraordinary? Might it not kill him as well as any other man?

406 Yet the other bodies fought so well (at St. Omer) that he (the Prince of Orange) lost not much, besides the HONOUR OF THE DAY.

He was used to that

407 these leading men ... spoiled the hopefullest session the court had had of a great while, before the court was well aware of it.

Court, court, rare style!

409 Lord Danby ... thought it was the Duke's interest to have it done ... if they saw his daughter given to one that was at the head of the Protestant interest, it would very much soften those apprehensions ... With all this the King was convinced.

Then how was the King for bringing in Popery?

Page	Burnet	Swift

413 with lifted up hands, Sharp promised by
the living God, that no hurt should come
to him, if he made a full discovery.

Malice

They thought both hands should be cut off.
Lord Rothes, who was a pleasant man,
said, How shall he wipe his breech then?
This is not very DECENT to be mentioned
in such a work, if it were not necessary;

As decent as a thousand
other passages; so he might
have spared his apology

414 But the judge, who hated Sharp, as he
went up to the bench, passing by the
prisoner, said to him Confess nothing,
unless you are sure of your limbs as well as
your life.

A rare judge

Nisbit, who had been King's Advocate,
and was one of the worthiest and learned-
est men of the age, was turned out: and
Mackenzie put in his place, who was a man
of much life and wit, but he was neither
equal nor correct in it: he has published
many books, some of law, but all full of
faults; for he was a slight and superficial
man.

Envious and base

416 Hickes (chaplain to Duke Lauderdale) ...
published a false and partial relation of
this matter, in order to the justifying of it
(Mitchell's trial).

A learned, pious man

425 Titus Oates a chaplain in one of the King's
ships, from which he was dismissed upon
complaint of some unnatural practices,
not to be named.

Only sodomy

434 Staley was brought to his trial, which did
not hold long ... He was cast:

Anglice, was found guilty

441 Maynard, an ancient and eminent lawyer,
explained the words of the Statute of 25
Ed. III. that the courts of law could not
proceed but upon one of the crimes there
enumerated: but the Parliament had still a
power, by the clause in that act, to declare
what they thought was treason:

Yes, by a new act, but not
with a retrospect; therefore
Maynard was a *knave and a fool,
with all his law*

442 this was ordinary in all treaties, where the
prince that desired a peace was made to
buy it. This indeed would have justified
the King, if it had been demanded above
board:

Style of a gamester

451 The approaches of death ... must needs
work so much on the probity and candour
which seemed rooted in human nature,
that even immoral opinions, maintained
in the way of argument, could not then
resist it.

Credat Judaeus Apella

Page	*Burnet*	*Swift*

455 The Earl of Shaftesbury proposed the excluding him simply . . . this was nothing but the disinheriting the next heir, which certainly the King and Parliament might do, as well as any private man might disinherit his next heir, if he had a mind to it.

That is not always true. Yet it was certainly in the power of King and Parliament to exclude the next heir.

457 Government was appointed for those that were to be governed, and not for the sake of governors themselves:

A true maxim and infallible

458 It was a maxim among our lawyers, that even an Act of Parliament against Magna Charta was null of it self.

A sottish maxim

459 But for a great while I thought the accepting the limitations was the wisest and best method.

It was the wisest, because it would be less opposed; and the King would consent to it; otherwise an exclusion would have done better

461 The Act that restrained the Press not being revived . . . it became very licentious against the Court and the clergy . . . the Bishops and clergy, apprehending that a rebellion . . . was designed, set themselves to write against the late times, etc. The chief manager of all those angry writings was Sir Roger L'Estrange,

A superficial meddling coxcomb

471 the guards, having lost thirty of their number, were forced to run for it:

For what?

475 Dangerfield, a subtle and dexterous man, who . . . in particular was a false coiner, undertook now to coin a plot . . .

Witty

478–9 the character of Godolphin.

All this very partial to my knowledge.

483 I laid open the cruelties of the Church of Rome in many instances . . . and I AGGRAVATED, though VERY TRULY, the danger etc.

A Bull!

Sprat had studied a polite style much: but there was little strength in it: he had the beginnings of learning laid well in him: but he has allowed himself in a course of some years much sloth, and too many liberties.

Very false

489 The much greater number were of opinion that he (Lloyd) ought to be silent (against Turbervill, a witness against Lord Strafford).

Damned advice

496 Jones stood upon a point of law, of the unseparableness of the prerogative from the person of the King.

A lawyer's way of arguing, very weak

509 in defence of these *ignoramus* juries a book was writ . . . in which both law and reason were brought to confirm it . . . by Somers.

Lord Somers

Page	Burnet	Swift
516	The Bishops were earnest for this (imposing the Test on all M.P.s) which they thought would secure them for ever from a Presbyterian Parliament . . . and that made many of the Court more zealous than ever for carrying through the Act.	And it was very reasonable
519	About eighty of the most learned and pious of their clergy (in Scotland) left all, rather than comply with the terms of this law . . . About twenty of them came up to England:	Enough to corrupt England
523	the rest was spongy, liker the lungs than the heart.	*Anglice,* more like
525	great applications were made to the Duke for saving his (Home's) life: but he was not born under A PARDONING PLANET.	A silly fop
526	All the Presbyterian party saw they were now disinherited of a main part of their birthright, of choosing their representatives in Parliament:	As much of Papists as of Presbyterians.
527	It was much questioned, whether those surrenders (of charters of towns) were good in law or not: it was said . . . they could not extinguish those corporations, nor part with any of their privileges etc.	What does he think of the surrender of the charters of abbeys?
528	The Nonconformists were now prosecuted with much eagerness. This was visibly set on by the Papists: and it was wisely done of them; for they knew how much the Nonconformists were set against them.	Not so much as they are against the Church
531	Lord Halifax and he (Lord Hyde) fell to be in ill terms: for he hated Lord Sunderland beyond expression, though he had married his sister.	Who married whose sister?
536	The truth is, juries became at that time the shame of the nation, as well as a reproach to religion: for they were packed, and prepared to bring in verdicts as they were directed . . .	So they are now
538	(Algernon Sidney) was ambassador in Denmark at the time of the Restoration, . . .	For Cromwell
543	One Rumbold, who had a farm near Hodsden, on the way to Newmarket, through which the King sometimes passed . . . he could have shot them both and rode away. Upon which they ran into much wicked talk about the way of executing that. But . . . all was but talk.	All plots begin with talk

Page	*Burnet*	*Swift*

548 Then he asked them if they had been in any consultations with lords or others in Scotland. Baillie faltered at this, for his conscience restrained him from LYING.

The author and his cousins could *not tell lies*, but they *could plot*

549 Next morning he (Lord Grey) went with him again to the Tower gate, the messenger being again fast asleep.

Is this a blunder?

553 for his man, thinking he (Lord Essex) staid longer than ordinary in his closet, said, he looked through the key-hole, and there saw him lying dead.

He was on the close stool

555 Finch summed up the evidence against him (Lord Russell): but . . . shewed more of a vicious eloquence than of solid or sincere reasoning.

After Earl of Aylsford, an arrant rascal

562 Only I offered to take my oath, that the speech (of Lord Russell) was penned by himself, and not by me.

Jesuitical

567 I knew Spanheim particularly, WHO WAS envoy from the elector of Brandenburg, WHO IS the greatest critic of the age in all ancient learning.

Who was—who is, pure nonsense

568 (Jefferies) was not learned in his profession; and his eloquence, though viciously copious, yet was neither correct nor agreeable.

Like Burnet's eloquence

572 At Sidney's trial, Finch aggravated the matter of the book, as a proof of his intentions, pretending it was an overt act; for he said, *scribere est agere.*

Yet this Finch was made Earl of Aylsford by King George

He told it to a person, from whom Tillotson had it, who told it me.

Admirable authority

577 The credit of the Rye-plot received a great blow by Halliday's confession . . . it was plain that it had gone no further, than that a company of seditious and inconsiderable persons were framing among themselves some treasonable schemes, that were never likely to come to anything.

Cursed partiality

579 The King had published a story . . . as the reason of this extreme severity against Armstrong: he said, that he was sent over by Cromwell to murder him beyond sea, and that he was warned of it, and challenged him on it; and that upon his confessing it he had promised him never to speak of it any more as long as he lived. So the King, counting him now dead in law, thought he was free from that promise.

If the King had a mind to lie, he would have staid till Armstrong was hanged

Page	Burnet	Swift
583	It ended in dismissing Lord Aberdeen, and making Lord Perth Chancellor, to which he had been long aspiring in a most indecent manner.	*Decent* and *indecent*, very useful words to this author
585	I saved my self out of those difficulties by saying to all my friends, that I would not be involved in any such confidence; for as long as I thought our circumstances were such that resistance was not lawful, I thought the concealing any design in order to it was likewise unlawful; and by this means I had preserved my self.	Jesuitical
	(Spence and Carstairs tortured) Upon what was thus screwed out of these two persons, . . .	Witty the second time
586	(Imprisonment of Baillie) He seemed all the while so composed, and even so cheerful, that his behaviour looked like the reviving of the spirit of the noblest of the old Greeks or Romans, or rather of the primitive Christians and first martyrs in those best days of the church.	For he was our cousin
587	The only excuse that was ever pretended for this infamous persecution was, that they were sure he was guilty:	Bishop of Rochester
588	Leightoun, brought to London by Burnet to see Lord Perth—he told me, he was very near his end. . . The next day Leightoun sunk so, that both speech and sense went away of a sudden . . . and then died without pangs or convulsions.	Burnet killed him by bringing him to London
	He retained still a peculiar inclination to Scotland:	Yet he chose to live in England
589	As to the administration (of the Church of England) he looked on it as one of the most corrupt he had ever seen.	Very civil
	He used often to say, that if he were to choose a place to die in, it should be an inn; it looking like a pilgrim's going home, to whom this world was all as an inn, and who was weary of the noise and confusion in it.	Canting puppy
590	Stearn, Archbishop of York, died in the eighty-sixth year of his age: he was a sour, ill-tempered man, and minded chiefly the enriching his family.	Yet thought Author of *The Whole Duty of Man*
591	Morley, Bishop of Winchester . . . was in many respects a very eminent man, zealous against Popery, and yet a great enemy to the Dissenters: he was considerably learned, and had a great vivacity of thought: but he	

Page	*Burnet*	*Swift*
	was too soon provoked, and too little master of himself upon those occasions.	
595	And now the tables were turned	This character is true Style of a gamester
596	I chose for my text these words: *Save me from the lion's mouth, thou hast heard me from the horns of the unicorns.* I made no reflection in my thoughts on the lion and the unicorn, as being the two supporters of the King's scutcheon: (for I ever hated all points of that sort, as a profanation of Scriptures:)	I doubt that
600	At a public supper . . . some hot words passed . . . which raised a sudden quarrel, none but three persons being engaged in it. Swords were drawn, and one was killed outright: but it was not certain by whose hand he was killed: so the other two were both indicted upon it.	The story is wrong told
604	There was at this time a new scheme formed, that very probably would have for ever broken the King and the Duke . . . Mr. May of the Privy Purse told me, that he was told there was a design to break out, with which he himself would be well pleased:	The bishop told me this with many more particulars
609	There were many very apparent suspicions of his (Charles II) being poisoned. . . . Short, another physician, who was a Papist, but after a form of his own, did very much suspect foul dealing.	One physician told me this from Short himself
611	After the battle of Worcester he wandered about England for ten weeks . . . shewed a temper so careless, and so much turned to levity, that he was then diverting himself with little household sports, in as unconcerned a manner as if he had made no loss, and had been in no danger at all.	This might admit a more favourable turn
613	His person and temper, his vices as well as his fortunes, resemble the character that we have given us of Tiberius so much, that it were easy to draw the parallel between them.	Malicious, and in many circumstances false
615	I have gone through all that I knew relating to his life and reign with that regard to truth, and what I think may be instructive to mankind, which became an impartial writer of history, and one who believes that he must give an account to God of what he writes, as well as of what he says and does.	He was certainly a very bad prince, but not to the degree described in this character, which is poorly drawn, and mingled with malice very unworthy an historian, and the style abominable, as in the whole history, and the observations trite and vulgar

Page	*Burnet*	*Swift*

Book IV

623 Because Chudleigh, the envoy there (Holland) had openly broken with the Prince, (for he not only waited no more on him, but acted openly against him; and once in the Vorhaut had affronted him, while he was driving the Princess upon the snow in a trainau, according to the German manner, and pretending they were masked, and that he did not know them, had ordered his coachman to keep his way, as they were coming towards the place where he drove;) the king recalled him, etc.

A pretty parenthesis

626 England now seemed lost, unless some happy accident should save it. All people saw the way for packing a Parliament now laid open.

Just our case at the Queen's death

638 And yet this forwardness to give in such a reign was set on by Musgrave and others, who pretended afterwards, when money was asked for just and necessary ends, to be frugal patriots, and to be careful managers of the public treasure.

A party remark

651 Goodenough, who had been under-sherriff of London when Cornish was sheriff, offered to swear against Cornish; and also said that Rumsey had not discovered all he knew. So Rumsey, to save himself, joined with Goodenough, to swear Cornish guilty of that for which the Lord Russel had suffered.

Goodenough went to Ireland, practised law, and died there

It gave a general horror to the body of the nation: and it let all people see, what might be expected from a reign that seemed to delight in blood.

The same here since the Queen's death

654 The Archbishop of Armagh had continued Lord Chancellor of Ireland, and was in all points so compliant to the Court, that even his religion came to be suspected on that account.

False

Yet, it seemed, he was not thought thoroughpaced. So Sir Charles Porter, ... a zealous promoter of every thing the King proposed, ... and being poor, was thought a person fit to be made a tool of, was declared Lord Chancellor of Ireland.

False and scandalous

669 Powis succeeded (Finch) as Solicitor General,—who was a compliant young aspiring lawyer, though in himself he was no ill-natured man.

Sir Thomas Powis, a good dull lawyer

Page	*Burnet*	*Swift*
670	it was an overturning the whole government, and the changing it from a legal to a despotic form, to say that laws . . . should at the pleasure of the prince be dispensed with: . . . so that the King could no more pardon that, than he could discharge the debts of the subjects, and take away property:	Wrong reasoning
672	All on a sudden Churchmen were disgraced, and the Dissenters in high favour . . . Some of them began to grow insolent upon this shew of favour.	The whole body of them grew insolent, and complying to the King
675–6	Sancroft lay silent at Lambeth. He seemed zealous against Popery in private discourse: but he was of such a timorous temper and so set on the enriching his nephew, that he shewed no sort of courage.	False as hell
681	But the Presbyterians, though they were now freed from the great severities they had long smarted under, yet expressed their unconquerable aversion to Popery.	Partial dog
682	He made the Earl of Tyrconnell Lord Lieutenant.	Lord Deputy
688	Nor were the clergy more diligent in their labours among their people, in which respect it must be confessed that the English clergy are the most remiss of any.	Civil that
690	He (the Prince of Orange) had no vice, but of one sort, in which he was very cautious and secret.	It was of two sorts—*male* and *female*—in the *former* he was neither cautious nor secret
691	When he found I was in my opinion for toleration, he said, that was all he would ever desire to bring us to, for quieting our contentions at home.	It seems the Prince even then thought of being King
692	This would lay the foundation of a perfect union between them, which had been of late a little embroiled:	By Mrs. Villiers, now Lady Orkney; but he proved a damned husband for all that
693	(The Princess) in a very frank manner told him, that she did not know that the laws of England were so contrary to the laws of God, as I had informed her:	Foolish
	Pen the Quaker came over to Holland. He was a talking vain man. . . . He had such an opinion of his own faculty of persuading, that he thought none could stand before it: . . . he had a tedious luscious way, that was not apt to overcome a man's reason, though it might tire his patience.	He spoke very agreeably and with much spirit

Page	Burnet	Swift
695	Cartwright was promoted to Chester. . . . He was ambitious and servile, cruel and boisterous and, by the great liberties he allowed himself, he fell under much scandal of the WORST SORT.	Only sodomy
696	He was looked on as a man that would more effectually advance the design of Popery, than if he should turn over to it . . . he never made that step, even in the most desperate state of his affairs.	He went to Ireland with King James, and there died neglected and poor
697	and now they resolved to attack Oxford . . . few will venture to dispute the (privileges of colleges and universities) much less to disturb them, when their title is good, and their possession is of a long continuance:	Yet in King George's reign, Oxford was bridled and insulted with troops, for no manner of cause but their steadiness to the Church
699	It was much observed, that this university, that had asserted the King's Prerogative in the highest strains . . . as must establish an uncontrollable tyranny, should be the first body to feel the effects of it most sensibly.	And their virtue and steadiness ought equally to be observed
701	I was still of opinion, that, though this (action against Magdalen College) was indeed an act of despotical and arbitrary Power, yet I did not think it struck at the whole:	He was a better Tory than I, if he spoke as he thought
	. . . the Presbyterians seemed reconcileable to the Church; FOR THEY LOVED EPISCOPAL ORDINATION AND A LITURGY,	A damnable lie
702	Both were enemies to this high prerogative that the King was assuming, and were very averse to Popery.	Style
	The more considerable among them (the several sects) resolved not to stand at too great a distance from the Court, nor to provoke the King so far, as to give him cause to think they were irreconcileable to him,	They all complied most shamefully and publicly, as is well known
703	The king's choice of Palmer, Earl of Castlemain (as ambassador to Rome) was liable to great exception.	Duchess of Cleveland's husband
705	since what an Ambassador says is understood as said by the prince whose character he bears, this gave the States a right to make use of all advantages that might offer themselves.	Sophistry
710	The restless spirit of some of that religion (Papist) and of their clergy in particular, shewed they could not be at quiet till they were masters:	All sects were of that spirit

Page	*Burnet*	*Swift*

716   when some of those who had been always moderate told these . . . that they would perhaps forget as soon as the danger was over, they promised the contrary very solemnly. It shall be told afterwards, how well they remembered this. — False and spiteful

726   I was to be married to a considerable fortune at the Hague. — A phrase of the rabble

. . . being now naturalized in Holland, my allegiance was, during my stay in these parts, transferred from his Majesty to the States. — Civilians deny that, but I agree with him

727   the year 1688 . . . produced an extraordinary and UNHEARD of revolution. — The Devil's in that, sure all Europe heard of it

730   If the King had anything to lay to my charge, justice should be done in their courts. The King took the matter very ill; and said, it was an affront to him, and a just cause of war. — Vain fop

731   I never possessed my own soul in a more perfect calm, and in a clearer cheerfulness of spirit, than I did during all those threatenings, and the apprehension that others were in concerning me. — A modest account of his own magnanimity

746   it seemed to be set up as a maxim, that the army by rendering itself odious to the nation would become thereby entirely devoted to the Court: but after all, though soldiers were BAD ENGLISHMEN AND WORSE CHRISTIANS, yet the Court found them too good Protestants to trust much to them. — Special doctrine

748   the Queen's delivery was the subject of all men's discourse. And since so much depends on this, I will give as full and as distinct an account of all that related to that matter, as I could gather up either at that time or afterwards. — All coffee-house chat

751   a resolution was taken for the Queen's lying in at St James's; — Windsor would have been more suspicious

752   a warming pan was brought. But it was not opened, that it might be seen that there was fire and nothing else in it: — This, the ladies say, is foolish

one Hemings . . . heard one coming into the neighbouring parlour, and say with a doleful voice, 'The Prince of Wales is dead:' . . . it was plain they were in a great consternation. — A most foolish story, hardly worthy of a coffee-house

Page	Burnet	Swift
753	it was not possible for them to think it was the same child. They looked on one another, but durst not speak what they thought.	So here are three children
762	The Lord Mordaunt was the first of all the English nobility that came over openly to see the Prince of Orange.	Now Earl of Peterborough
	The Earl of Shrewsbury . . . seemed to be a man of great probity, and to have a high sense of honour.	Quite contrary
763	the Lord Lumley, who was a late convert from popery, and had stood out very firmly all this reign.	He was a knave and a coward
	Mr. Sidney, brother to the Earl of Leicester . . . was a man of a sweet and caressing temper, had no malice in his heart, but too great a love of pleasure.	An idle, drunken, ignorant rake, without sense, truth or honour
764	I recommended a kinsman of my own, Johnstoune, whom I had formed, and knew to be both faithful and diligent.	An arrant Scotch rogue
	. . . Earl of Nottingham, who had great credit with the whole church party: for he was a man possessed with their notions.	That is, Church notions
765	Lord Churchill—he had no fortune to set up on: this put him on all the methods of acquiring one.	A composition of perfidious-ness and avarice
	So he resolved, when the Prince should come over, to go in to him; but to betray no post etc.	What could he do more to a mortal enemy?
769	But this did clearly prove, that such an alliance (with France) was made:	And who can blame him, if in such a necessity he made that alliance?
772	the King of France thought himself tied by no peace; but that, when he suspected his neighbours were intending to make war upon him, he might upon such a suspicion begin a war on his part.	The common maxim of Princes
776	In the declaration prepared for Scotland . . . the Prince by an implication declared in favour of presbytery. He did not see what the consequences of those were, till I explained them. So he ordered them to be altered. And by the declaration that matter was still entire.	The more shame for King William, who changed it
782	He took God to witness, he went to England with no other intentions, but those he had set out in his declaration:	Then he was perjured; for he designed to get the crown, which he denied in the declaration
783	We looked upon our escape as a mark of God's great care of us, who though he had not changed the course of the winds and	Then still it must be a miracle

Page	*Burnet*	*Swift*

seas in our favour, yet had preserved us while we were in such apparent danger, beyond what could have been imagined.

784 An order was also sent to the Bishop of Winchester, to put the President of Magdalen College again in possession. Yet, that order not being executed when the news was brought that the Prince and his fleet were blown back, it was countermanded;

The Bishop of Winchester assured me otherwise

785 the Court thought it necessary, now in an AFTER GAME, to offer some satisfaction (as to the birth of the Prince of Wales).

And this was the proper time

786 It was much observed, that Princess Anne was not present. ... So it was looked on as a colour that shewed she did not believe the thing, and that therefore she would not by her being present seem to give any credit to it.

I have reason to believe this to be true of the Princess Anne

790 Among the first to come in to the Prince at Exeter were the Lord Colchester and the Lord Wharton,

Famous for his cowardice in the Rebellion of 1642

791 Soon after that . . . the Duke of Ormond . . . left him and came over to the Prince,

Yet how has he been since used?

792 In a little while a small army was formed about (the Princess) who chose to be commanded by the Bishop of London; of which he too easily accepted.

And why should he not?

lero, lero lilibulero said to be Irish words,

They are not Irish words, but better than Scotch

795 So the queen took up a sudden resolution of going to France with the child. The midwife, together with all who were assisting at the birth, were also carried over, or so disposed of, that it could never be learned what became of them afterwards.

That is strange and incredible

796 With this his reign ended: for this was a plain deserting his people, and the exposing the nation to the pillage of an army, which he had ordered the Earl of Feversham to disband.

Abominable assertion, and false consequence

797 if (the King) had got clear away, by all that could be judged, he would not have had a party left . . . But what followed upon this gave them a colour to say, that he was forced away and driven out.

So he certainly was, both now and afterwards

They made great havock of many places, not sparing the houses of ambassadors. But none were killed, no houses burnt, nor were any robberies committed.

Don Pedro de Ronquillo's house was plundered and pulled down; he was Spanish ambassador

Page	*Burnet*	*Swift*
	Jefferies, finding the King gone, saw what reason he had to look to himself . . . had disguised himself. But he fell into the hands of some who knew him . . . after many hours tossing him about, he was carried to the Lord Mayor; whom they charged to commit him to the Tower,	He soon after died in the Tower by drinking strong liquors
798	So he sent to Oxford, to excuse his not coming thither, and to offer the association to them, which was signed by almost all the heads, . . . even by those who became afterwards his most implacable enemies.	Malice
799	I was affected with this dismal reverse of the fortune of a great Prince, more than I think fit to express.	Or than I will believe
800	since the Earl of Feversham, who had commanded the army against the Prince, was come without a passport, he was for some days put in arrest.	Base and villanous
801	asked them if the King should go to Rochester. . . It was very visible, that this was proposed in order to a second escape.	And why not?
802	Some said . . . the person of the King was now struck at, as well as his government: and this specious undertaking would now appear to be only a disguised and designed usurpation.	All this is certainly true
803	Old Sergeant Maynard came with the men of the law. He was then near ninety . . . The Prince took notice of his great age, and said, that he had outlived all the men of the law of his time: he answered, he had like to have outlived the law it self, if his highness had not come over.	He was an old rogue for all that
804	In the western counties of Scotland, the Presbyterians . . . generally broke in upon the episcopal clergy with great insolence and much cruelty . . . Nor did they treat those of them, who had appeared very zealously against Popery, with any distinction.	To reward them for which, King William abolished Episcopacy
805	The Episcopal party saw themselves under a great cloud: so they resolved all to adhere to the Earl of Dundee,	He was the best man in Scotland
806	Londonderry and Iniskillen refused to receive a Popish garrison . . . resolved to stand to their own defence and stay till supplies should come to them from England.	He should have mentioned Dr. Walker, who defended Derry

Page	Burnet	Swift
		Swift

807 Those who were employed by Tyrconnell to deceive the Prince, made their applications by Sir William Temple, who had a long and well established credit with him.

A lie of a Scot; for Sir William Temple did not know Tyrconnell

Others thought that the leaving Ireland in that dangerous state, might be a mean to bring the convention to a more speedy settlement of England; and that therefore the Prince ought not to make too much haste to relieve Ireland.

That is agreed to be the true reason, and it was a wicked one

810 Archbishop Sancroft was a poor-spirited and fearful man; and acted a very mean part in all this great transaction.

Others think very differently

811 The greatest part of the clergy declared themselves for it (a regency).

And it was certainly much the best expedient

The third party was made up of those who thought that there was an original contract between the kings and the people of England etc.

I am of this party, and yet I would have been for a regency

813 By this proposition of a regent, here were to be . . . two kings at the same time . . . This was both more illegal and more unsafe than the method they proposed.

There is something in this argument

814 It was believed that those of the King's party, who were looked on as men of conscience, had secret orders from him to act upon this pretence etc.

This is malice

Others thought it enough to say that in extreme cases all obligations did cease; and that . . . by reason of the late ill government, and by King James's flying over to the enemy . . . had put the people of England on the necessity of securing themselves upon a legal bottom.

This was the best reason

815 But this was a critical dispute (about the word *abdicate*): and it scarce became the greatness of that assembly, or the importance of the matter.

It was a very material point

it was urged, that by the law, the King did never die; but that with the last breath of the dying king the regal authority went to the next heir.

This is certainly true

816 Those who insisted on the abdication said, that, if the King dissolved the tie between him and his subjects to himself, he dissolved their tie likewise to his posterity.

This is sophistry

Page	Burnet	Swift

I was ordered to gather together all the presumptive proofs (of the birth of the pretended Prince of Wales) . . . these did not amount to a full and legal proof: yet they seemed to be such violent presumptions, that, when they were all laid together, they were more convincing than plain and downright evidence:

Well said, Bishop

817 if there was no clear and positive proof made of an imposture, the pretending to examine into it and not being able to make it out . . . would strengthen the pretension of his birth.

They thought it would be a good security . . . to oblige our princes to govern well, while they would apprehend the danger of a revolt to a pretender still in their eye.

I have used more than ordinary care to gather together all the particulars that were then laid before me as to that matter.

Wisely done
I think this was no ill design; yet it hath not succeeded in mending Kings

And where are they?

818 I desired to be disengaged, that I might be free to oppose this proposition (to make the prince King) with all the strength and credit I had. He answered me, that I might desire that when I saw a step made: but till then he wished me to stay where I was.

Is all this true?

819 I heard no more of this; in which the Marquis of Halifax was single among the peers: for I did not find there was any one of his mind . . . except Lord Culpepper.

The Princess continued all the while in Holland, . . . so that she came not to England till all the debates were over.

Yet was not the same thing done in effect, while the King had the sole administration? Why was she [not] sent for till the matter was agreed? This clearly shews the Prince's original design was to be King, against what he professed in his Declaration.

820 He said, he came over, being invited, to save the nation: he had now brought together a free and true representative of the kingdom: he left it to them to do what they thought best for the good of the kingdom: and, when things were once settled, he should be well satisfied to go back to Holland again.

he would not be regent . . . they must look out for some other person for that post:

Did he tell truth?
Was not this a plain confession of what he came for?

821 he thought the issue of Princess Anne should be preferred, in the succession, to any issue he might have by any other wife than the Princess.

A great concession truly

Page	*Burnet*	*Swift*

822 The poor Bishop of Durham . . . was now prevailed upon to come, and, by voting the new settlement, to merit at least a pardon for all that he had done: which, all things considered, was thought very indecent in him, yet not unbecoming the rest of his life and character.

This is too hard, though almost true

The power of the Crown to grant a *Nonobstante* to some statutes was objected.

Yet the words continue in patents

824 The Prince's success against King James gave him the right of conquest over him. and by it all his rights were transferred to the Prince etc.

The author wrote a paper to prove this, and it was burnt by the hangman, and is a very foolish scheme

Book VII

Vol. II

525 all those who appeared for this large and comprehensive way were reproached for their coldness and indifference in the concerns of the church; and in that I had a large share;

Dog

526 so catching a thing is this turbulent spirit, when once it prevails among clergymen, that the same ill temper began to ferment and spread itself among the clergy of Ireland . . . the clergy were making the same bold claim there, that had raised such disputes among us;

Dog, Dog, Dog,

580 Prior had been taken a boy out of a tavern by the Earl of Dorset, who accidentally found him reading Horace; and he, being very generous, gave him an education in literature:

Malice

581 this was done with much art, but WITH NO REGARD TO TRUTH, in a pamphlet entitled the *Conduct of the Allies and of the late Ministry*;

It was all true

The Jacobites did with the greater joy entertain this prospect of peace . . . which made them conclude, that it was to have a happy effect with relation to the Pretender's affairs.

The Queen hated and despised the Pretender, to my knowledge

583 I said to the Queen if any such peace should be made (which would deliver up all Europe into the hands of France) she was betrayed and we were all ruined: in less than three years' time she would be murdered, and the fires would be again raised in Smithfield:

A false prophet in every particular

Page	*Burnet*	*Swift*
589	It was said, that the Queen could not send a message to any one House to adjourn, when the like message was not sent to both Houses etc.	Modern nonsense
591	The House of Commons . . began with Walpole, whom they resolved to put out of the way of disturbing them in the House.	He began early, and has been thriving twenty-seven years to January 1739
609	some of these addresses mentioned the Protestant succession . . . with zeal; others did it more coldly; some made no mention of it at all. It was universally believed . . . no addresses were so acceptable to the ministers as . . . the last sort.	Foolish and factious
610	The Duke of Ormonde had given the States such assurances . . . that he was let into the secrets of all their counsels, which, by that confidence, were all known to the French:	Vile Scot, dare to touch Ormonde's honour, and so falsely
612	Duke of Hamilton and Lord Mohun both killed in a duel—neglecting the rules of art, they seemed to run on one another, as if they tried who should kill first . . .	Wrongly told
614	Godolphin never once suspected of corruption—his estate was not increased by him to the value of 4000 pounds.	A great lie
669	The pleasures of sense I did soon nauseate;	Not so soon with the wine of some elections

THE LIFE OF THE AUTHOR by Thomas Burnet

Facing title:		A rude, violent party jackanapes
719	in a letter from Tillotson, dated Oct. 23, 1694: The account given of Athanasius's creed seems to me no wise satisfactory; I wish we were well rid of it.	(Against this Swift has drawn a pointing finger)
722	The character I have given his wives, will scarce make it an addition to his, that he was a most affectionate husband. His tender care of the first, and his fond love to the other two . . .	Three wives
723	The Bishop was a kind and bountiful master to his servants, . . . and peculiarly happy in his choice of them; especially in that of the steward to the bishopric and his Courts, William Wastefield Esq. . . . and of his domestic steward, Mr. Mackney.	A Scot, his own countryman

12. CLARENDON, EDWARD HYDE, EARL OF: *HISTORY OF THE REBELLION*, 1707

VOL. I. *On the first board, according to Scott, but now disappeared:*
Finished the 4th time, April 18, 1741

On the recto of the blank leaf before the title:
Judicium de authore

(*This seems not to have been written, but beneath on the same page:*)
The cursed Hellish Vilany, Treachery, Treasons of the Scots were the chief Grounds and Causes of that execrable Rebellion

THE WORD OF A KING. This Phrase is repeated some hundred times; but is ever foolish, and too often false

Page	Clarendon	Swift
Preface		
v.	LOVE OF ARBITRARY POWER	what king doth not love and endeavour at it?
vi.	the People may not always be restrained from attempting by force to do themselves Right, tho' they ought not.	They ought
vii.	WITHOUT he can satisfy	except
viii.	the Soveraignty of our Seas, so naturally, so anciently, and so justly the true defence of this Kingdom;	←
ix.	whereas the Fleet of England hath been renown'd, through so many Ages, for the honour and security of this Kingdom, in these latter days, by an unaccountable improvidence, our care has been more industriously applied to the raising . . . Land Forces,	←
xviii.	every Man's Expectation, THAT had laboured	who
9, ll. 1–4	all men being Inhibited . . . by the Proclamation at the Dissolution of the Parliament in the Fourth year, so much as to mention or speak as if a Parliament should be called	great Weakness
31, l. 13	where his Person and Presence WAS	were
47, l. 9	Robert Carr, a *Scots*-man	a Scottish King makes a Scottish Favorite
48, ll. 19–34	the Earl of Carlisle . . . had wrought himself into a particular interest with his Master, and into greater affection and esteem with the whole *English* Nation, than any other of that Country; by choosing Their friendships and conversations and preferring it to any of his Own.	A Miracle in a Scot

Page	Clarendon	Swift
58,	l. 10f. from the Dissolution of the Parliament in the Fourth year, to the beginning of this Parliament, which was above twelve years, this Kingdom . . . enjoy'd the greatest Calm, and the fullest measure of Felicity, that any People in any Age, for so long time together, have been bless'd with; to the wonder, and envy of all the other parts of *Christendom*.	Partial
59,	l. 5 *Scotland* (which was but the WILDERNESS of that Garden)	Dunghill
	l. 43 the Power of Kingdoms is more reverenced than their Justice by their Neighbours: and it may be this Consideration might not be the least Motive, and may not be the worst Excuse for those Counsels.	too arbitrary
60,	l. 2–3 a Time . . . wherein those two Adjuncts, . . . *Imperium & Libertas* were as well reconciled, as is possible.	Nego
74–5	INNOVATIONS in Religion.	
	Bishop Williams publish'd a Discourse and Treatise against the matter, and manner of the Prosecution of that Business; a Book so full of good Learning, and that Learning so close and solidly applied . . .	Is that Book to be bought, or borrowed?

THE SECOND BOOK

88,	ll. 42–9 no man ever enquired what was doing in *Scotland*, nor had that Kingdom a place or mention in one Page of any Gazette;	Should Bridewell News be in any Gazette?
	That People after they had once begun, pursued the business vigorously, and with all imaginable Contempt of the Government;	Scottish scoundrels
94,	ll. 22–5 (the Scots) desired nothing but to be admitted into the Presence of their gracious Soveraign, to lay their Grievances at his Royal Feet.	Scotch Dogs
96,	l. 32 the Marquis of Hamilton	a cursed true Scot
100,	l. 32 the *Scots* got so much Benefit and Advantage by it	Confounded Scots
101,	l. 45 The Earl of Argyle joins with the Covenanters, notwithstanding his great Obligations to the King.	All Argyles, cursed Scottish Hell-hounds for ever
103,	l. 1 A Letter intercepted from some of the Scottish Nobility to the French King.	Scottish Traytors
	l. 45 the general Aversion over the whole	

Page	*Clarendon*	*Swift*

Kingdom to the *Scots*, and the Indignation they had at Their presumption in their design of Invading *England*, made it believ'd that a Parliament would express a very sharp sense of their Insolence and carriage towards the King,

cursed Hellish Scots for ever

104, l. 2 Writs for the meeting of Parliament on the Third day of April next

April 3d for Knaves the 1st for Fools

116, l. 34 The Convocation continued after the Parliament: —makes Canons.

Convocations of the Clergy are as legal and as necessary as those of the Layety

122, par. 1 The Scots petition the King: upon it a Treaty appointed at Rippon, only popular men entrusted with it

a cursed Committee

l. 34 *Alexander Henderson* their Metropolitan

a cursed Fanatick

123, l. 15 *English* Commissioners receive the Scottish proposals that the Archbishop, the Earl of *Strafford*, and the Marquis of *Hamilton* . . . should be removed from the King.

Cursed Hellish Scots

124, l. 40 Besides those the King had nobody to consult with but the Lord Keeper *Finch*, the Duke of *Richmond*, the Marquis of *Hamilton*, the Earl of *Strafford*, and Sir *Harry Vane*,

Bad Councillors

125, l. 42 fifty thousand pounds a month for the *Scots* army but thirty for the King's;

Greedy Scotch Rebellious Dogs!

129, l. 21 it must not be DOUBTED that there were many particular Persons of Honour of that Nation who abhorr'd the Outrages which were committed, and retained very Loyal wishes for his Majesties Prosperity;

I doubt it

for they were Scots!

130, l. 1 NOT VERY RICH Nobility of *Scotland*

Beggarly, Beggarly

THE THIRD BOOK

148, l. 24 Mr. Saint-John (being A NATURAL SON of the House of Bullingbrook)

a Bastard

151, l. 17 The Earl of *Rothes* had been the chief Architect of that whole Machine from the beginning, and was a man very well bred, of very good parts, and great address;

a Scottish free-thinker

152, l. 28 an Order was carefully entred, 'that upon all occasions the Appelation should be used of OUR BRETHREN OF SCOTLAND

cursed Scots
Brethren in Iniquity

153, l. 9 That the Charge against the Earl of *Strafford* . . . being to make a Treason evident out of a complication of several ill Acts; That, he must be traced through many dark paths, etc.

As a boy

Y

Page	Clarendon	Swift
153, l. 37	at his coming from *Ireland* the Earl had said in Council there; That if he ever return'd to that Sword again, he would not leave a *Scotish*-man in that Kingdom.	And it was a good Resolution
	the Lord Mayor and some Aldermen . . . not giving that Satisfaction was expected . . . he should tell the King That it would never be well till he hang'd up a Lord Mayor of *London* in the City to terrify the rest.	At worst, onely a rash Expression
155, l. 15	Divers new Privy-Counsellors sworn of the Popular Party, the Earl of *Hertford* . . . the Earl of *Bedford* etc.	All but the first
161, l. 39	When a Multitude of Hands was procured, the Petition it Self was cut off; and a New One framed, suitable to the Design in hand, and annex'd to the long List of Names which were subscribed to the Former.	Dogs, Villains, almost as bad as the cursed Scots
167, l. 1	*Saint-John* made Sollicitor General . . . a Gentleman of an Honourable Extraction (if he had been Legitimate)	the Bastard before mentioned
183, l. 4	Saint-John's argument 'upon want of Proof' in the case against Strafford— Private Satisfaction to each man's Conscience was sufficient, although no Evidence had been given at all:	Bp. Atterbury
187, l. 45	Bill for extirpating Bishops, Deans, and Chapters . . . none so importunately press'd the Reading of it as *Saint-John*,	the Bastard
199, l. 9	The Explanation of the Protestation concerning the meaning of the words 'true reform'd Protestant Religion, express'd in the Doctrine of the Church of *England*.	true Popish evasion Fanatick Dogs
202, l. 41	The Earl of *Strafford* himself writes to the King to assent to the Bill against him.	Great Magnanimity
203, l. 1	This absolv'd the King from any scruple . . . so in the end they extorted from him to sign a Commission to some Lords to pass the Bill	weak and wrong
l. 28	his ROYAL CONSORT	a most unhappy Marriage
204, l. 39	At the same time an Act for the continuing this Parliament; no hope of borrowing in the City, since no security if the two Houses should be dissolv'd	Cursed stupidity and Hinc illae lachrymae
205, l. 16	that This Parliament should not be Adjourn'd, Prorogued, or Dissolv'd, but by Act of Parliament	The fatal stroak

Page	Clarendon	Swift

l. 43 The Lords consented and the King induced to include that Bill in the Commission with the Act of Attainder

I wish the Author had enlarged here upon what Motives the King passed the Bill. The King by this Act utterly ruined

207, l. 47 And so in expectation and confidence, that they would make glorious additions to the State and Revenue of the Crown, his Majesty suffer'd himself to be Stripp'd of All that he had left.

Great weakness in the King

225, l. 24 These Acts of Parliament ... will be acknowledg'd, by an Incorrupted Posterity, to be Everlasting Monuments of the King's Princely and Fatherly Affection to his People;

Rather of his Weaknesse

BOOK IV.

237, l. 21 A general Insurrection of the *Irish* spread itself over the whole Country; in such an inhumane and Barbarous Manner, that there were Forty or Fifty Thousand of the *English* Protestants murther'd,

at least

243, l. 39 That which should have been an Act of Oblivion, was made a Defence and Justification of whatsoever They had done: Their first Tumults . . . and suppressing both Courts of Justice and Session

Scot, Scot, Scot, for ever Scot.

244, l. 51 His Majesty having never receiv'd any considerable Profit from *Scotland*, cared the less for what he parted with there; and, it may be, being resolv'd They should be no more Charge to him in his Court here (for surely he had then very hard thoughts of a great part of the Nation)

How could he, from Scottish Rebels and Beggars?

Who can doubt of it?

257, l. 6 Propositions made from *Scotland*, 'for the sending ten thousand men from Thence, into *Ulster*, to be paid by the Parliament, were consented to; whereby some Soldiers were dispatch'd thither, to defend Their Own Plantation; and did in truth, at Our Charge, as much Oppress the *English* that were There, as the Rebels could have done;

send cursed rebell Scots who oppressed the English in that Kingdom as the Irish Rebels did, and were Governors of that Province &c.

271, l. 50 Dr. Williams published, by his own Authority, a Book against the using those Ceremonies (*countenanced by the Archbishop of Canterbury*) in which there was much good Learning, and too little Gravity for a Bishop.

Where is that Book to be had?

Page	Clarendon	Swift
275, l. 16	(Dr. Williams) being then an Archbishop, did in Person assist the Rebels to take a Castle of the King's;	I have heard say he did . . . ght (? fight)
l. 31	the great hatred of this Man's Person and Behaviour, was the greatest invitation to the House of Commons so irregularly to Revive that Bill to remove the Bishops;	How came he to be so hated by that faction he is said to favor?
276–7	The Petition and Protestation of the Bishops to the King and the House of Lords	I see no Fault in this Protestation
280	Articles of High-Treason against Lord Kimbolton and five Members of the House of Commons	It proved a long and vexatious affair
281	The King goes to the House of Commons to demand the Persons accused of High Treason	Too rash and Indiscreet The second great and fatal Error.
282, l. 2	He declared to them, that no King of *England* had been ever, or should be more careful to maintain their Privileges, than He would be . . . and ASSURED THEM IN THE WORD OF A KING, that he never intended any Force etc.	Never to be relyed upon
284, l. 1	a Proclamation for the Apprehension of all those whom he had accused of High Treason, forbidding any Person to Harbour them;	A very weak and wrong Proceeding in the King, which had many bad Consequences. What was their Crime?
322, l. 50	The Petition to the House of Commons of many thousands of Poor People . . . in *London*.	Who was the Author?
334, l. 42	The King persuaded to pass the Bill against the Bishops Votes and also concerning the Militia	Too great a weakness, and attended by a heap of gross Follyes
336, l. 27	an Ordinance for the settling the Militia was agreed on by both Houses, . . . the most avowed Foundation of all the Miseries that followed.	The most ruinous Consequence of the King's Weakness or Cowardice
364, l. 7	he assured them IN THE WORD OF A KING,	I cannot endure that Phrase any more
365, l. 20	what greater earnest of his trust, and relyance on his Parliament could he give, than the passing the Bill for the continuance of this Present Parliament? The Length of which, . . . he hoped, would never . . . invite his Subjects So much to abuse his Confidence, as to esteem any thing fit for this Parliament to do, which were not fit, if it were in his power to Dissolve it to Morrow.	like a very weak Prince Yet, that was his Ruin.
366, l. 20	a design to send the Prince beyond the Seas, and to MARRY HIM TO SOME PAPIST	as it fell out

Page	*Clarendon*	*Swift*
384, l. 21	IN THE WORD OF A KING	How long is that Phrase to last?
419, l. 27	yet all those PIKES and Protestations,	What are those Pikes?
427, l. 31	on the WORD OF A KING	a frequent foolish word
428, l. 1	We do engage unto you solemnly THE WORD OF A KING, that etc.	batterd as a Phraze
472, l. 41	he expressed a great Trust in his two Houses of Parliament; which was a just, necessary, and proper Prerogative.	Proved his Ruin
543, l. 6	(Sr *Richard Gurney*) was by their LORDSHIPS, in the presence of the Commons, adjudged 'to be put out of his Office of Lord Mayor of *London*;	Dogs

VOLUME II

Page	*Clarendon*	*Swift*
7, l. 32	We promise, in the WORD OF A KING, all safety	very weak
10, l. 22	*The Answer of the Lords and Commons unto the King's last Message*	I do not much dislike this Answer
17, l. 13	Attacks of the people on the persons and property of Sir *John Lucas* and the Countess of *Rivers* in *Essex*.	As bad as Scots
18, l. 3	There are Monuments enough in the seditious Sermons at that time printed, and in the Memories of Men, of others not printed, of such wresting and perverting of Scripture to the odious purposes of the Preacher, that pious Men will not look over without trembling.	I wish I could find them
20, l. 22	at *Worcester* . . . two or three *Scotish* OFFICERS, were taken Prisoners.	Dogs
33, l. 19	Faction in the King's Army between the General and Earl of *Lindsey* and Prince *Rupert* . . . the King was so indulgent to him, that he took his advice in all things relating to the Army,	A great Mistake in the King by too much indulgence to Prince Rupert
40, l. 39	(The Earl of *Lindsey* bore heavily that restriction) which was put upon him by the Commission granted to Prince *Rupert*, and by the King's preferring the Prince's opinion, in all matters relating to the War before His.	I blame the Kings Partiality
51, l. 19	the Marquis of ARGYLE	Always a cursed Family of Scots
59, ll. 41–6	*a 6-line parenthesis in a long sentence marked*	too long a Parenthesis
62, l. 36	two of their most eminent Chaplains, Dr. *Downing* and Mr. *Marshal*, publicly avow'd, that the Soldiers lately taken Prisoners at *Brentford*, . . . released by the King upon their Oaths that they would	

Page	Clarendon	Swift
	never again bear Armes against him, WERE NOT OBLIGED BY THAT OATH; but, by Their power, ABSOLVED THEM THEREOF.	Perfect Popery
65, l. 42	he doubted not the Duty and Affection of his SCOTISH Subjects would have so just a resentment,	cursed Scots to trust them
66, l. 20	of whose Courage and Loyalty, he SHOULD LOOK to make use	in vain, and never found
l. 48	He could not DOUBT, a dutiful concurrence in his Subjects of *Scotland*, in care of his Honour, and just Rights, would draw down a blessing upon that Nation too.	a Scots blessing
67, l. 4	and other fruit of their Allegiance he expected not, than that they should not Rebel.	but they did
81, l. 34	and sollicite Our Subjects of SCOTLAND, to enter this Land with an Army against Us:	Damnable Scots
91, l. 36	*The Propositions of the Lords and Commons.*	
	4. That your Majesty will be pleased to give your Royal Assent unto the Bill for taking away the superstitious Innovations; . . . for abolishing Archbishops, Bishops etc. and all other under Officers, out of the Church of *England*.	a thorow Sweep
l. 46	Bill for consultation . . . with GODLY, RELIGIOUS, and LEARNED Divines.	i.e. cursed Fanaticks
99, l. 52	a Garrison of two hundred SCOTS; who, upon the approach of Sr *Ralph Hopton*, as kindly quit *Saltash*, as the others had *Launceston* before.	Loyall Scots—ever cursed
101, l. 25	RUTHEN, (a *Scotch*-man, the Governour of *Plymouth*)	A cursed Scottish Dog
103, l. 10	The Earl of *Stamford* had not the same patience to abide the other Party at *Tavistock*,	A Rogue, half as bad as a Scot
134-7	Petition of the General Assembly of the Kirk of *Scotland*	
134, l. 33	(our not vain, but just GLORIATION)	Scotch Phrase
40	Papists declared to be far better Subjects than ∧ Protestants	Scotch
135, l. 2	TO CHANGE THE FACE of your two Kingdoms of SCOTLAND and England, into the similitude of miserable *Ireland*;	←
l. 18	to FALL DOWN AGAIN BEFORE YOUR Majesty	rise against
l. 24	Commissioners may be sent from THIS KIRK;	Hell

Page	*Clarendon*	*Swift*

136, l. 9 the strongest LET, till it be taken out of the way, is the Mountain of Prelacy: l. 28 and joyn with OTHERS in the way of Reformation)

Scottish Dogs
i.e. Scots

l. *b.* The National Assembly of this Kirk, from which We have our Commission, ^

from Satan

138–143 *His Majesty's Answer to the late Petition...of Our* CHURCH *of Scotland*

Kirk

139, l. 9 unbecoming in itself for Them to require, the ancient, happy, and establish'd Government of the Church of England to be alter'd, and conform'd to ... ANOTHER CHURCH

a Scotch Kirk

140, l. 37 To which (Synod) We shall be willing that some learned DIVINES OF OUR CHURCH OF SCOTLAND may be likewise sent

to confound all

142, l. 35 the Conversion of OUR DEAREST CONSORT ... so much our desire,

a thorow Papist

199, l. 42 And there being no evidence against Mr. HAMBDEN

Which Hambden? Not the Rebel Hamden · No, it was one Alexdr Hambden

201, l. 48 many Officers (of the Scottish Army) betook themselves to the Service of the Parliament; whereof divers were Men of good Conduct, and Courage;

cursed Scots for ever

Colonel *Hurry* commanded those Horse at *Edge-hill* which had preserv'd their Army there; . . . feeling himself afterwards not so well regarded . . . he resolv'd to quit them and go to the King;

A miracle. Colnel Urry was an honest valiant loyal Scot, repenting his mistake

203, l. 51 But the Man was in his nature proud, and imperious; had raised many Enemies; was a Man of Licence, etc.

A mixture of the Scot

219, l. 7 On the brow of the Hill there were Breast-works, on which were pretty Bodies of small shot, and some Cannon; on either Flank grew a pretty thick Wood towards the declining of the Hill . . . at the Rear, was a very fair Plain etc.

silly stile

244, l. 2 the Garrison of *Glocester* . . . do conceive our selves wholely bound to obey the Commands of his Majesty, signified by both Houses of Parliament:

Cursed Rogues

261, l. 48 Sr *Anthony Ashley Cooper,*

E. of Shafsbury by C.2d. a great Vilain

262, l. 29 the flexibility and instability of that Gentleman's nature, not being then understood, or suspected.

Shafsbury, an early Rogue

l. 36 the King would not put an affront upon his Nephew.

Too fond of those Nephews

Page	*Clarendon*	*Swift*

270, l. 26 In this unhappy Battle, was slain the Lord Viscount *Falkland*; a Person of such prodigious parts of Learning and Knowledge, of that inimitable sweetness and delight in Conversation, of so flowing and obliging a humanity . . . that if there were no other barnd upon this odious and accursed Civil War, than that single loss, it must be most infamous, and execrable to all Posterity.

←

271, l. 43 two large discourses . . . with that sharpness of Style, and full Weight of Reason, that the Church is depriv'd of great Jewels in the concealment of them, . . .

ten thousand pityes that they are not to be recovered

277, l. 16 Thus fell that incomparable young Man, in the four and thirtieth year of his Age, etc.

It moves grief to the highest Excess

l. 49 as firmly united to one and the same end, as their Brethren the *Scots*;

Deceitfull Scots

282, l. 46 the Earl of *Holland*—his own GENEROUS Nature

treacherous

283, l. 2 he resolv'd to make what hast he could back to the Parliament, and to spend the remainder of his life in Their Service: which Action, so contrary to his own natural discretion and GENEROSITY, . . .

Treachery

l. 36 they had called an Assembly of their Kirk, and a Convention of their Estates, Without, and expressly Against the King's Consent;

Diabolicall Scots for ever

284, l. 16 those Politick arguments would have no influence upon the People, who had such a natural Affection and Loyalty to their Sovereign . . . there were many well-wishers to him, and maligners, in their hearts, of the present Reformation;

Cursed Scots

l. 45 MARRIAGE between the Parliament and the *Scots*

Satan was Parson

285, l. 37 for, Dr *Featly* (upon whose Reputation in Learning, they had raised great advantages to themselves) having made many Speeches in the Assembly in the behalf of the order of Bishops etc and inveighed against 'the liberty that was taken in matter of Religion, by which etc. had so far incurr'd their displeasure, and provoked their jealousy, that an ordinary fellow (so well Confirm'd in Spirit, that they fear'd not his failing or conversion)

A long confounding Period

Page	*Clarendon*	*Swift*

was directed to make application to him in cases of Conscience, and after he had got sufficient credit with him (which was no hard matter) to intimate to him etc.

287–9 A Copy of the Covenant

288, l. 16 3. We shall endeavour . . . to preserve and defend the King's Majesty's Person, and Authority   Damnable Rebel Scots

l. 50 6. . . . this Cause, which so much concerneth the Glory of God . . . and the HONOUR OF THE KING;   by Martyrdom

289, l. 10 We have not, as we ought, valued the inestimable benefit of the Gospel, that We have not labour'd for the purity, and power thereof; . . . other Sins and Transgressions so much abounding amongst Us: All very true

l. 16 our true and unfeigned purpose, desire and endeavour . . . each ONE TO GO BEFORE ANOTHER in the example of a real Reformation;   ←

291, l. 14 In the end, they very devoutly extolled the Covenant, magnified the *Scotish* Nation, with all imaginable Attributes of Esteem and Reverence, 'a Nation that had engaged itself to God . . .   Most diabolicall Scots

292, l. 26 Of Sir *Harry Vane*—there need no more be said of his Ability, than that he was chosen to cozen, and deceive a whole Nation which was thought to excell in craft and cunning: could outcheat a Scot

293, l. 18 Duke *Hamilton* (whose advice and orders, the King himself had required them to observe; unhappily still believing him to be faithful)   that Duke was a hellish Treacherous Villain of a Scot

316, l. 6 nothing troubled the King so much, as the Intelligence he received from *Scotland*, that they had already form'd their Army, and resolv'd to enter England in the Winter Season.   cursed Scots

l. 30 all the Peers in the King's Service might subscribe a Letter to the Council of State in *Scotland*, . . . which possibly might make some impression upon the Nation of *Scotland*,   Scottish Dogs

318, l. 41 Proclamation was issued out, . . . mentioning the League of *Scotland* to invade the Kingdom; which was the most universally odious, and detestable;   Hellish Scots

339, l. 49 a FORREIGN NATION, upon the very point of invading it.   cursed Scotland

Page	Clarendon	Swift

340 l. 40 The Earl of *Essex*'s Answer.

Essex was a cursed Rebel

341, l. 8 An Extract of the Declaration of the Kingdom of *Scotland*—'It was necessary, that everyone, against all doubting, should be perswaded in his mind of the lawfulness of his Undertaking, and of the goodness of the Cause maintain'd by him —the good of Religion in *England*, and the deliverance of their Brethren out of the depths of Affliction;

Abominable, damnable Scotch Hellish Dogs for ever. Let them wait for Cromwell to plague them, and enslave their Scabby Nation

l. 26 'the Question was not . . . whether they might propagate their Religion by Armes; but whether . . . they ought to assist their Brethren in *England*, who were calling for their help,

Diabolical Scots for ever—

342, l. 27 An Extract of the Declaration of *England* and *Scotland*—being confident that this War, wherein both Nations were so firmly united, and deeply engaged, WAS OF GOD, they resolve etc.

An error, mistaking the Devil for God
The Devil made the damnable Scots Covenant

343, l. 5 they proclaim'd 'a Pardon to all those who would before such A DAY DESERT THE KING, and adhere to them, and ∧ take the Covenant;

the Devil to take the Covenant

l. 22 after this time that the Earl (of Essex) declined this opportunity of declaring himself, HE NEVER DID PROS-PEROUS ACT IN THE REMAINDER OF HIS LIFE;

I am heartily glad of that

l. 50 at least the world might see, that they did, in PLAIN ENGLISH, refuse to admit of any Peace.

Scotch

347, l. 49 That all his Majesty's Subjects . . . of *England* and Wales are bound to resist and repress all those of Scotland who should enter as Enemies of the State;

execrable Scots

348, l. 12 The Lords and Commons, who had given their consents to the present coming in of the *Scots* in a Warlike manner, had committed High Treason:

Rebel Scots

l. 29 the Invasion which THE SCOTS MADE in the depth of Winter,

cursed Scots ever inflaming

351, l. 18 the violent Party, whereof the Earl OF ARGYLE was the Head

odious Dog and so are all his Descendants

l. 40 no part should be communicated to Duke *Hamilton*;

an arrant Scot

352, l. 44 to cause GOOD ELECTIONS to be made

what? in Scotland?

353, l. 44 *Jo. Pym*; who died with great Torment and Agony of a disease unusual, and therefore the more spoken of, *Morbus pediculosus*,

I wish all his Clan had dyed of the same disease

| *Page* | *Clarendon* | *Swift* |

THE EIGHTH BOOK

382, l. 36 Sr *Anthony Ashley Cooper*
a Rogue all his life

385, l. 43 *Weemes*, a *Scotch*-man, had been as much obliged by the King, as a Man of His condition could be, and in a manner very unpopular: for he was made Master Gunner of *England*,
a cursed Hellish Scot, why was not the Rogue hanged?

387, l. 4 Sr *Edward Walker* (Garter King at Arms and Secretary to the Council of War)
A very mean Author

388–9 that Party of the King's Horse which Charged the *Scots*, so totally routed and defeated their whole Army, that they fled all ways for many miles together, and were knocked on the head, and taken Prisoners by the Country
I am glad of that

420, l. 37 Colonel *Hurry*, a *Scotch*-man, quitted the Parliament and perform'd some signal Service to the King . . . quitted the Service: . . . and made a discovery of all he knew of the King's Army,
Mentioned before; and then I was deceived by him, but now I find him a cursed true Scot

427, l. 16 after the Battle of *York*, the Scots return'd to reduce *New-castle*; which they had already done; and all other Garrisons which had held out for the King;
most damnable Scots

l. 21 The King's Army less united than ever; the old General set aside, and Prince Rupert put into the Command, which was no popular Change:
too fond of his Nephews

l. 38 Goring, who was now General of the Horse, was no more gracious to Prince Rupert, than Wilmot . . .
Caracter of Wilmot and Goring

453, l. 10 The question of the command of the Militia; . . .

30 without which they looked upon themselves as lost, and at the King's mercy; not considering that He must be at Theirs, if such a power was committed to them.
The case seems doubtfull, the Point should be moderated

454, l. 42 one hundred thousand pounds, had been sent in one entire Sum into ʌ *Scotland*,
cursed

457, l. 13 that the SCOTS would insist UPON ʌ the whole Government of the Church, and in all other Matters would DEFER TO the King;
to destroy

betray

l. 50 in the particular which concern'd the Church, THE SCOTS would never depart from a tittle;
Scots Hell-Hounds

Page	Clarendon	Swift

466, l. 17 the SCOTISH ARMY march'd North-wards, to reduce the little Garrisons remaining . . .

cursed Dogs

    38 the MARQUIS OF ARGYLE, who had then the Chief Government of *Scotland*;

A most damnable false Dog, and so are still their Family

478, l. 30 The Parliament had, some Months before, made an Ordinance against giving Quarter to any of the *Irish* Nation which should be taken Prisoners,

Barbarous Vilains and Rebels

THE NINTH BOOK

484, l. 25 the Age . . . which did produce as many Men eminent for loyalty and incor-rupted fidelity to the Crown, as any that had preceded it.

not quite

485, l. 40 THE MARQUIS OF ARGYLE was now come from *Scotland*,

A cursed Scotch Hellhound

501, l. 43 Resolutions taken to fall upon the *Scotch* Army in *York-shire*,

cursed Scots still

516, l. 22 one *Brabant*, an Atturney at Law, . . . being brought before Sr *Richard Greenvil*, was immediately, by his own direction, without any Council of War, because he said he was disguised, hanged as a Spy:

This Rogue would almost be a perfect Scot

521, l. 22 (After several paragraphs with a number of parentheses, one of more than seven lines is marked.)

long parenthesis

574, l. 30 and whether THE SCOTS had ever a thought of doing him Service.

No more than Beelzebub

579, l. 31 the Cardinal was well assured, that THE SCOTS would behave themselves henceforwards

Damnable Scots

Vol. III.   THE TENTH BOOK

At the bottom of the half-title, in ink:

That frequent Expression, UPON THE WORD OF A KING, I have always despised and detested, for a thousand Reasons.

Dedication (c.1ʳ) putting him (Charles II) on the thoughts of marrying some ROMAN CATHOLICK LADY, who might As he did engage those of that Religion . . . in his Majesty's Interest;

As he did

2, l. 11 Lord *Jermin* had promised a Body of five thousand Foot . . . under the Com-mand of *Ruvignie*,

Father to Ld Galloway a Huguenot

6, l. 47 the chief reason before was, that he would put himself into the SCOTS hands;

He could not do worse

Page	*Clarendon*	*Swift*

7, l. 2 the King was by this time known to be in the SCOTS Army.

And these Hellhounds sold him to the Rebels

11, l. 36 That they had press'd the king to do many things, which he had absolutely refused to do; and that thereupon they had put very strict Guards upon his Majesty,

The cursed Scots begin their new Treachery

14, l. 25 The Paper Montrevil sent to the King, being a promise for the Scots receiving the King, Apr. 1.

Montrevil might as safely promise for Satan as for the Scots

l. 45 Many days had not passed after the sending that Express, when he found such chagrin, and tergiversation in some of those he had treated with, . . . that he thought himself obliged with all speed to advertize his Majesty of the foul change

Will Montrevil trust them again?

15, l. 27 the two Princes might follow the King, with such other of his Servants as were NOT EXCEPTED FROM PARDON;

and why those? bacause the Scots were part of the Rebells.

16, l. 12 They tell me that they will do more than can be express'd,

So the Scots did, with a Vengeance

l. 20 they will do all in their power to hinder him falling into the hands of the English.

by delivering him up for money. Hellish Scottish Dogs

l. 24 Montrevil signed that Engagement upon the FIRST OF APRIL

April fool

17, l. 16 In this perplexity, he chose rather to commit himself to the *Scots* Army

to be delivered up for money which would betray him, though his Countrymen

24 whether he would go to the SCOTS Army

37 WENT INTO THE SCOTS ARMY BEFORE NEWARK,

Prodigious weakness to trust the malicious Scotch hellhounds

49 assuring them 'that all their Orders would meet with an absolute obedience in their Army:

no doubt of it.

(?) Scots

18, l. 35 From the text of the sermon preached before the King, on the march Northwards: ii Sam. chap. 19, v. 42. *And all the men of* JUDAH *answered the men of Israel, Because the King is near of kin to us: wherefore then be ye angry for this matter?*

Scotch

21, l. 9 there should be an Army of THIRTY THOUSAND MEN immediately transported into *England,*

Gasconade

23, l. 20 the Council of *Scotland* seem'd to answer with Courage enough, and insisted most on those Arguments of the King's legal Rights,

by the Event they proved true Scots

l. 38 they made great profession of their Duty and good purposes, 'which they

Page	Clarendon	Swift
	said they would manifest as soon as it should BE SEASONABLE;	See the Event still Scots
	l. 44 The King sends to the Marquis of *Montrose* to disband; which he did.	The onely Honest Scot
23-4	if his Majesty would have been induced to have satisfied them (in consenting to the extirpation of Episcopacy in *England*, as he had in *Scotland*) they would thereupon have declared for the King	rather declare for the Devil
24, l. 14	Whilst the King stayed at *New-Castle*, the French Embassadour . . . came to his Majesty,	Kings are generally ? ? ?
26, l. 34	When the *Scots* had secured the peace and quiet of their own Country,	Cursed Scots
	50 an eternal Infamy would lie upon them and the whole Nation, if they should deliver the King;	Damnable Scots
27, l. 14	though they would observe their own method, they would in the end do somewhat for his Service.	Ditto Cursed Scots
	The King upon the *Scots* desire, sends Orders for the surrender of *Oxford*, and all his other Garrisons.	Cursed, abominable, hellish Scottish Villains everlasting Traitors. &c. &c. &c.
28, l. 4	The *Scots* . . . used all the rude importunity and Threats to his Majesty, to perswade him freely to consent to all:	Most Damnable Scots
	l. 12 The Chancellor of *Scotland* told him, 'that the consequence of his Answer to the Propositions, was as great, as the ruin, or preservation of his Crown or Kingdoms: . . .	Cursed Scots Chancellor ←
	l. 31 General Assembly of the Kirk had petition'd . . . 'that if the King should refuse to give satisfaction to his Parliament, he might not be permitted to come into *Scotland*.	Scots inspired by Beelzebub
29, l. 11	The *Scots* agree to deliver up the King.	cursed Scot, sold his King for a Groat
	l. 17 In this infamous manner that excellent Prince was, in the end of *January*, given up, by his Scots Subjects, to those of his *English* who were entrusted by the Parliament to receive him;	Hellish Scots From this Period the English Parliament were turned into Scotch Devils
31, l. 40	Sir Harry Killigrew was most zealous in opposing all the extravagant proceedings of the Parliament. . . . He stood up and said, 'he would provide a good Horse, and a good Buff Coat, and a good pair of Pistols, and then he doubted not he should find a good Cause; and so went out of the House,	Another loyall Man used the like saying

Page	Clarendon	Swift

53, l. 18 many years after, when (James II) was sent out of *England*, he made the full relation of all the particulars *to Me*, with that commotion of Spirit, that it appear'd to be deeply rooted in him;

Yet he lived and dyed a rank Papist, and lost the Kingdom

55, l. 1 And no Men were fuller of professions of Duty, and a resolution to run all hazards, than the *Scotish* Commissioners . . . loudly complained of the presumption of the Army in seising upon the Person of the King;

False Scots they did (?)

The Scots Dogs delivered up their King

64, l. 37 MR ASHBURNHAM HAD SO GREAT A DETESTATION OF THE SCOTS, that he expected no good from their fraternity, the Presbyterians of the City;

so have I

68, l. 42 Hammond removes the King's old Servants from about him.

A detestable Villain, almost as wicked as a Scot

76, l. 9 After the King had been so infamously deliver'd up to the Parliament by the SCOTS at *New-Castle*,

Detestable Scots

l. 48 the malice and power of the Marquis OF ARGYLE,

Always a cursed Family

77, l. 1 confident that all *Scotland* would rise as one Man for his Majesties defence and vindication;

A strange Stupidity to trust Scots at any Time

79, l. 10 an Act of Parliament . . . for the suppressing the opinions and practices of Anti-Trinitarians, Arians, Socinians, Anti-Scripturists, Anabaptists, Antinomians, Arminians, Famylists, Brownists, Separatists, etc.

What a medley of Religions

80, l. 4 all Armies should be disbanded; and in case this should not be granted, that Declarations should be emitted by the Kingdom of *Scotland* . . . against the unjust proceedings of the two Houses of Parliament towards his Majesty . . .

They would rather be hanged than agree

l. 14 an Army should be sent out of *Scotland* into *England*, for the preservation and establishment of Religion; for defence of his Majesties Person,

Scotch Impudence

81, l. 46 and to give a relish to all the rest, the King engaged himself to imploy those of the *Scots* Nation equally with the English in all Foreign Imployments and Negotiations; and that a third part of all the Offices and Places about the King, Queen, and Prince, should be conferr'd upon some Persons of that Nation;

Impudent Scottish scoundrels

Page	Clarendon	Swift

83, l. 12 the Presbyterians, by whom I mean the *Scots*,

Hellish Scotch dogs

85, l. 27 (Cromwell) compelled the *Scots* Army to depart the Kingdom, with that circumstance as must ever after render them odious and infamous.

He out-cunning'd the Scots

86, l. 49 the delivery of the King up, besides the infamy of it, was, in view, destructive to all that could be thought their Interest.

That Infamy is in the scurvy Nature of a Scot and the best part of their (?) pride

89, l. 18 the vile Artifices of the *Scotish* Commissioners to draw the King into their hands, and then their low and base compliance, and gross folly, in delivering him up, . . .

vile treacherous Scots for ever

THE ELEVENTH BOOK

97, l. 52 *Argyle* found it would be to no purpose directly to contradict or oppose it.

an infamous dog, like all that Family

108, l. 52 having sent his Brother, THE DUKE OF YORK, with all his Family to the *Hague*, to remain there.

a sorry Admiral

109, l. 1 Though the Duke was exceedingly troubled to leave the Fleet, . . . he submitted to the determination; and was well content to remain with his Sister,

Popery and Cowardice stuck with him all his life

l. 23 the Prince came prepared and disposed from the Queen, to depend wholly upon the Presbyterian Party, which, besides the power of the *Scots* Army . . . was thought to be possessed of all the strength of the City of *London*;

Curse on the Lyars

l. 39 the Prince would have been directed . . . to have followed all the advice which should have been sent from the *Scots*.

so much the worse, to rely on the cursed Scots

112, l. 44 *Argyle* . . . desired that, if they were to have any Command in the Army, they might presently take the Covenant;

That Scotch Dog

113, l. 48 they entreated them with all imaginable importunity, that they would take the Covenant;

their damned Covenant

117, l. 32 Sir *Philip Musgrave* . . . carried a list with him of the names of many Officers in their Troops who had been compelled to take the Covenant . . .

Confound their damnable Covenant

129, l. 35 that defeat of the Scots Army, which must break all their measures, and render the condition of the Prince and the whole Kingdom, very deplorable, and leave that of the King in the utmost despair.

I cannot be sorry

l. 49 and, that all respect might be

Page	*Clarendon*	*Swift*

shewed to the Parliament of *Scotland*, he (the Earl their messenger) had a Chair allow'd him to sit upon.

Respect to a Scotch Parliament with a Pox &c. &c.

133, l. 13 Orders were sent out of *Scotland* for the delivery of *Berwick* and *Carlisle* to the Parliament; in which Orders there was not the least mention of making conditions for the *English*.

Cursed Scots

l. 42 It was generally believ'd, that the Marquis of *Argyle* earnestly invited him (Cromwell)

that eternall Dog Argyle

141, l. 6 *Cromwell* had written to his Friends, . . . and conjured them to continue firm in that resolution.

a cursed Hell-Hound

142, l. 27 When there appeared some hopes that the *Scots* would raise an Army for the relief of the King,

Trust them not, for they are Scots

145, l. 18 He betook himself to his Armes for his defence, but quickly found that his Friend had betrayed it, . . .

base

155, l. 15 the Council had inclined the Prince to that designation (to be with the Fleet) out of ill will to his Highness, . . .

The Duke's Courage was always doubtfull

157, l. 15 (*Parenthesis marked of* 11 *lines*)

167, l. 5 And two of them very plainly and fiercely told the King, 'that if he did not consent to the utter abolishing of Episcopacy, he would be damn'd;

very civil

168, l. 13 (The King) with much reluctancy, offered to suspend Episcopacy for three years, . . .

Prudent Concessions

l. 22 he consented to all that he had offer'd . . . with reference to the Government of the Church; and that Money should be raised upon the sale of the Church Lands, and only the old Rent reserv'd

Scotch Principles

l. 49 in all Cases, when the Lords and Commons shall declare the safety of the Kingdom to be concern'd unless the King give his Royal Assent to such a Bill for raising Money, the Bill shall have the force of an Act of Parliament, as if he had given his Royal Assent.

English Dogs as bad as Scots

170, l. 43 he had condescended to so many things which gave himself no satisfaction, he would give full satisfaction to the Parliament . . . and the Kingdom that Peace and security he desired.

After so many Concessions the Commissioners shewed themselves most damnable Villains

Z

Page	Clarendon	Swift
172, l. 38	he did concur with them in their distinction of Bishops, and if they would preserve the Scripture-Bishop, he would take away the Bishop by Law.	Indeed a great Concession
174, l. 33	such Agreements as should be made by both Houses with that Kingdom, in the security of such thereof who had assisted or adhered to those of the Parliament of *England*,	A most diabolical Allyance
175, l. 45	The King had begun a Letter to the Prince his Son . . . in his own hand, and contained above six Sheets of Paper;	The whole Letter is a most Excellent Performance
176, l. 4	if the Parliament had been able to have resisted the wild fury OF THE ARMY,	Diabolical Vilains
177, l. 45	It cannot be imagin'd how wonderfully fearful some Persons in *France* were that he should have made his Escape,	French Villains
180, l. 15	And thither they sent their well tryed SERGEANT WILD, to be the sole Judge of that Circuit; (at Winchester)	An Infernall Dog
l. 45	Young Sr *Harry Vane* had begun the Debate with the highest Insolence, and Provocation;	A cursed insolent Vilain, worse than even a Scot, or his own Father
183, l. 35	Many of the Members entring into the House seised upon by the Soldiers.	Damnable Proceeding
184, l. 3	The remaining Members Vote the contrary to their former Votes.	cursed Rogues
189, l. 46	The King . . . was receiv'd by Colonel Harrison with a strong Party of Horse; . . . HARRISON WAS THE SON OF A BUTCHER	The fitter for that Office
195, l. 21	The King told them, he would first know of them . . . who gave them power to judge of his Actions, for which he was accountable TO NONE BUT GOD;	very weak
198, l. 38	He was always a great Lover of the *Scotish* Nation,	There I differ from Him— who were the Cause of his Destruction like abominable Scotch Dogs
199, l. 20	Belov'd by his Subjects in general when he was Murther'd.	onely common Pity for His Death, and the manner of it
208, l. 26	*Cromwell*, who had known him (Lord Capel) very well, spoke so much good of him, and profess'd to have so much kindness and respect for him,	cursed Dog
210, l. 23	Lord Capel commends the Prince— of exemplary Piety: not to be shaken in his Religion: and had all those Princely Virtues, which could make a Nation happy:	He should have (?) (?) (?)

Page	*Clarendon*	*Swift*

THE TWELFTH BOOK

217, l. 10 contrary to the DISSENT and Protestation of that Kingdom the late King was remov'd . . . his lawful Successor, was become their true and lawful King: but upon condition of his good behaviour etc.   Cursed Scots in every Circumstance
l. 41 The Character of this Duke *Hamilton*.   A Scotch Duke celebrated by the Author: a perfect Miracle

218, l. 44 As well the Assembly of the Kirk as the Parliament, renew'd the sense they allways had of REPROACH IN THE DELIVERY OF HIS PERSON,   The Scots were the Cause and chief Instruments of the King's Murder, by delivering him up to the English Rebels
l. 47 And the Marquis OF ARGYLE had had too deep a share in that wickedness,   A true Argyle

222, l. 38 ARGYLE meant only to satisfy the People,   Ever detestable vilain

224, l. 50 had the confidence to desire the King, that the Marquis of *Mountrose* (whom they called *James Graham*) might be forbidden to come into his Majesty's Presence, or Court,   Abominable Scotch Dogs

225, l. 2 a worthy *Scotish* Divine, Dr *Wishart*, who was then Chaplain to a *Scotish* Regiment,   A prodigious Rarity
l. 44 The earl of *Lautherdale* told him he could not imagine, or conceive the barbarities and inhumanities Mountrose was guilty of . . . that he had in one Battle kill'd FIFTEEN HUNDRED OF ONE FAMILY, of THE CAMPBELLS, of the blood and name of *Argyle*,   That Earl was a Beast I mean Lauderdale / not half enough, of that execrable Breed

228, l. 51 one *Dorislaus*, bred at Leyden afterwards liv'd long in London, sent as Envoy to Holland from the Parliament.   A Dutch fellow employ'd by those Regicides who murdred the King

237, l. 30 The Prince of Orange wish'd the King would offer . . . to refer all matters in controversy concerning Religion to a National Synod; in which there should be admitted some foreign Divines from the Protestant Churches;   I do not approve it

249, l. 6 the Lord Lieutenant . . . was at last compell'd to draw off the whole Army . . .   Ormonds Army discomfited

265, l. 37 the Council of *Scotland* . . . to send again to the King to *Jersey*, to invite him to come . . . not without a rude insinuation that it was the last invitation he should receive.   Scots / still cursed Scots

267, l. 12 The King himself, and all who should attend upon him, were first TO SIGN THE COVENANT before they should be admitted to enter the Kingdom.   Damnable Scottish Dogs

Page	Clarendon	Swift

268, l. 20 *Argyle* would immediately deliver up the Person of the King into the hands of *Cromwell*

That Scotch Dog was likely enough to do, and much worse

l. 36 the Embassadours in *Spain* . . . had a strong aversion that the King should ever venture himself in the hands of that Party of the *Scotish* Nation, which had treated his Father so perfidiously.

Damnable nation for ever

269, l. 25 BUT NOW THAT HE WAS POSSESSED OF ONE WHOLE KINGDOM, in which no Man appear'd in Armes against him, a Kingdom which had been famous for many war-like Actions etc.

Yet all cursed Vilains
A possession of the Devils Kingdom, where every Scot was a Rebel

l. 48 (that Nation) which was predestinated for a greater chastisement and mortification of that People, as it shortly after prov'd to be.

That is good News

270 l. 1 The Marquis of *Mountrose* goes for *Hamburg* to sollicite for Forces.

He was the onely Man in Scotland who had ever one Grain of Virtue; and was therefore abhorred and murdered publickly by his hellish Countrymen.

l. 12 MANY OFFICERS OF GOOD NAME . . . of the *Scotish* Nation, who were grown rich in *Sweden*.

Impossible

271, l. 9 *Mountrose* knew that of the two Factions there . . . EACH OF THEM WERE EQUALLY HIS IMPLACABLE ENEMIES . . . THE WHOLE KIRK, OF WHAT TEMPER SOEVER, BEING ALIKE MALICIOUS TO HIM;

Very certain

Scots damnable Kirk

272, l. 2 (Mountrose's friends) assur'd him that they would meet him with good Numbers; and they did prepare so to do, some really; AND OTHERS, with a purpose to betray him.

much the greater Number

l. 38 the Tyranny of *Argyle*, and his having caused very many to be barbarously murther'd, without any form of law or justice, who had been in Arms with *Mountrose*,

That perpetual inhuman Dog and Traytor, and all his Posterity to a Man Damnable Vilains

273, l. 5 all the Country desiring to merit from *Argyle* by betraying all those into his hands which they believ'd to be his Enemies.

The Virtue and Morality of the Scotts

l. 18 *David Lesley* treated the Marquis with great insolence,

A Tyrannical Scottish Dog

274, l. 7 that FOR THE LEAGUE AND COVENANT, HE HAD NEVER TAKEN IT, and therefore could not break it:

The Devil, their God, I believe had taken it

Page	*Clarendon*	*Swift*

l. 31 to be hanged upon a Gallows thirty foot high, for the space of three hours, and then to be taken down, and his head to be cut off upon a Scaffold . . .

Oh, if the whole Nation to a Man were but so treated, but begin with Argyle and next with the Fanatick Dogs who teised him with their Kirk Scurrilityes

l. 41 their Ministers came presently to insult over him with all the reproaches imaginable; pronounced his damnation etc.

Mad treacherous damnable infernall Scots for ever

275, l. 2 He told them, 'he was prouder to have his head set upon the place it was appointed to be, than . . .'

A perfect Hero, wholly un-Scotified

l. 14 and prayed, 'that they might not betray Him, as they had done his Father'.

A very seasonable Prayer—but never performed

l. 47 Argyle, who wanted nothing but HONESTY AND COURAGE to be a very extraordinary Man,

Trifles to a Scot

276, l. 10 the proceeding against the late Marquis of *Mountrose* had been for his Service.

Impudent lying Scottish Dogs

THE THIRTEENTH BOOK

285, l. 13 WITHOUT He likewise consented to those.

bad

286, l. 18 The king was received by the Marquis of *Argyle* with all the outward respect imaginable

That Dog of all Scotch Dogs

l. 35 Daniel ONeile banished the Kingdom, and obliged to sign a paper, by which he consented to be put to death, if he were ever after found in the KINGDOM.

In Scotland with a Pox

287, l. 14 the King's table was well serv'd

with Scotch food &c.

300, l. 51 the Duke of *York* should conform himself entirely to the will and pleasure of the Queen his Mother, MATTERS OF RELIGION ONLY EXCEPTED.

Yet lost his Kingdomes for the sake of Popery

301, l. 12 which wrought that effect upon him, that none of them had that credit with him, that

3 that

l. 39 The Duke was full of Spirit and Courage, and naturally lov'd designs . . .

Quantum mutatus!

304, l. 8 only Sr *George Ratcliff* undertook to speak to him about it, who could only make himself understood in *Latin*, which the Duke cared not to speak in,

because he was illiterate, and onely read Popish Latin

305, l. 42 The Queen bid him 'assure the Duke of *York*, that he should have a free Exercise of his Religion,'

who unkinged himself for Popery

Page	Clarendon	Swift
	306, l. 1 all his hopes must be in the ROMAN CATHOLICKS, AND THE PRESBYTERIANS;	A blessed Pair
	l. 29 and was fortified with a firm resolution never to acknowledge that he had committed any error.	No, not when he lost his Kingdoms for Popery
	311, l. 7 The King granted a Commission to the Duke of *Buckingham* . . . The Duke had lost much ground by having broken off all Friendship with Duke *Hamilton,* and the Earl of *Lautherdale* . . .	Vix intellego
	318, l. 16 The King's defeat at Worcester	September 3d always lucky to Cromwell
	339, l. 49 There was no need of Spurs to be employed to incite THE DUKE; who was most impatient to be in the Army.	How old was he when he turned a Papist and a Coward?
	340, l. 13 The Duke pressed it with earnestness and passion, in which HE DISSEMBLED NOT;	Dubitat Augustinus
	343, l. 20 The Duke goes to the Army, where, in a short time, he got the reputation of a Prince of very signal Courage,	But proved a Cowardly Popish King
	348, l. 49 But the designation of them to this *Scotish* Intrigue . . . shook that foundation of Peace . . .	Scots
	349, l. 12 by the frequent resort of the *Scotish* Vicar to him 'that there was some secret in hand which was kept from her' (the Queen).	The little Scottish scoundrel conceited *Vicar*

THE FOURTEENTH BOOK

386, l. 10 (*Scotland*) was reduced under the GOVERNMENT OF THE ENGLISH LAWS, and their Kirk, and Kirkmen, entirely subdued to the obedience of the State . . .	I am glad of that
387, l. 11 Cromwell's Parliament meets Sept. 3. 1654	His lucky day
394, l. 35 The Highlanders made frequent incursions in the night into the *English* Quarters; and kill'd many of their Soldiers, but stole more of their Horses:	Rank Scotch Thieves
413, l. 47 gave occasion for a bold Person to publish, amongst the Amours of the *French* Court, a particular that reflected on the Person of the King.	Bussy Rabutin amours de Gaules
414, l. 5 a Lady of great beauty, . . . that captivated those who were admitted into her presence;	A Prostitute whore
420, l. 19 The Chancellor of the Exchequer's discourse to the King concerning his going into *Scotland.*	The Chancellor never thought so well of the Scots before
l. 33 His Majesty discoursed very calmly	

Page	*Clarendon*	*Swift*

of that Country . . . and 'how impossible it was for him to live there with security or with health; . . . he should in a short time BE BETRAYED AND GIVEN UP.'

But the King knew them better.

425, l. 47 they perswaded many in *England*, and . . . abroad, that his Majesty was in truth a Papist:

which was true

443, l. 14 and the Wretch, soon after, receiv'd the reward due to his Treason.

In what manner?

THE FIFTEENTH BOOK

469, l. 48 But that which made a noise indeed, and crown'd his Successes, was the Victory his Fleet, under the Command of *Blake,* had obtain'd over the *Spaniard*;

I wish he were alive for the Dogs the Spaniards sake—instead of our worthless H— (*much underlined and marked in the margin*)

489, l. 30 The Address of the Anabaptists to the King

495, l. 3 We humbly beseech your Majesty , . . never to erect, nor suffer to be erected, any such Tyrannical, POPISH, AND ANTICHRISTIAN HIERARCHY (EPISCOPAL, PRESBYTERIAN, or by what name soever it be call'd)

Honest, though Fanaticks

501, l. 17 Marshal *Turenne,* accompanied with the Duke of *York,* who would never be absent upon those occasions . . . riding so near the Line very frequently, that some of his Company were Killed . . .

James the 2d a fool and Coward

502, l. 14 a Rumour in the French Army, that the Duke of York was taken Prisoner by the *English,* . . . found they were mis-inform'd; which if they had not been, they would have enlarg'd him; so great an Affection that Nation own'd to have for his Highness.

Yet he lived and dyed a Coward

THE SIXTEENTH BOOK

523, l. 20 The Gentleman accused was Sr *Richard Willis*; who . . . was universally thought to be superior to all temptations of infidelity.

Doubtful

539, l. 33 if it had not been for the KING'S OWN STEADINESS, of which he gave great indications

of which in Religion he never had any

540, l. 10 The Duke of York invited into Spain as *El Admirante del Oceano*—'but would never be suffered to go to Sea under any title of Command, TILL HE FIRST CHANGED HIS RELIGION;

as he did openly in England

Page	Clarendon	Swift

559, l. 20 General Monk sends a Letter to the Parliament.

   52 there being scarce a Bone-fire at which they did not roast a Rump,   The Army

561, l. 11 & 31 (Rump's Paper carefully marked and underlined especially the following:)

   settlement UPON COMMON-WEALTH FOUNDATIONS   ←

   certainly IT MUST LYE IN A COMMONWEALTH

562, l. 20 for the full Establishing of this Commonwealth, without a King, single Person, or House of Lords.   ←

   l. 44 a Commonwealth establish'd in such a Model as *Holland* was, WHERE HE HAD BEEN BRED;   ←

583, l. 28 Charles II's *Declaration*: let all our subjects RELY UPON THE WORD OF A KING, by which, UPON THE WORD OF A KING, We will be advised.   usually good for Nothing provided he be an honest and sincere Man

585, l. 18 Letter to the Fleet: God Almighty will heal the Wounds by the same Plaister that made the Flesh raw;   a very low comparison

586, l. 9 those who would SUBJECT OUR SUBJECTS to a Government they have not yet devised,   Cacofonia

587, l. 6 though offer'd all the Authority that *Cromwell* had enjoyed, and the Title of King, he (Monk) used all his endeavours to promote and advance the Interest of his Majesty: ←

593, l. 29 YOUR PIETY AND GOODNESS HATH   have

595, l. 8 Proclamation of the King: and thereunto We most humbly and faithfully do submit, and oblige our Selves, our Heirs, and Posterity for ever.   Can they oblige their Posterity 10000 years to come?

596, l. 18 Cromwell . . . taking his hand in his, and putting the Pen between his Fingers, with his own hand writ Richard Ingoldsby, he making all the resistance he could: and he said, 'if his Name there were compared with what he had ever writ himself, it could never be look'd upon as his own hand.'   A mistake for it was his own hand writ without any one's restraint

602, l. 41 the nine and twentieth of May, AND HIS BIRTH-DAY, HE (Charles II) ENTER'D LONDON;   a lucky Circumstance

APPENDIXES

A

LETTER

FROM THE

Grand Mistress

OF THE

FEMALE FREE-MASONS

TO

Mr. *Harding* the Printer.

Ixion the Impious, Lewd Profane,
Bright *Juno* Woo'd but Woo'd in Vain.
Long had he sigh'd for th' Heavenly Dame;
'Till *Jove* at length to quench his Flame;
Some say for Fear, some say for Pity,
Sent him a Cloud like *June* Pretty,
As like as if 'twere drawn by Painters,
On which he got a Race of *Centaurs*.
A Bite quoth V E N U S —— —— ——

*a.   b.   c.   Lib.*6th.

DUBLIN:

Printed by *John Harding* in *Molesworth*'s
Court in *Fishamble-Street*, 1724.

A

LETTER, &c.

Mr. *Harding*,

SEEING it is of Late become a Fashion in Town, in Writing to all the World, to Address to YOU, our Society of *Female Free-Masons* has also Chosen you for our *Printer*; and so without Preface, Art, or Embelishment, (for Truth and a short Paper needs none of 'em) our *Female Lodge* has the whole Mistery as well as any *Lodge* in *Europe*, with proper Instructions in Writing; and what will seem more strange to you, without the least Taint of *Perjury*. By this Time any *Reader* who is a *Mason*, will, I know, laugh, and not without Indignation. But that matters not much, our Sex has long ow'd yours this good Turn: You refused to admit Queen *Elizabeth*, and even *Semiramis* Queen of *Babilon*, tho' each of 'em (without *Punning*) had a great Deal of *Male Flesh* upon their Bodies; but at last you will be forc'd to own we have it; and thus it was we came by it.

A Gentleman who is a great Friend to all our Members, who has since instructed and form'd us into a *Lodge*, and whom we therefore call our *Guardian*, fell in lately with a *Lodge* of *Free-Masons* at O——h in V——r. They press'd him hard to come into their Society, and at length prevailed. They wanted an *Old Testament* to Swear him by. The *Inn-keeper*'s Bible having both *Old* and *New* bound up together, wou'd not do: For the *Free-Masons* Oath being of much older Date than the *New Testament*, that is from the Building of *Soloman*'s Temple, (for 'till then it was but a Protestation well Larded over with *Curses* and *Execrations*) they are always Sworn on the *Old Testament* only. They offer to buy the Fellow's *Bible*, he Consents; but finding they were to Cut away the *New Testament* from the *Old* concluded them at once a Pack of Profane Wretches, and very Piously Rescu'd his *Bible*. This Custom of Swearing on the *Old Testament* only, is what has given Birth to the Vulgar Error, That *Free-Masons* Renounce the *New Testament*. So they proceed on the Rest of the Ceremony, Deferring the Oath till next Morning, One of 'em having an *Old Testament* for the Purpose at his House hard by. This 'tis true was a heinous Blunder against the Canons of *Free-Masonry:* But the Gentlemen were far gone in *Punch* and *Whisky*. In short our Friend and present Guardian is made a *Free* but *Unsworn Mason*, and was Three Hours gone on his Journey next Morning before the Merry *Free-Masons* awoke to send for their *Old Testament*; and what was worse, they had taught him the Form of the Oath against he was to Swear in the Morning.

Now as to the Secret Words and Signals used among *Free-Masons*, 'tis to be observ'd that in the *Hebrew* Alphabet (as our Guardian has inform'd our *Lodge* in Writing there are Four Pair of Letters, of which each Pair is so like, that at first View they seem to be the same, *Beth* and *Caph*, *Gimel* and *Nun*, *Cheth* and *Thau*, *Daleth* and *Resch*, and on these Depend all their Signals and Grips.

Cheth and *Thau* are shap'd like Two standing Gallowses (of Two Legs each) when Two *Masons* accost each other, one Cries *Cheth*, the other answers *Thau*, signifying that they wou'd sooner be Hang'd on the Gallows than Divulge the *Secret*.

Then again *Beth* and *Caph* are each like a Gallows lying on one of the Side-Posts, and when used as above, imply this Pious Prayer: *May all who Reveal the* Secret *hang upon the Gallows till it falls down*. This is their *Master Secret*, generally call'd the *Great Word*.

Daleth and *Resch* are like Two Half Gallowses, or a Gallows cut in Two at the Cross Stick on Top, by which, when pronounced, they Intimate to each other, that they wou'd rather be half hang'd than Name either *Word* or *Signal* before any but a *Brother* so as to be understood.

When one says *Gimel*, the other answers *Nun*; then the first again joyning both Letters together repeats Three Times, *Gimel-Nun*, *Gimel-Nun*, *Gimel-Nun*, by which they mean that they are united as one in Interests, Secresy, and Affection.

This Last Word has in Time been depraved in the Pronunciation from *Gimel-Nun* to *Gimelun*, and at last into *Giblun*; and sometimes *Giblin*, which Word being by some Accident discover'd, they now adays pretend its but a *Mock Word*.

Another of their Words has been maim'd in the Pronunciation by the Illiterate, that is the Letter *Lamech*, which was the *Hush-Word*, for when spoke by any *Brother* in a *Lodge* it was a Warning to the Rest to have a Care of Lisseners. 'Tis now corruptly pronounced *Lam*, but the *Masons* pretend this also is a *Mock-Word* for the same Reason as *Giblin*: This Play with the *Hebrew* Alphabet is very antiently call'd the MANABOLETH.

When one *Brother* orders another to walk like a *Mason*, he must walk Four Steps backwards; Four, because of the four Pair of Letters already mentioned, and backwards because the *Hebrew* is Writ and Read Backwards.

As to their *Misterious Grips*, they are as follows: If they be in Company where they cannot with Safety Speak the above Words, they take each other by the Hand, one Draws one of the Letters of the *Manaboleth* with his finger on the other's Hand, which he returns as in Speaking.

It is worth observing, that a certain *Lodge* in Town Publish'd sometime ago a Sheet full of *Mock-Masonry*, purely to puzzel and banter the Town, with several false Signs and Words as *Mada* or *Adam*, Write backwards, Boas, *Nimrod*, *Jakins*, *Pectoral*, *Guttural*, &c. But not one Word of the Real ones, as you see by what has been said of the MANABOLETH.

After King *James* the Sixth's Accession to the Throne of *England*, he reviv'd *Masonry*, of which he was *Grand-Master*. Both in *Scotland* and *England* it had been entirely suppress'd by Queen *Elizabeth*, because she cou'd not get into the Secret, all Persons of Quality after the Example of the King got themselves admitted *Free-Masons*; but they made a Kind of MANABOLETH in *English*, in Imitation of the True and Ancient One; as I.O.U.H. a Gold Key, that is, *I owe you each a Gold Key*; H CCCC his Ruin. *Each foresees his Ruin.* I C.U.B. YY for me. *I see you be too wise for me.* And a great Deal more of the same foolish Stuff, which took its Rise from a Silly *Pun*

upon the Word *Bee*; for you must know, that ————
———— A *Bee* has in all Ages and Nations been the Grand
Hierogliphick of *Masonry*, because it excells all other living
Creatures in the Contrivance and Commodiousness of its
Habitation or *Combe*; as among many other Authors Doctor *Mc
Gregor* now Professor of Mathematicks in *Cambridge* (as our
Guardian informs us) has Learnedly demonstrated; nay
Masonry or *Building* seems to be of the very Essence or Nature
of the *Bee*, for her Building not the ordinary Way of all other
living Creatures, is the Generative Cause which produces
the Young Ones (you know I suppose that *Bees* are of *Neither
Sex*.)

For this Reason the Kings of *France* both *Pagans* and
Christians, always Eminent *Free-Masons*, carried three *Bees* for
their *Arms*, but to avoid the Imputation of the *Egyptian*
Idolatry of Worshipping a *Bee*, *Clodevaus* their first Christian
King call'd 'em *Lillies* or *Flower de Luces*, in which notwithstanding the small Change made for Disguise Sake, there's
still the Exact Figure of a *Bee*. You have perhaps Read of a great
Number of Golden Bees found in the Coffin of a *Pagan* King
of *France* near *Brussels*, many Ages after CHRIST, which
he had ordered should be Bury'd with him, in Token of his
having been a *Mason*.

The *Egyptians*, always Excellent and Antient *Free-Masons*,
paid Divine Worship to a *Bee* under the outward shape of a
Bull, the better to conceal the Mistery, which *Bull* they call'd
Apis, is the *Latin* Word for a *Bee*, the *Enigma* of Representing
the *Bee* by a *Bull* consists in this; that according to the Doctrine
of the *Pythagorean Lodge* of *Free-Masons*, the Souls of all the
Cow-kind transmigrate into Bees, as one *Virgil* a Poet, much
in Favour with the Emperor *Augustus*, because of his profound
Skill in *Masonry*, has describ'd; and Mr. *Dryden* has thus
English'd.

———— ———— ———— *Aristeus*

Four Altars raises, from His Herd he Culls
For Slaughter, Four the fairest of his *Bulls*,
Four Heifers from his Female Store he took,

All Fair, and all unknowing to the Yolk;
Nine Mornings thence with *Sacrifice* and *Prayers*,
The Gods invok'd he to the Grove repairs:
Behold a Prodigy! for from within
The Broken Bowels and the Bloated Skin
A buzzing Noise of *Bees* his Ears alarms,
Straight issue thro' the Sides assembling Swarms, *&c.*

What *Modern Masons* call a *Lodge* was for the above Reasons by Antiquity call'd a HIVE of *Free-Masons*, and for the same Reasons when a Dissention happens in a *Lodge* the going off and forming another *Lodge* is to this Day call'd SWARMING.

Our Guardian is of Opinion, that the present *Masonry* is so tarnish'd by the Ignorance of the working, and some other illiterate *Masons*, that very many, even whole *Lodges* fall under the Censure of the venerable *Chinese Brachman*, whose History of the Rise, Progress, and Decay of *Free-Masonry*, writ in the *Chinese* Tongue, is lately Translated into a Certain *Europenan* Language. This *Chinese* Sage says, the greatest Part of Current *Masons* Judge of the Misteries and Use of that Sacred Art, just as a Man perfectly Illiterate judges of an Excellent Book, in which when open'd to him he finds no other Beauties than the regular Uniformity in every Page, the Exactness of the Lines in Length, and Equidistance, the Blackness of the *Ink*, and Whiteness of the *Paper*, or as the Famous *British Free Mason* MERLIN says of the Stars in the Firmament, when view'd by a *Child*, &c. But I shall not trouble you with the Length of the Quotation at present, because *Merlin* and Fryar *Bacon* on *Free-Masonry* are soon to be dress'd up in Modern *English*, and sold by our Printer Mr. *Harding*, if duly encourag'd by Subscribers; and also a Key to *Raymundus Lullius*, without whose Help our Guardian says it's impossible to came at the Quintessence of *Free Masonry*.

But some will perhaps Object, how come your unsworn Guardian by this refin'd and uncommon Knowledge in the great Art? to which I answer that,

The Branch of the *Lodge* of *Soloman*'s Temple, afterwards call'd the *Lodge* of St. *John of Jerusalem* on which our Guardian fortunately hit, is as I can easily prove, the Antientest and Purest now on Earth. The famous old *Scottish Lodge* of *Kill-winnin* of which all the Kings of *Scotland* have been from Time to Time Grand Masters without Interruption, down from the Days of *Fergus*, who Reign'd there more than 2000 Years ago, long before the Knights of *St. John* of *Jerusalem* or the Knights of *Maltha*, to which two *Lodges* I must nevertheless allow the Honour of having adorn'd the Antient *Jewish* and *Pagan Masonry* with many Religious and Christian Rules.

Fergus being eldest Son to the chief King of *Ireland*, was carefully instructed in all the Arts and Sciences, especially in the natural Magick, and the Caballistical Philosophy (after-wards call'd the *Rosecrution*) by the *Pagan Druids* of *Ireland* and *Mona*, the only true *Cabalists* then Extant in the *Western* World. (For they had it immediately from the *Phenecians*, *Chaldeans*, and *Egyptians* (which tho' but a Woman can prove). The *Egyptians* probably had it immediately from *Abraham* as the Scripture Plainly hints in the Life of that Patriarch; and' tis allow'd I am told by Men of Learning, that the *Occult* as well as *Moral* Philosophy of all the *Pagans* was well be-sprinkl'd and enrich'd from the Caballistical School of the Patriarchs, and afterwards by the *Talmudists* and other Inferior *Rabbins*, tho' the prevailing Idolatry of those Days much depraved and vitiated it.

Fergus before his Descent upon the *Picts* in *Scotland* rais'd that famous Structure, call'd to this Day *Carrick-Fergus* after his Name, the most misterious Piece of Architecture now on Earth, (not excepting the Pyramids of the *Egyptian* Masons, and their *Hierogliphicks* or *Free Masons* Signs) as any Skillful *Free-Mason* may easily perceive by examining it according to the Rules of the Art; he built it as a *Lodge* for his College of *Free Masons* in those Days call'd *Druids*, which Word our Guardian assures us signifies an *Oak* in the *Greek* Language, because *Oak* is one of the best Timber-Trees for Building, of which especially the Marine Architecture, the *Druids* were the only Masters, tho' your Modern Term of *Mason* implys no more than a Worker in Stone, erroneously enough indeed, or at least far short of the true and antient Term of *Druid*, since

2A

the Marine Architecture the most useful Branch of the Sacred Art, corresponds naturally and perfectly with the Word *Druid* or *Worker* in *Oak*, and had nothiog at all to do with Stones of any Kind, 'till *Jason* a famous *Druid* or *Free-Mason* used the *Load-stone* when he went in Quest of the *Golden Fleece* as it is call'd in the Enigmaticall Terms of *Free-Masonry*, or more properly Speaking of the *Cabala*, as *Masonry* was call'd in those Days. The use of the *Load Stone* was then and long after kept as Secret as any of the other Misteries of the Art, till by the unanimous Consent of all the Great *Lodges*, the use of it was made publick for the Common Benefit of Mankind. *Jason*'s artificial *Frog* had it fixt in his Mouth, and having a free Swing in an oaken Bowl half fill'd with Water, always faced the *North* Pole, which gave rise to the Poetical Fable; That *Jason*'s Frog was a *Little Familiar* or *Sea Demon* presiding over the Navigation like any other Angel Guardian. For *Free-Masons* in all Ages, as well as now, have been look'd upon to deal with *Sprites* or *Demons*, and hence came that Imputation, which they have in many Nations lain under, of being *Conjurors* or *Magitians*; Witness *Merlin* and Fryar *Bacon*.

'Tis perhaps further worth Remarking, that *Jason* took one of the Two Sacred Vocal *Oaks* of the Grove of *Dodona* to make the Keel of the *Argus*, for so his Ship was call'd, misteriously Joyning together *Architecture* or *Masonry*, and the *Druidical* Priesthood or Power of Explaining the Oracle. For our Guardian will have it so, that the *Pagan* Priesthood was always in the *Druids* or *Masons*, and that there was a perceivable Glimering of the *Jewish Rites* in it, tho' much corrupted, as I said, that the *Pagan* Worship was chiefly in Groves of *Oak* that they always lookt upon the *Oak* as Sacred to *Jupiter*, which Notion is countenanced (making Allowance for the *Paganism*) by the *Patriarchs*, for you see in *Genesis*, that *Abraham* Sacrificed under the *Oaks* of *Mamre*. *Joshua* indeed took a great Stone and put it up under the *Oak*, Emblematically joyning the Two great Elements of *Masonry* to raise an Altar for the LORD.

Our Guardian also says, that *Cæsar*'s Description of the *Druids* of *Gaul* is as Exact a Picture of a *Lodge* of *Free Masons* as can possibly be Drawn.

His Reasons for the *Manaboleth* are the better worth discovering, that I believe there are even some *Masons* who know nothing of it, *viz.* that is has been an Antient Practice among the *Cabalistick Philosophers* to make every *Hebrew* Letter a *Heirogliphick* Misterious in its Figure above all other Letters, as being thus Shap'd and Form'd by the immediate Directions of the *Almighty*, whereas all other LETTERS are of *Humane Invention*.

Secondly, that the *Manaboleth* has a very close and unconstrain'd Analogy with *Masonry* or *Architecture*, for that every Letter of the *Hebrew* Alphabet, as also of the *Syriac*, *Chaldaic*, *Runic*, and *Irish* Alphabets, derived from it, have their Names from *Timber-Trees*, except some few who have their Names from *Stones*; and I think its pretty plain, that *Timber* and *Stone* are as much the Elements of *Masonry* as the Alphabet is of *Books*, which is a near Relation enough between *Architecture* and *Learning* of all Kinds, and naturally shews why the *Druids*, who also took their Title from a Tree, kept *Learning* and *Architecture* joyntly within themselves.

Next Week shall be Publish'd the *Free Mason*'s Oath, with the Remarks upon it of a Young *Clergyman* who has Petition'd to be admitted *Chaplain* to our *Lodge*, which is to be kept at Mr. *Painter*'s Female Coffee-House every *Tuesday* from Nine in the Morning to Twelve, and the Tenth Day of every Month in the Year; where all Ladies of true Hearts and sound Morals shall be admitted without Swearing.

I think it Proper to Incert the *Free-Mason*'s SONG commonly Sung at their Meetings, tho' by the By, it is of as little Signification as the Rest of their Secrets. It was Writ by one *Anderson* as our Guardian informs me, just to put a Good Gloss on the Mistery, as you may See by the Words.

SONG

I.

COME let us prepare
  We Brothers that are
Assembled on merry Occasion,

Let's Drink, Laugh and Sing,
Our Wine has a Springs;
Here's a Health to an accepted MASON.

II.

The World is in Pain
Our Secrets to gain,
And still let them wonder and gaze on,
They ne'er can Divine
The Word or the Sign
Of a Free and an Accepted MASON.

III.

'Tis this and 'tis that,
They cannot tell what;
Why so many Great Men of the Nation,
Shou'd Aprons put on,
To make themselves one,
With a Free and an Accepted MASON.

IV.

Great Kings, Dukes and Lords,
Have laid by their Swords,
Our Mistery to put a Good Grace on,
And ne'er been Asham'd,
To hear themselves Nam'd
With a Free and an Accepted MASON.

V.

Antiquity's Pride
We have on our Side,
And it maketh Men Just in their Station,
There's nought but what's good,
To be understood
By a Free and an Accepted MASON.

VI.

Then Joyn Hand in Hand,
To each other firm stand;
Let's be merry and put a Bright Face on,
What Mortal can boast,
So noble a Toast,
As a Free and an Accepted MASON.

POSTSCRIPT

Mr. *Harding,*

OUR *Lodge* unanimously desire you'll give their Sincere Respects to your *Ingenius* DRAPIER, to whose *Pen* we, as well as the Rest of the Nation, own our selves oblig'd. If he be not already a *Free-Mason,* he shall be welcom to be our *Deputy-Guardian.*

Your Humble Servant,

Tsrif eht Lirpa Nilbud

Thalestris

In the Dublin 1762 edition of 'A Letter from the Grand Mistress' there is a footnote:

'*Tsrif eht Tsugua Nilbud.*'

'*DUBLIN, *August the* first. *Those who understand* Irish, *may find some other Meaning.*'

1. MEMORANDA
FROM FORSTER MS. 519

MEMORAND OF THINGS TO BE DONE IN THE CITY

Note at the top of the page: 'Memds Those onely done wch are crossed.'

Full anthems, and Dr Crofts book
of anthems.

        in Fleet-street about
a Clock for St Patr's Cathedrall.

Spectacles for 70 years old   4 pair   X

Fenocchio and Brocali original seeds, and
the whole direction about planting them.

Melon seeds, and any othr garden curiosity

Some presents fluid   X

A pair of Spectacles for 60 and a large
reading glass for Mr Worrall.   X

My Grandfathers tomb

Pay Pothecary in Country and town   X
and pay the Pirmont water   X

To buy 200 ll. in some Stock   X

Godfrey in Southampton Street, Hungary
water and palsy drops.
Pay lodging. 1l - 11s - 6d   X
How to pay Mr Rolt's money   X

On the top of the recto of the second leaf there is one more note which seems to refer to some story to be passed on to Sheridan:

Full anthems, and Dr Croffs book
of anthems.

in Fleet-ftreet about
a Clock for St Pat: Cathedral
Spectacles for 70 years old   4 pair
Peaches and Brocoli original feeds, and
the whole direction about planting them.
Melon seeds, and any other garden curiosity
Some prefents fund   ×

A pair of Spectacles for 60. and a large
reading glafs for Mr Worrall. ×

My Grandfathers tomb

Pay Pothecary in Country and town.
and pay the Permant water ×

To sell buy 2d. in fome Stock ×

Godfry in Southampton Street, Hungry
water and palfy drops
Pay Lodging. 1^d - 11^s - 6
How pay Mr Rolls money

First page of Notebook, containing *Holyhead Journal*

Rememb the Abbot when you write to S——
and on the verso of the last leaf, turned upside down, is a list in pencil—

> Male Toasts
> Bp. Bath and Wells
> Erasmus Lewis
> Mr Bromley
> Bp Rochestr
> Mr Pulteney

2. FROM EGERTON MS. 201:

Egerton MS. No. 201, f. 1.

Call for watr. bring up p e complains it stinks, all watr stinks at sea, drink it, feel a t— why di[d] you bring a toast with it.

A woman crying opium a dose: desires a mending, for she's poor &c.

At the 4 crosses, cut in wood on an old Inns window

> Fleres si scires unum tua tempora mensu[m]
> Rides, cum non sit forsitan una dies.

A woman makes a young husband a cuckold; will she not make an old one so. If this be done in the green tree, what will they do in the dry.

A Fryar had got 5 nuns with child: his excuse to the Bp was, Ld then had trusted 5 talents. I have made them 10

Scarrons Verses on the destructions made by time; the Pyramids destroy, Rivers, Touns Empires &c decay, and shall I repine that a scurvy black wastcoat, when I worn it 2 years, is out at elbows. to the vulgar some poet says vos &c moderatius iste sub umbras The thought borrowd from Lucretius tu vero dubitabis

Your Ice is best [?], your bread is ill bred, and yr Oranges are not civil.

Egerton MS. No. 201, f. 1b.

Flirtation   following a woman, playing with her fan &c
                 it differs very little from dangling.

Frescamenti

Dolinc   a Turkish dish—forc'd meat stew'd in
                 Cucumb[er]

Kabob

Oddity

quite   absolute and papist[?]

Clever

Buzzleers   Slight nothing, well pronouncd, of cates a
                 quack a Lover. masculine a tenincue [?]

M.r[?]   onelyest way

Curcazo   stewd beef with rice the first Tastiest dish

[Patlego]

Bumblecasters

Arburman—a Roaring drunken feller

Tim—a nice finicale man in dress & manner

Ralph. Not quite so civil as a Tim

Roger. A downright rough fellow

Dangle—that dangles & leads out Ladyes, at an Opera

Fustyes—poor contemptible disagreable Cousins

    Godfry a Chymist in Southampton Street 10.
       for Drugs to . . . world[?] &c.

A MODEST
DEFENCE
OF A LATE
POEM

By an unknown Author, call'd,
The LADY's *Dressing-ROOM.*

A Poem, or Pamphlet published in this Kingdom without
a Name, will not long want one, if the Paper makes
any Noise.

There is a certain *Person* of Distinction among us, who is
conjectured to have written many Things, both in Prose and
Verse, for the Service of the Nation, which, undoubtedly,
were published with his own Consent. It is also believed, that
he hath composed others occasionally, for the Amusement of
himself and a few intimate Friends; which by the Indiscretion
of others, were, from stolen and uncorrect Copies, *dragged into
Light.*

But, I hold it for certain, that a much greater Number have,
by the Boldness of *Printers*, and the Want of Judgment in
Readers, been charged upon that *Author*, wherein he never had
the smallest Finger, as I am assured he hath often declared;
and, which is remarkable, was as free in disowning some
Writings charged upon him, of which he had no Reason to be
ashamed, as he could be of the meanest Productions of *Hibernian Grub-street:* Of which I shall instance only one Pamphlet,
which hath been very well received, as it justly deserved. It is
entitled, *An Infallible Scheme to pay the Nation's Debts, by a Tax
upon Vice*; which he disclaimed any Share in, at the same Time
giving it due Praises. And, I find, the *true Author* of that

Pamphlet lyes yet concealed; which is a Happiness that few *Writers* of any Distinction can arrive at, whether by their own Indiscretion, or that of their Friends I shall not determine.

As to those *fatal Verses* called the *Lady's Dressing-Room*, which have so highly inflamed the whole Sex, (except a very few of better Judgment) as I can by no Means justify the vulgar Opinion, that seems to fix it upon a Person, so well known for Works of a very different Nature; so I cannot but lament the prevailing ill Taste among us which is not able to discover that useful Satyr running through every Line, and the Matter as decently wrapp'd up, as it is possible the Subject could bear.

Cleanliness hath, in all polite Ages and Nations, been esteemed the chief corporeal Perfection in *Women*, as it is well known to those who are conversant with the antient *Poets*. And so it is still among the young People of Judgment and Sobriety, when they are disposed to marry. And I do not doubt, but that there is a great Number of young Ladies in this Town and Kingdom, who in reading that Poem, find great Complacency in their own Minds, from a Consciousness that the Satyrical Part in the *Lady's Dressing-Room*, does not in the least affect them.

Wherefore it is manifest, that no *Poem* was ever written with a better Design for the Service of the *Sex:* Wherein our *Author* hath observed to a Tittle, the Precepts of his Master *Horace*; or, indeed, rather hath gone very far beyond him, in the Article of *Decency*.

That great *Poet*, instructing us what Actions are fittest to be produced openly upon the *Scene*, and which are most proper to be only related to the Audience, goes many Lengths beyond the *Author* of the *Lady's Dressing-Room*; for at the same Instant when he says, some Actions should not appear as done upon the Stage, he allows, they may be *recited* with *Pleasure* and *Elegance*; and yet when he comes to Particulars, his Recital is extreamly gross, and so are his very *Precepts* which forbid the Actions: That if our infinitely more modest *Author* had imitated his *Master's Stile*, the whole World might with great Appearance of Reason, have been up in Arms against him.

Therefore, to set these two *Poets* in a true Light, I have ventured, for the Satisfaction of both Sexes, to translate, as literally as I could, ten Lines in *Horace*, upon the very same Subject, which our *Author* hath handled with a Decency so far superior to his *Roman* Master.

To justify the Truth of my Translation, I desire all fine Gentlemen and Ladies will appeal from me to the Information of the Learned, that I may be wholly clear from the least Censure of misrepresenting so great an Authority; for, indeed, if I have been guilty of any Fault, it is in palliating the gross Expressions in the Original, and soft'ning them very much to the *Politeness* of the *present Age*.

The *Latin* is Word for Word as follows.

> *Aut agitur res in scenis, aut acta refertur.*
> *Segnius irritant animos demissa per aurem,*
> *Quam quæ sunt oculis subjecta fidelibus, & quæ*
> *Ipse sibi tradit spectator. Non tamen intus*
> *Digna geri promes in scenam: Multaq; tolles*
> *Ex oculis, quæ mox narret facundia præsens.*
> *Nec pueros coram populo* Medea *trucidet;*
> *Aut humana palam coquat exta nefarius* Atreus.
> *Aut in avem* Progne *vertetur,* Cadmus *in anguem.*
> *Quodcunq; ostendis mihi sic, incredulus odi.*

The literal Translation whereof is thus.

> Some Ladies *do their Need* before your Face;
> Some only tell the *Action*, and the *Place.*
> Our Mind is less provok'd by what it hears,
> Than when the *Fact* before our Eyes appears.
> In Closet dark, your *Cedar-box* be hid;
> Not in a Parlour shown without the Lid.
> Some *Actions* must be always out of Sight,
> Yet *elegantly told*, may give Delight.
> Nurse must not hold the Child, and cry *Eee, Hee,*
> When Madam and her Friends are o'er their Tea.
> *Atreus*, with Ladies by, mistakes his Wit,
> In new-born T——s to run a red-hot Spit.

Miss *Progne* must not cry, *a Bird, a Bird!*
Before good Company, and shew a ——
Cadmus, who voids out Worms of monst'rous Size,
In mere good Manners should deceive our Eyes;
Must do his dirty Work behind the Scene,
And e'er he shews the *Vermin*, wipe them clean.
To bring such odious Objects full in View,
Though *Fools* may laugh, will make a *wise Man* spew.

I desire the Reader will compare the least exceptionable Lines in the *Lady's Dressing-Room* with the least offensive of these in *Horace*; although purged by me, as much as could consist with preserving the true Sense of the Original: Yet this was the great *Master of Politeness* in the *Roman* Empire, at the Time it flourished most in *Arts* and *Arms*.

Horace, you see, makes Use of the plain slovenly Words, which our decent *Irish Poet* industriously avoids, and skips over a Hundred dirty Places, without fowling his Shoes. *Horace*, on the contrary, plainly calls a *Spade*, a *Spade*, when there was not the least Necessity; and when, with equal Ease as well as Significancy, he might have express'd his Meaning in comely Terms, fit for the nicest Ears of a *Queen* or a *Dutchess*.

I do, therefore, positively decide in favour of our *Hibernian Bard*, upon the Article of *Decency*; and am ready to defend my Proposition against all Mankind; that in the ten Lines of *Horace*, here faithfully and favourably translated, there are ten Times more *slovenly Expressions*, than in the whole *Poem* called the *Lady's Dressing Room*; and for the Truth of this Proposition, I am ready to appeal to all the young Ladies of the Kingdom, or to such a *Committee* as my very Adversaries shall appoint.

FINIS.

A Copy of the Paper with which several Persons of the Liberty of St. *Patrick*'s attended the Rev. Dr. *J. Swift*, Dean of St. *Patrick*'s *Dublin*, in the Name of themselves and all the Inhabitants of the said Liberty, as well as of the Neighbourhood, on *Tuesday*, the 8th of this Instant *January*, 1733-4.

WE the Inhabitants of the Liberty of the Dean and Chapter of St. *Patrick*'s, *Dublin*, and the Neighbourhood of the same, having been informed, by universal Report, that a certain Man of this City hath openly threatened and sworn, before many hundred People, as well Persons of Quality as others, that he resolves upon the first Opportunity, by the Help of several Ruffians, to murder or maim the Reverend the Dean of St. *Patrick*'s, our Neighbour, Benefactor, and Head of the Liberty of St. *Patrick*'s, upon a frivolous unproved Suspicion, of the said Dean's having written some Lines in Verse reflecting on the said Man.*

Therefore we, the said Inhabitants of the said Liberty, and in the Neighbourhood thereof, from our great Love and Respect to the said Dean, to whom the whole Kingdom hath so many Obligations, as well as we of the Liberty, do unanimously declare, that we will endeavour to defend the Life and Limbs of the said Dean against the said Man, and all his Ruffians and Murderers, as far as the Law will allow, if he or any of them presume to come into the said Liberty with any

* The lines were these:

> Thus at the Bar that [Booby *Bettesworth*]
> Tho half a Crown oerpays his sweat's worth,
> Who knows in Law nor text nor Margent,
> Calls Singleton his brother Serjeant.

wicked or malicious Intent, against the House, or Family, or Person, or Goods of the said Dean. To which we have chearfully, sincerely and heartily set our Hands.

January 8, 1733.

William Anyon,	*Joseph Hopkins,*
John Anyon, sen.	*Moses Lewis,*
John Anyon, jun.	*Pat. Laughlin,*
Jonathan Anyon,	*John Owens,*
James Classon,	*Thomas Allen,*
George Simpson,	*John Benn,*
James Simpson,	*Ralph Spencer,*
John Baptist Curville,	*Allexander Tickel,*
James Curville,	*Thomas Coleman,*
John Spencer,	*Robert Jones,*
James Spencer,	*William Reily*
Daniel Dowd,	*Thomas Murphy,*
Edward Byrne,	*John Pinckney,*
Francis Carthy,	*Timothy Pinckney,*
William Singleton,	*Joseph Copstone.*
Samuel Jackson,	

The Dean being in Bed, and extremely ill of a Giddiness and Deafness, not being able to receive the said Persons, was pleased to dictate the following Answer.

Gentlemen,

I Receive, with great Thankfulness these many kind Expressions of your Concern for my Safety, as well as your declared Resolutions to defend me (as far as the Laws of God and Man will allow) against all Murderers and Ruffians, who shall attempt to enter into the Liberty with any bloody or wicked Designs upon my Life, my Limbs, my House or my Goods. Gentlemen, my Life is in the Hand of God, and whether it may be cut off by Treachery or open Violence, or by the common Way of other Men; as long as it continues I shall ever bear a grateful Memory for this Favour you have shown, beyond my Expectation, and almost exceeding my Wishes.

The Inhabitants of the Liberty, as well as those of the Neighbourhood, have lived with me in great Amity for near Twenty Years; which I am confident will never diminish during my Life. I am chiefly sorry, that by two cruel Disorders of Deafness and Giddiness, which have pursued me for four Months, I am not in a Condition either to hear, or to receive you, much less to return my most sincere Acknowledgments, which in Justice and Gratitude I ought to do. May God bless you and your Families in this World, and make you for ever happy in the next.

Printed in the Year, MDCCXXXIII.

MEMORANDUM ON
MR. GRATTAN'S WALK AT BELCAMP

MR. GRATTAN'S Walk, called *The Revenge Walk*, was from the gate going in, to Gordon's house-door, by gross computation, 1740 feet; out of the length of this walk, he made a lease for ever of 595 feet, with a field adjoining to Mr. Deering, a stranger. Therefore Mr. Grattan's walk is now in length only 1245 feet. It was the greatest folly of a private domestic kind, that I ever remember: for that walk was the only convenience in his garden or grounds about it, and the only agreeable circumstance that could make the place tolerable.

CHARACTER OF ARISTOTLE

ARISTOTLE, the disciple of PLATO, and tutor to ALEX-ANDER the GREAT. His followers were called *Peripateticks* from a *Greek* word which signifies *to walk*; because he taught his disciples *walking*. We have not all his works; and some of those which are imputed to him, are supposed not genuine. He writ upon *logick*, or the art of reasoning; upon *moral* and *natural philosophy*; upon *oratory, poetry*, &c. and seems to be a person of the most comprehensive genius that ever lived.

From the DUBLIN NEWS-LETTER

Jan. 4 and Jan. 18, 1736-7

DUBLIN

THE DEAN, who is never last in encouraging the *honest* and *industrious* Trader of *IRELAND*, has earnestly recommended the melancholy Case of Mr. *Godfrey* and *Anthony Green* in the following Words, to whose Reliefs beside his own Contribution and that of the Chapter of St. Patrick's, other Gentlemen have generously contributed.

THERE being a Collection intended, thro' the City and Suburbs of *Dublin*, for the Relief of the Sufferers by the accidental burning of the Sugar-House in St. *Mary*'s *Abby*; and the Clergy of the several Parishes resolving to recommend the said Collection to their Parishioners, the Dean of St. *Patrick*'s having been desired to second, and encourage the same good Design in the Liberty of the said Dean and Chapter; He, the said Dean, doth therefore very heartily recommend to the Inhabitants of the said Liberty, the distressed Case of the Sufferers, that they would contribute, according to their Abilities, in the Case of a Calamity from which no Family can promise themselves to be secure.

Jonathan Swift.

ADVERTISEMENT

For the HONOUR *of the* KINGDOM *of* IRELAND.

THIS *is to inform the Publick, that a Gentleman of long Study, Observation and Experience, hath employed himself for several Years in making Collections of Facts, relating to the Conduct of* Divines, Physicians, Lawyers, Soldiers, Merchants, Traders, *and* Squires, *containing, an Historical Account of the most remarkable* Corruptions, Frauds, Oppressions, Knaveries *and* Perjuries; *wherein the Names of all the Persons concerned shall be inserted at full Length, with some Account of their Families and Stations.*

But, whereas the said Gentleman cannot compleat his History, without some Assistance from the Publick, he humbly desires, that all Persons who have any Memoirs, or Accounts, relating to themselves, *their* Families, their Friends *or* Acquaintance, *which are well attested, and fit to enrich the Work, will please to send them to the Printer of this Advertisement: And, if any of the said Persons, who are disposed to send Materials, happen to live in the Country, it is desired their Letters may be either franked, or the Post paid.*

This Collection is to commence with the Year 1700, *and be continued to the present Year* 1738. *The Work is to be entitled,* The Author's Critical History of his own Times.

It is intended to be printed by Subscription, in a large Octavo; each Volume to contain five hundred Facts, and to be sold for a British Crown: *The Author proposeth, that the whole Work (which will take in the Period of thirty eight Years) will be contained in eighteen Volumes.*

Whoever shall send the Author any Account of Persons who have performed any Acts of Justice, Charity, Publick Spirit, Gratitude, Fidelity, *or the like, attested by indubitable Witnesses within the same Period; the said Facts shall be printed by the Way of* Appendix *at the End of each Volume, and no Addition to the Price of the Work demanded. But, lest such Persons may apprehend, that the relating of these Facts may be injurious to their Reputations, their Names shall not be set down without particular Direction.*

N. B.   *There will be a small Number printed on Royal Paper for the Curious, at only two* British *Crowns. There will also be the* Effigies *of the most eminent Persons mentioned in this Work, prefixed to each Volume, curiously engraved by Mr.* Hogarth.

SUBSCRIPTIONS *are taken in by the Printer hereof, and by the Booksellers of* London *and* Dublin.

TEXTUAL NOTES

1. AN ABSTRACT OF THE HISTORY OF ENGLAND

First printed probably from Swift's manuscript by Deane Swift in *Works*, London, 4to., 1765, Vol. VIII, p. 123; from which the present text is taken. Reprinted by Faulkner in *Works*, Dublin, 8vo., 1765, Vol. XII, p. 195.

A FRAGMENT OF THE HISTORY OF ENGLAND

First printed by Deane Swift in *Works*, London, 4to., 1768, Vol. XIII (or Vol. IV of the Correspondence), p. 253; from which the present text is taken. Reprinted by Faulkner in *Works*, Dublin, 8vo., 1768, Vol. XIX, 279.

2. OF PUBLICK ABSURDITYES IN ENGLAND

Here printed from Swift's autograph manuscript in the Victoria and Albert Museum Library—Forster, no. 534, 48. G. 6/2, 4 quarto leaves paged 1–8. The first four pages are written out across the whole leaf with scarcely any margin; the second two leaves are folded in half again vertically and the text is written in the right hand column only, except on p. 5, where a sentence intended to be inserted is entered at the head of the left hand blank column. Twice endorsed at the top of page 8—'Absurdityes in Engld.'

First printed by Deane Swift in *Works*, 4to., 1765, VIII, 117 where Swift's peculiarities of spelling and punctuation are modified and his capitalization eliminated. Reprinted by Faulkner with no alterations in *Works*, Dublin, 8vo., 1765, XII, 185.

The manuscript seems to be a first draft, and there are a good many alterations and changes written between the lines. There were so many on page 4 that when he began the next leaf he folded it and left the left half blank for additions.

Page	Line	Text	MS alterations
79	19	wise and	wise (men that *del.*) and
	23	results	resolu *del.*
	6 f.b.	which is a point	are points of *del.*
	b.	are often	almost *del.*
80	4	their Clymate	the Cly *del.*
	11	State	*written above* publick
	28	may	can *del.*
	4 f.b.	designs	intentions *del.*
	2 f.b.	consisted,	

Here Deane Swift inserted as a parenthesis, introduced by 'as', the sentence I have enclosed in square brackets, which Swift inserted at the top of the blank half of page 5, without indicating where it was to be placed in the text. There is a pen-point in the margin of page 4, opposite the words 'Prince and Country', but this may be due to the editor. The insertion is obviously related to this sentence and does not belong to the next paragraph, as printed by Temple Scott.

Page	Line	TEXT	MS ALTERATIONS
81	5	And surely this is full as requisite etc.	

Swift originally wrote: is at least as proper as Jurymen ex vicinia; since such persons are etc.

Then above the first six words he crowded in: full as requisite a Circumstance to a Legislator, as to a

and after Juryman: who ought to be if possible

(N.B. *Other editors conflate*: this is at least full as requisite D.S.; this is at least as proper, and full as requisite T.S.)

Page	Line	TEXT	MS ALTERATIONS
	23	corn or hay	hay or *del.*
	2 f.b.	full of industrious	full of (thriving *del.*) of industrious
82	1	to have themselves and servants	to (be exempt from Lawsuits and arrests is manifestly absurd *del.*) have exe *del.* have themselves etc.

3. OF MEAN AND GREAT FIGURES

Here printed from Swift's autograph manuscript in the Victoria and Albert Museum Library—Forster, nos. 537, 538; Forster 48. G. 6/2. Each consisting of two folded quarto leaves of four pages,
537 endorsed on p. 4 across the top of the right hand half:
Great and small figures
538 endorsed similarly; but on both halves of the outer blank page:
Of Mean and great Figures
made by Severall Persons
First printed by Deane Swift in *Works*, 4to., 1765, VIII, pt. 2, p. 241. Reprinted by Faulkner in *Works*, Dublin, 8vo., 1765, XIII, 253.

Page	Line	TEXT	MS ALTERATIONS
83	11	Time	Hour *del.*
		the Moment he expired.	his last *del.*
84	19	to dy.	not to live *de* .
	26	lay down to	and *del.*

MS. 538 seems more like a fair copy, as there are no deletions, but on page 5 a letter or two which had been omitted are added above the line; and on page 6 the following phrases seem to have been squeezed in later.

85	28	and he bore it with Patience	
86	4	upon which she drew it out, and flung it on the Ground	
	6	the Time of	
	15	at fifty years old,	

4. THE HUMBLE REPRESENTATION OF THE CLERGY OF DUBLIN, 1724

First printed by Deane Swift in *Works*, 4to., 1765, VIII, pt. i, p. 226; from which the present text is taken. Reprinted by Faulkner in the same year in Dublin, *Works*, XII, 341.

5. A LETTER TO THE WRITER OF THE OCCASIONAL PAPER, 1727

First printed from an unfinished manuscript by Deane Swift in *Works*, 1765, VIII, pt. i, p. 111, from which the present text is taken. Reprinted by Faulkner in the same year in Dublin, *Works*, XII, 175.

6. AN ACCOUNT OF THE COURT AND EMPIRE OF JAPAN, 1728

First printed by Deane Swift in *Works*, 1765, VIII, pt. i, p. 101, from which the present text is taken. Reprinted by Faulkner in the same year in Dublin, *Works*, XII, 159.

7. PREFACE TO VOLTAIRE'S *ESSAY UPON THE CIVIL WARS OF FRANCE*, 1728

Voltaire's Essay was first printed in London in 1727. Swift probably arranged with Hyde for its publication in Dublin, and provided this prefatory note in response to Voltaire's request for assistance in Ireland, in his letter to Swift of Dec. 14, 1727.

The text printed here is from the Hyde edition of 1728, which was not signed by Swift. But when the essay was reprinted in Dublin for William Ross, in 1760, he added on the title-page:

To which is Prefixed,
A short Account of the AUTHOR
By J.S.D.D.S.P.D.

8. THE ANSWER OF THE RIGHT HON. W. PULTENEY TO THE RT. HON. SIR ROBERT WALPOLE, 1730

First printed by Deane Swift 'from the Originals' in 1768, at the end of Vol. IV of the edition of Swift's *Letters*, sometimes numbered Vol. XIII of the *Works*, 4to., 1768, p. 245. Reprinted the same year by Faulkner in Dublin, *Works*, 8vo., XIX, 265.

9. PREFACE AND MEMOIRS OF CAPTAIN CREICHTON, 1731

The Advertisement to the Reader and the Memoirs are printed from the first edition, the title-page of which is reproduced facing p. 120. The Memoirs were first reprinted among the works of Swift by Faulkner in Dublin, *Works*, 1762, X, 179, with a long note written by Faulkner, in which he says that the Captain waited on the Dean with his Papers, 'from whence he compiled the following MEMOIRS.' They were printed in London in *Works*, 4to., 1764, VII, pt. i, 109, with the following alterations in *The Printer's Advertisement*:

Page	Line	Faulkner's Note	Printer's Advertisement, 1764
120	7	but who was	but was
	9	from them, and was	from it. As he was
	10	which moved Dr. Swift very much, who made	Dr. Swift made
	23	Then Dr. Swift	The good dean
	29	from whence he compiled the following MEMOIRS, in which he seems particularly attentive to support the Character of the Person in whose Name they were published; and to write in the natural, unadorned, and even in the homely Style of a plain old Soldier.	and related many adventures to him; which the dean was so kind as to put in order of time, to correct the style, and make a small book of, entitled, The MEMOIRS of CAPTAIN JOHN CREICHTON.
	3f.b.	was very considerable and got the Captain	raised for the captain

10. AUTOBIOGRAPHICAL PIECES
(i) FAMILY OF SWIFT

Printed from Swift's autograph manuscript, deposited by Deane Swift in Trinity College Library, Dublin. I have tried to indicate in the text Swift's alterations, corrections and marginal additions.

Further marginal notes added in a MS copy now in the Pierpont Morgan Library, New York, are given below. (Ms) N.B.—The marginal observations are not the Dean's. It was first printed by Deane Swift in the Appendix to his *Essay upon the Life, Writings, and Character, of Jonathan Swift*, in 1765, with annotations and corrections, some extracts from which are also reprinted here (DS).

Page	Line	TEXT	NOTES
187	2	Yorkshire	I never heard the name of the old estate: perhaps the Earl of Eglington mentioned below could give some information. (Ms)
	3	a noted Person	Barnam Swift, Esq.; created viscount (not baron) of Carlingford, in the realm of Ireland, March 20, 1627, anno 3 Caroli regis. (DS)
	21	William Swift	In that dedication (of the sermon) we find that Thomas Swift, the father of William, was presented in the year 1569, to the parish of St. Andrew in the city of Canterbury: And moreover, that upon the decease of Thomas, William Swift, in the year 1591, succeeded his father in the same parish. Not in the list of Prebendaries. (DS)
	24	sermon	It is a good sermon, I have read it: there is a Dedication which clears up a point. (Ms)
	28	a Yorkshire Gentleman	Rather a Gentleman of Kent: for Thomas the father of William, who was also a clergyman of Canterbury, was the first who came from Yorkshire; and in all probability his son never went into those parts. (Ms)
		considerable estate	It is said £1500 a year. (Ms)
	4f.b.	several instances	Some very pleasant ones. (Ms)
188	2	Goodrich	and two other neighbouring parishes, viz. *Marstow* and *Llangarran*. (DS)
	5	great-great grandson	Deane Swift, Esquire. (DS) (Ms)

Page	Line	Text	Notes
	6	Godwin Swift	This Gentleman is now dead; the pictures are in the hands of his widow (DS) (Ms)
	18	Thomas	was a clergyman, as appears from his picture, in 1623, aetatis suae 28. (DS)
	20	one or two miles	Within four miles of Ross (DS) (Ms)
	21	another church living	The living of Wilton adjacent to the town of Ross. He was likewise (I think) a Canon of Hereford. (Ms)
	26	The house	The date upon one of the Pillars is 1636 (DS) (Ms)
	31	Landlord	Deane Swift. (Ms)
	b.	another in folio	The last book he refers to was written by (I believe) Walker, whose name I have often heard the D. mention upon this occasion: and I know he was angry with the Earl of Clarendon for not taking notice of his Grandfather. (Ms)
189	4	above fifty	I was told by his Grandson of the female line who lived all his life-time upon the spot, that the precise number of times was 52. (Ms)
	5	gatherd	This word is so defaced in the original, that I could hardly pick it out, yet as the sense is clear, it is of little or no consequence (Ms—*this proves that the copy was taken from Swift's autograph*).
190	6	a fanatical saint	One Gyles Rawlins succeeded him in the parish of *Goodrich*: but the fanatical saint here mentioned, succeeded Rawlins some time before the month of October, 1657; his name was William Tringham. (DS)
	20	the year of his age	63ᵈ, as it is plain from his original picture drawn an. Dom. 1623, aet. 28. (Ms) (DS)
	30	ten sons	vide Mercurius Rusticus, ten children and their names postea.
	32	inner Temple	Of Gray's-*Inn* (DS) my authority is Guillim (Ms)
191	2	co-heiress	sole heiress (DS) (Ms)

Page	Line	TEXT	NOTES
	4	have all estates	that is, the eldest son of each several wife was left an estate, and his second son by his first wife. Besides these five there were three more who grew up to be men who had no estates, the sons of his last wife, who was sister to Sir John Meade, and one of the most beautiful Women of her age, the two elder of whom went into the army and the youngest was bred an Attorney: One of them, Captain Thomas Swift, who was killed at the battle of Almanzo, having inherited the complexion and beauty of his Mother, was supposed to have been the handsomest man in the Queen's Army. But this note is of little consequence since they all three dyed childless. (Ms)
	16	a near relation	Aunt (Ms) (DS)
	27	his death	at the age of about five and twenty. (DS)
192	8	born on St Andrews day	1667 (DS) (Ms)
	7 f.b.	batchlor	of Arts (Ms)
	3 f.b.	College	University (Ms)
		Speciali Gratia	I have been told, that within these few years, by order of the Fellows and Provost this circumstance hath been erased from the books, as a thing they were ashamed of. The Dean went afterwards to Oxford ad eundum, whereupon shewing his Testimonial they understood Speciali Gratia as a Compliment from the University for his extraordinary Diligence and Parts: the Dean never undeceived them. It seems this is an Academick Phrase Peculiar to the University of Dublin. The Dean studied at Hart-Hall in Oxford, which within these few years has been made Hartford College. The Dean took his Master of Arts Degree at Oxford, and his Doctor's of Divinity in Dublin. (Ms)

Page	Line	TEXT	NOTES
193	4	to the Family,	His Mother's family. (Ms)
194	6	under twenty-one years	It was first written, but afterwards erased in the original manuscript *three and twenty years old*, which in all probability was right; for, Dr. Swift was twenty-one years old the last day of November 1688, and before that period there could have been so such bill under consideration. (DS)
	11	converse with Courts	I have heard the Dean say, when he was a young man, he thought he should be the happiest person in the world if he could but once converse with a crowned head; but that after his curiosity had been satisfyed, his reverence towards Princes was much abated. And the Dean has told me, that he has often walked and conversed with K. William in Sir W. Temple's garden, Sir William himself not being able to attend his Majesty having been confined by the gout: and particularly, that K. William taught him to cut Asparagus, which was a vegetable his Majesty was fond of. (Ms)
	20	the Prince obligeth himself to consent to all Laws, etc.	The Dean's opinion of this point will appear clearer in the suppressed paragraph of the Sentiments of a C. of England man &c. (Ms)
	21	*Quas vulgus elegerit.*	This whole paragraph was written by the D. after this imperfect sketch of his life was finished, as appears by its being written on the opposite Column in the original. I need not observe that if it were wholly omitted, the transition from the former paragraph to that which succeeds next would be much easier. (Ms)
	3 f.b.	a legacy——	these words scratched out thus in the original which although I have defaced a little too much was certainly £100. (Ms)

Page	Line	Text	Notes
			which according to the best conjecture I can make, was five hundred pounds; or else the legacy and what he made by sir William Temple's works amounted to that sum; for in the year 1699 he was just worth so much and no more. (DS)
195	*b.*	thirty years old	he was then upwards of two and thirty years old; for it was in the month of February, 1699/1700, that he was presented to the rectory of Aghar, and the vicarages of Laracor and Rathbeggan, in the diocese of Meath. (DS)
			Either Indolence, Sickness, Old Age, or carelessness, hindered the Dean from proceeding further in these Memoirs: yet Mrs. W. says that she has seen a fairer Copy than the one I have taken them from. If there be such a one upon earth Lyon must have it: and if it be possible, I will get a sight of it. (Ms)

The manuscript in the Orrery Correspondence in the Morgan library also contains a copy of the passage from Mercurius Rusticus concerning the persecution of the Rev. Thomas Swift and his family, which is printed by Deane Swift in his Appendix, pp. 11–19.

An edition of *The Fragment of Autobiography of Jonathan Swift* was prepared with Notes and Appendices by W. Victor Whatton. Toronto, 1950, M.A. thesis.

(ii) ACCOUNT OF HIS MOTHER'S DEATH, 1710

Taken from the entry in Swift's account book of Personal Expenses for the Year 1710–11, where it was entered on the page which contains his expenses for May, 1710, when he was at Laracor. The leaf is now missing from the account book in the Forster collection. The present text is therefore taken from *Works*, ed. Nichols, 1801, X, 104.

(iii) TREATY WITH MRS ANNE LONG; and DEATH OF MRS ANNE LONG

'The Decree for Concluding the Treaty between Dr. Swift and Mrs. Long' was first printed by Curll in *Tales, Poems* etc., 1718 from which the present text is taken.

The account of the Death of Mrs Long is printed from a note book—Forster 48. D. 34/4 no. 508—containing the *Private Expenses of Jonathan Swift*, 1711–12, entered in Swift's own hand. Written in his smallest script at the top of the recto of fol. 2, and facing an account of his gains and losses at Picquet and Hazard and Ombre with Mrs. Van., Lady Masham, Ld Treas., Lewis etc.

(iv) PETITION TO THE HOUSE OF LORDS AGAINST THE LORD BLANEY

Printed from the autograph manuscript, probably a first draft, from a volume of *Autograph Letters of Jonathan Swift*, now in the Pierpont Morgan Library. I have not found any reference to this petition having been presented to the House of Lords, in their Journals. On the other hand there is a record on Feb. 7, 1715, that 'the Lord Baron Blayney be recommended to His Majesty's Favour and Protection, that he may be provided for in the new Levies, now to be raised in this Kingdom'. It was first printed by Sheridan in his Life of Swift, 1784.

(v) HOLYHEAD JOURNAL

Printed from the autograph manuscript—Forster, no. 519–48. D. 34/10, pp. 10–23 of the book Swift said he had stolen from 'the Right Honrble George Dodington Esqr, one of the Lords of the Treasury, June 1727.,' adding

But the Scribblings are all my own.

I have printed here also the contents of pp. 6–7, but not the verses on the leaves before and after. Memoranda on the first and last leaves are given in Appendix B. There are no alterations in the manuscript of any account, nothing that did not reach the paper as he wrote, except

P. 204, l. 15 a while
l. 23 there
205, l. 27 a slice of *instead of* a little
l. 28 yesterday
206, l. 4 Mountain *instead of* hill
l. 13 in worse rain

11. CHARACTERS

(i) CHARACTER OF PRIMATE MARSH

First printed in *Miscellanies*, Vol. X, 1745, pp. 169–71. Reprinted in *Works*, London, 4to., Vol. VI, pt. ii, p. 176. There are no substantive variants, so I follow the text of the *Works*, 1755, from which most of the other pieces in this group have to be taken.

(ii) CHARACTER OF MRS HOWARD, 1727

First printed by Deane Swift in *Works*, 4to., 1765, VIII, pt. i, p. 244, from which the present text is taken. Reprinted by Faulkner in Dublin in the same year in *Works*, XII, 373.

(iii) CHARACTER OF DOCTOR SHERIDAN; HISTORY OF THE SECOND SOLOMON

First printed by Deane Swift in *Works*, 4to., 1765, VIII, pt. i, pp. 247–54, from which the present text is taken. Reprinted by Faulkner in Dublin in the same year in *Works*, XII, pp. 379–90.

The BLUNDERS AND MISFORTUNES OF QUILCA were first printed in the *Miscellanies*, Vol. X, 1745, from which the present text is taken. Pp. 164–8. Reprinted in *Works*, 4to., 1755, VI, and by Faulkner in Dublin in *Works*, 1763, X, 383–7.

(iv) ON THE DEATH OF MRS JOHNSON: BON MOTS DE STELLA

First printed by Deane Swift in *Works*, 4to., 1765, VIII, pt. i, pp. 255–64, from which the present text is taken. Reprinted by Faulkner in Dublin in the same year in *Works*, XII, pp. 391–406.

The *Bon Mots* de Stella were first printed in *Miscellanies*, 1745, X, pp. 243–7 from which the present text is taken. The presence of certain characteristic spellings, e.g. writ, extreamly, corkt, which are normalized in the later reprints, suggest that it was printed from Swift's manuscript.

It was reprinted by Faulkner in Dublin, in the next year, in *Works*, VIII, 348–50; and afterwards in London in *Works*, 4to., 1755, Vol. VI, pt. ii, pp. 185–6, with the omission of the last one about the Quaker apothecary, which was added in London edition in 1779.

APPENDIXES

A. LETTER FROM THE GRAND MISTRESS OF THE FEMALE FREE-MASONS, 1724

Printed from a photographic facsimile of Tract No. 12, Box 171, of the Haliday Collection in the Royal Irish Academy, Dublin.

The Letter was originally addressed to Mr. *Harding* the Printer; and it was printed by him with the same imprint and in the same year as he printed the *Drapier's Letters*: Printed by *John Harding* in *Molesworth's Court* in *Fishamble-Street*, 1724. Harding's spellings and misprints have been preserved.

It was first reprinted in the London edition among a number of the unpublished pieces which are included in this volume in 1755, in Vol. VI, pt. ii, p. 187, but on the title-page, in the text and in the postscript, the well-known name of George Faulkner was substituted for John Harding. And it was reprinted in this form by Faulkner himself in Dublin in the *Works*, 1762, Vol. X, p. 367. It has some careless omissions, and changes in spelling and punctuation. It also provides a footnote at the end elucidating the date: DUBLIN, *August* the first. *Those who understand* Irish, *may find some other Meaning.*

It seems to me to belong with other pieces addressed to Harding at this time, such as *A Letter from a Lady of Quality to Mr. Harding the Printer*, etc., dated August 22, 1724. But it is curious that it was printed among Swift's Works in the eighteenth century, and is still accepted in some quarters. See *The Lodge of Research, No. CC., Ireland. Transactions for the Year 1924*, Dublin, 1931, 'Free-masonry in Ireland, 1725–31', pp. 107 ff.

B. MEMORANDA FROM FORSTER MS 519 and EGERTON 201, 1727

Printed together here from the manuscripts, since it has been shown that the Egerton leaf probably belonged to the same volume as that containing the *Holyhead Journal*. See George P. Mayhew, *A Missing Leaf from Swift's 'Holyhead Journal'*, Bulletin of the John Rylands Library, Vol. 41, No. 2, March 1959, p. 388.

C. A MODEST DEFENCE OF THE LADY'S DRESSING-ROOM, 1732

Printed from the first edition printed by Faulkner in 1732 and referring to 'a Late Poem By an unknown Author', though he printed the Poem himself in the same year, and claimed on the title-page that it was taken from the Original Copy, and was 'By D——n S——t'. He afterwards included it in Swift's *Works*, 1746, Vol. VIII, p. 181. It was reprinted in London by John Nichols in his *Supplement to Swift's Works*, 1779, pp. 408–12.

D. DECLARATION OF THE INHABITANTS OF ST. PATRICK'S, 1733–4

Printed from the original Broadside, in the National Library of Ireland. The Declaration is dated January 8, 1733–4, with the imprint: Printed in the Year, MDCCXXXIII.

It was included by Faulkner in 1762, in *Works*, Vol. X, pp. 323–5, with the following prefatory note:

Mr. B——*sw*——, Serjeant at Law, and Member of Parliament, a professed Enemy to the Clergy, having been reflected on by the Dean, in a humorous Poem, intitled, *Brother Protestants*, &c. and thinking himself highly injured thereby, resolved to be revenged on Dr. *Swift*, as the Author of the said Poem. With this Design he engaged his Footman and two Ruffians to attend him, in order to secure the Dean wherever they met him, until he had gratified his Resentment either by maiming or stabbing him. Accordingly he went directly to the Deanery, and hearing the Dean was at a Friend's House*, followed him thither, charged him with writing the said Verses, but had not Courage to put his bloody Design into Execution. However as he had the Assurance to relate this Affair to several Noblemen and Gentlemen, the Inhabitants of the Liberty of St. *Patrick*'s, waited upon the Dean in Form, and presented the following Paper, signed by thirty of them, in the Name of themselves, and the rest of their Neighbourhood.

E. MEMORANDUM ON MR. GRATTAN'S WALK AT BELCAMP

First printed by Nichols from MS annotations to Hawkesworth's *Life*, in his *Supplement to Dr. Swift's Works*, 1779, p. 746.

The memorandum was probably written during one of Swift's visits to Belcamp in 1733 or 1734; see *Corr.* vi, 227.

F. NOTE ON ARISTOTLE

Printed by Deane Swift in his *Essay on the Life and Character of Dr. Swift*, 1755, note to p. 283.

G. ADVERTISEMENTS

(i) *The Dublin News-Letter*, no. 1, Jan. 1–4, 1736–7
     repeated in   no. 5, Jan. 15–18, 1736–7
Printed from copies of the newspaper in the National Library, Dublin.

(ii) For the HONOUR of the KINGDOM OF IRELAND.
I have not been able to find a copy of the original advertisement which seems to have appeared in 1738, but the file of Faulkner's *Dublin Journal* is incomplete for that year. It was reprinted by Faulkner in 1746 in Swift's *Works*, Vol. VIII, pp. 177–8, from which the present text is taken.

THE INDEX

Abingdon, Montagu Bertie, 2nd Earl of, Macky's character of, 259

Abraham, 329

Acheson, Sir Arthur, xvii, 120

Acheson, Lady, xviii

Actium, 85

Addison, Joseph, Secretary to the Earl of Wharton, xxiv, 200; and Stella, 229, 235; as Secretary of State, xxxiii; his *Freeholder*, xxxiii, 251–255

Adela, Adelicia, daughter of William the Conqueror, 41, 263

Adelais, of Lorrain, second wife of Henry I, 41

Adrian, Pope, 76

Advertisement for the Honour of the Kingdom of Ireland, 346–7

Aglionby, Dr., Envoy to Swiss Cantons, Macky and Swift on, 261

Airs-Moss, battle at, 147

Albemarle, Arnold Keppel, Earl of, Macky's character of, 259

Albemarle, Stephen, Earl of, nephew of William I, 20, 54

Alexander the Great, 83; pupil of Aristotle, 345

Algiers, Dey of, 93

Anabaptists, address to the King, 319

Anandale, Earl of, 162

Andeli, 39

Angers, siege of, 67

Angles, 5

Anjou, Geoffrey, Earl of, invasion of Normandy, 51, 59; 39, 41, 48, 63; death of, 66

Anjou, 38

Anne, Queen of England, 85, 126, 213, 289; Act for better collecting Charity money, 91; hated Pretender, 293; death of, 12, 284

Anselm, Archbishop of Canterbury, 16, 28; exiled, 17; death of, 34

Antioch, 22

Antiochus, 86

Antony, Mark, xi, 85, 86

Apulia, 27

Arthur, King of England, 'if not a fable', 4

Arbuthnot, Dr. John, xxvii

Argyle, Archibald, 7th Earl of, character by Burnet and Swift, 266

Argyle, Archibald, 8th Earl and Marquis, invades Scotland in support of Duke of Monmouth, 158; captured and beheaded, 160; 'greatest villain of his age', 269; character by Clarendon and Swift, 308, 311, 312, 315–17

Argyll, Archibald, 1st Duke of, character by Macky, 261

Aristotle, character of, 345

Armstrong, conspirator against Charles II, 281

Arran, Earl of, sent to Tower, 165

Artois, 43

Arundel, 57, 58

Asia, prime ministers in, 117

Ashburnham, Mr., opinion of Scots, 311

Ashe, Dr. St. George, Bishop of Clogher, friend of Stella, 233

Athole, or Atholl, John Murray, first Marquis of, 129, 134, 158

Atterbury, Francis, Bishop of Rochester, 272, 282; 298, 335

Augustine, St., 4

Aylmer, Colonel Matthew, Vice-Admiral, Macky and Swift on, 261

Ball, Dr. Elrington, xiii, xv

Bacon, Francis, Lord Verulam, xi, xl, 85

Bacon, Friar, 328

Baillie, a cousin of Burnet, 282

Baker, Sir Richard, *A Chronicle of the Kings of England*, x

Balfour, a murderer of the Archbishop of St. Andrews, 135

Bangor, 202

Barfleur, 40

Baronius, Caesar, *Annales Eccl.*, x, xxxvii

Bath-Gate, near Edinburgh, 131

Beaumont, John, 196

Becket, Thomas a, Archbishop, death of, 78
Bedford, captured by Stephen, 52
Belcamp, residence of the Grattans, 344
Bell, Sir John, Provost of Glasgow, 141
Bentley, Dr. Richard, 201
Berkeley, Charles, 2nd Earl of, Lord Justice in Ireland, 195; Macky and Swift on, 259
Bernard, Dr., Bishop of Limerick, xxxiii
Berwick, 313
Bettesworth, Sergeant, 341
Bible, St. Matt. vi. 3, quoted, 90
Bigod, Hugh, 48
Billingsgate, 113
Bishops, rights of investing, 30
Blackmore, Sir Richard, Addison's remarks on, xxxiii; 201
Black Prince, The, xi
Blackwell, Sir Lambert, Envoy to Tuscany, Macky and Swift on, 261
Blair, Laird of, 172
Blake, Admiral, Clarendon and Swift on, 319
Blayney, Lord, xxiv; Petition against, 199–200
Blois, Theobald, Earl of, 41, 47, 51
Brooke, parson, of Dublin, 207
Bodin, Jean, *Six livres de la République*, xxxii, 244
Bodleian Library, Oxford, 187
Bolingbroke, Viscount, *see* St. John
Bolton, Charles, 3rd Duke of, Macky and Swift on, 258
Bothwell-Bridge, xx, 131, 139, 141
Bowes, Sir Jerome, ambassador to Muscovy, xi, 84
Bowood, Wiltshire, Marquis of Lansdowne's library, xxxvi
Boyle, Henry, Lord, Chancellor of the Exchequer, 260
Boyle, Michael, Dean of Cloyne, afterwards Archbishop of Armagh, Burnet and Swift on, 284
Boyle, Hon. Robert, 'a very silly writer,' 271
Brabant, an attorney, hanged as a spy, 308
Brent, Mrs., Swift's housekeeper, xviii

Brennus, army of, 100
Bridewell, 94, 116
Bristol, 53
Britain, language of, 5; early Britons, 3, 80
Bromley, William, Speaker of the House of Commons, 335
Brown, Dr. Peter, Bishop of Cork, friend of Stella, 233
Browne, Sir John, *Essays on Trade and Coin of Ireland*, xxxiv, 256
Brydges, James, Lord Chandos, father of the Duke, 260
Buckingham, George Villiers, 2nd Duke of, Burnet and Swift on, 268, 275; Clarendon on, 318
Buckinghamshire, John, Duke of, Macky and Swift on, 257
Bunting, Major, 170
Burnet, Gilbert, Bishop of Salisbury, Swift's relations with, xxxvi, xxxvii; his account of Pretender's birth, 183; arguments for a regency, 291; 'canting puppy', 282; comments on clergy, 293; eloquence, 281; 'the King knew him right', 276; Lord Arran's governor, 165; malice to Laud and Sharp, 268, 271, 290; his misrepresentation, 146; 'modest' account of his appointment as Professor, 274; paper to justify William III's rights, 293; 'silly fop', 280, 287; style, 272, 274; 'three wives', 294; 'treacherous villain', 276; 'witty', 279; Burnet and Cromwell, 267: Macky and Swift on, 260; *History of his own Times*, x, xix, xx, xxxvi, 139, 266–94
Burnet, Thomas, *Life of Gilbert Burnet*, 294
Butler of Weston, Charles, Lord, afterwards Earl of Arran, 260

Cabalists, 329
Cardrosse, Lord and Lady, 137
Caesar, Julius, 3, 86, 207, 330
Callidon, 125
Cambridge, 162, 217
Cameron, the 'famous Covenanter', killed, 148
Cameron, Sir Owen, 158, 170

Canterbury, 35; St. Andrew's Church, xxiii; Prebend at, 195; Archbishop of, see Anselm, Corbois, Lanfranc, Theobald, etc.

Canutus, king of Denmark, 5 f.

Capel, Henry, Lord Deputy of Ireland, 194, 314

Cardiff, castle, 33

Carlingford, Cavaliero Swift, Baron, 187

Carlisle, 27, 49, 66, 75, 313

Carlisle, Charles Howard, Earl of, 258, 295

Carmichael, Sir John, 146

Carnwarth, Lady, 174

Caroline, Princess of Wales, afterwards Queen of George II, xxvii, 213, 214, 226

Carr, Robert, 295

Carrick-Fergus, 329

Carstairs, William, 262

Carteret, John, 2nd Lord, afterwards Earl of Granville, xxix, 207, 217, 223

Carthage, 36

Castle maine, Palmer, Earl of, Burnet and Swift on, 286

Catholics, Roman, 318

Cato, the younger, xi, 84

Cavan, free-school of, 218; county of, 224

Chandos, James Brydges, Duke of, Macky and Swift on, 260

Charles I, King of England, xxxviii, 84, 86, 162, 188; final concessions, 313; indulgence to Prince Rupert, 301; delivered up, 312; 'the word of a King', 295, 300–1, 308; Clarendon and Swift on, 296, 297, 300

Charles II, King of England, xxxiv, 85, 120, 130, 162, 308, 312–3, 320; severity against Armstrong, 281; death of, 283; Burnet and Swift on, 277

Charles V, Emperor, 85, 86

Charles XII, King of Sweden, 11, 85

Cherbury, Edward, Lord Herbert of, xxxii-iii

Cherrytree, Lady, 130

Chester, xxiv-v, 20, 201, 203, 206, 208

Chester, Earl of, 58, 66, 71

Chesterfield, Philip Stanhope, Earl of, Macky and Swift on, 259

Cholmondeley, Hugh, Lord, Swift on, 260

Christendom, unity of against the Turks, 23

Chronicle, Saxon, 36

Church of England, bishops, xx, 298; electing, 31; proposal to abolish, 302, 310; revenues of vacant sees belong to the Crown; 15; relations with government, 37

Churchill, Charles, Colonel, 214

Churchill, George, Vice-Admiral, 261

Churchill, John, Lord. *See* Marlborough, Duke of.

Cicero, 83; Swift's copy of his *De Officiis*, xxxi

Cincinnatus, 83

Clarendon, Edward Hyde, first Earl of, compared with Burnet, 267; his *History of the Rebellion*, x, xxxviii f., 295, 304

Claudius, Emperor, 3

Clavers, Captain, 140, 141

Clayton, Mrs., afterwards Lady Sundon, 214

Clement VII, Pope, 86

Cleopatra, 85

Clermont, Council at, 21

Clifford, Thomas, Lord, 274

Clodevaus, first Christian King of France, 327

Common Law, introduced by Edward the Confessor, 6

Commons, House of, Charles I's indiscreet visit, 300

Compton, Dr. Henry, Bishop of London, Burnet and Swift on, 289

Coriolanus, 86

Cockburn, Lieutenant Colonel, 129

Comines, Phillippe de, *Historie*, xxxi; *Memoirs*, xviii & *n*. 122

Conway, 202

Cooper, Sir Anthony Ashley, Earl of Shaftesbury, xxxix; Clarendon and Swift on, 303, 307

Coote, Sir Charles, *see* Montrath

Corbois (Corbeil), William, Archbishop of Canterbury, 48

Cork, Sheridan's sermon at, xxix

Cornwall, 4

Covenant, Solemn League & 'the devil made it', 305, 306, 316

Covenanters, 124, 180

Craftsman, The, xii, xiv, xvi, 93, 116, 118
Creichton, Alexander, of Dumfries, 125
Creichton, Capt. John, his forebears, 125; his dreams, 154; a 'Persecutor of the Saints', 123; loyalty to Church, 124; appointed Lieutenant to Capt. Stuart, 135; nearly killed at Airs-Moss, 148–9; returns to Ireland, 152; Captain's commission, 167; loyalty to James II, 168; imprisoned at Edinburgh, 171; threatened with hanging, 172; settled in County Tyrone, 180; his *Memoirs,* xvii f., 160; Faulkner's note on, 120
Crewe, Lord, Bishop of Durham, 293
Crispin, William, 39
Crockat, Gilbert, *Scotch Presbyterian Eloquence,* 130
Cromwell, Oliver, 84, 85; Clarendon and Swift on, 312, 313, 318, 320
Crusades, 21
Ctesias, 243
Culross, in Fife, 131
Cutts, John, Lord, Macky and Swift on, 261
Cyrus, King, 36

Dalhousie, Lord, kindness to Creichton, 151
Dalziel, Thomas, General of forces in Scotland, xix, 130, 139; rebukes Duke of Monmouth, 142; account of, 155–7
Daniel, Samuel, *Collection of the History of England,* ix, x
Dartmouth, William Legg, Earl of, Macky and Swift on, 259
D'Avenant, Dr. Charles, Agent at Frankfurt, Macky and Swift on, 261
Davenant, Sir William, 191
David, King of Scotland, invades England, 49; besieges York, 53; his defeat, 54–5; joins Prince Henry, 66; barbarous invasion of Northumberland, 52
Danes, 5
Deane, Admiral, Richard, 191
Declaration of the Inhabitants of the Liberty of St Patrick's, xxiv, 341–2
Delamair, Lord, 164

Delany, Patrick, xxviii–ix
De la Warr, John, Macky and Swift on, 259
Delgarno, Elizabeth, wife of Captain Creichton, 129
Denmark, 5
Dennis, John, 201
Derby, James Stanley, Earl of, Macky and Swift on, 258
Devizes, 56
De Witt, John, Pensionary of Holland, murder of, 275
Dinan, Alan, Count of, 56
Dingley, Mrs. Rebecca, xxix, 220
Dissenters, Burnet and Swift on, 285
Dobbs, Dr., Fellow of Trinity, 206
Dodington, George Bubb, one of the Lords of the Treasury, xxv, 214
Donegal, 129
Dorislaus, Dr., 315
Dorset, Charles, 6th Earl of, Macky and Swift on, 258
Douglas, who refused to quit his burning ship, 84
Douglas, James, General of Scottish army for James II, 161, 163, 169
Douglas, Lord William, 175
Dover, 53, 71
Downing, Dr., Army chaplain, 301
Druids, 3, 329
Drumclog, 136
Drummond, Lieut. Gen., 155
Dryden, John, 191, 327
Dublin, xxiv, 206, 228; castle of, 223; clergy of, 87
Dublin News Letter, 346
Ducklane, London, xxxix, 201
Dumfries, Lady, 125
Dunbarton, Earl of, 162–3, 159
Dunboyn, 218
Dundee, John Graham of Claverhouse, 1st Viscount, 136, 161 f.; threatens reprisals if Creichton harmed, 172; death of, 173; Burnet and Swift on, 290
Dundee, Lady, 170
Dungannon, school of, xix, 129
Dunkirk, demolition of, 113
Dunmore, Charles Murray, 1st Earl of, 162 f.
Dunstan, Abbot of Glastonbury, 263
Dutch, 'too dear at 10/- apiece', 275

Edgar Atheling, 5, 6, 16
Edinburgh, Castle, held for James II, 169; Tolbooth prison, 171
Edred, King, suffers penance from the Abbot of Glastonbury, 263
Edrick, traitor at Ashdon, 263
Edward, Prince of Wales, the Black Prince, 84, 263
Edmond Ironside, 6
Edward the Confessor, 6; his laws, 28, 60
Egbert, King of the West Saxons, 4
Eglington, Alexander, 8th Earl of, his connection with the Swift family, 187
Egypt, 85, 327
Eikon Basilike, 'I think the King did not write it', 268
Eleanor, wife of Louis le Jeune, her marriage to Prince Henry, 67
Elizabeth, Queen, 11, 117, 324, 326
Ely, bishop of. See Nigellus.
England, standing army an absurdity, 80; army service under Norman kings, 20; tyranny and injustice, 236; Parliament, House of Lords, 244; House of Commons, election of members, 80; triennial, 193; septennial, 277; Bill not to dissolve Parliament, 194; 298
Epaminondas, 83
Epicurean philosophy, 231
Epte, river, 38
Erick, Mrs. Abigail, Swift's mother, 191
Essex, Algernon Capell, 2nd Earl of Essex, Macky and Swift on, 259
Essex, Arthur Capell, 1st Earl of, his suicide, 281
Essex, Robert Devereux, 3rd Earl of, Parliamentary General, 306
Ethelbert, King of South Saxons, 4
Ethelred, 5, 6
Eugenius VI, Pope, 68
Europe, courts of, 117
European Magazine, xxxvi
Eustace, son of King Stephen, Duke of Normandy, 51, 60, 61, 67; his death, 69
Evreux, Count d', 41
Exclusion, Bill of, 264, 279
Exeter, 50

Fairfax, Thomas, General, 86, 267
Falkland, Lucius Cary, Viscount, Clarendon's character of, xxxix, 304
Faulkner, George, printer, xxxi, 347
Featley, Dr., 304
Feilding, Robert, 'Beau', xi, 86, 187
Fenton, Mrs., 196
Fergus, King of Scotland, 329
Feversham, Louis, Earl of, General of James II's forces, 162 f.; Burnet and Swift on, 290
Fielding, Beau. *See* Feilding.
Finch, Heneage, afterwards Earl of Aylsford, Burnet and Swift on, 281
Finch, Heneage, Solicitor-General, 284
Flanders, Charles, Earl of, 38, 43, 71
Flemings, soldiers of fortune employed by Stephen, 70, 72, 74
Fletcher, of Saltoun, Andrew, 262
Fleury, Cardinal, lampoon on, parodied, xvi
Forbes, Lord, afterwards Earl of Granard, sent to Tower, 165
Ford, Charles, of Woodpark, his copy of Savile, x; letters to, xxxii
Fountaine, Sir Andrew, xxiii
Frankland, Sir Thomas, Postmaster General, Macky and Swift on, 260
Frederick Augustus, Elector of Saxony, King of Poland, 85
Freemasons, 314 f.; Hierogliphick of, 327; song of, 331-3

Galway, Henri Massue de Ruvigny, 1st Earl of, 308; Macky and Swift on, 261
Gauls, 80
Gay, John, xvi, xxv, xxvii, xxviii, 201; ballad of *Molly Mog,* 225
Geoffrey, of Anjou, son of Henry I, 74-5
George I of England, Elector of Hanover, xxxiii, 11, 92, 101, 215, 245, 286; 'grand Funeral' at Hanover, 265
George II, 102 f., 119, 214, 226
Geneva, 274
Genoa, 274
Germany, 5, 12, 34, 36
Gibb, James, 145-6
Gilbraltar, 95, 113

Gillicranky, battle of, 173
Gizors, castle of, 38
Glasgow, 4; attacked by rebels, 138
Gloucester, 16, 59
Gloucester, Robert, Earl of, 52, 53, 57; withdrew to Normandy, 55, 63, 64; death and character of, 65
Godfrey, Duke of Lorraine, crusader, 21–2
Godfrey, chemist in Southampton Street, London, 334, 336
Godfrey, Mr. of Dublin, 346
Godolphin, Sidney, Earl of, Lord Treasurer, Burnet and Swift on, 279, 294
Godwin, Earl, 6
Goodenough, under-Sheriff of London, 284
Goodrich, in Herefordshire, 188
Gordon, George, 1st Duke of, in command of Edinburgh Castle, 169
Goring, George, Clarendon and Swift, on, 307
Goths, 3, 36
Graevius, xxxvii
Grafton, Charles Fitzroy, Duke of, Macky and Swift on, 258
Graham, John. *See* Dundee.
Graham, Cornet Robert, 137
Grant, a Highland gentleman, 131
Grattan, family, the, 344
Greenvil, Sir Richard, 308
Gregory, Pope, 4
Grey of Werke, Ralph, Earl, Macky and Swift on, 260
Griffin, Edward, Lord, Macky and Swift on, 260
Gronovius, xxxvii
Grubstreet, 201
Gué Nicaise, battle at, 39
Guildford, Francis, Lord, Macky and Swift on, 260
Gurney, Sir Richard, Lord Mayor of London, Clarendon and Swift on, 301
Gyllenborg, Count de, Swift's letter to, ix, 11

Hakluyt, Richard, *Principal Navigations*, xi & *n.*
Halifax, Charles Montagu, Earl of, Macky and Swift on, 258

Halifax, George Savile, Marquis of, 164; Burnet on, 280, 292
Hamilton, James, Duke of, Macky and Swift on, 261
Hamilton, James, third Marquis and first Duke of, Clarendon and Swift on, 296, 297, 305, 306
Hamilton, James, 4th Duke of, friendship for Creichton, 154, 158; 167, 173; Macky and Swift on, 261
Hamilton, William, 2nd Duke of, Clarendon and Swift on, 315, 318
Hamilton, Sir William, of Preston, 136
Hammond, Colonel Robert, Clarendon and Swift on, 311
Hanmer, Sir Thomas, under name of 'Ramneh', 103
Hannibal, 83, 86
Hanover, royal house of, 114, 115; court of, 213
Hardicanute, 6
Harding, John, Dublin printer, 323–4
Harley, Sir Edward, father of Robert, his papers, 190
Harley, Robert, afterwards Earl of Oxford, xi, 84, 190, 275; Macky and Swift on, 260
Harley, Henrietta, Countess of Oxford, daughter of Duke of Newcastle, 258
Haro. *See* O'Hara.
Harold, son of Earl Godwin, 6 f.
Harrison, Colonel John, the regicide, Clarendon and Swift on, 314
Harrison, Mary, afterwards Mrs. Deane Swift, xxxv
Hartington, William Cavendish, Marquis of, Macky and Swift on, 258
Hastings, William, baron, pension from Louis XI, 246
Haxton, murderer of Archbishop Sharp, 148
Helie, Count de la Flèche, 23
Henderson, Alexander, 297
Henrietta Maria, Queen of Charles I, 86; Clarendon and Swift on, 298, 317
Henry I, King of England, history of his reign, 27–47; called Beauclerc, 27; his charter, 28; death of his son William, 40; last voyage to Normandy, 45; his death and character, 46–7

Henry II, King of England, his birth, 44; 63, 65, 66, 70; history of his reign, 73–78; his character, 77

Henry IV, King of France, 84

Henry V, Emperor, 34

Herbert, Edward, Lord Cherbury, *Life and Raigne of Henry VIII*, 247

Herbert, Thomas, *Relation of some yeares travaile into Africa*, etc., xxxii, 243

Hereford, 20, 53

Herodotus, Swift's copy of his *History*, xxxi; his judgment of it, 243; no English Herodotus yet, xxxvii

Heylin, Peter, notions of royal power, xxxiv; *History of the Presbyterians*, xxxiii, 255–6

Hickes, George, Dean of Worcester, Burnet and Swift on, 278

Hill, Richard, Envoy to Savoy, Macky and Swift on, 261

Historiographer Royal, Swift's qualifications for, x

Hobbes, Thomas, errors of, 231

Hogarth, William, 347

Holinshead, Raphael, *Chronicles*, x

Holland, Squire Ned, 202

Holland, Earl of. *See* Rich, Sir Henry.

Holyhead, xxiv-v, 202; Vicar of, 204; Sacrum promontorium, 206

Hook, 41st child of his mother, tomb of, 202

Horace, xxv, 201; compared with Swift, 338–40

Hostreham, Henry II landed at, 73

Howard, Charles, Earl of Suffolk, 215

Howard, Henrietta, afterwards Countess of Suffolk, her character, xxvii-viii, 213–5; Swift's letter to, quoted, xv

Howard of Escrick, Lord, Burnet and Swift on, 276

Howells, William, *Medulla Historiae Anglicanae*, xxxv; 'a cursed writer, damned Dunce', 262 f.

Howth, 199

Hugh the Great, brother of Louis VI, King of France, 21

Hume, or Home, Charles, 8th Baron, imprisoned in Castle of Edinburgh, 175

Huntingdon, Henry, Earl of, son of David, King of Scotland, 50, 54, 55

Hurry, or Urrie, Colonel, 303, 307

Husige, anagram of Whigs, 99 f.

Iceni, 263

Infallible Scheme to pay the Nation's Debts, by a Tax upon Vice, An, 337–9

Intelligencer, The, xxx

Ireland, 3, 125; condition of in 12th c., 75–6; Primates and Governors of, 92; Church of, First Fruits, xxvii; Parliament, House of Lords, 199; loved by Stella, 235

Irvin, Captain, afterwards Sir Gerard, 126–7, 152, 154

Irvin, Dr., 152

Italy, 37, 80

Jacobites, the, 115

James I of England, and James VI of Scotland, 125, 326

James II, formerly Duke of York, 85, 86, 120, 153, 157, 162 f.; Howells on, 264; Burnet and Swift on, 286, 289 f.; Clarendon and Swift on the Duke of York, 311–13, 317–19

James, son of James II, called the Pretender, his birth, 292

Japan, 99 f.

Jason, 330

Jefferies, George, Lord Chief Justice, imprisonment and death, 290

Jermyn, Henry, Lord, 308

Jerusalem, 21, 22, 23, 27

Jervas, Charles, the Painter, 237

Jews, 3

John, King of England, 86

John, King of France, prisoner of the Black Prince, 84

John V, King of Portugal, 126

Johnson, Hester (Stella), xiii, xxii; her character, 227 f.; at Quilca, xxix, 219; advice to Sheridan, 222; her progress in reading, 231; her receipt of oyster shells, 203; Verses to quoted, xxvi; her death, 227; *Bon Mots*, xxvi, 229, 237–8

Johnstone, William, 1st Marquis of Annandale, 125

Johnstoun, James, Macky and Swift on, 262

Jones, master of the packet-boat to Dublin, 205

Kells, 219
Kemp, Corporal, 163
Kensington, Swift sent to King William III at, 193
Kent, Henry de Grey, Earl of, Macky and Swift on, 259
Kent, William d'Ypres, Earl of, 61, 74
Kent, recovered by William II, 14
Keynes, William de, 59
Kilkenny, its Grammar School, 192
Killigrew, Sir Harry, Clarendon and Swift on, 310
Kilsythe, Lord, Colonel of Dunmore's Dragoons, 166, 169, 175; intention to carry off the regiment, 171
Kimbolton, Lord, 300
Kinard, or Callidon, in Ireland, 125
King, John, 132, 136; capture of, 143–4
King, William, Archbishop of Dublin, *The humble Representation of the Clergy of Dublin*, 87 f.; described, xi, xii
Kirkwood, minister in Galloway, his experience of the 'Godly', 178
Kit-Cat-Club, 197 *n.*

Lanfranc, Archbishop, 13–14
Langueveny, 202
Lauderdale, John Maitland, Earl afterwards Duke of, messenger from the Parliament of Scotland, 313; Clarendon and Swift on, 315, 318; Burnet on, 276, 278
Leicester, 196; Swift joins his mother, at, 193
Leicester, Robert Dudley, Earl of, 117
Leicester House, xxvii, 213
Leicester Fields, xxiii
Leightoun, Robert, Archbishop of Glasgow, killed by Burnet's bringing him to London, 282
Lelop-Aw, anagram of Walpole, 103 f.
Lepidus, 85

Lesley, David, Clarendon and Swift on, 316
Lestrange, Sir Roger, 'A superficial meddling coxcomb', 279
Letter from the Grand Mistress of the Female Freemasons, 323
Letter from Sir R. W. to W.P. Esq., etc., 111
Levingston, Sir Thomas, 167, 169, 171
Lewis, Erasmus, 335
Lexington, Robert, Lord, Ambassador at Madrid, Macky and Swift on, 259
Lilliput, crown of, xxvii
Lincoln, 56, 58, 66
Lindsay, Dr. Thomas, Bishop of Kilaloe, later Archbishop of Armagh, 233
Lindsey, Robert, 4th Earl of, 301; Macky and Swift on, 259
Lindsey, Dr., 152
Linlithgow, George Livingstone, 3rd Earl of, 129, 164
Lisbon, 126
Little Britain, xxxix
Lives of those who suffered persecution for King Charles I, 188–9
Livy, xxxvii
Lloyd, Dr. William, Bishop of Killala, friend of Stella, 233
Lockhart, Lady, 176
London, 28, 62, 163; desctruction by Danes, 5; council of clergy, 44; Swift's last visit to, xxiv
Long, Mrs. Anne, xxiii; *Treaty between Dr. Swift and*, 197–8; death of, 198
Lothian, Lord, Commissioner from William III, 179
Louis VI, king of France, 38, 42
Louis VII, king of France, 66
Lucas, Charles, Lord, Governor of the Tower, Macky and Swift on, 259
Lucretius, 335; Swift's copy of *De Rerum Natura*, 1631, xxxi
Ludlow Castle, 53, 55
Ludlow, Edmund, *Memoirs*, 121
Lumley, Lord, Burnet and Swift on, 288
Lyndsay, Mr., verses to Davy Morice, 202
Lynn, in Norfolk, 198
Lyon, Rev. John, Swift's copy of Burnet's *Memoirs*, xxxvi
Lycurgus, 36

McCarthy, Charles, of College Green, Dublin, xii, 87
Macartney, General George, 261
Macclesfield, Thomas, Earl of, 265
McCoy, Major General, 170, 173
Mackenzie, Sir George, King's Advocate, Burnet and Swift on, 278
Macky, John, *Characters of the Court of Britain*, xxxiv-v, 257 f.
McDonnel, a Highland Laird, 160–1
Mahomet, xi
Malcolm III, King of Scotland, 16; slain with his son at Alnwick, 18
Malcolm IV, King of Scotland, 75
Malmesbury, 68
Malta, Knights of, 329
Manley, Francis, xxxv
Mans, (Le) 23
Mansel, or Mansell, Sir Thomas, Lord of the Treasury, Macky and Swift on, 260
Mar, or Marr, John, Earl of, Macky and Swift on, 262
Marble Hill, residence of Lady Suffolk, xxvii
Marches, Welsh invasion of, 34
Margaret, Queen of Scotland, death of, 18
Marius, Gaius, Roman general, 84
Market-Hill, in County Armagh, residence of the Achesons, xvii, xxx, 120
Marlborough, John Churchill, Duke of, 85, 162; Macky and Swift on, 257; Burnet and Swift on, 288
Marlborough, Sarah, Duchess of, 85
Marr, Episcopal clergyman, 177
Marsh, Narcissus, Archbishop of Dublin, afterwards of Armagh, character of, xxvi-xxvii, 211–2
Marshall, Mr., Army chaplain, 301–2
Marvel, Andrew, *Rehearsal Transprosed*, 273
Mary, wife of William III, Queen, 292
Mary, wife of James II, Queen, 289
Mary, Queen of Scots, and Bothwell, 86
Mason, William Monck, *History and Antiquities of St. Patrick's, Dublin*, xxi
Matilda, Queen, daughter of Malcolm of Scotland, wife of Henry I, 29

Matilda, or Maude, wife of Stephen, Queen, 60, 61
Maude, daughter of Henry I, wife of the Emperor, Henry V, 34, 41; tax for her portion, 35; struggle with Stephen, 55, 57; at Winchester, 61; at Oxford, 63; returns to Anjou, 65
Maurice, Archdeacon, 126
Maxwell, Ann, mother of Creichton, 129
Maynard, Sergeant, Burnet and Swift, on, 278, 290
Media, 36
Melvil, Secretary of Scotland, 173–4
Mercurius Rusticus, 188
Merlin, 328
Methuen, Sir Paul, Ambassador to Portugal, Macky and Swift on, 261
Meulant, Earl of, 41
Mews, Peter, Bishop of Winchester, Burnet and Swift on, 289
Middleton, Charles, Earl of, 165; Macky and Swift on, 262
Militia, importance of, Clarendon and Swift, 307
Milton, John, his description of Uriel, quoted, xvii, 116
Mohun, Charles, Lord, Macky and Swift on, 259
Monk, General, 320
Monmouth, Duke of, Commander in-Chief at Edinburgh, 139; at Bothwell Bridge, 140 f.; his defeat, 160
Montagu, Ralph, 1st Duke of, Macky and Swift on, 258
Montfort, Hugh de, 41
Montrath, Charles Coote, Earl of, 126
Montrèville, Monsieur, Clarendon and Swift on, 309
Montrose, James Graham, Marquis, afterwards Duke of, 162; Macky and Swift on, 262; Clarendon and Swift on, 310, 315 f.
Moor Park, near Farnham, 193
More, Sir Thomas, xi, 84
Morley, George, Bishop of Winchester, Burnet and Swift on, 282
Mortain, Earl of, 30, 31, 33
Mowbray, Robert. *See* Northumberland.
Murray, Lieutenant, 169, 171

Murray, Captain, 169, 171.
Muscovy, 85, 130
Musgrave, Sir Philip, 312

'Nena', anagram of Anne, 99 f.
Nero, 3, 85
Nerva, xxxix
Neumarché, castle of, 67
Newcastle, 21, 49, 75
Newcastle, John Holles, Duke of, Macky and Swift on, 258
New Forest, 23, 24
Newgate, 94, 116
Newmarket, xi, 85
Newspapers, party, 95
Nice, 22
Nigellus, Bishop of Ely, 56
'Nomptoc', anagram of Compton, 103
Normandy, 6, 23, 36, 38, 51, 71; invasions of by William II, 15, 19; conquest by Henry I, 40; visits by Henry II, 78
Northampton, Stephen's court at, 66
Northumberland, George Fitzroy, Duke of, Macky and Swift on, 258
Northumberland, Robert Mowbray, Earl of, 18, 20
Norway, 5
Norwich, 50
Nottingham, Daniel Finch, Earl of, 245; Macky and Swift on, 258; Burnet on, 288

Occasional Paper, writer of, 93
Odo, Bishop of Bayeux, 13 f.
Ogleby, Lord, afterwards Earl of Airly, 162
O'Hara, Sir Charles, Lieutenant General, Macky and Swift on, 261
Orange, Prince of. *See* William III.
Orange, Princess of. *See* Mary II.
Orkney, Elizabeth Villiers, Countess of, mistress of William III, 285
Orkney, George Hamilton, Earl of, Macky and Swift on, 261
Ormonde, James, Marquis, afterwards 1st Duke of, 190, 315
Ormonde, Marchioness, afterwards Duchess of, 190

Ormonde, James, 2nd Duke of, Lord Lieutenant of Ireland, xxvii; Macky and Swift on, 257; Burnet and Swift on, 289, 294
Ostend Company, 95
Oxford, 61, 63–4, 217; Parliament at, 56; steadiness to the Church, 286; surrender of, 310
Oxford, Earl of. *See* Harley.

Painter's Coffee House in Dublin, 331
Palestine, crusades for recovery of, 21
Papists, disabilities of, 281; under James II, 286
Parliament, injustices and absurdities of, 79; origin and character of, 35–37; election of members, 81; privileges of members and their servants, 82
Parker, a Lancashire gentleman, 150
Parkgate, 206
Parsons, Robert, *A Conference about the next Succession to the Crown of England*, xxxi; annotations to, 241–2
Pascal II, Pope, 30, 33, 34
Patrick, Symon, bishop of Chichester and Ely, *A friendly Debate*, 273
Pearce, Edward, xxxi
Pembroke, William, 3rd Earl of, 85
Penmenmawr, 201
Penmany, Owen Tudor's tomb at, 202
Penn, William, the Quaker, Burnet and Swift on, 285
Pepys, Samuel, *Diary* cited, xi *n.*
Percival, Mr., 196
Perseus, King of Macedon, 85
Persia, Queen of, 83
Peter, the Hermit, 22
Peterborough, Charles Mordaunt, Earl of, Macky and Swift on, 259; Burnet and Swift on, 288
Pettencrife, Laird of, 175, 176
Philip I, King of France, 15, 19
Philip II, King of Spain, 85
Picts, Wall, 4
Plantagenet, Geoffrey, Earl of Anjou, married to Henry I's daughter, 42
Plato, 231, 345
Plutarch, *Lives*, xix; importance of small circumstances, 124
Pocammock, 134
Poddishaw, Laird of, 133

Pollock, Laird of, 172
Polybius, 36
Pompey, 85
Pope, Alexander, xxiv, xxv, 201, 205
Pope, The. *See* Adrian, Pascal II, Eugenius III.
Porter, Sir Charles, Lord Chancellor of Ireland, Burnet and Swift on, 284
Portland, William Bentinck, Earl of, 193, 194; Macky and Swift on, 258
Portmahon, 95, 113
Portsmouth, 29, 57
Portugal, King of. *See* John V.
Poulet, John, Lord, afterwards Earl, Macky and Swift on, 259
Powis, Sir Thomas, Solicitor General of Ireland, Burnet and Swift on, 284
Presbyterians, 183; lose Parliamentary franchise, 280; Burnet and Swift on, 285–6; Clarendon and Swift on, 312, 318
Press, liberty of, 96
Prior, Matthew, Macky and Swift on, 260
Protestants, under James II, 286
Proverbs quoted, 221, 238
Ptolemy, 206
Pulleyn, Dr. Tobias, Bishop of Dromore and Cloyne, friend of Stella, 233
Pulteney, William, xvi, 111 f., 335
Putland, John, a surgeon, his copy of Macky's *Memoirs*, xxxv
Pym, John, death of, Clarendon and Swift on, 306

Queensberry, Douglas William, 1st Duke of, 145, 173
Quilca, xxix, *Deficiencies of*, 219–21

Rabutin, The Count de Bussy, 86; *Amours des Gaules*, 318
Raby, Thomas Wentworth, Lord, afterwards Earl of Strafford, Macky and Swift on, 261
Ralph, Bishop of Durham, 26, 28
'Ramneh', anagram of Hanmer, 103
Ranelagh, Richard, Earl of, Macky and Swift on, 259
Rathfarnam, Sheridan's house at, 216, 223–4

Reading, Scotch horse at, 163
'Regoge', anagram of George, 99 f.
Regulus, return to Carthage, 83
Reimond, count of Toulouse, crusader, 22
Restoration, The, xl
Revolution, of 1688, The, Burnet's account of, 184; Burnet and Swift on, 287
Rich, Sir Henry, first Earl of Holland, Clarendon and Swift on, 304
Richard II, King of England, 85
Richmond, Charles Lennox, Duke of, Macky and Swift on, 258
Richmond, James Stuart, 1st Duke of, 297
Richmond, xxvii, 227
Ridland, 201
Rivers, Richard Savage, 4th Earl, Macky and Swift on, 258
Robert, Duke of Normandy, eldest son of William I, struggle with William Rufus, 13 f.; his part in the Crusades, 23, 27 f.; achievements in the Holy Land, 34; defeat and imprisonment, 33
Roger, bishop of Salisbury, 56–7
Rolt, Mr., husband of Swift's cousin Patty, 334
Romans in Britain, 3 f.
Rome, Church of, 17, 18; Papal Court, 30, 34; sends legates to Ireland, 75; see of, 86
Rome, empire of, 36, 68
Romney, Henry Sidney, Earl of, 'an old illiterate rake', 195; Burnet and Swift on, 288; Macky and Swift on, 258
Ronquillo, Don Pedro, Spanish ambassador, 289
Rosamond, of Woodstock, 77
Rothes, John, 7th Earl, afterwards 1st Duke of, 142; Burnet and Swift on, 278; Clarendon and Swift on, 297
Rouen, 32, 39; Archbishop of, 57
Ruthen, Governor of Plymouth, 302

St. Andrews, Archbishop of. *See* Sharp, James.
St. Denys le Forment, 46
St. James', court of, 213; Palace, 237
St. John, of Jerusalem, 328

St. John, Henry, afterwards Viscount Bolingbroke, xii f.; preaching at St. Patrick's in Swift's dream, xxv, 205; Swift's letter to, xl

St. John, Oliver, Solicitor General, 297 f.

St. Johnstoun, 172

St. Patrick's Cathedral, Dublin, 205, 334; Liberty of, 341

St. Paul, his precept to accept the *Powers that be*, 124

Salisbury, 162; Bishop of. *See* Roger, Burnet, Hoadly

Sancroft, William, Archbishop of Canterbury, Burnet and Swift on, 277, 285, 291

Sandwich, Edward Montague, Earl of, Macky and Swift on, 259

Saracens, in Spain, 21

Savile, Sir Henry, *Rerum Anglicarum scriptores post Bedam*, x

Saxons, 4

Scarron, Paul, his verses, 335

Schomberg, Marshal Frederick, Duke of, xix, 267

Schutz, Mr., 214

Scipio, the elder, 83

Scotland, Church of, General Assembly, 302–3, 310; Episcopal clergy, xx, 168, 179; Presbyterian, 168; Council of, 315–6; Parliament of, 313; Roman conquests in, 4

Scots, demands of King Charles I, 311; and Parliament, 304; treachery, 309, 319; in Ulster, 299; Swift's dislike of, xxxviii, 296 f., 306

Scott, Sir Walter, xxi, xxxvi

Sedley, Sir Charles, Burnet and Swift on, 273

Semiramis, Queen of Babylon, 324

Severus, Emperor, 4

Shaftesbury, Anthony Ashley Cooper, 1st Earl of, xl, 274

Sharp, James, Archbishop of St. Andrews, 135

Shelburne, Lord, afterwards Marquis of Lansdowne, xxxvi

Sheldon, Gilbert, Archbishop of Canterbury, Burnet and Swift on, 272

Sheridan, Rev. Thomas, xiii, xxviii-xxx; character of, 216–8; best instructor of youth, 216; sermon at Cork, 223; birthday song for the Queen, 226; satire of Swift, 222; Stella's *Bon Mots* on, 237, 238; his wife, 222–3; *Ballyspellin*, 225

Sheridan, Thomas, son of Dr. Thomas, 217

Shrewsbury, 20, 53.

Shrewsbury, Charles Talbot, Earl, afterwards Duke of, 164; Macky and Swift on, 257; Burnet and Swift on, 288

Shrewsbury, Robert, Earl of, 30, 31

Sidney, Algernon, Ambassador in Denmark for Cromwell, 280

Smith, Rt. Hon. John, Macky and Swift on, 260

Socrates, 83

Solomon, temple of, 328

Somers, John, Lord, Macky and Swift on, 258; Burnet and Swift on, 279

Somerset, Charles, Duke of, Macky and Swift on, 257

Sophia, Princess, Electress Dowager of Hanover, xxxv

Spain, 37

Spaniards, 80

Sparta, 36

Sprat, Thomas, Bishop of Rochester, Burnet and Swift on, 279

Stamford, Henry Grey, Earl of, Parliamentary General, 302

Stamford, Thomas Grey, 2nd Earl of, Macky and Swift on, 259

Stanhope, General James, 1st Earl of, 261

Stanhope, Colonel, son of James, Macky and Swift on, 261

Standard, war of the, 54

Stearn, Dr. John, Dean of St. Patrick's, afterwards Bishop of Clogher, 233

Stearn, Dr. Richard, Archbishop of York, Burnet and Swift on, 282

Steele, David, leader of rebels captured and killed, 154–5; his monument, 157, 158

Steevens' Hospital, Dr., 236

Stella. *See* Johnson, Hester

Stephen, Earl of Albemarle, 20–1

Stephen, Earl of Boulogne, afterwards King of England, his reign, 47–73; 41, 75; elected, 48; licence to build castles, 49; causes of revolt, 50–51; invasion of Scotland, 52; defeat, 59; truce, 69; death and character, 71–2

Stephens Hospital. *See* Steevens.

Stepney, George, envoy to Emperor of Austria, 260

Stirling, 4, 129, 136

Stobow, Adam, 131

Strafford, Thomas Wentworth, Earl of, 84, 297 f.; trial of, 279

Stuart, Francis, Captain of Dragoons, 135, 141

Stuart, Sir Robert, 126, 128

Sweyn, King of Denmark, 5

Swift, Mrs. Abigail, mother of the Dean, xxiii, 191 f., 95

Swift, Adam, 191

Swift, Deane, grandson of Godwin, editor of Swift's Works, ix, xii, xxvi, *Essay upon the Life, Writings and Character of Dr. Jonathan Swift*, xxii

Swift, Dryden, 191

Swift, Sir Edward, 187

Swift, Godwin, uncle of the Dean, xxii, 190 f.

Swift, Jonathan, father of the Dean, 191

Swift, Dr. Jonathan, Dean of St, Patrick's, born St. Andrew's Day 1667, 192; ordained in Ireland, 194; invited to Court of Sweden, 11; Dean, 346; assisting at the bog, 219; perpetually storming, 220; Drapier, xxiv, 333; design of a history, 11; well versed in history, 194; in favour of regency, 291; on King Henry VIII, 247–51; relations with Burnet, xxxvi, xxxvii; with Sheridan, 225; his library, xxxiii; attributions, to, 337; *Abstract of History*, ix, 1–7; *An Account of the Court and Empire of Japan*, 99; *Advertisement to Creichton's Memoirs*, xviii, 121; *Answer of Pulteney to Walpole*, xv, xvi, 111; *Answer to Declaration of Inhabitants of Liberty of St. Patrick's*, 342–3; *Appendix to Dr. Swift's Works*, xxxiii; *Autobiography*, ix; *Blunders of Quilca*, xxix, 219; *Bon*

Mots de Stella, 237; *Character of Mrs. Howard*, 213; *Character of Primate Marsh*, 211; *Character of Sheridan*, ix, xxx, 216; *Conduct of the Allies*, 293; *On the Death of his Mother*, 196; *On the Death of Stella*, xxv-vi, 227; *Treaty with Mrs. Long*, 197; *On the death of Mrs. Long*, 198; *Drapier's Letters*, xi, xxxiv; *Examiner*, xiv; *Family of Swift*, xxii, 187; *Fragment of History of England*, x, 9; *Gulliver's Travels*, xi, xiv, xix, xx; *History of the Four Last Years of Queen Anne*, xxxvi, xl; *History of the Second Solomon*, xxviii, 222; *Holyhead Journal*, ix, xxiv-v, 201; *Journal to Stella*, xxv; *The Lady's Dressing-Room*, 338; *Letter addressed to Writer of the Occasional Paper*, xii f., 93; *Marginalia*, xxx f., 241 f.; *Of Mean and Great Figures made by several Persons*, x-xi, 83; *A modest Defence of the Lady's Dressing Room*, 337; *Petition against the Lord Blayney*, xxiv, 199; *Of public Absurdities in England*, x-xi, 79; *Presbyterian's Plea of Merit*, xxxix; *Sentiments of a Church of England Man*, xxxiv; *Short Remarks on Burnett's History*, xxxvi, 183; *Verses on the Death of Dr. Swift*, xxviii

Swift, Rev. Thomas, Vicar of Goodrich, xxii-iii; family of, 190; his loyalty, 189–90; his tomb, 334

Swift, Thomas (2nd in orders), 191

Swift, Thomas (3rd in orders), Rector of Puttenham, 191

Swift, William, xxii-iii; 187, 191

Swift, Mrs. W., heiress of Philpot, Yorkshire, 187

Suetonius, *Vitae Caesarum*, xxxi-ii

Sunderland, Robert Spencer, 2nd Earl of, turns papist, 86

Sunderland, Charles Spencer, 3rd Earl of, Macky and Swift on, 259

Sussex, 6

Sutherland, John Gordon, Earl of, 262

Tallard, Maréchal, French Ambassador, 204

Tankerville William of, 41

'Tedsu', referring to Hanover, 100

Temple, Sir John, a great friend of the Swift family, 193

Temple, Sir William, xxvii, 193; Master of the Rolls in Ireland, 194; Burnet and Swift on, 276, 291; *Introduction to History of England*, ix; *Letters and Miscellanea*, 194

Tenerchebray, 32

Tenison, Dr. Thomas, Archbishop of Canterbury, 'the dullest, good for nothing man I ever knew', 271; Macky and Swift on, 260

Test Act, Burnet and Swift on, 280

Teviot, Sir Thomas Livingstone, Viscount, Macky and Swift on, 261

Thanet, Thomas Tufton, Earl of, Macky and Swift on, 259

Theobald, Archbishop of Canterbury, 67 f.

Theobald, Count of Blois, 38

Thierrie, Earl of Alsace and Flanders, 43

Thurstan, Archbishop of York, 53

Tickell, Thomas, secretary to Carteret, xxix

Titus, Colonel, 'greatest rogue in England', 266

Tories, The, 113. *See* Yortes.

Tower of London, 27

Townshend, Charles, 2nd Viscount, Macky and Swift on, 259

Trinity College, Dublin, 192, 217

Tudor, Owen, tomb of, 202

Turenne, Marshal, 319

Turks, their encroachments in Spain, 21

Twysden, Roger, *Historiae Anglicanae Scriptores decem*, x

Tyrconnell, Earl of, Lord Deputy of Ireland, 285

Tyrrel, Walter, 24

Urban II, Pope, 21

Uxbridge, James II's forces at, 163

Vandals, 3

Vane, Sir Harry, 'a dangerous, enthusiastic beast', 270; Clarendon and Swift on, 297, 305, 314

Van Homrigh, Mrs. G., 197-8

Van Homrigh, Ginkell, Vanessa's brother, xxiv, 198

Vanhomrigh, Hester (Vanessa), xxxii, 197-8

Virgil, xi, xxv, 84, 201

Vitellius, 85

Voltaire, François de, *Essay upon the Civil Wars of France*, 109

Vortigern, 4

Wales, 4, 24; princes of, 40

Walker, Sir Edward, 307

Walker, Dr. George, Bishop of Derry, 290

Wallingford, 64

Walpole, Sir Robert, Prime Minister, xii, xiii, xiv, 97, 101, 213, 214; ill success of defenders, 112; threats against opponents, 118; Lelop-Aw, 103 f.; Burnet and Swift on, 294

Wat, Swift's servant, xxv, 202-8

Waters, Peter, 117

Waristoun, Lord, 'a fit uncle for Burnet', 271

Weemes, Parliamentary gunner, 307

Weems, David, Earl of, 262

Welch, Mrs., innkeeper at Holyhead, 202, 207

Westminster, coronation at, 73; prebend at, 195

Westminster-Hall, 27

Westminster School, 217

Wharton, Thomas, 1st Earl and Marquis of, 197, 289; Lord Lieutenant of Ireland, xxiv, 200; Macky and Swift on, 259

Whelden, a mathematician, 206

Whigs, The, 194; their polemical tracts, 113. *See* Husige.

Whitehaven, 177, 192

Whiteway, Mrs. Martha, xxii

Whitworth, Charles, afterwards Lord, ambassador to St. Petersburg, 85

Wild, Sergeant, 314

William I, formerly Duke of Normandy, 3, 6 f.

William II, 'Rufus', 11; history of his reign, 13 f.; expedition against Welsh, 20; relief of Mans, 23; death of, 24; character, 25 f.

William, son of Henry I, 39

William, son of Robert of Normandy, 38, 41, 43, 44

William, son of Stephen, 69, 70

William III, King of England, Prince of Orange, xxxv, 85, 120, 161, 164, 173, 180, 195, 242, 275, 285, 288, 315; lands in England, 162; Prince and Princess of Orange, proclaimed King and Queen, 166; original design to be King, 292; and Scotland, 179, 270, 290; his death, the ruin of English interests, 296

Williams, John, Bishop of Lincoln, Archbishop of York, Clarendon and Swift on, 296, 299 f.; *Life of*, 202

Williamson, David, described in *Scotch Presbyterian Eloquence*, 130

Willis, Sir Richard, 319

Wilmot, John, Earl of Rochester, Clarendon and Swift on, 307

Wilson, Captain of the rebels, captured by Creichton, 144

Winchelsea, Charles Finch, Earl of, Macky and Swift on, 259

Winchester, 5, 13, 24, 29, 60, 69, 73

Winchester College, Library, v, xxxi

Winchester, Henry, bishop of, youngest brother of Stephen, 48, 57

Windsor, 41, 287

Windsor Castle, 27

Wishart, Dr. William, 315

Wolsey, Cardinal, 'not the son of a butcher', 263

Wood, William, xii

Woodstock, labyrinth at, 77

Woolly, Edward, bishop of Clonfert, 273

Worcester. battle of, 130, 154, 318

Worrall, Rev. John, Vicar of St. Patrick's, 334

Worrall, Mrs., of Leicester, 196

Wright, Sir Nathan, Lord Keeper, Macky and Swift on, 258

Wycherley, William, 206

Wynne, John, Bishop of Bath and Wells, 335

Xenophon, 36

York, 66. Archbishops of. *See* Sharpe, Thurstan, Williams.

Yorkshire, 187

'Yortes', anagram of Tories, 99 f.